This Blessed Wilderness

Archibald McDonald, c. 1846, a daguerreotype now in the National Archives of Canada (PA143221).

Edited by Jean Murray Cole

This Blessed Wilderness

ARCHIBALD MCDONALD'S LETTERS
FROM THE COLUMBIA, 1822-44

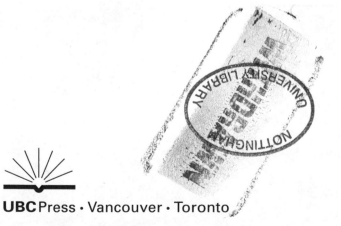

UBC Press · Vancouver · Toronto

Printed in Canada on acid-free paper ∞
ISBN 0-7748-0832-2
ISSN 0847-0537 (The Pioneers of British Columbia)

Canadian Cataloguing in Publication Data

McDonald, Archibald, 1790-1853.
  This blessed wilderness

  (The pioneers of British Columbia)
  ISBN 0-7748-0832-2

  1. McDonald, Archibald, 1790-1853–Correspondence. 2. Hudson's Bay
Company–Biography. 3. Fur traders–Northwest, Canadian–Correspondence.
4. Northwest, Canadian–Biography. I. Cole, Jean Murray, 1927- II. Title.
III. Series: Pioneers of British Columbia.

FC3213.1.M22A4 2001	971.2′01′092	C00-911376-2
F1060.8.M22A4 2001		

This book has been published with the help of a grant from the Humanities and
Social Sciences Federation of Canada, using funds provided by the Social Sciences and
Humanities Research Council of Canada.

UBC Press acknowledges the financial support of the Government of Canada through
the Book Publishing Industry Development Program (BPIDP) for our publishing
activities.
Canadä

We also gratefully acknowledge the support of the Canada Council for the Arts for our
publishing program, as well as the support of the British Columbia Arts Council.

UBC Press
The University of British Columbia
2029 West Mall, Vancouver, BC V6T 1Z2
(604) 822-5959
Fax: (604) 822-6083
E-mail: info@ubcpress.ca
www.ubcpress.ca

100252 4764 T

For A.O.C.C.

'We clamb the hill thegither'

Contents

Illustrations

This Blessed Wilderness

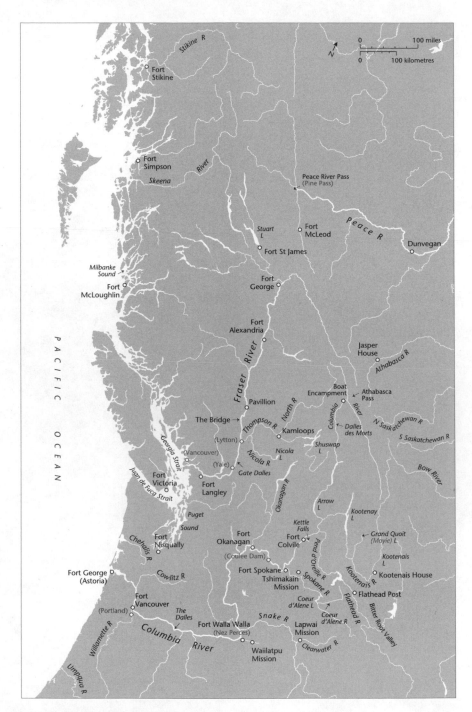

The Columbia District in McDonald's era.

Introduction

Change was in the air when Archibald McDonald first arrived in the Pacific Northwest in 1821. The merger of the Hudson's Bay Company (HBC) and the North West Company (NWC) that year dramatically altered the conduct of the fur trade in British North America, and nowhere were the vibrations felt more than in the Columbia District.

McDonald was one of the first two HBC men to go west of the mountains after the merger. He remained there, serving in progressively senior positions at various posts in the Columbia District until late in 1844. Just over a year later the signing of the Oregon Treaty established the boundary that separated the British and American territories.

These were important years in the history of the Pacific slope, and McDonald's many letters, gathered from archives and collections in Canada, the United States, and Great Britain, provide a perceptive picture of people and events as seen from his privileged vantage point. What gives distinction and interest to his writing is his frankness, the fullness of his accounts, and the originality of his literary style. His candid observations and his ironic wit, especially when writing informally to old friends, are both entertaining and illuminating. The tone of his letters is diverse, set by his relationship with his correspondents. The annual letters to his old friend Edward Ermatinger are intimate and confiding, full of news and gossip about fur trade colleagues along with rare glimpses into family life, which include vivid vignettes of his beloved wife Jane Klyne and their children – 'the greatest treasure I have.' In contrast there was a somewhat hearty deference, along with affability and even affection, in letters to Governor George Simpson. With John McLoughlin, who reigned over the Columbia, he maintained a respectful cordiality. And there are revealing letters to fellow HBC officers and to subordinates that demonstrate clearly the hierarchy of the HBC.

At the time of the merger of the two companies in 1821, the regions west of the mountains had long been dominated by the NWC, although there was opposition from American 'mountain men' and from both American and Russian ships trading on the north Pacific coast. Few HBC men had ventured beyond the Rockies. Joseph Howse and a small party made one foray through the mountains from the Athabasca Territory in 1810-11, but unfriendly Natives made it so unproductive that it was not repeated.

Years of conflict and competition between the HBC and the NWC in the central regions of Rupert's Land had created much waste and duplication, resulting in dwindling profits for both. The coalition brought about a new era. Men who had been bitter enemies were suddenly colleagues; others were declared redundant because of the closing of posts throughout the fur country where the rivals had long manned establishments within short distances of each other to court the Native fur hunters. It took a leader of great tact and skill, and one not involved in the old antagonisms, to oversee the changes.

Andrew Wedderburn Colvile, a member of the HBC London Committee, had been a moving force in the negotiations between the two companies. It was his protégé, George Simpson, who was named governor of the Northern Department, and to Simpson fell the task of uniting these unlikely bedfellows. With only a year's experience in the fur country, he assumed control firmly and moved quickly to assert his authority and to familiarize himself with all aspects of the trade. He determined to visit all the districts east of the mountains as soon as possible, but the far-flung regions of the NWC's Columbia Department required attention before he could find the time to go there himself.

His choice of an emissary was Archibald McDonald, with whom he had spent the 1820-21 season in the Athabasca District, a baptism into the fur trade for both young men. 'We possess little information about the Columbia. I have therefore sent Archd McDonald thither in the capacity of accountant and requested him to give a full and accurate report of it which will be transmitted to the committee,' Simpson wrote to Colvile, 8 September 1821. 'This young man has been a long time in the country – he possesses good abilities and I think his situation should be ameliorated.'

McDonald was well known to Colvile, whose brother-in-law, the earl of Selkirk, had sent the young Scot from the well-known Glencoe family out to his Red River Colony (now Winnipeg) in 1813 as leader of the second large group of settlers. A year of furthering his education in London under Selkirk's direction – studying a variety of scientific pursuits from map making to medicine – had prepared McDonald for a special role in the colony. Little did he suspect how soon he would be called upon to make use of his training. While still en route to Hudson Bay typhus struck the *Prince of Wales* passengers with deadly results, and McDonald was forced to take charge of the party when the doctor to whom he had been apprenticed fell ill and succumbed to the disease.

At twenty-three, the young highlander was responsible for those who remained of the ninety-four settlers who had set off from Stromness. Landed abruptly at Churchill by an unfeeling ship's captain, the weary and ailing settlers were forced to set up camp for the winter on nearby Churchill Creek. It was McDonald's job to care for the sick and cajole the remainder of the restless group into assisting with chores about the camp. As the winter wore on, he prepared them for their long walk from

'Leacantuim,' the house in the valley of Glencoe, Scotland, where Archibald McDonald was born. Photographed in 1962. Most of the glen is now owned by the National Trust for Scotland, and Leacantuim is a hostel for mountain climbers and hikers.

Churchill to York Factory in the spring and thence to the settlement at Red River.

Once at the settlement, the growing overt opposition of the NWC to the colonists created serious tensions. Some defected and were transported to Upper Canada in NWC canoes. Those who remained endured repeated attacks by NWC men and their Métis allies. McDonald was in Montreal, en route from England, when the final blow came – the murder of recently arrived Governor Robert Semple and nineteen of the settlers at Seven Oaks in June 1816 by a mounted party of Métis led by Cuthbert Grant.

McDonald served in many capacities at the colony through the ups and downs of its early years, including as a member of the Council of Assiniboia and, for a short period, as acting governor. However the prolonged litigation over the settlement's troubles with the NWC, along with Selkirk's declining health and resultant lack of interest in the colony, led McDonald to join the HBC in 1820.[1]

Archibald McDonald arrived at the mouth of the Columbia River with Chief Factor John Dugald Cameron, a former Nor'wester, and Chief Trader John Lee Lewes, a fellow HBC man, on 8 November 1821. Two other experienced former NWC officers, Chief Factor John Haldane and Chief Trader James McMillan, were also appointed to the district. Within days of their appearance McDonald and Lewes began the inventory of the headquarters establishment at Fort George (Astoria). By 6 April 1822 McDonald had completed his report to the council covering all four posts in the Columbia District – Fort George (Astoria), Spokane House, Fort Walla Walla (Nez Percés), and Thompson River (Forts Okanagan and Kamloops).

It was soon revealed that all the former NWC posts had been characterized by a combination of self-indulgence and wastefulness that bore little resemblance to the practices laid down by the new regime. First there was the large roster of officers, clerks, servants, Iroquois, and Owhyhee (Sandwich Islanders, or Kanakas, now known as Hawaiians) employees who carried on the work involved in the fur trade. Then the detailed inventories listed not only trading goods, but also the stores of foodstuffs, medical supplies, and even the titles of books in the Fort George library. Imported luxury items and foods such as dried meat, pease, and grains had been stockpiled and were deteriorating. Simpson was shocked

---

[1] See Jean Murray Cole, *Exile in the Wilderness* (Toronto/Seattle: Burns and MacEachern/ University of Washington Press, 1979).

to learn of the extravagance and prodigality that had been endemic in these remote outposts during the NWC regime; he was determined to introduce austerity to the district and to encourage greater reliance on their own produce, cutting off supplies of expensive European provisions that had hitherto been taken for granted.

When the two companies merged, the HBC London Committee created 100 shares in the new organization, forty of which were to be shared by the officers in the field, two each for the chief factors and one each for the chief traders who had charge of the day-to-day operations at the trading posts. Although the HBC was dominant, it was the former Nor'westers who were blessed with the majority of the commissions. Fifteen of the twenty-five factorships and seventeen of the twenty-eight chief traders' positions went to the old rivals, creating awkward jealousies and even hostilities among the 'partners' in the new concern. Some of the older men would retire soon so that clerks could aspire to promotion, but it was some years before the perceived wrongs were righted.

Cameron was sent out to the Columbia to share the command with Haldane. It was a short-lived arrangement. Haldane returned east in the spring of 1822, being replaced by Chief Factor Alexander Kennedy, a senior HBC man. When Cameron left early in 1824 Kennedy took over the whole management of the district and remained in charge until Simpson came out to the coast on his 1824-25 tour of inspection.

The governor's arrival at Fort George on 8 November was marked by his usual flourishes – voyageurs bedecked in their finest and most colourful garments, singing lustily to the paddles' rhythm as the big canoe swept down the Columbia to the river's mouth. A touch of asperity can be detected in Simpson's journal where he described the scene: rather than finding all hands at the wharf with the traditional ceremonial welcome, he found both Chief Factor Kennedy and his accountant Archibald McDonald out on the water 'amusing themselves boat-sailing.'

All in all Simpson was not well pleased with what he found at the Columbia headquarters. 'The establishment of Fort George is a large pile of buildings covering about an acre of ground well stockaded and protected by Bastions and Blockhouses ... altogether an air or appearance of grandeur and consequence which does not become and is not at all suitable to an Indian Trading Post ... extravagance has been the order of the day,' he recorded in his diary.

Following Simpson came Chief Factor John McLoughlin, yet another leading light of the old NWC, who took over the reins and became the driving force in the Columbia when the governor returned east the following spring. McLoughlin was trained as a medical doctor, but his

Governor George Simpson made
several trips to the Columbia District
and was a long-time colleague and
correspondent of Archibald
McDonald. (Hudson's Bay Company
Archives 363-s-25/5)

assignment now was management. Kennedy left with Simpson in April
of 1825. From that time, under McLoughlin's direction, affairs west of
the mountains took on greater stability, although a growing friction that
built up between the chief factor and the governor caused problems.

Meanwhile Simpson directed sweeping changes in the operations of the
department during his winter on the scene. He had stopped at Spokane
House and Fort Walla Walla en route to the coast, discovering for himself their dependence on costly European provisions when they could well
be raising their own crops with great savings to the HBC. From the beginning of his tenure Simpson insisted that each fort should attempt to produce as much of its own food as possible. Before the governor left the
district in April 1825 he arranged the removal of Spokane House north
to Kettle Falls on the Columbia River, where Fort Colvile was established, and a large farm was soon prospering in the wide fertile valley.

One of the governor's first decisions on his arrival at the coast was
to move the headquarters from Fort George on the south side of the
Columbia River (not far from its entry into the Pacific) to Bellevue
Point on the north side near the mouth of the Willamette River, ninety
miles from the sea. There he established Fort Vancouver on land upon
which extensive gardens and field crops could flourish. He sent James
McMillan north to explore the Fraser River with the intention of building a new headquarters there, should the Americans begin to extend settlement into the Oregon Territory. The ten-year-old 1818 Treaty of Joint
Occupancy between the British and Americans was still in force, but the
HBC was well aware of American ambitions. The Fraser River, less
threatened by the Americans, would be more centrally located for the

coasting trade. If the upper rivers proved to be passable, then it would also provide easier access to the northern posts of New Caledonia, which Simpson decreed should henceforth be a part of the Columbia Department rather than be served from York Factory on Hudson Bay. At the same time, as another cost-cutting measure, he pared down the complement of officers and men from 151 to eighty-three.

Simpson was dissatisfied with the performance of Chief Trader John McLeod at Thompson River, and before leaving the district he appointed McDonald to take over the charge. 'This young gentleman has not had much experience as an Indian Trader,' he wrote to McLoughlin on 10 April 1825, 'but from his manner and address I think he would very soon gain popularity; he knows the value of property and I have every reason to believe would turn it out to the best account; he appears thoughtful, steady and discreet and I am satisfied he will spare no pains or exertion to put things on a proper footing and give satisfaction.' The move was held up until the arrival of Edward Ermatinger, who was to take over the accountant's duties at headquarters in the autumn of 1825, and McDonald stayed on to show the ropes to his successor. 'We have them [the accounts] now in order & we ought to endeavour to keep them so,' McLoughlin wrote on 9 November 1825, explaining the delay to McLeod.

With all the changes in command in the Columbia during those first few years, McDonald had remained a constant at Fort George, keeping the accounts and managing the stores and trade goods. He came to accept the permanence of his isolated post, so remote from family and former friends. Although he had once harboured hopes of marrying the daughter of a family connection in Scotland, he realized that this was impossible as long as he remained in the fur country, and he had no other prospects. Like many another lonely trader in the northwest, he decided to take a country wife – his choice, Princess Sunday, also known as Princess Raven (Koale Koa), was the youngest daughter of the Chinook chief Comcomly, who, since the days of John Jacob Astor's Pacific Fur Company, had been one of the best known Natives on the Pacific slope.

According to their son Ranald, who heard an account of the wedding years later from an eyewitness,[2] much pageantry accompanied the

---

[2] Ranald MacDonald was to gain recognition in later years when he shipwrecked off the coast of Japan in 1848, then the forbidden kingdom. He was taken prisoner but treated as a guest and, in the ten months he spent there, taught English to fourteen government officials, thus providing interpreters for Commodore Matthew Perry when he made his historic venture into Japan in 1853. See W.S. Lewis and Naojiro Murakami, eds., *Ranald MacDonald: The Narrative of His Early Life* (Spokane, WA: Eastern Washington State Historical Society, 1923; reprinted, Portland, OR: Oregon Historical Society, 1990).

ceremony at Comcomly's lodge, 'a long, one-storey, gothic-roofed, very large house of wood with doors and windows and other conveniences, and adornments outside, including a monumental totem pole by way of a royal flagstaff.' A path of furs, prime beaver and otter, lined the path from the shore to the lodge, according to the report. 'Along this golden pathway, as a guard of honor, were three hundred of the slaves, so-called, of the King. On the arrival of the bridegroom and his party ... they walked the furry path ... the King, with royal grace and dignity, in silence, handed over the evidently not unwilling bride.' Sadly, the bride did not long survive the birth of her son in 1824, and McDonald was again left alone, mourning her loss. The infant was turned over to an aunt and lived throughout his babyhood in Comcomly's lodge.

About a year later McDonald remarried 'in the custom of the country,' this time to Jane Klyne, daughter of Michel Klyne, postmaster at Jasper House in the Rocky Mountains. Some say Jane came to the coast in Simpson's entourage, but it is not known how or where she and McDonald met. Jane had grown up in the Rocky Mountain region; although her father was a French-Canadian from the parish of Montreal, her mother, Suzanne LaFrance, a Métis, was a member of a long-time fur trade family.[3]

With the move to the Thompson River District, McDonald was able to establish his family for the first time in their own home. When Jane arrived at Kamloops in September 1826 she brought with her their month-old first-born son Angus and young Ranald, who was then two years old. Also in the party were the wife and little son of Francis Noel Annance, with whom the McDonalds would share the officers' quarters. In spite of the isolation and the roughness of the habitation, it was an idyllic time. 'Nothing could be more congenial to man than the winter [at Kamloops] ... and the fall and spring are perfectly free from that raw and heavy atmosphere so common to other parts west of the Rocky Mountains,' wrote McDonald in his report that year.

[3] Joseph LaFrance, 'a French Canadese Indian,' son of a French-Canadian trader and an Ojibwa mother, born at Michilimackinac, was Arthur Dobbs's informant and drew the original map for him when he wrote *An Account of the Countries Adjoining to Hudson Bay* (London: J. Robinson, 1744). LaFrance 'traveled thro those Countries and Lakes for three years from 1739 to 1742.' The name reappears in fur trade records through succeeding generations, but it is not known which was Suzanne's father. François LaFrance was with Edward Ermatinger's York Factory Express crew when Michel and Suzanne Klyne and their family travelled with the party from Jasper to Fort Edmonton in the spring of 1827.

The Thompson River District had two posts – the main depot at Okanagan, on the Columbia, where the correspondence and reports were gathered each spring to be taken east by the York Factory Express canoes, and Kamloops, a twelve- or fourteen-day journey north on horseback, which was kept up as a winter trading post. The officer in charge was in residence at Kamloops from late August or September until March or April, when he brought the fur returns down to Okanagan to be taken on down to Fort Vancouver for shipment to England in the summer.

After McDonald took over in February 1826, Thompson River also served as the connecting link between the Columbia District headquarters at Fort Vancouver and the New Caledonia District. Previously, trade goods had been shipped from Hudson Bay via the Athabasca route to Fort St James on Stuart Lake and Alexandria on the upper Fraser River. Furs gathered in that productive northern region went back the same way to the east. Simpson believed that transportation costs could be cut in half by bringing the trade goods and supplies up the Columbia from Fort Vancouver to Okanagan by boat and from there, via Kamloops, to Alexandria on horses in the fall. Canoes carried on up the Fraser from Alexandria to Fort St James. The fur returns came down in the spring in reverse fashion, to be shipped back to England around the Horn by the HBC supply ship from Fort Vancouver.

One of McDonald's responsibilities at Kamloops was to see that there were enough healthy horses – sometimes as many as 120 – on hand to facilitate these New Caledonia brigades in the spring and fall, along with provisions for the men accompanying them. Parties were sent frequently in the fishing season to the Fraser River to bring back quantities of salmon to be processed at the fort; indeed it sometimes seemed that there was more trade in salmon than in furs. Thompson River returns had been declining over the years, and by the time McDonald took over he discovered that 'even the name of a Beaver is scarcely heard among the Natives ... A person can walk for days together without seeing the smallest quadraped, the little brown squirrel excepted.' In spite of this Simpson wanted to keep Kamloops going because of its strategic importance to the northern traders.

Another assignment given to McDonald when he took over at Thompson River involved exploring the navigation possibilities of the Fraser River, with the hope that this river would prove amenable to Simpson's projected plan to establish a post at its mouth in order to be prepared in case the Americans moved to take over the lower Columbia River. The HBC committee members in London were sanguine in their belief that, when the boundary was eventually established between the

American and British territories, the British would continue to hold the regions north of the Columbia River, and Simpson held the idea that the Fraser River would be the most central route for the shift in trade to the north. McDonald set off on horseback in September 1826 with the Upper Okanagan chief Nicolas[4] to explore the (Thompson) river to its confluence with the Fraser, and, although he reported that there were hazards, he felt that they could be overcome by not-too-formidable portages. As a result of these explorations McDonald produced the first map of the interior of British Columbia. According to A.L. Farley, in his *Historical Cartography of British Columbia*, 'Even with precise observations, the intricate drainage patterns and generally difficult topography associated with what is now British Columbia rendered mapping especially complex ... McDonald unquestionably made use of information from other traders. Unlike others, however, he was apparently interested in mapping and possessed no mean ability as a draughtsman.' (unpublished monograph, BCA)

McDonald's sketch map accompanied his 1826-27 post journal and report of the district.[5] The report also included detailed information on the affairs of the district, along with McDonald's observations on the neighbouring Native tribes, for which he listed population statistics and the names of all the tribes and their 'principal men.' The fort journal records, on 18 December 1826: 'They furnished me with a small piece of stick for every grown man of their community ... with few exceptions each has a wife, seldom more.' He also described Native ceremonials – for example, the Nez Percé 'horse fair' in the summer of 1826 and the 'grand entertainment' given by the Shuswap for their Coutamine neighbours in December that same year.

Another of his continuing interests was natural history, and in one of his early letters to Andrew Colvile he refers to 'a Box or two of curiosities and preserved Birds' that he was sending by ship to John Halkett, an influential HBC stockholder and naturalist. McDonald continued for many years to collect plant and animal specimens to send to the British

[4] In Francess G. Halpenny and Jean Hamelin, eds., *Dictionary of Canadian Biography*, vol. 8 (Toronto: University of Toronto Press, 1985), Mary Balf gives his name as Hwistesmetxe'qen and his dates as 1793-1859. Nicolas, who was also known as N'Kuala, became a staunch friend of McDonald and the HBC.

[5] The 'Thompson River District Report, 1827' is published in Appendix A, E.E. Rich, ed., *Simpson's 1828 Journey to the Columbia: Part of a Dispatch from George Simpson ESQr Governor of Rupert's Land,* Simpson's 1828 Journey to the Columbia (Toronto/London: Champlain Society/Hudson's Bay Record Society, 1947).

Museum or Kew Gardens. When, under the protection of the HBC, the Scottish botanist David Douglas was sent out to Fort Vancouver in 1825 by the Horticultural Society of London to gather specimens from the Pacific Northwest, he was befriended by McDonald. In succeeding years the two travelled together on a number of occasions, sharing their enthusiasms.

The first group of McDonald's letters that follow here cover the years from his arrival in the Columbia (including his initiation at Fort George and his tenure at Thompson River) until his first journey back east in the spring of 1828, when, with his new appointment as chief trader, he was invited for the first time to take his place at a meeting of the Northern Council. He went east with the York Factory Express, conducted by his friend Edward Ermatinger, who was about to leave the HBC, later to take up a career in business and politics in St Thomas, Upper Canada (now Ontario).

McDonald returned to the Columbia that summer in the governor's party, a journey often described in fur trade literature.[6] His annual letters to Ermatinger, covering the years from 1830 until he left the Columbia for retirement in the fall of 1844, were preserved by the Ermatinger family[7] and give a vivid picture of domestic life on a remote trading post, along with news of the fur trade, much casual chat about old acquaintances, and a running commentary on Upper Canadian politics. When Simpson's party arrived at the recently established post at Fort Langley on the Fraser River on 10 October 1828, McDonald took over from Chief Factor James McMillan, who, with the governor, carried on down the coast to the Columbia River and Fort Vancouver.

The second group of letters in this volume (1828-34) deals with the Fort Langley years. They were years of challenge and growth for McDonald in his fur trade career, and they were a time of contentment and joy in his family life. By the time Jane and the children (Ranald, nearly five; Angus, three; and Archibald, one-and-a-half) arrived at the fort on the HBC ship *Cadboro* from Fort Vancouver in July 1829, McDonald had enlarged the palisaded compound and finished building the 'Big House,' which had comfortable quarters for his family. Even with children so young, he soon established a schoolroom where he tutored his wife along

---

[6] See Malcolm McLeod, ed., *Peace River: A Canoe Voyage from Hudson's Bay to the Pacific by the Late Sir George Simpson in 1828. Journal of the late Chief Factor Archibald McDonald ... who accompanied him* (Ottawa: Durie and Son, 1872).

[7] Originals now with the British Columbia Archives.

with the boys (two more were born at Langley, Alexander in October 1829 and Allan in May 1832), taking great pride in their progress, as his letters eloquently attest.

McDonald felt sadly neglected by headquarters during his first winter and spring on the Fraser River. Communication was virtually non-existent, and although he sent Native couriers both via Okanagan and the Puget Sound-Cowlitz Portage route with letters to McLoughlin, no replies were forthcoming. Finally, in March, when the weather improved, he sent his assistant James M. Yale, interpreter Francis Noel Annance, and 'ten of our best men' down to Puget Sound to find a Native courier to go on to Fort Vancouver with the fort journal, reports, and accounts, along with many requests for the wherewithal to expand and improve his operations at Langley. He needed more blankets and other trade goods to keep up the competition against American coastal ships trading for furs along the coast, and he hoped for a cooper to enable them to produce sound barrels to preserve the teeming salmon that the local Natives harvested from the river. He had seen the abundance of the fall run, and the summer run was known to be even better.

When the *Cadboro* finally arrived at the mouth of the Fraser in July, McDonald was somewhat mollified to learn that McLoughlin had attempted unsuccessfully to get messages through to him and that one of the main reasons for the delay was that the HBC's English ship *William and Ann* had gone down as it crossed the bar at the Columbia River mouth early in March, with the loss of captain, crew, and cargo. It meant less liberality in Langley's share of trading goods, but they would make do.

During two weeks of his first summer at Fort Langley McDonald calculated that his handful of men preserved nearly 8,000 fish, averaging six pounds each, for a total of twenty-three tons of salmon. This cost the HBC a mere thirteen pounds, nineteen shillings, and ten pence worth of trade goods. The following year he reported that between 25 August and 15 September they procured 15,000 fish. McDonald carried on many experiments with salting and curing fish for export during his years at Fort Langley. At the same time he saw the potential in the fine stands of timber; by mid-October 1829 his men had 10,000 cedar shingles and 300 two-inch planks ready to ship to Fort Vancouver, along with a large quantity of barrel staves prepared to provide containers for the next year's salmon. Kitchen gardens flourished, and although flooding was a problem – and later caterpillars wreaked havoc – field crops, grains, and potatoes were productive.

Official communication continued to be a problem, although apparently

McDonald's personal correspondence was voluminous; in February 1831 he received a packet from Vancouver containing thirty-two letters from eastern friends, delivered by a succession of couriers via the Cowlitz route. McDonald went to headquarters to confer with McLoughlin in November 1829 and was rewarded by a letter from his chief on his return, saying: 'You may depend upon your suggestions and plans settled on while here being followed up.'

Unfortunately troubles continued to plague McLoughlin. The following spring, another ship, the brig *Isabella*, was lost, and it was that year, 1830, that the Chinook of the lower Columbia were attacked by a virulent epidemic of 'intermittent fever' (malaria). Nearly three-quarters of them succumbed within the next few years. McLoughlin reported fifty-two of his own men on the sick list, though they were better able to fight off the disease than were the Natives, and none of the HBC people died.

The letters herein describe relations with neighbouring Native tribes and encounters with the more war-like Native peoples from Vancouver Island and the Gulf of Georgia, who appeared in the lower Fraser River with considerable frequency.[8] In spite of the difficulties and interruptions, Fort Langley grew and prospered in those years. The increasing importance of the coastal vessels, the establishment of Nass (Fort Simpson) to secure the HBC presence on the north coast, and the agreement with the Russian-American Company all contributed to the HBC gradually shifting its activities northward in preparation for the final boundary settlement with the American government.

When the time came for McDonald to move on from Fort Langley, he left the fort in charge of his successor, James M. Yale, and went down to Vancouver via Puget Sound, where he stopped with his men for twelve days. On McLoughlin's orders he had paused there on his way back from headquarters in November to select a site for the new Fort Nisqually, which was intended to become the principal establishment in the Columbia. It was time to make a start on some of the buildings there. Here he met his botanical friend David Douglas, and the two continued on to headquarters together, leaving a handful of men to continue the work on the fort. In late May he was back at Nisqually supervising the completion of the fort buildings. (Nisqually never did take on the prominence that was intended for it, but it did serve as the centre for the Puget Sound Agricultural Company, an HBC subsidiary formed in 1839.)

---

[8] For more detail see Morag Maclachlan, ed., *The Fort Langley Journals 1827-30* (Vancouver: UBC Press, 1998).

Part 3 begins with the move to Fort Colvile,[9] near Kettle Falls. After the isolation of Fort Langley, this was a welcome change. It was a port of call for all 'comers and goers.' The eastbound Express parties assembled there before heading up the Columbia to Boat Encampment and proceeding through the Rocky Mountains to Jasper House. Kootenay House and the Flathead District came under Colvile's wing, and there was frequent communication with Walla Walla, Okanagan, and Kamloops. Travelling botanists from Great Britain and exploring parties sent out from Washington enlivened the scene. After the arrival of the American missionaries from New England and the 1839 establishment of the Tshimakain mission sixty miles to the south, even the women and children paid social visits back and forth.

McDonald took over at Colvile in the autumn of 1833 and spent the winter there before leaving the following March for a long-anticipated furlough abroad. Ranald remained at John Ball's school at Fort Vancouver so that he could accompany his father east in the spring, while Jane took the other children to stay with her family, the Klynes, at Jasper for the winter months (MaryAnne, the McDonalds' only daughter, was born at Jasper House in February 1834).

In the spring, all went to the Red River Settlement, where the boys (including Ranald) were enrolled in the new school there. Jane lived with the Reverend William Cockran (the Anglican missionary) and his family, while McDonald returned to Great Britain for the first time since 1818. He spent a few days in London in October, reporting to the committee at Hudson's Bay House, before heading north to Scotland. He visited family in the highlands and then returned via Glasgow, where he met Professor William Hooker of Glasgow University (later to be Keeper of Kew Gardens, Sir William was knighted in 1836) and other leading botanists, and he was recruited to collect specimens for them when he returned to the Pacific Northwest.

After a quick trip to Paris and back to North America via New York and Montreal, in June McDonald was back at Red River where his family awaited his return. There he attended the annual meeting of the Northern Council, and he and Jane were formally married by Reverend William Cockran before they set off for the Columbia with the two youngest children, leaving Ranald and the three other older boys at the Red River Academy.

---

[9] The site of old Fort Colvile now lies beneath the waters of Lake Roosevelt, about thirty-five kilometres south of the Canada-US border. The valley was flooded by the building of the Grand Coulee Dam in 1941.

McDonald's last ten years west of the mountains were spent being in charge at Fort Colvile. His correspondence reveals the regular rhythms of the year's activities – the comings and goings of the Kootenay and Flathead trading parties; the arrival of the eastbound Express from Fort Vancouver in March and the attendant flurry of northern visitors from New Caledonia and Thompson River; ploughing and planting in April and May as the Colvile farm was extended year by year, with livestock being added (some even brought through the mountains from St Louis) and a mill being built. Farm exports increased, especially to help in fulfilling a contract the HBC had made in 1839 to supply Russian posts on the Northwest Coast in return for trading rights along the Russian-controlled stretch between Fort Simpson and the Lynn Canal. Part of the chronicle too were the seemingly frequent disasters – loss of life in the treacherous waters of the Columbia, fires, Native attacks, accidents, illnesses. It was during the long winter months that McDonald did much of his writing – official reports and journals and innumerable long letters to many personal correspondents near and far.

There were many highlights. McDonald developed real friendships among the local Natives wherever he lived, and he came to depend upon their help and cooperation, as he had at Fort Langley with 'the Doctor' and at Kamloops where Nicolas was a stalwart supporter. At Colvile he frequently expressed his warm feelings towards Cornelius (Bighead), the Lower Spokane chief, in letters to his neighbours at the Tshimakain mission.

The coming of the American missionaries signalled a new era in the fur country, and for Jane McDonald it provided an opportunity to associate for the first time with White women who had grown up in a vastly different society than her own. It was the beginning, too, of the wave of American settlement that was to change forever the position of Great Britain and of the HBC in the Oregon Territory. McDonald had mixed feelings about the effects of encroaching 'civilization.' The Methodist and Roman Catholic missionaries saw each other as rivals; he told Hooker (2 April 1843) that the 'sectarian doctors' were 'thick as blackberries, in some instances doing good, in others causing confusion worse confused.'

As communities sprang up around missions on the Willamette River, in the Cowlitz Valley, and the Bitter Root region, McDonald saw a threat to the wildlife and natural environment. When the HBC established the Puget's Sound Agricultural Society at Nisqually, he wrote to James Douglas (11 January 1840): 'The moment the freehold grant is obtained I move that the Clallam district in a line from Hood's Canal to the Pacific be barred up and appropriated to the preservation of the poor expiring Beaver race, still leaving country enough for the ostensible objects of the agricultural company in rearing Merino sheep, horned cattle & all the rest of it.'

The year 1841 was a particularly eventful one. It began badly with a destructive fire at the Tshimakain mission in January, followed by the murder of Chief Factor Samuel Black by a Native at Kamloops a month later, and the death of Chief Trader Pierre Pambrun at Walla Walla (after a fall from a horse) a few weeks after that. All of these events demanded assistance from Colvile. The governor was making another visit, and for months before his expected arrival letters went back and forth between McDonald and John Rowand at Fort Edmonton, John McLoughlin at Fort Vancouver, and various other colleagues, discussing Simpson's route and plans to facilitate his journey. At the same time James Sinclair and a party of settlers from Red River were making their way westward to establish a community in the Cowlitz Valley under the auspices of the HBC. In June McDonald played host to a party from the American government exploring expedition led by Charles Wilkes. In August Simpson appeared, followed in a few weeks by Jane's younger brother Joseph, who brought messages from the Sinclair settlers. And in November Father Pierre DeSmet came from his newly established Jesuit Mission to the Flatheads in the Bitter Root Valley, seeking supplies and assistance.

All these events brought change west of the mountains. For McDonald the changes intensified his long-held desire to return to what he still thought of as 'the civilized world.' He was a product of his times, and he was appalled at the rise of republican spirit in the Americas; his loyalties still remained with the British Crown. From the time of his return from his furlough in 1835, his concern mounted for the future of his children, four of whom he had left at the Red River school 'without guide or protection' of their parents. A move to the east became a continuing theme in his correspondence. As early as 1838 he wrote to Ermatinger: 'I have never yet come to any fixed principle as to the proper mode of governing our American colonies: so far however I am influenced by an inherent love for everything that lends to the glory of Great Britain & the prosperity of its descendents.' To James Hargrave at York Factory he wrote: 'Despite all you hear of the charms of Oregon I am by no means disposed to become a citizen of that will-be new section of the great American Republic.'

Health problems began to plague him, and his old vigour diminished after thirty years of life in the fur country. His plan was to establish a home in the east as a base for his children so that he and Jane could 'set ourselves down with them in time & to endeavour to bring them up in habits of industry, economy & morality [rather] than aspire to all this visionary greatness for them.' With his promotion to chief factor in 1841, and the consequent doubling of his income and of his potential retired income, it all became possible. As preparations went ahead, he remained three more years in 'exile in the wilderness.'

In September 1844 the McDonald family left Colvile to recross the mountains for the last time. There was a short pause because of dangerously high waters on the river, and McDonald detoured briefly on Lake Kootenay to gather ore samples from a deposit he thought had a high silver content (later the Riondel Mine) and send them back to James Douglas to be tested in England. From Boat Encampment on the west side they made their way on foot and on horseback through the mountains until they reached the Athabasca River, where they were able to go on by canoe, a blessing for Jane, who was pregnant again and expecting the new baby within weeks. They were heading for Fort Assiniboine, but by 23 November, when the baby (Benjamin) arrived, ice was forming on the river and they were still far from their destination. McDonald decided to go down to Fort Edmonton, where Simpson had suggested they might spend the winter. There tragedy struck, and within ten days in May 1845 three of their little boys died of scarlet fever. The family moved east in June, a melancholy group.

The McDonalds lived in and near Montreal until McDonald purchased his property, 'Glencoe,' on Lake of Two Mountains near Carillon, Lower Canada (Quebec), in 1847. There he was again able to have all his children around him, and the family (increased by another son, Angus, in November 1846) settled contentedly, becoming an integral part of the community. McDonald died there, suddenly, of pneumonia on 15 January 1853, in his sixty-third year. Jane Klyne McDonald stayed on at Glencoe until all the children were grown, when she moved to a cottage in the nearby village of St Andrews East. She died there in 1879.

The letters in this volume represent only part of the body of McDonald's correspondence that has been located, and they have been edited to preserve their continuity and authenticity. In some instances parts (or whole letters) are omitted to avoid repetition or irrelevancies (e.g., I have included only a few of the discussions regarding George Simpson's proposed route through the mountains in 1841, and only a sampling of the many accounts of Samuel Black's murder and its aftermath that were sent to colleagues near and far). The letters to the Tshimakain missionaries that appear here have been chosen to give the flavour of the correspondence, which was frequent and touched on many intimate aspects of their daily round.

Punctuation has been maintained, except for eliminating most of the dashes that McDonald used liberally and inserting a comma or period for clarification. In general I have standardized spelling, with the exception of a few names, such as 'Wallamette' and 'Whilatpu,' where I have retained McDonald's contemporary spelling in the text of the letters. To conserve space I have, for the most part, omitted the often fulsome salutations that begin and end each letter.

The letters themselves come from a variety of repositories. The Hudson's Bay Company Archives (hereafter HBCA), Winnipeg, are a prime source, particularly the post journals, the Thompson River District and Fort Langley letter books, and Simpson's Letters Inward. They also contain letters to Hudson's Bay House, London, and several of McDonald's reports to the governor and Northern Council, which are used for reference but are not reproduced in this volume. The McDonald Papers containing the original Fort Colvile journal and letter books, the Ermatinger Papers containing McDonald's letters to Edward, and the John McLeod Papers also containing McDonald letters are in the British Columbia Archives (hereafter BCA) in Victoria. The large collection of letters to the missionaries Walker and Eells that are excerpted here are in the Walker-Whitman Papers, Coe Collection, Beinecke Rare Book and Manuscript Collection, Yale University. The letters to Sir William Jackson Hooker are in the Kew Gardens Library, Richmond, Surrey, England. I am grateful to all these institutions for their assistance and for their permission to include the letters in this volume.

Jean Murray Cole

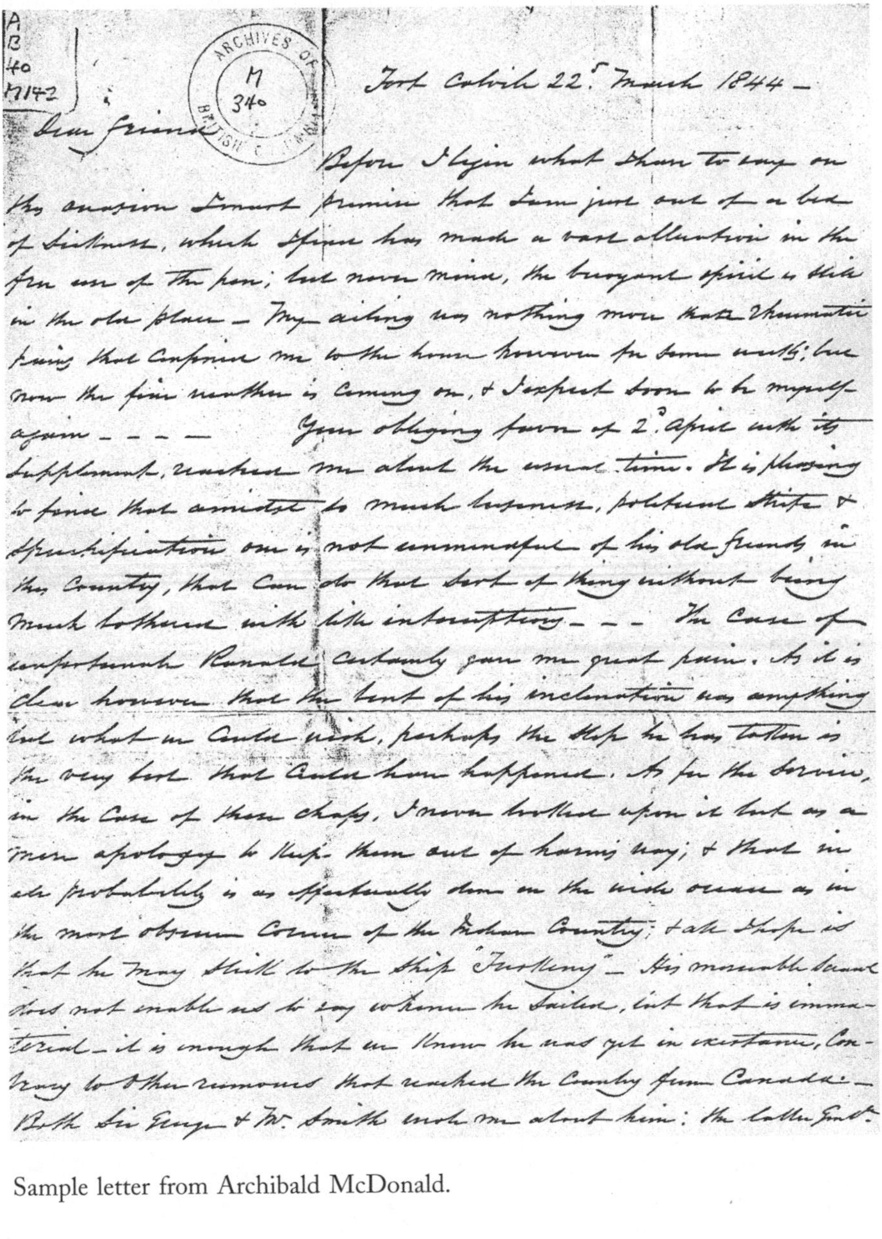

Fort Colvile 22d March 1844 –

Dear Friend

Before I begin what I have to say on this occasion I must premise that I am just out of a bed of sickness, which I fear has made a vast alteration in the free use of the pen; but never mind, the buoyant spirit is still in the old place – My ailing was nothing more than rheumatic pains that confined me to the house however for some weeks; but now the fine weather is coming on, & I expect soon to be myself again – – – Your obliging favor of 2d April with its supplement, reached me about the usual time. It is pleasing to find that amidst so much business, political strife & speechification one is not unmindful of his old friends in this Country, that can do that sort of thing without being much bothered with like interruptions – – The Case of unfortunate Ranald certainly gave me great pain. As it is clear however that the bent of his inclination was anything but what we could wish, perhaps the step he has taken is the very best that could have happened. As for the service, in the case of those chaps, I never looked upon it but as a mere apology to keep them out of harm's way; & that in all probability is as effectually done on the wide ocean as in the most obscure corner of the Indian Country: & all I hope is that he may stick to the ship "Tuckling" – His miserable scrawl does not enable us to say whence he sailed, but that is immaterial – it is enough that we know he was yet in existence, contrary to other rumours that reached the Country from Canada – Both Sir George & Mr. Smith wrote me about him: the latter Gent.

Sample letter from Archibald McDonald.

PART I

Fort George and
Thompson River, 1822-28

McDonald was sent to the west coast headquarters at Fort George in November 1821 to take an inventory of the NWC posts in the Columbia District that had been acquired with the merger of the NWC and the HBC earlier that year. His role at that time did not involve correspondence or keeping the post journal, and although there are many account books in his hand, only two of his letters have been located from the years before he took charge of the Thompson River District in February 1826.

The first letter in the section that follows was written to accompany the detailed inventory of Fort George, Spokane House, Nez Percés (Walla Walla), and Okanagan (Thompson River), and it was completed in the months after his arrival. The second was written in the fall of 1825, when McDonald was awaiting the arrival of the new accountant, Edward Ermatinger, who was to take over the accounts and leave him free to assume his new charge of the Thompson River District (Kamloops and Okanagan). Governor Simpson had completed his 1824-25 tour of inspection and had returned to the east, leaving behind instructions for a mass of sweeping changes in the management of the district.

The Columbia had been the sole preserve of the NWC, and the old officers were firmly in charge when McDonald and Chief Trader John L. Lewes, another HBC man, arrived. With them came Chief Factor John D. Cameron, who was to share the Columbia command with Chief Factor John Haldane, both of them former NWC officials who had received commissions under the 1821 merger agreement. Within a year both Haldane and Cameron returned east, and the charge of the district was left to Chief Factor Alexander Kennedy, who remained at the helm until George Simpson arrived in November 1824. According to Kennedy, the total complement of the fort was then thirty-seven officers and men (including eight men from the interior with the governor's canoe), twenty extra men, thirty-seven women, and thirty-five children.

In his last report from Fort George before the headquarters was moved ninety miles upriver to Fort Vancouver, Kennedy described the new location as both 'beneficially situated for trade' and 'capable of raising grain, cattle and other livestock to provide beef, pork and butter to supply any demand.' Thus he was able to fulfil Simpson's orders to reduce the consumption of imported produce and place more reliance on homegrown supplies. Kennedy left the newly established Fort Vancouver with Simpson in the spring of 1825. Dr John McLoughlin, who had come west in Simpson's wake a few months before, was left in charge of the Columbia District, beginning a reign that was to last for more than twenty years.

For McDonald, the years between 1821 and 1826 were not uneventful. Aside from his accounting work, which also included managing the trading stores on the post, there were momentous changes in his personal life. In 1823, in the 'custom of the country,' he took a Native wife, Princess Raven – Koale Koa – daughter of the influential Chinook chief Comcomly. And early in 1824 a son, Ranald, was born to them. Raven did not long survive the baby's arrival, and Ranald was sent to live with his aunts in Comcomly's lodge. Sometime that year McDonald met and fell in love with young Jane Klyne, daughter of Michel Klyne, the postmaster at Jasper House. She became his country wife, and when he moved to Kamloops in February 1826, he was to prepare a home to welcome her the following summer.

McDonald was comfortable at Kamloops, with his family (including young Ranald, Jane's first-born son Angus, and [later] Archibald, born at Kamloops in February 1828) and congenial colleagues like Frank Ermatinger and Francis Annance around him. He enjoyed the climate and the landscape, and he relished being given the charge of a district. As he bragged to Andrew Colvile, at last he began to hope he might aspire to a chief tradership in the near future. He was able to pursue his interest in natural history, sending a box of specimens back to John Halkett in London in April 1926 and renewing his acquaintance with botanist David Douglas, who was travelling in the region.

Kamloops was the link between New Caledonia and Fort Vancouver. Simpson had decreed that the New Caledonia District would now be part of the Columbia, and furs from the Fort St James and Alexandria trade were to be transported south to Fort Vancouver rather than east to Hudson Bay. Thompson River (with its posts at Kamloops and Okanagan) was expected to be self-reliant as well as to provide a good supply of fresh horses for the pack trains and rations of dried salmon for the New Caledonia men as they made their way down in the spring with their loads of furs. As these letters reveal, it was a challenge that sometimes caused friction and frequently led to ingenious solutions.

With the exception of one personal letter to Andrew Colvile, found in the Selkirk Papers (National Archives of Canada), and the letters to Simpson taken from Simpson's Correspondence Inward in the HBCA, Winnipeg, the main body of letters from Thompson River are in the post letter book (appendix to the fort journal), which is also in the HBCA.

Fort George, Columbia River, 6 April 1822

To the Governor & Council of the Northern Department,
Rupert's Land
Gentlemen:

In pursuance of orders received last fall from Governor [George] Simpson, I accompanied Messrs [John Dugald] Cameron and [John Lee] Lewes to this place where we arrived on 8th November, and in a few

Fort George (Astoria), at the mouth of the Columbia River, painted by Henry Warre in September 1845. (National Archives of Canada C1626)

days after, commenced taking inventory of the property at Fort George which is now enclosed and forwarded for your consideration. As no specific directions were given as to the prices, form or distinction to be observed in making out the inventory, I have taken the liberty of closing the different descriptions of goods under six separate heads, in case such distinction might afterwards be required in the final arrangement of them.

The first column shows the quantity of old stock *actually* found here last fall, the second the amount of the Interior inventories taken collectively from the Book of Remains last spring, and the third column the aggregate amount of what was sent to the Interior including New Caledonia from 15th March to 12th November. So that the total, with the addition of what was sold to servants and otherwise disposed of … last year at Fort George (of which no distinct acct was kept) ought to constitute the Remains of the North West Company in this River last spring, as taken out by Mr James Keith. With respect to the other section of the inventory, altho it is to be presumed that the whole amount is at once charged to the present Hudson's Bay Company, we have nevertheless exhibited in separate columns what was found here last fall, as well as the proportion of that Outfit which was issued for the Inland trade, and will in like manner correspond with the whole of the importation less what was previously used at Fort George last summer along with the other goods. It may not be improper to remark that the last year's Outfit under the mark [F] was found perfectly *entire*. The items inserted under the mark NW [M] include the Boston invoice[1] which is chiefly in the article provision, the whole is now thrown into old stock, and priced in sterling money according to the two last years consignments. There is in like manner a few articles included in this inventory that were manufactured at Fort George out of materials mentioned on the remains of spring list such as oil cloths, Bags, Salops, Iron works, &c and can only be considered as to the good in lieu of the difference in those articles. The [items] with the remarks prefixed were taken out from here last spring after the inventory was taken and are of course charged to the English River department. There is no further explanation in my opinion that is required. The few items among articles of an old stock from China, and another distinguished by the names of Inglis Ellice & Coy are all included with the general stock on hand last spring. [You will find] the same distinction as in the trading goods with respect to

---

[1] The NWC had a contractual arrangement with Perkins and Company of Boston to ship furs from the Columbia to Canton, to return with supplies for their own needs, and to fulfil their obligations to Russian and Spanish coastal settlements.

date of importation. The articles in use, new stock, &c are all put down in the usual form.[2] Gentlemen, as I am aware that anything in the shape of fresh intelligence to promote your common interest in the prosperity of the fur trade must always be acceptable, I hope I may not be considered as deserting from the duties of my department in life, if hereafter I should take the liberty of offering any remarks from the Columbia committee with the subject.

Aboard the brig William and Ann, *15 October 1825*[3]
Report to HBC Secretary William Smith, London

In pursuance of Mr C.F. McLoughlin's command ... I came down here [to the coast] to enquire into the supposed theft of the Beaver skins on board the *William and Ann* and the means by which the sailors became in possession of other furs seen with them when the Beaver in question were searched for.

I have now to state for the information of the Honbl Committee that Michael Laframboise, the interpreter, instead of 30 left but 20 skins on board the brig, as clearly ascertained from his own subsequent confession and the recollection of the Indian who delivered them to him, and certainly the only palliative that can be offered for so glaring a mistake on the part of the interpreter is the circumstance of his perceiving on returning to the vessel that his skins were handled during his absence and one actually exchanged. But in justice to William Light this exchange of the Beaver skin was not without its being previously proposed by him to Laframboise altho the latter did not give it his consent as may be inferred by Light's own note to me on the subject. Mr C.F. McLoughlin also refers to furs found with the seamen when searching for the ten Beaver skins. I have in like manner investigated into this affair along with Capt [Henry] Hanwell – after they had all given their furs to him ... It appears the Captain thro the medium of his Chief Mate intimated to the seamen that they should not be allowed to trade furs or any other private trade on the coast but many of them have positively asserted that no formal notice of the kind was given them ... it is admitted that two or three might plead ignorance of this kind but the Captain has no

[2] For detail on accounts that accompanied this letter, see HBCA B.76/d/4.
[3] McDonald was sent from Fort Vancouver to Fort George by McLoughlin to investigate the reported disappearance of some furs from the coastal vessel. HBC employees were forbidden to conduct any private trade with Native peoples, as this would have been a serious breach of the HBC's Licence of Exclusive Trade. Contained here is an abbreviated account of McDonald's views on the incident and one of the relatively rare acknowledgments in official documents of the presence of women on the scene.

doubt in his own mind but the whole of them are fully aware of its being prohibited by him altho he did not got to the length of reading Mr McLoughlin's letter to them or telling them there was an Act of Parliament against it ...

Allusion is also made ... to Blankets & other articles that appeared deficient in the Outfit sent on the coasting trade but from all I have been able to collect ... I am not inclined to implicate the ship's company particularly. I would however humbly suggest that another time property sent for trade of this kind should be more conveniently arranged and secured when the vessel arrives on the coast.

... Among the ship's stores left us here by Capt Hanwell is a sextant of his *own* which I believe I shall be able to make use of, but the size is one great inconvenience in carrying it about, probably the Honbl Board of Directors may not conceive it improper to send me a more portable one.

P.S. 16 October 1825

Since yesterday afternoon we have had a further clue to the affair of the Blankets which by the evidence of one of the Sandwich Islanders went to prove that two of his companions had each taken one after the vessel came back to the river and which one of them now with me confessed to be the case. I must however still take the liberty of suggesting that the property so situated in future ought to be well secured and out of temptation ... Herewith I send a list of material deficiency: 8 plain blankets 3 pts; 1 plain blanket 2½ pts; 1 blue capot 4 ells; 12 yds HBC strouds; 3 calico shirts.

McKenzie's encampment, Monday A.M.

To Capt Hanwell

If I recollect right I believe you told me the first day when Laframboise went on shore to look after the property, that the sailors still had everything that was sold to them before you last came down to the fort ... now Michael informs me for the first time that he had seen on shore four Blankets with the women of Mr [John Pearson] Swan [First Mate of the *William and Ann*], George, William (the Cook) and Duncan. It is a pity we were not acquainted with all this when the investigation was going on below. He says he told all to Mr Swan and the Doctor when you and I were away sounding ...

Fort Vancouver, 19 October 1825

To Capt Hanwell

In case it is possible you may not be over the Bar when Mr [Alexander] McKenzie is likely to get down I shall briefly state the result of an active inquiry I set on foot among the Owhyhees [Hawaiian employees of the HBC who had been helping load the brig] on my arrival here about 4 o'clock this morning ... I left the [Sandwich] Islanders that were with me a short distance below the fort and immediately commenced searching all their boxes ... but not the slightest shadow of suspicion could be brought home to them. Tourawhyheene on my interrogating him as to the 3 yds HB strouds I gave him on his advances of which he has now but one, told me at once he gave Capt Brown's daughter the rest – [John] Cox positively denies having given Blankets to his own wife ... with respect to James Canton and Kakarrow, America's information against them went merely to say that these fellows had taken Blankets at the ship, and it is true Canton exchanged a plain Blanket for a green one with an Indian – but all this was some time after they had their advances from me. Kakarrow in like manner owns that he gave one of his Blankets to [Jean Baptiste] Dubreuilles woman – Towai positively denies having taken the beads – Morrouna admits his having helped himself to a Blanket at the time Harry [Bell Noah] took his ... the plain matter of fact is that they and the women they kept while allowed to live in the hold with the property must have taken the deficiency in the Outfit.

THOMPSON RIVER DISTRICT

Thompson River (Kamloops), 14 March 1826
To William Connolly,[4] Alexandria, New Caledonia

Contrary to Governor Simpson's arrangement prior to his leaving the Columbia last year, the early arrival of the Company's ship for the coast and other circumstances connected with the Department generally did not admit of my proceeding to this place with the Outfit in the summer, and even my arrival in the winter was not so early perhaps as Mr Chief Factor McLoughlin in his letter from Nez Percés might at that time have given you to understand. After Mr McLoughlin's return to Vancouver the arrangement was such that I should endeavor to be at Nez Percés about the time Mr [Donald] Manson was expected to be there with the Express [from Fort Vancouver] ... Accordingly I left Vancouver on the 7th January and found the packet at Nez Percés on the

---

[4] Chief Factor William Connolly was in charge of the New Caledonia trade from 1824 to 1831. A wintering partner in the NWC, he was made a chief trader in the new HBC after the merger in 1821 and was promoted to chief factor in 1825.

14th which intimated a deficiency in the number of horses and agrès [harness] required for the use of New Caledonia as well as the state of this place. To supply these wants without interrupting the other great essential work of procuring the salmon, I lost no time in coming in with 26 horses of all ages I found with Mr [Samuel] Black [at Walla Walla] altho their poor condition forced me to leave five at Spokane and the other nineteen at Okanagan – myself reached here on the 13th February and Mr [John] McLeod started for Fort Vancouver on 19th. I now regulate myself in great measure by your letter of November addressed to myself and the answer to it by McLeod & the return of Mr [John] McBean. With respect to the horses, appèchements [buffalo hide saddle cloths] and saddles I am satisfied that in conformance with your memo of wantages, these are not far short – the pack cords I believe are complete, but of the Saskatchewan leather I can say nothing. I am aware that at the time Mr McLeod wrote, he could not have determined as to the time of my departure from here … I have it now in my power to acquaint you that Mr [John Warren] Dease *can* without risk of want employ all his people inland and that to great advantage in removing everything to Fort Colvile[5] in the spring and consequently we shall all rendezvous at Okanagan, unless Mr C.F. McLoughlin will find it advisable to direct that a Boat's crew from the interior should accompany down the extra Boat he may send with the Express the length of OK … however I trust that in either case you will find everything on this communication fully to your satisfaction.

I leave this tomorrow with the Returns and upwards of 2,000 salmon, so as to meet the Express at OK where I shall have further instructions from Mr McLoughlin; in the meantime Mr Francis Ermatinger[6] remains at this place with the interpreter & 2 good men expecting daily to hear from Alexandria … the 2 men you were to send to replace the old hands we agreed to forward for your purpose the length of Alexandria, and when they do come no time will be lost in dispatching ours ([Étienne] Grégoire & [Jean] Gingrais … I go down with 7 men instead of 10.

[5] En route back east in April 1825 Governor Simpson stopped at Spokane House and made arrangements to move that post north to Kettle Falls on the Columbia River in order to avoid the sixty-mile overland trip to and from Walla Walla with furs and supplies. The new post was given the name Fort Colvile.

[6] Francis (Frank) Ermatinger and his brother Edward joined the HBC as clerks in 1818. McDonald first met them when they crossed to Hudson Bay on the same ship in the summer of 1818, and both brothers became his lifelong friends. Both came to the Columbia in 1825. Edward retired from the fur trade in 1829, but Frank remained in the Columbia District and served with McDonald at Thompson River and, later, at Fort Colvile.

I now leave 10 horses here exclusive of 2 of your own ... with 20 I expected to have reached here from OK before my departure all to be at your disposal on arrival here: or indeed in the event of Mr Ermatinger hearing that relief horses may be required even before you get this length he will dispatch some to meet you. Whether or not I go down to the sea before your arrival at OK I shall always have time to send up a few of the best horses I now take down, so as to enable you to remove *all* the salmon, should you determine on leaving none for the ingoing. Mr E. will also take down the few goods if they are not required for your quarter. While at Nez Percés I also selected for you from the goods left there and originally intended for the Snake country, a few capots, trousers, vests, shirts, red baize, calico, &c &c and made them up into two Bales which I left with the horses at OK, but will I expect be here with these horses hourly expected. Herewith I enclose you all the charges against New Caledonia I could pick up on the way – to those from Nez Percés I have taken the liberty to annex a few notes in explanation. The charges from Spokane ... we shall undertake to make good – there are now 36 appèchements and 15 saddles at this place and at OK 105 appèchements and 10 saddles ... On inquiry I find that should the water be too high at the Forks of Okanagan River, it can always be crossed in Indian canoes or even the main river is generally fordable between the Forks and the Doglake, otherwise I would have taken precautions to accommodate you from OK with a Boat.

If one Boat at least does not come up with the Express one, I fear the number inland will be too few for taking down the Returns. Mr C.F. McLoughlin is advertised on the subject of those intended for the trip down; 4 old ones are at OK which I shall endeavour to put in the best possible repair, altho we have no man that knows much in that way. Making no allowance for the salmon that may be traded during the spring, there is now here in store:

for taking down your Brigade	1,500
for the journey ingoing	2,500
for the present estab. to end of May	1,000
Rations 3 per diem at Okanagan when I got down	7,000
Total	12,000

For present use, these are all tolerable good salmon, but I fear the quantity appropriated for taking you in from here to Alexandria cannot at that season of the year be good. Mr Erm. will point out a certain portion for that purpose better preserved than the generality. Wishing you a safe and speedy conveyance to the banks of the Columbia.

Okanagan, 10 April 1826

To William Connolly, Alexandria

As I was on my way up to the Forks of Spokane in company with Mr C.T. John McLeod and the York Factory Express canoe, your several communications of 6th Feb. 5th & 11th March and Mr G[eorge] McDougall's letter of 22nd of last month were handed to us late last night. I need scarcely observe that the disastrous tale they contained of the fate of the horses was most painful to us both.

I returned immediately to this place so as to dispatch the bearer of the packet back to Thompson River with as little delay as possible, trusting that Mr [James] Yale will not leave that place until he has some satisfactory account for your information of what he can still do to insure the transport of the furs to the Columbia. Indeed by Mr McDougall's statement of *36 able horses fit for service* being still absolutely required, I conceive it would be imprudent in Mr Y. to return before he heard from here, as with the exception of 2 of the horses I brought on in the winter ... I am aware from the hardship they suffered going up last month, they are in no condition to be relied on as affording so many of the number required. I have therefore sent off 12 of the best horses I brought down with me two weeks ago ... to Alexandria, the rest of my Brigade was composed of mares that are just now beginning to drop their foals, but I trust that this 12 and the 12 I left above including 2 of your own with what number Mr Erm. can procure from the Indians will contrive to bring you the length of Kamloops, and from thence with the help of the young horses I conceive unfit for the journey to Alexandria and with whatever number not less than 25 Mr Dease can spare from Spokane, I think we can yet venture to entertain sanguine hopes of seeing you on the banks of the Columbia by the 10th of June ...

When I return from the Forks of Spokane, where Mr Dease is at present so far on his way with bag and baggage [family] to establish Fort Colvile at the Kettle Falls, I go down to Walla Walla with 2 Boats and all the disposable hands that come up in company with the Express so as to be employed in preparing the removal of that Establishment also, and from thence I proceed by land to Fort Vancouver with 30 or 40 horses upon which depends the certain return of Mr [Peter Skene] Ogden with his furs [from Snake River] in the month of August ... I think it essential to acquaint you that our stock of salmon at this place is 1,500 less than I was aware of. There is another very heavy demand in that commodity, altho I have not had it in any official way from Mr C.F. McLoughlin. Mr [Samuel] Black, who is to have the men above alluded to attached to his place until you descend, desires me to furnish them with salmon, otherwise he will use corn and pease left there by the Snake expedition last fall ...

As horses are so scarce I suppose you will at once decide on leaving at Kamloops for the summer the salmon appropriated for your going in from there. I shall soon see Mr Black [at Walla Walla] on my way down, and will of course lay before him your correspondence on the affairs of New Caledonia and will not fail to urge the necessity of buying horses, altho in fact orders to that effect are in constant force with the Gentlemen at Walla Walla ever since Gov Simpson left us last year, but I am sorry to remark that the Natives of that quarter seem to feel great reluctance in parting with animals so much in admiration among themselves. I understand that 106 was the original number of skins from the Saskatchewan last fall and that 94 only were forwarded. Your letter to the Saskatchewan Gentlemen just arrived in time to cross by the Express canoe. Two of our men are busily employed about the Boats and I think there will be as many as we are likely to require. I hope they will also be able to block out paddles, but there would be no harm in your men themselves looking after those things as they come along. I start for the Spokane Forks early tomorrow morning, and I trust Mr Dease will have it in his power to afford you considerable assistance in getting on from Kamloops to here.

Forks of Spokane, 15 April 1826

To Andrew Colvile Esqr, London

Unwilling to intrude myself too much on your attention I have not even acknowledged the receipt of your much esteemed letter two years ago, on the subject of my prospects in the present concern ... To Governor Simpson's special friendship I owe a great deal. I am quite pleased with this part of the Indian country, where am now stationary for these five years, & in fact am considered an *old hand* on this side the Rocky Mountains now. Last year the Govr & Council at York Factory were good enough to confer on me the charge of a District, so that I am now (& indeed the only HB man) associated with a long chain of N.Westers in the conduct of the Columbia trade, altho alas! I hear nothing of my Chief Tradership.

I have a Box or two of curiosities and preserved Birds going home in the first ship for Mr [John] Halkett[7] & should he not be in England

[7] John Halkett, a member of the HBC London committee and (like Colvile) a brother-in-law of McDonald's former patron Lord Selkirk, had a long-standing interest in natural history and gathered specimens for his friends at the British Museum.

himself at the time they arrive, they ought not to be allowed to remain any time unexposed.

The principal object of my troubling you now is the little money due to me by the Fur Trade which, from the circumstance of my being situated in this remote part of the country ever since the new arrangement I have been deprived of the opportunity of formally directing, should be put in the hands of the Honbl Hudson's Bay Company for bearing the interest usually allowed their other old clerks, but year after year finding no accumulation from interest, and that an objection is lately made by the Honbl Committee to receive any further sums of that nature above a certain amount, I trust if my application already to Mr Secty Smith on the subject has not brought about the transfer, that my soliciting your kind interference may not be considered presumptuous. If no interest can be obtained from the Company I beg leave to leave to your own better judgement the mode of employing it to the best advantage; the amount this spring is about 440 pounds.

In this part of the world I hear but little from Red River, however I am sorry to say, that by my H.B. correspondents on the east side the mountains I am not flattered with any favourable account of our Buffalo Wool concern.[8] A Mr Henderson forwarded to me last year from York Factory a charge of 200 pounds due to the estate of the late Earl of Selkirk the nature of which I am unable to comprehend. Mr Pritchard never writes to me.

Forks of Spokane, 16 April 1826

To Governor, Chief Factors and Chief Traders

The circumstances of my having succeeded Chief Trader John McLeod in the charge of the Thompson River district last February requires that I should intrude upon your attention with a few lines of the annual conveyance, but as McLeod himself is about starting for headquarters, and will of course exhibit the result of last year's trade &c &c before the Council, it is only necessary for me to advert particularly to the facility that Gentleman and myself have been labouring to afford to Mr Chief Factor Connolly for getting across to the Columbia with the Returns of New Caledonia this spring and to give you the best idea of the preparations in progress for that purpose; I beg leave to refer you to a copy of my letter for Mr Connolly before I left Thompson River, and which

---

[8] The Buffalo Wool Company was established at Red River after the coalition to process hides supplied by the HBC, under the management of former Nor'wester John Pritchard. Many of the HBC officers and clerks, including McDonald, held shares; unfortunately, the venture was never successful.

is not likely to find its way to York Factory by any other route this season. [Enclosure, see letter of 14 March]

So far I apprehended no serious obstacle to the Brigade getting out
in due time, but unfortunately the contents of an Express lately received
from New Caledonia has frustrated these arrangements, altho I hope not
totally defeated the main object. To show the extent of the difficulties
we have now to obviate, I beg leave to enclose copies of the last communication from Mr Connolly, and as my reply to these letters embrace
the only alternative left with us at this season of the year, I also take it
upon me to transcribe it for your information. [Enclosure, see letter of
10 April]

I arrived here on the 12th and Mr Dease lost no time in coming in to
the last arrangement proposed to Mr Connolly as far as it rested with
him, and accordingly the following day we dispatched 20 horses for OK
and with 10 or 12 more I may be able to obtain from our men I trust to
make out the number of 30, which will leave that place about 1st May
so as to have 10 days to recruit at Kamloops before the Brigade comes
in. Under all those circumstances, and however much the risk in passing
and repassing with any sort of security the horses we are obliged to have
constantly in the way, and on which now depends everything, I am still
in hopes that we shall ultimately find [that] Mr Connolly with the remainder of the furs will effect the journey to Okanagan by the 10th June.
Mr F. Ermatinger wrote to me 3rd April (the day after Mr Yale arrived)
that about the 15th that Gentleman was preparing to return to Alexandria with all the horses they could muster about Kamloops, but Jacques
[Lafentasie], our interpreter, who came down with the Express did not
think he would start before his return. Mr Dease joins with me in the
propriety of using at Walla Walla the salmon intended for Mr Connolly's
voyage from Okanagan to Kamloops in lieu of the corn and pease Mr
Black will otherwise be obliged to resort to. Instead of 2 Boats as Mr
McLoughlin directs, I can only for want of a steersman take down one,
which will answer all our purpose, because after the different parties are
sent off to Kamloops and 2 men to accompany myself from Walla Walla
Mr Black will only have 10 men exclusive of his own 5 summer men.

Okanagan, 19 April 1826

To Francis Ermatinger, Thompson River

I arrived here from the Forks of Spokane this morning, accompanied
by your brother [Edward Ermatinger] and Mr [John] Work. Edward &
I depart tomorrow for the sea [Fort Vancouver] & Mr Work takes Mr
Annance's place [at Okanagan] (who in like manner goes down with us)

until you arrive & will then in conformance as I have already observed with Mr Chief Factor McLoughlin's arrangement take charge for the summer.

You already sufficiently well know the nature of our situation at Okanagan to render minute directions unnecessary – I would like however to lay considerable stress on the provisions and means of subsistence at the post for the winter without having recourse to Kamloops or Fraser River. Therefore the salmon is the first consideration, which I believe can be traded to some extent in the months of July & August. The garden is the next object & I am sanguine enough to hope that my own pains in seeing the crop put in the ground & Mr Work's assiduous attention no doubt to that department also, ultimately joined by your own talent & zeal for promoting so laudable an object will almost ensure us a *thriving crop*. Berries & everything else that will serve as part rations ought to be traded on a particular scale. You may also trade a few good horses if not too dear.

The most unlimited assistance is to be given to Mr Connolly & party. In a few days Jos Deslard & the New Caledonia men with an Indian will leave this with thirty horses. The three sent by the men are expressly for carrying *packs*, and at the risk of the Company. I hope this reinforcement will enable you all to get on swimmingly.

Of course you are aware how destructive insects have been about this post during the summer season & will guard against as much as possible. The six Kegs potatoes we could muster here are in the ground, but one I had from Spokane will be sent up by Deslard for enlarging our field at Kamloops – [Jacques] Lafentasie and [Antoine] Bourdignon are the two men that will summer with you. I left open memoranda with Mr Work & you will attend to the things required to go down by the Brigade to be returned to the general store, besides the few furs that may be got in before their departure.

Nez Percés, 17 July 1826

To Francis Ermatinger

We arrived here two days ago after a journey of eleven days from Fort Vancouver. Mr [William] Kittson with three Boats now proceeds to Fort Colvile & in meantime brings you a Bale leaf tobacco which I presume is the only article of trading goods you may stand in need of.

Messrs Work, Annance, the two Douglases [James and David] & myself [along with an interpreter, twenty-eight men and an Indian chief named Charlie] are on the eve of starting to the horse fair at Nez Percés

Forks, and do not expect to be back here before the 25th.[9] Consequently our arrival at Okanagan will be at least as late as the 5th or 8th of next month.

I have nothing particular to say in the business of the place. However, that an opportunity *did* offer, I thought you might drop me a line this length.

Nez Percés, 30 July 1826

To Governor George Simpson

It is with infinite pleasure I anticipate your speedy return to the shore of the Pacific, altho there is great reason to apprehend that the unexpected high waters this year will not admit of your descending from the mountains quite as early as was first calculated upon, still everyone is in the full persuasion of seeing you as soon as it is at all practicable.[10]

Hitherto this season everything has gone on well in the Columbia, however before we could all proceed to our respective destinations the unaccountable mortality in the New Caledonia horses last winter has again subjected us all to delay in the Nez Percés River, where Messrs Work, [James] Douglas, Annance and myself have now procured upwards of 70, which with our remaining stock at Okanagan ought to suffice for all parties in the Interior, and I believe in all conscience, enough is at hand for the low country. I return from here tomorrow, expecting to join Mr Connolly at Walla Walla in a couple of days. I think we ought to reach OK by the 10th. He of course loses no more time there than is indispensable so I suppose there is no chance of *his* seeing you this season but as my presence is not so very urgent at Thompson River so early I am authorized by Mr McLoughlin to await your arrival to at least the 20th or 25th as the winter operations in our quarter will altogether depend upon the settled plans of the ensuing year for the extension of trade.

[9] After a sweltering six-day journey from Walla Walla up the Snake River to Nez Percés Forks the group joined a party of about 600 Native people, 'a camp of three different nations … the Pierced-Nose Indians, the Chewhapton and the Chamniemuchs,' according to David Douglas's journal. After partying and gift-giving late into the first night, the parleying began on the second day, followed by several days of 'singing, dancing, haranguing and smoking, the whole party being dressed in their best garments.' The proceedings were interrupted by an altercation between the interpreter and one of the chiefs that nearly led to warfare. Fortunately the affair was settled amicably, and on the sixth day of the encampment the HBC party set off with a train of seventy healthy new horses.

[10] Apparently Simpson was expected that year, but in fact he did not return to the Columbia until 1828.

This being the case and as it becomes an object to gain knowledge of every sort of communication between the inland posts and the sea, I propose after Mr C's departure to proceed with a few men across as far as the headwaters of Puget Sound which if necessary may be found a convenient communication from that quarter with this part of the Columbia. As I do not consider the distance long, I expect I may be back before the 25th ...

Nez Percés, 30 July 1826

To John Warren Dease, Fort Colvile

The extreme scarcity of leather[11] at Ft Vancouver this year has rendered our plan entirely dependent on Ft Colvile and in addition to the 14 elkskins I had in the spring, I trust you will be able to supply us per the fall canoe with 12 more, a few parchment skins & 200 fathm pack cord, in case Mr Connolly may require the greatest part of what we had in the spring.

In consequence of an order to have Boats built in our quarter this winter [Pierre] LaCourse is again appointed to Thompson River and as I believe we are destitute of almost everything for that purpose I am in hopes you will afford us all the assistance you can in the way of tools &c &c ... I believe LaCourse expects his family down to Okanagan immediately on arrival of Mr Work.

Okanagan, 13 August 1826

To Francis Noel Annance[12]

Although the usual time of proceeding to Thompson River with the Outfit is arrived, certain circumstances will not admit of such a measure at present; however, as it is desirable that some of our people should accompany Mr Connolly & the New Caledonia Brigade as far as Kamloops you & two men are appointed for that purpose.

• Your first & principal object will be to secure as much salmon & berries or anything else in the shape of provisions as possible.

---

[11] Leather hides were used to wrap the fur bales for shipping.

[12] Francis Noel Annance, clerk and interpreter, was McDonald's assistant in the Thompson River District in 1826-27 and, later, at Fort Langley, where he had been one of the founding party. He joined the HBC at the time of the merger in 1821, after a year's service with the NWC. He was part Abeneki from Quebec, was well educated, and spoke several languages. He retired to Montreal in 1834. In 1845 he returned to the Abenaki village of St Francis.

- The potatoes planted there in the spring will of course require attention if not already destroyed by the Natives.
- As tis possible you will have to move about a little I would wish you to ascertain where the best & most convenient wood for Boat building can be found.
- With respect to the Natives, you are already aware that we have had no reason to be too well satisfied last spring with those in the neighbourhood of the fort. You will therefore treat them (particularly Court Apath & Tranquille [Shuswap chiefs]) with all the indifference consistent with prudence & your own safety. You will have tobacco enough to give them the necessary smoak & all their Beaver trade will be put off until my arrival with the Outfit, not later than the 10th of next month.
- Of course anything you can get done to repair the fort & buildings will be desirable.

Okanagan, 22 August 1826

To John McLoughlin, Fort Vancouver

Something like us all, you are no doubt in momentary expectation of seeing Governor Simpson's arrival, but I fear it will all be in vain now – at least until we see the fall Express.

Mr Chief Factor Connolly & myself got here on the 10th with 4 Boats having previously proceeded to Fort Colvile where Mr James Douglas had arrived three days before with sixty of the horses traded at the Nez Percés Forks, of which 15 were made over to Thompson River, & with the remaining 45, & 75 already at this place, Mr Connolly was able to make a start on the 13th with a Brigade of 120 excellent horses including those sold to the men, and about insure his arrival at Alexandria in little more than 20 days. Mr Annance & two of our people accompany them the length of Kamloops & will give what assistance may be required there besides attending to our little interest until I get up.

... You are aware it was my intention to have awaited the governor at this place till at least the 20th and by way of making something of the delay with our men I once thought, had we arrived in time, of making a trip across land towards the headwaters of Puget Sound, but our late arrival, & the idea of being absent should he cast up in the interval prevented the undertaking ... [Instead] five of our men were employed on a trip of six days down to the Piscahoes River, from whence they are just returned with about 500 salmon, enough to keep us all afloat here for a few days, & enable me to take what may suffice for the journey to

Kamloops, which I mean to undertake in 3 or 4 days. By Indian report
we are informed that everything there is ruined, but I am of opinion tis
something of the old story with a little more exaggeration altho of the
potatoes from the circumstance of its being left entirely to its own fate,
I am not at all too sanguine.

At this place, if the quantity of potatoes be not overabundant it is certainly sufficiently good to reward all the labour bestowed upon it … cab-
bages are beyond expectation, turnips, beet root, onions, peas & melons
are worth trial another year. Of Indian corn we shall have a few good
heads. Barley may not be wholly hopeless another season, but the wheat
has completely failed.

In reference to your letter of 17th ultimo & the man expected for
our place, I have now to inform that *two* are required to complete the
complement of last year for Louis Satakarota was given to the Rocky
Mountain Boat before your letter reached me at Nez Percés Forks, &
since that time we have given another Iroquois (Lasard) to Mr Connolly
to replace a sick man of his, who is now here & will be sent down in
the fall if not in a fit state to go about. As we are not overstocked with
effective horses, for the greatest part of those that came to our share of
those from Nez Percés were unfit to proceed on the journey, I hope more
coming for us may be provided at Walla Walla … It is much to be regretted that the mares cannot be more moderately used at Thompson River
– last fall 21 took the stud but this summer we have hardly the prospect
of half dozen colts.

LaCourse accompanies me to Kamloops, but nothing will be attempted
in the way of Boat building until we hear from you or some other again.
Meantime however I send you a small memo of all that may be required
from below, should we meet with some little assistance from Ft Colvile
– even from LaCourse['s] own information I am satisfied there is no
absolute necessity of having a Blksmith on the spot. I am afraid the transport of Boats from Big OK Lake to the Shuswap Lake will be attended
with insurmountable difficulties.

Okanagan, 23 August 1826

To Samuel Black,[13] Walla Walla

Should there be any men your way bound for this place from Ft Vancouver, you will be good enough to supply them with horses on acct of

[13] Samuel Black, who served with the NWC from 1804 until the merger, harboured
resentment towards the HBC, partly because his appointments as clerk (1823) and,
later, chief trader (1824) were delayed due to his reputation as a troublemaker. He

the district, or if you have a superabundance of them you can now forward a couple by the Indians that accompany Mr Douglas, & in so doing will promote the interest ...

Okanagan, 23 August 1826

To John Warren Dease, Fort Colvile

Mr [David] Douglas safely arrived here yesterday morning with your trusty Robidou. He at his own choice embarked in a small canoe with 2 Indians this forenoon that will carry him the length of Walla Walla, where tis to be hoped he will meet with no difficulty to protract his journey downwards.

Robidou will have his leave to return tomorrow & he brings you back in the saddlebags the piece of Russia shirting & ½ doz 14 inch files sent down here as part of your disposable goods last winter ...

Having understood from Mr Douglas that you were much at a loss for plough irons this fall, to extend your already thriving fields at Fort Colvile, I shall be happy to let you have the use of a set I had up this summer, & which I cannot myself apply to any improvements this season either here or at Kamloops. Meantime will answer your purpose & Robidou is also the bearer thereof. It is gratifying to hear that your potatoes is in such a thriving state; here there is no reason to complain of the little put in the ground.

Mr [Francis] Ermatinger sends up two or three gunlocks that require some trifling repair at the hand of Pierre Philippe Degras. I cannot say with you that our Beaver trade is tolerable, for as yet nothing could be more miserable. I mean to leave this on the 28th when I shall give up all idea of seeing anyone across the mountains before the usual time of the fall Express. On questioning LaCourse as to the tools required I believe all we shall trouble you for will be a small [illegible] hammer, 2 cold chisels, 1 punch & an old line for making oakum ...

Okanagan, 27 August 1826

To Governor George Simpson

It being now upwards of two weeks since my arrival here & I may say in daily expectation of seeing you, I further delay to no purpose. It was Mr Chief Factor McLoughlin's particular desire that I should this long

---

became a chief factor in 1837. Black was in charge at Walla Walla (Nez Percés) from 1825 to 1830 and at Kamloops from 1830 until 1841, when he was murdered at the fort by a Native. He was apparently a rather prickly character, and McDonald's letters to him frequently reveal his impatience with Black's demands.

postpone my journey to Thompson River, conscious of the advantage an interview with you might have given us in the event of establishing Fraser River & opening the inland communication by our route.

I leave this tomorrow accompanied by 8 men,[14] & in course of the fall … will endeavour to visit Thompson River down as far as its confluence with the main stream [Fraser River] …

Thompson River, 30 September 1826

To John McLoughlin, Fort Vancouver

In conformance with your desire of the 4th July to examine the nature of the water communication from this part of Thompson River down to its confluence with the main stream, I set out accompanied by 8 men & Nicolas [Hwistesmetxe'qen, also known as NKuala], the Upper Okanagan Chief, on Monday the 18th Inst and am happy to inform that in seven days we were back after performing the desired object, an object which I hope may prove satisfactory in the event of the anticipated plans of extending the trade to the northward being carried into execution. They must be considerably facilitated by finding these two rivers navigable for Boats, which I have no hesitation to say is the case, altho not at all seasons of the year.

This river to the mouth of the Coutamine is not bad, & indeed to the little rivulet Nicaumchin there are no very dangerous places; but from there for about five miles down, even when I was there and when the water was greatly fallen, it was nothing but a continuation of cascades & strong rapids. Earlier in the season it would of course present a more formidable appearance, but if this place was the only obstacle, it could with additional exertion be overcome at any time. The fact is, that the nature of those two rivers, rolling down with great rapidity in a narrow bed between immense mountains, generally speaking render their ascent

---

[14] Not mentioned here is that McDonald was also accompanied by his wife Jane Klyne and her new son Angus, born 1 August at Okanagan; two-year-old Ranald; Annance's wife and son; and the families of seven of the eight men in the party. (Joseph Deslard, Antoine Bourdignon, Alexis Laprade, Joseph Moreau, Jacques Lafentasie and Pierre LaCourse all brought their wives and, among them, a total of ten children. By the following spring four more babies were born at the fort.) After a journey of thirteen days (200 miles), they arrived at Kamloops on 9 September at the head of a train of fifty horses carrying the annual Outfit for the fort. According to McDonald's Journal of Occurrences at Thompson's River, 1826-27 (HBCA B.97/a/2), the Outfit, valued at 200 pounds, included 'Guns, Ammunition, Tobacco, Blankets, Strouds, Brass Kettles, Beaver Traps & Axes.' They were greeted by Annance and two other men who had gone ahead to prepare the fort for their homecoming.

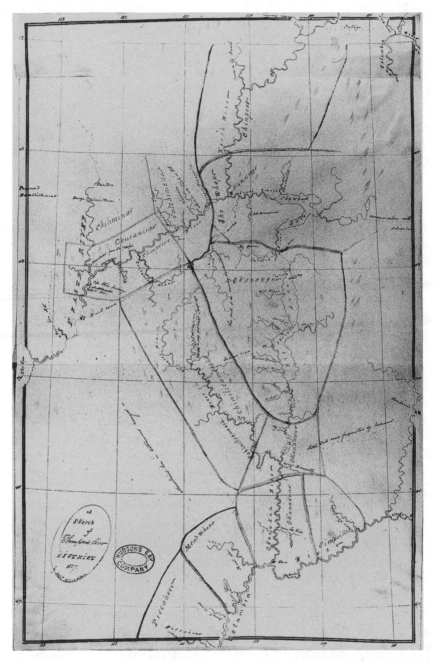

This map of the Thompson River District was drawn by Archibald McDonald in 1827 and was the first map of the interior of British Columbia. On it McDonald outlined the territories occupied by various native tribes in different coloured inks. (Hudson's Bay Company Archives B.97/a/2 fo. 40)

most laborious, & in places in the main river perhaps impossible except at low water.

The two rivers, after their junction, form a stream hardly equal to the Columbia before the Forks of Spokane, & in its progress downwards meets with no considerable water except one river from the N.W. not far from the sea. The last mentioned river is not likely to furnish an easy outlet with the Interior, but the Indians speak of plenty Beaver being along its banks. There is a short communication with it either by the Fokonote River, or from the Bridge by way of the lakes near which it takes its rise.

On arrival at the Forks I was anxious to see the state of the water, but the canoe furnished, & the only one there, proving inefficient we could not go on. I then left the Indian Chief & 4 men with the horses and our little property, & proceeded by land with the interpreter & three Bouts [steersmen] for the span of about 8 miles, which comprehended what the Natives called 2 rapids & one of their dangerous places; on viewing that part of it the rapids proved mere ripples, and when we returned was nothing more than something similar to our little Dalles on the Columbia River, but rather longer with good hauling room at either side.

While at the Dalles, the Natives pointed out to us about 6 leagues off a mountain to the south east at which there was a village where two Chiefs have had some intercourse with Nicolas this summer across land. To that place they said there were no worse places than we had seen, & believe it to the sea the only out & that always passable with the line at low water.

With respect to Fraser River *above* the Forks, I am satisfied from every information I could collect, that the same low state of the water which is necessary for ascending the main river, will also admit a free passage for Boats as high up at least as the Bridge is where we trade our salmon. Nicolas himself once came down by water from there to the Forks.

A convenient land communication from these rivers with the bank of the Columbia being also an object of attention, on my return I left Thompson River at the Nicaumchin & came by the Indian track that leads to the upper Forks of the Okanagan River the length of Nicolas' lodge, which, so far, is passable enough & may with safety be adapted with horses instead of going round by Kamloops. However in parting as high up as the mouth of the Coutamine there would be less danger from the Natives to the craft coming here, & the road across land is equally good & convenient from there.

During the trip we had the good fortune to see but few Indians: their salmon fishing was over, and by that time they were back in the mountains after the deer. Some however more anxious to gain our favour represented all the absentees as off for Beaver. Nicolas showed himself among them very jealous for the whites. He exercised his rhetorical fancy among them two or three different times & as I was told much to the purpose: above all things to avoid quarrelling with us. I have advised this Indian to continue his friendship with the two Chiefs from below & to bring them to the fort next time they come his way. By an intercourse of this kind we may soon make a very favourable impression upon the numerous tribes of Indians in the lower part of the river.

About 40 Beaver skins we got in the vicinity of them that came from below to meet us at the Dalles: for a Blanket of blue stroud or one of 2½ pts. they at once gave 6 Beaver & 5 for each of two traps I had & which the Indian from below eagerly caught. Giving the goods at this rate, I conceive no sacrifice made; those, with ammunition & tobacco, were the favourite articles.

It may not be unnecessary to remark that as far as I had seen, the face of the country is wretchedly barren, wholly unfit for any kind of gardens & indeed after the first day's journey, it might be a matter of difficulty to find *room* enough for a fort except at the Forks itself & that would be but a very disadvantageous site for an Establishment.

Herewith I forward a sketch of the river,[15] & the other objects referred to in this report. I had a few good observations for the Lat. and I have reason to suppose that the Long. of the Forks cannot be far wrong. This place is about the same meridian with Okanagan which the inland travellers have placed on or about 120 degrees & I believe the mouth of Fraser River is not far from 123 on Vancouver's survey of the coast. The distance between the triangles or *Trepieds* represent one day's journey on this trip, as well as the ordinary march with loaded horses from Okanagan to here.

P.S. 24 October 1826. On reference to the sketch you will find dotted off my track from Thompson River the other day by Schimilicameach [Similkameen] & where I assumed the Indian path not far from where I left it when coming up the Coutamine. What I have seen of the country there would not discourage me from adopting that passage in preference to go round by Kamloops. I had with me but two men & the Indians were inclined to give some trouble, however with a more formidable force I am convinced they would be passive enough.

[15] HBCA B.97/a/2.

Thompson River, 8 October 1826

To William Connolly, New Caledonia

During my absence from here on 20th ult your son arrived here from below on his way to New Caledonia & was off a couple of days before my return. It however happened that his Indian was unwilling to proceed beyond the Traverse, & they both came back to the fort about three days after. They now again make a fair start and trust nothing will interfere to prevent them reaching your quarter in safety. I am sorry to add that somehow or other William drop'd his letters somewhere between Okanagan & this, if Mr McLoughlin *did* say anything on business cannot refer to his letter. I go down to OK myself on the return of Mr Annance from Fraser River,[16] & hope to find there sufficient directions should the contemplated plan of extending the trade be adopted. There will be horses enough to attend to your memo should the leather & cord be still forwarded by way of the Columbia.

Agreeable to Mr McLoughlin's orders I visited this river down to the Forks, which is perfectly navigable for Boats when the state of the water suits the working of them in other parts of the communication[17] ... the Natives however say that a worse place is near to the sea, but always with the advantage of using the line coming up & never necessary to carry the Boats going down. So much for navigation in lower part of the river – tis to be hoped that the upper will not prove insurmountable.

Thompson River, 8 October 1826

To James M. Yale, Fort Alexandria

I forward you a note, although I have nothing particular to communicate; William [Connolly Jr] will verbally give you the news all the way from Fort Vancouver to Alexandria & poor fellow he'll require it for

---

[16] Annance had gone with a party of men to Fraser River to procure a supply of salmon from the Natives fishing there.

[17] This proved to be untrue. When McDonald went down the Thompson and Fraser Rivers with Simpson in October 1828, according to his journal they found the route to be a treacherous series of rapids, whirlpools, and eddies 'at least half the distance embedded in solid rock.' See Malcolm McLeod, ed., *Peace River: A Canoe Voyage from Hudson's Bay to the Pacific, by the late Sir George Simpson in 1828. Journal of the late Chief Factor Archibald McDonald ... who accompanied him* (Ottawa: Durie and Son, 1872). Simpson pronounced it unsuitable as a 'practicable communication ... having three of the most experienced Bowsmen in the country ... I consider the passage down to be certain Death, in nine attempts out of Ten.' See E.E. Rich, ed., *Simpson's 1828 Journey to the Columbia: Part of a Dispatch from George Simpson ESQr Governor of Rupert's Land* (Toronto: Champlain Society and London: Hudson's Bay Record Society, 1947).

unluckily he dropt on the way up from OK to here all his written news
… The Indian that accompanied him received payment from 12 to 15
skins. It is unnecessary to return by the Indian the identical horse for I
suppose some will be required this fall again by your people to go from
here to Alexandria.

Thompson River, 12 October 1826

To the Officer Commanding HBC at Mouth of Fraser River

I am just returned from examining the river down to a short distance
below the Forks, which am happy to acquaint you is so far likely to
answer our purpose. I send this by two Indians I invited up from there,
& who promise to forward it without fail should they hear of the Whites
being established at the mouth of the river.[18] All is well in this quarter.
I go down to Okanagan in a couple of days, & then expect to hear of
the intended operations for the ensuing year.

Okanagan, 17 October 1826

To John Warren Dease, Fort Colvile

… I came down to meet the Express after returning from an expedition down Fraser River, & Mr Annance and three men making another
trip for the salmon to the usual place. I was fortunate to get here 24
hours before the arrival of Mr McMillan & friends, when I was kindly
favoured with yours. I have now to thank you for the effort made to procure us the leather, am however rather disappointed not sending us that
pack cord, an article so much required in the present transport of salmon,
& of which, some are now sent down with several Bales to Walla Walla
out of the few we had & more will be required for that purpose in course
of the season. Parchment we can do without but at the expense of shut-
ting up all our windows. However we are aware of your own great demand
this year in that article …

Okanagan, 24 October 1826

To John McLoughlin, Fort Vancouver

The anxiety I felt at Thompson River increased by the loss of the last
letter, induced me to make a trip this length immediately on the return
of our people from Fraser River and arrived two days ago. Then & only
then I found every document addressed to me both by yourself & Mr
Black in the subject of tobacco, salmon, boat rivets &c &c.

---

[18] McDonald thought Fort Langley was being built that year, but it was delayed until
the summer of 1827.

The arrival of tobacco from the other side obviates that part of the subject, but Mr Black's Bale is nevertheless sent down. As for the salmon, it is clear that I could not have any idea of the scarcity at Walla Walla ... However of 1,600 that came down for goers & comers, 500 are sent by Mr McMillan & Mr Black is informed that he can have any quantity he may require at this place by middle of December. With respect to the building of Boats, I find it can be dispensed with for one year: yet, the certainty of their being required the following season may render it desirable that something towards that object might be attended to this winter also, but this nor any other real improvements cannot be commenced without a small summer Establishment, when a couple of men would be quite secure.

By the Minutes of Council it would appear that many changes are in contemplation with respect to the Columbia Gentlemen ... I am not likely to be here any more this season. We have no copy of the Minutes of Council, but took a few extracts of such as may in part be applicable to ourselves.

The present conveyance affords the opportunity of forwarding to you a short report with a rough sketch of the country from Thompson River Establishment down to the Forks of Fraser River, which agreeable to your request I visited this fall. The result of which I have also transmitted for the information of Mr Chief Factor Connolly.

Okanagan, 24 October 1826

To Samuel Black, Walla Walla

On my arrival here two days ago, I was favoured with the various communications made by yourself & Mr McLoughlin on the subject of tobacco, salmon, &c. And have now to acquaint you that the Bale of leaf consigned to you in the summer ... is sent down ...

When I left Thompson River of course I would not have been aware of the scarcity at Walla Walla & consequently made no provision for you; however of 1,600 salmon that came down, Mr McMillan takes 500 in the Boats for you & as I apprehend no want in our quarter, you may send up here for any quantity by the 15th or 20th of December.

What I said to you of horses meant nothing more than merely to facilitate the journey of such people as are expected up, especially as I anticipated they would be encumbered with iron works. As it is, not furnishing *one* horse to carry the rivets here, occasioned their being left a second time on the way, & only arrived three days ago after being sent for to Priest's Rapid & incurred expenses equal to half the price of a horse ...

Thompson River, 22 November 1826

To James M. Yale, en route from New Caledonia

Late this evening the Indian safely handed me the packet with your kind note dated at the *Pavilion* on the 19th and it is with infinite satisfaction I learn that so far you descended this river well & found it possible to be navigated with Boats. The lateness of the season is certainly against the undertaking, but with favourable change in the weather of late & the probability of meeting with fewer obstacles the nearer you get to the Forks will enable you to make a good march ere the Indian can return to the *Pavilion*. He tells me you have settled to meet him in ten days, but whether at the same place or higher up at the Falls I cannot make out. However we shall endeavour as much as possible to put off signing accounts with him here that he may have an inducement of his own to carry you the returned packet [of letters]. One of our men will accompany him unless Mr Annance (whom of course you must have fallen in with) will judge that the Indian alone cannot but find you out. Our people left this on the 15th & they must have been at Fraser River about the 19th.

I shall be happy to hear of your further success. Letters left anywhere between the *Pavilion* & the Falls will be sure to find the way here.

Thompson River, 23 November 1826

To William Connolly, New Caledonia

An Indian arrived here late last night from Mr Yale ... Mr McMillan & friends arrived safe at Okanagan where I met them on the 24th ... The warlike passion which at present rages so fatally among the Indians of Alexandria and the surrounding tribes is unfortunate & cannot fail to produce consequences highly detrimental to the trade.[19] If the Returns fail at Thompson River we must trace the cause to some other source, which [I] am afraid is not so easily removed, as a reconciliation is brought about with the hostile party; with us the Beaver have actually vanished.

As tis possible there will be no other conveyance between us this winter, I take it for granted that the arrangement of last spring will be adopted in the ensuing one, as far as regards our having a sufficient force to take care of the provisions until your arrival & find the means of forwarding the outgoers to Okanagan, whom I presume are not likely to be here before I leave. You may rely on finding some fresh horses at this place & perhaps we may have it in our power to send a vessel or two to

---

[19] Both the Carrier in the vicinity of Fort St James and the Babine farther west had a long history of hostile behaviour towards European traders.

meet the Brigade at North River Traverse. We have now a couple under
way altho they are not actually required for the first season, but the Boat
builder is on the spot & we may as well give them a trial. It is possible
Mr McLoughlin will authorize this man to be left here for the summer,
as something of the kind is indispensable another year.

Thompson River, 3 December 1826

To John McLoughlin, Fort Vancouver
    ... I am now happy to inform that less what the post of Okanagan
itself may require, about 3,000 salmon is sent down [for Samuel Black]
on this occasion. The last trip however to Fraser River has not been so
successful as we anticipated. Mr Annance found the Natives more troublesome than heretofore & nowise inclined to trade with their usual unre-
served disposition. Without giving them any offence on his part, the next
morning after he got there, he had the mortification to find that two of
our horses were shot by them during the night and assigned as the reason, without asking the malcontents, that it was in revenge of former
grievances received at the hand of the whites. Mr James Yale & eight
men from New Caledonia happened to arrive at our people's camp that
very day & they all thought the best plan was to procure the salmon in
mean time, but even this was effected with some difficulty & shyness on
the part of the Natives and ultimately traded not above ⅔ of the quantity required. On the eve of their departure our people again had some
trouble with them & to extricate themselves the party would be compelled to fire; but as good luck would have it the New Caledonians after
destroying their canoe & giving up the idea of returning by water, again
unexpectedly joined our people, when all [the Indians] were obliged to
scamper, but not before 2 or 3 of them had got some corporal chastise-
ment & two others suspected of being concerned in the killing of the
horses were deprived of their guns. Thus rests the business at present.
    It may be proper to observe that since the reduction in our Establish-
ment of men, it was customary to send no more than six for the salmon,
which were considered few enough; but the last trip Mr A. was under
the necessity of leaving one on the way in consequence of his having
received a kick from one of the horses & this reduced his party to five.
The next time we send, which will be some time in Febry the party will
consist of a Gentleman and at least eight men. Before that time as the
trip to F.R. may be unsuccessful, we shall try down this same stream
where, from appearances in the fall, we may get some salmon. I am aware
of the advantage a good supply in this article would give us in the upper
part of the Columbia next spring, but unless we succeed in getting at

least 6,000 pieces yet, we cannot be relied on to furnish any to the Express or Walla Walla. Exclusive of what is going down now we have at present in store 5,000 salmon.

With respect to Beaver I am sorry to say that present appearances only confirm that they fall short of last year's trade in the same proportion that Thompson River returns have diminished within these four years back. The Natives seem well disposed & many of them during the fall made unsuccessful efforts; the fact is this, Beaver have been incredibly scarce.

By a perusal of Mr Chief Factor Connolly's general letter to the Factors & Traders herewith forwarded ... we are acquainted with the probability of his being this year at Okanagan by the first of June, & the quantity of salmon required to take him hence to there, & I hope nothing depending upon us will protract their progress. We shall in like manner provide for their retiring servants but they ought not to leave this later than the 1st of April so as to reach Okanagan by the 12th, which period the Express may probably find late enough. As for myself, unless I am directed by you to the contrary, I shall leave this with a few men about the 15th or 20th of March, so as to be some days at Okanagan before the arrival of the Express.

Mr Yale, agreeable to directions from Mr Chief Trader [Joseph] McGillivray, came down Fraser River the length of the Bridge, where he found our people. He wrote to me by an Indian from the *Pavilion* (15 miles above the Bridge) dated 19th Nov. in which he says 'The river thus far is navigable by Boat but not without much difficulty & danger: for these three days back it was full of drifting ice; it is now however nearly clear again.' The Indian was returned the morning of the 24th with the N. Caledonia letters ...

The 4 Boats left at Okanagan last autumn will be forthcoming, which with 2 at Fort Colvile are all I believe we have to depend on, unless one or two left at Walla Walla might be made to answer if required. Here we have all the wood necessary for two new ones brought home & sawed; they may possibly be of service in the spring to meet the New Caledonians up North River, however they must be left to the mercy of the Indians if a couple of men, as I have already hinted, are not to remain for the summer. Till that is the case, neither will it be worthwhile to make any further attempts at gardening.

Thompson River, 3 December 1826

To John Warren Dease, Fort Colvile
Three of our men are just about starting for Okanagan with salmon

for Mr Black so as to meet his people [from Walla Walla] there about the 15th, the time we have reason to expect letters from below ...

As usual in our hammering about after salmon, Mr Annance a few days after my return made another trip to Fraser River, but was not quite so successful as we had reason to expect. The Indians all along the upper part of that river were in a complete state of warfare & it would seem the flame in great measure has caught those we visit in this lower part also ... While our people were at Fraser River they fell in with Mr Yale & eight men from Alexandria visiting the river ... In his descent he did not see the Indians with whom it was also an important object to have a conference on the nature of the commotions among them in the vicinity of Alexandria ...

As the old Boats will require much repairing, we shall expect gum down by the first opportunity.

Thompson River, 3 December 1826

To Samuel Black, Walla Walla

... we now send down 2,800 salmon of which Mr Ermatinger is directed to let your people have from 1,500 to 2,000 if you require them, & possibly in the spring we may be able to let you have a few hundred more.

By the public correspondence of Messrs Connolly & McGillivray you will see the extent of their trouble with the Indians in that quarter & we ourselves have had some difficulty with those of Fraser River also ...

Thompson River, 3 December 1826

To Francis Ermatinger, Okanagan

Our people returned from Fraser River about six days ago, altho their trip was not to the full extent of our expectations, yet I hope [André] Picard will be at you to a day, that Mr Black's people, should he send up for the salmon, may not be detained a single hour. To avoid any misunderstanding as to the quantity intended for him, I have left my letter open for your guide ...

Lafentasie comes up in the room of Picard & I see no necessity for their remaining in expectation of the Express from below later than the 25th ... Should any letters from Fort Vancouver ... arrive after that date, perhaps to avoid unnecessary expense with Indians you could find it convenient to come up with them yourself. Keep down such horses as you think will not be in good condition to accompany me in March; I fear some of them are affected with the strangles as is the case with many of those here now.

Thompson River, 23 December 1826

To Joseph McGillivray, Fort Alexandria

... the Indian entrusted with the letters ... at length, about ten days ago ... cast up with his packet &, according to his own story, a deplorable account of his privations during a fruitless chase after Mr Yale, who in my opinion was rather sanguine in expecting [to be] back to the ... river by the 24th, the Indian that left him at the *Pavilion* on 19th ...

In sending the letters now, I avail myself of the return of another Indian from your own quarter who tells me that the object of his returning is pressing – no less than the laudable purpose of apprising you of a meditated plan of the Tsilcoutines [Chilcotins] to attack your fort & in particular to revenge some insult offered to their tribe of late by John, your interpreter, whose relations here urge the speedy departure of the bearer ... We are at present honoured with the company of all the idle Indians on those streams from below the forks to the very Rocky Mountains. They are now engaged in one of their grand Banquets [*] at the special invitation of Court Apath and altho they are by no means troublesome yet our attention is diverted from any other object.

Following is an excerpt from McDonald's Journal of Occurrences at Thompson River, 1826-27.

Sunday 17th [December] – During the night & this morning 3 to 4 inches of snow fell ... but still mild weather ... Had an early visit from 30 of the Coutamines ... traded about 20 Beaver, a few pieces dried salmon & eight dogs ... smoaked with us the whole day ...

Monday 18th – Ascertain total number of population (Coutamines) – they furnished me with a small piece of stick for every grown man of their community, with few exceptions each has a wife, seldom more, children must be averaged from more accurate statement taken of other tribes.

Wednesday 20th – Everything being prepared to commence the grand banquet, we all had an invitation from Court Apath this afternoon, but for the present myself only and one of the Canadians attended. It is much to be regretted that the object of this kind of jubilee (not uncommon among the Natives here) is not better understood by the Europeans, & am sorry to say that I am not likely to throw any additional light on the subject – not a word of the Native language here can anyone attached to the Company's service speak. All our little dealing with them is done thro the medium of the Okanagan ...

On arrival at the camp I saw for the first time the Basin [hollow depression] the Chief had constructed for the express purpose of this entertainment – its dimension at base is 45 feet square with an upright

wall of about 4, and then the roof running to a point in the centre, to
answer the purpose of a door. To this aperture is fixed up nearly perpen-
dicular, a stout stick of about 18 ft. notched at convenient distances to
serve as a ladder ... gang of stark naked fellows actively engaged in low-
ering down by means of slings from 20 to 25 of their waterproof baskets,
smoaking hot with thin soups, none of them less than 10 gallons & some
considerably more. In mean time as many were already busily employed
below cutting up the most excellent dried Beaver & venison laid up at
the expense of much labour & privation to themselves solely for the purpose since autumn – bear's fat, both raw and melted ... & roots of every
description peculiar to this part of the country ready for distribution.

The guests, near upon 300 men, sat upon the ground as thick as they
could ... round & round this subterranean habitation, leaving very little
space for the attendants, who by the bye let it be observed were not the
most contemptible of the Shewhaps & even Court Apath himself was by
no means an idle spectator altho his labour did not extend beyond mere
superintendence. Every man was furnished with the cheekbone of salmon
for his spoon, & the soup kettles, consisting of berries, roots, grease,
pounded fish, salmon roe, &c &c being planted here & there among
them, they fell to & soon emptied their dishes. These spacious reservoirs
the Shewhaps Chief & other personages in attendance made it a point
to taste a portion of each before the hungry visitors commenced the attack.
The next course was each a lump of suet, after which the Beaver & venison with a raw piece of bear's fat; & lastly the roots. This ceremony occupied about two hours, when I enabled them to resume the pipe, which
being some time indulged in, the devouring organs were again called to
action & to continue alternately with the pipe for at least 24 hours.

It is a universal rule with them on such occasions that the guest must
eat all put before him, & if this task be too much another is imposed –
that of carrying it with him. This (being liberally supplied with the most
substantial part of the eatables) was unluckily the case with myself today,
but the constant dry salmon at home rendered [it] more agreeable than
painful. Those who come from a distance are by this law much beholden
to their good appetite & to their still better powers of digestion, but I
believe before the feast is over seldom the latter is found capable of performing its functions, & the consequence is what naturally might be
expected. This heaving up scene affords the host (evidence absolutely
necessary) the most convincing proof of their being treated to their heart's
content.

They have been dancing for the last 48 hours, which I believe necessarily carries with it a system of fasting. During the dance presents were

exchanged. The Coutamines gave 3 or 4 horses, Guns & Hayques [hai-qua shells used as currency]. The Shewhaps returned the compliment with Guns, Robes, Beads & a few Beaver traps. I observed hung up in the Banquet Hall what they told me were appendages belonging to some of the deceased relations of Court Apath & friends, which in the progress of the dance were often saluted with loud peals of mourning & lamentations. During this rendezvous it is also an object with them to pledge their friendship with each other, altho religion is no doubt the primary consideration.

Before quitting this grand affair, I acknowledged the good behaviour of the Coutamines when I was among them [and] intimated our intention of soon going that way again for salmon, & the probability of the whites by & bye passing thro their country with Boats &c &c, all of which seemed to leave them with sentiments of additional regard for us. The rest of our people crossed to the camp in the evening. None of the Okanagans attended & but very few of the Schimilicameach [Similkameens].

Thursday 21st – A few of the Coutamines left the camp early this morning, but those good fellows that swallowed most of last night's emetic are still on the ground.

Friday 22nd – The six principal Indians from below came across this morning to see us before their departure – took their names & gave each a ½ yard green Beads, a corn scalper & ½ head leaf tobacco.

Thompson River, 30 December 1826

To Chief Factor Connolly and Chief Trader McGillivray, Alexandria

Five days after the opportunity that last occurred to Alexandria, the Fort Vancouver winter Express arrived, which we forward without delay. Meantime I transmit our account this season with New Caledonia & the few articles supplied [to] individuals, which latter are charged at the winter price, but should it be more regular to charge the District with the whole at the 70 p.c. we are agreeable. I am not informed how such accounts are disposed of at our depot, & I beg Mr McGillivray may be good enough to acquaint me by the first conveyance. Our Boatbuilder is recalled to Fort Colvile for it is supposed that craft will still be required next summer for the Columbia. I see Mr McLoughlin is anxious that Fraser R. should be examined in the spring, but with the returned packet he is acquainted with all the information I have had from Mr Yale on that head.

Thompson River, 6 January 1827

To John McLoughlin, Fort Vancouver

I was favoured with yours of the 18th Novr on the return of our

people from Okanagan 30th Ult & as Mr Annance, who was then absent
with six men at the Coutamine for salmon, did not return before the 4th,
LaCourse was not, agreeable to your request, to have taken his departure for Fort Colvile before now. A partial failure in the last trip having
subjected us to another attempt to Fraser River for the salmon when our
horses are sufficiently recovered, but perhaps at a time it would be too
late for him to answer your purpose below. I also give Mr Annance himself his leave now, that they may go in company to Okanagan. I trust
Lafentasie & myself will do what is to be done till the spring. This
moment we have not quite 5,000 salmon in store here, & but a few
hundred at OK. By Mr Black's tone of perfect indifference about this
article, I should almost think he is putting us to unnecessary trouble ...

Our Returns here may possibly come up with last year's trade yet, but
Okanagan is miserable. I beg your advice in the spring how we are to
take credit for the horses charged to this Outfit last year. An Indian left
us with the New Caledonia packet on the 1st & is now not far from
Alexandria. I perceive your anxiety to have Fraser River examined down
to the Forks; it must therefore afford you much satisfaction in perusing
my last to see that that task was already performed at the desire of Mr
Chief Factor Connolly; & Mr Yale's note to me ... will now tend to
remove many of your serious apprehensions on that head.

With respect to the men whose time will expire in the spring 1828
(none are free in 1827) & bound by their last contract to give twelve
months' notice of their intention then, I beg leave to submit for your
information the following list & reply viz:

> Jac. Lafentasie – Interpreter – In debt – has no thought of leaving the country
> Pierre LaCourse – Boatbuilder – At present is of opinion to visit Canada
> Alexis LaPrade – Middleman – Will reengage & trusts no objection to him as Bout
> Ant. Bourdignon – Middleman – Finds himself getting weak for the service
> Laurent Karonhitihigo – Bout – A good Bout & might be employed
> Louis Shoegaskatsta & Lasard Onahargon – Middlemen – These two are not
>   adapted for this place & should go out
> Pierre Satakarass – from N.C. is a noneffective man

P.S. On second thought, if nothing below absolutely requires his presence, I have directed Mr Francis Ermatinger to come up, that one of us
may accompany the people to Fraser River, & especially to reconcile our
late difference with the Natives there. Indeed am of opinion that another
year the post of Okanagan might be kept up without a Gentmn resident
there at all.

Thompson River, 6 January 1827

To Francis Ermatinger, Okanagan

I make no doubt you will be surprised at seeing two of our principal personages at Kamloops pop in upon you, but such are the orders from headquarters by the last packet. LaCourse proceeds without delay to Fort Colvile & his plan is to be supplied by a middleman from Mr Work. Now if you have nothing particular requiring your presence at Okanagan & your health perfectly recovered I should be glad to see you up here on arrival of Mr Annance, who continues his journey to Fort Vancouver, where Picard is joined by the man coming from Ft Colvile. Mr A. has time enough and can remain at least 20 days. Should he go down by land let him take Mr Black's mare, or if she is unfit, you can give another in her stead, that we may have no more horses changed so in this season. In mean time let Mr B. *again* be informed that we are absolutely in want of the pack cords. Send Mr Work an account of the boat irons we have at OK in case he may require them. Get LaCourse to examine the Boats below, & secure what hoops, nails &c may be required for their repair. Bring up all the saddles with their proportion of appèchements, & what cords you can gather. We also want up 10 yds blue strouds & the same quantity of red baise. With further reference to Mr Annance.

Thompson River, 5 February 1827

To Francis Noel Annance

On leaving this I was not aware of any particular objection to your proceeding to Fort Vancouver immediately on the arrival at Okanagan of the man coming from Fort Colvile in the room of LaCourse, but I have now to request, in consequence of directions contained in Mr Chief Factor McLoughlin's memorandum … that you remain at Okanagan until the return of Mr Ermatinger from hence …

Thompson River, 12 February 1827

To Francis Noel Annance

There being no chance of any letters arriving from New Caledonia in time to go down to Fort Vancouver before the departure of the Express, you will of course proceed with the Flathead & Fort Colvile letters without delay. Mr Ermatinger expects to get down in ten days.

Thompson River, 12 February 1827

To John McLoughlin, Fort Vancouver

… behold, on the evening of the 7th our Indian returned with only a couple private letters from Mr McGillivray which did not in the least hint that he had forwarded the packet ... or that he was at all aware of the importance you attached to an answer. It is therefore in vain to look for any returned letters from that quarter before the outgoers come on, & Mr Ermatinger accordingly leaves us tomorrow, that Mr Annance may proceed with the Flathead & Fort Colvile letters without delay.

This conveyance affords me the opportunity of giving you an exact idea of our stock of salmon now, which my last two letters left entirely in suspense. Before the arrival of Mr Ermatinger, the interpreter & seven men had safely returned from Deases River with 3,000 and we are now enabled to meet all demands, should you even appropriate enough to take the Express on to Fort Colvile & 5 or 600 yet to Nez Percés (if required) to save the conveyance of grain from below. It is with satisfaction I also add that our people are again well received by the Indians & that matters touching the old troubles have been amicably settled.

By the last account from Alexandria dated 16th Janry their horses were in good condition, & but little snow then on the ground. Mr McGillivray also intimated that all their endeavours to bring about a reconciliation with the Natives have proved unavailing – the Chilcotins refused their presents & interference altogether.

Thompson River, 14 March 1827

To George McDougall, New Caledonia

As I understand you are to pass this way in a few days with the New Caledonia retiring servants so as to be at Okanagan by the 10th or 12th April to meet the Columbia Express, I hope my being away will be no disappointment. Lafentasie, the interpreter, who remains here, is directed to give you every requisite accommodation as far as salmon for the party to go down with & horses to carry it, besides a horse or two for your own use may be considered as such. I leave this tomorrow & will be happy to see you at Okanagan by the appointed time.

P.S. I am sorry I have not the pleasure of your company down, & am afraid the lateness of the time proposed for your people to meet the Express leaves but little chance of your being with us any time before their arrival from below. I request you will without ceremony help yourself out of what little stores I leave here.

Thompson River, 14 March 1827

To William Connolly, Alexandria

Your packet of the 6th February is just arrived here, which however is too late to reach Mr Chief Factor McLoughlin before the departure of the York Factory Express.

I am exceedingly sorry to find that you have the mode of conducting these Expresses so universally condemned.[20] With respect to myself and the peculiar situation of the two posts under my charge ... I hope I shall always be found an avowed advocate for due economy. I am aware of woollens being the invariable demand about Okanagan, but if it is insisted upon to be less, I fear our Indian couriers will be more uncertain than they have been.

I also beg leave to exonerate myself as to time. Mr McLoughlin's packet of the 20th Novr reached Okanagan 13th Decr & left this on 1st January, upwards of ten weeks ago; I take the liberty of making this comparison to show that delay is not entirely confined to that part of the communication south of this, & I believe Mr McLoughlin will attribute *his* disappointment to something of this kind also. I sincerely hope that the conspicuous situation in which I am placed myself, & of course a good share of every conspicuous remonstrance levelled against any misconduct or inattention on the communication, justifies this explanation.

I leave this tomorrow morning, but two men remain in charge of the salmon until your arrival. It is also probable that some of us will meet you at the North River Traverse with a canoe by the 10th May. From the favourable account of Alexandria we make no provision here for transport to Okanagan. All ours [horses] are exceedingly poor & several died.

P.S. The letters arrived late in the evening by one of our Indians on *horseback*, who fell in with the regular courier in the morning, unable to gain the fort today.

Okanagan, 9 April 1827

To John McLoughlin, Fort Vancouver

Independent of our little accounts which are already closed & forwarded, I now send you all the public documents connected with Thompson River which I conceive required by the Governor & Council. To the Journal is subjoined all the correspondence and a Map of the District. Agreeable to your request the Report is also transmitted.

[McDonald's Thompson River District Report, dated at Okanagan, 5 April 1827 (HBCA B/97/e/1), is published in Simpson's 1828 *Journey to the Columbia: Part of a Dispatch from George Simpson ESQr to the Governor & Committee of the Hudson's Bay Company London*, by the Champlain Society and Hudson's Bay Record Society in 1947.]

---

[20] The preceding letters illustrate the difficulties and pitfalls of the communication system in the Columbia; often letters were slow to pass from hand to hand, and sometimes they failed to reach their destination at all.

Chief Trader Archibald McDonald Descending the Fraser River, 1828, by A. Sherriff Scott. (Hudson's Bay Company Archives P-408 N8093)

PART 2

Fort Langley,
1829-33

In March 1828 McDonald left his charge at Thompson River and went down to join Edward Ermatinger and the eastbound Express party at Okanagan. He had been invited, for the first time, to attend the annual meeting of the Northern Council, where he was to receive his coveted appointment as chief trader. He returned to the Columbia that fall in the entourage of Governor George Simpson, a journey well documented in McDonald's journal, edited by Malcolm McLeod, and published in 1872 under the title *Peace River: A Canoe Voyage from Hudson's Bay to the Pacific*. (It has since been reissued by Cole's [1970] and Hurtig [1971].)

Simpson's westbound party arrived at Fort Langley on 10 October. A few days later the governor continued on to Fort Vancouver, taking with him Fort Langley's chief factor James McMillan, while McDonald remained to take charge of the post. There he was to remain for the next four and a half years.

Fort Langley had been established by McMillan the previous year, in the hope that the Fraser River would prove to be a navigable route to the coast, a substitute for the Columbia should the Americans assert control over the southerly route. It was destined never to achieve the prominence originally intended for it. After experiencing the hazards of the journey down from Thompson River, Simpson immediately declared the Fraser to be 'certain Death, in nine attempts out of ten. I shall ... no longer talk of it as a navigable stream.'

McDonald found that he was isolated at Langley. From the time of his arrival in October 1828 until the following summer the only contact he had from outside was a letter from Simpson, sent by a Native courier as he travelled east with the spring Express. In February 1829 he wrote to John McLoughlin at headquarters expressing his concern about the long silence, sending his message up the river by courier to Okanagan, to be forwarded down the Columbia. In March he dispatched his two clerks, James M. Yale and Francis Noel Annance, with a party of ten men down to Puget Sound with another packet, containing his report to the Northern Council, to find 'a trusty Indian' to carry it to Fort Vancouver.

It was not until mid-July, when Captain Aemilius Simpson arrived with the *Cadboro*, that McDonald finally received any communication from Fort Vancouver: a letter bringing word from McLoughlin that the HBC supply ship from England had sunk at the mouth of the Columbia with the loss of the entire crew and the Outfit for the coming year. Meantime American trading ships moved up and down the coast gathering furs that the HBC traders missed because of a shortage of trading goods and delays in their ship's appearance among the Natives. Meeting this competition was one of the reasons for Langley's existence, but it was several years before the HBC gained control over the scene.

Meanwhile, the salmon fishery was so bountiful that McDonald urged that more skilled tradesmen be sent to Langley to enable him to process

Jane Klyne McDonald in Montreal, c. 1846. The daughter of fur trader Michel Klyne and his Métis wife Suzanne LaFrance, she became McDonald's wife in 1825. With their large family she retired to St Andrews East, near Montreal, twenty years later. (Cheney Cowles Museum/Eastern Washington State Historical Society)

and ship the thousands of salmon that the Natives brought in to barter. Another potential source of revenue was timber, and in September 1830, along with large quantities of dried and pickled salmon, he shipped to Fort Vancouver 10,000 dressed cedar shingles as an example of what his men could do by hand, without even the benefit of a small sawmill.

When the *Cadboro* arrived at the fort in July 1829 with its cargo of trade goods, it also brought Jane and the children (now three boys) from Fort Vancouver to join McDonald at his new post. The family became a happy diversion, and McDonald was soon conducting what he called a 'thriving school,' with his wife and little boys as the star pupils. Two more sons, Alexander and Allan, were born at Fort Langley. McDonald's vignettes of domestic life on this remote outpost provide a glimpse of the informal side of the fur trade rarely encountered elsewhere.

Numerous personal letters survive from this period, among them the earliest in the series of annual epistles to Edward Ermatinger, the first written in March 1830. McDonald's warm friendship with Ermatinger had grown over the years since 1818, when they had first met on board ship en route from England to Hudson Bay, and it sustained him. Edward became his link to the 'civilized world' to which he hoped some day to return. Ermatinger was the sounding board for McDonald's hopes and dreams, and the recipient of his thoughts and feelings about his family, his colleagues, and events in the daily round of the fur trade.

Edward Ermatinger, a former fur trader who settled in St Thomas, Ontario, preserved the long and interesting letters written to him by McDonald between 1830 and 1846. (Elgin County Pioneer Museum)

Fort Langley, 20 February 1829

To John McLoughlin, Fort Vancouver

By a packet we are about dispatching up the river by means of Indians, so as to reach Okanagan if possible before the York canoes pass, I address you these lines, in case it may be the only communication we can have with the Columbia before the Outfit is sent ...

As the people send no order of their own now, suitable equipments can be made up for them by a reference to their movements of last year ... Louis Boisvert is the only one of them that has any notion of leaving the place before March '30 – he says tis part of his agreement to be allowed to cross the mountains this fall.

One book of the accounts ... will be sent up by this conveyance ... Before we closed the accounts for last Outfit, 15th Inst the Returns were up to 1,400 skins. Everything is quiet here and we live in plenty.

Fort Langley, 11 March 1829

To John McLoughlin, Fort Vancouver

Although I had no positive assurance from Governor Simpson last fall that I should have heard from you even by this time, yet I confess I thought it more than probable and was in daily expectation of having seen the *Cadboro* for the last three weeks ... now that hardly a chance remains of seeing the vessel in time to return with any degree of certainty before the York Express leaves you, I dispatch Messrs Yale and Annance and ten men with a Boat tomorrow morning to the south end of the [Puget] Sound, where I am in hopes they will have no difficulty in confiding the packet to the hands of a trusty Indian that will carry it to Fort Vancouver at least before the governor starts. In this case I remain with but six men – a complement certainly not too formidable, nor is the party going along the coast unnecessarily strong. Still my extreme anxiety for their safety induces me to make rather a stretch on their behalf. And I hope we have nothing to fear here so early in the season until their return, which cannot be above 8 or 10 days.

The district accounts are forwarded with blank columns ready to be filled up on reaching you. The men's advances however are priced according to last year's Tariff ... There being but few trading goods on hand except Blkts the requisition for ensuing year is perhaps heavy in exceeding three hundred pounds ... but going this length I conceive that a few Bales extra from the manner in which the supplies are sent me can hardly be a fault – besides the fellows we have to deal with are yet so capricious in their fancy that a variety is necessary ...

Fort Langley, 11 March 1829

To Governor and Northern Council

From the short time I have been at this Establishment and the other circumstances connected with it since last season, it is not to be expected that I should now go into any particulars. I feel it incumbent upon me however to relieve your anxiety by informing you at this late date that everything is going on well, & that from all appearances we are likely to continue on good terms with the Natives.

Having had no communication with the Columbia since the York Express came in, we are quite unprepared with means of closing our accounts or a sure mode of forwarding them such as they are. The only alternative left is to send a strong party with a packet as far as the south end of Puget Sound where I am in hopes that a trusty Indian will be found to carry it to the Columbia before the departure of Governor Simpson.

The returns you will find have increased to upwards of 1400 skins and from the reduction made in the complement of men as well as the discontinuance of the other avoidable expense attending a new Establishment I trust that Fraser River will always give satisfaction.

Fort Langley, 22 March 1829

To Governor and Northern Council

... I am now enabled to say that our force is again united, and that Messrs Yale and Annance with their party have safely returned from the Cowlitz portage without experiencing any annoyance from the Natives of that quarter. Not so however when nearer home, for on entering this river yesterday morning, they had to encounter a most daring attack from those of the Gulf of Georgia ... It may be observed that the southern branch of the two main ones into which the river separates a few miles from the coast again divides itself within half a league to the mouth. Coming up the least of these channels ... our party discovered a number of canoes crowded with people on a point to the right hand exactly at the forks evidently wishing to conceal themselves behind, with the exception of two canoes each about 30 men – these boldly stood out into the stream with the manifest intention of amusing the Boat. But by this time everything being made snug on board and a resolution made to rush thro with the flag up and a cheerful song, the Gentlemen kept their eyes upon them. Finding there was no chance of decoying them or passing down with safety they instantly put about and stemmed the current, and now ... a half moon formed out in the river by 9 canoes as the Boat gained the point. No shot was fired until our people were fairly within the point and right in front of the canoes, that at that time might have been about 150 yards off – as they commenced the firing they began to approach gradually. The Boat now getting out of slack water had to contend with a brisk current along side of a steep bank, of which the Savages took immediate advantage and the very two canoes that first reconnoitred made for the shore. A battle now becoming inevitable, the [HBC] Boat also dropped to shore, but from some neglect amongst themselves all were thrown into an alarming dilemma for a moment by allowing it to shear out again when but seven men had been landed. These however kept the Indians below at sufficient distance until the two Gentlemen with the other three men hook or by crook got ashore with the ammunition, and rendered the position taken so formidable to the bloodthirsty villains that in about 15 minutes the whole Brigade of not an Indian under 240 was completely repulsed, and down the main branch into the open gulf before our party reembarked. Altho their guns carried well, loaded with plenty powder, tis most fortunate that none of our people was hurt; nor can we say with the exception of Mr Annance and his rifle shot, our small guns are likely to have made very great execution among the Indians. The Blunderbusses if they did not carry their length at least made a noise. Whether they had a fixed design upon the Establishment or the party, or merely came to catch what they could, is more than we can say. However had they even appeared before the fort while I was here with six men, I flatter myself they would require to fight more determined than they seem to have done to gain much by it.

All the Indians within the river have come to congratulate us on the wonderful triumph over the invincible Yewkaltas [Euclataws/Lekwiltoks] and are most desirous to become our allies when tis their turn. The Coutamine Chief from Thompson River Forks that came down with Governor Simpson last fall fortunately happens to be here this moment and has great encouragement to take this letter to Thompson River House, in case it may possibly overtake the governor at Fort Colvile.

[Covering letter] To Gentleman in Charge, Thompson River

The packet accompanying this being of importance it is expected that every exertion will be made to push it on to Fort Colvile before the governor can leave that place. I believe he is not to take his departure from Fort Vancouver before the 1st of April and may possibly pass by the plains from Walla Walla.

To John McLoughlin, Fort Vancouver

I have the pleasure to acknowledge rct of your letter of 17th June which was handed to me at the mouth of the river on 8th Inst and was the very first intimation I had of the melancholy event in the Columbia [the sinking of the *William and Ann* with the loss of all hands and cargo on 10 May 1829]. Indeed, although I did not apprehend calamities to the extent that have happened, I could not persuade myself that all was well with you after the governor's communication of the 19th Feby and the certainty of our opposition [American trading ships] being all over the coast made this delay still more unaccountable. To thwart the views of that opposition ourselves from here, situated as we then were with the hostile Indians of the Gulf hovering over us, was impossible. Besides tis clear that our stock of goods would not admit of a competition with them. The ruinous effect of this rivalship did not operate here before the arrival of the *Cadboro,* yet good policy suggested to ourselves the expectancy of reducing the Blanket to 3 skins and the Guns to 10 or 12, but even this will fall far short of expectation now.

At the time we made out our requisition, I was actuated by a spirit of economy and every measure that could tend to raise the credit of the Establishment, consequently the demand for goods was very moderate, but on the present mode of doing business, had we even had all that was demanded it would be little. How much more then must the Outfit fall short, when the three principal articles are entirely wanting: the duffles – cotton twine – & Beaver goods. Serious as this blank will prove, it would in some measure have been obviated had a few of the minor articles been augmented, such as capots, knives, rings, lookg glasses, or in fact anything there may have been enough of. Conceiving it my duty, I have said this much with respect to the supplies, conscious however that the whole of us must experience a share of the misfortunes that have happened ... We shall endeavour to do best we can with what there is, and probably may come in for some pickings should the vessel again come this way before next season.

The expediency of reducing this Establishment to twelve men now will not do, and I am happy that in some degree you have left this measure to my own discretion, as our actual compliance would have thrown us into a very dangerous situation. Still we send you [Amable] Arquoitte and [Louis] Boisvert which leaves the place two men less than the complement settled upon by the governor and my predecessor [James McMillan] last fall. And I have to beg that the equipments of the three other men pointed out for removal in your letter I sent per first opportunity. Their wages here I am convinced will be no great loss; they and as many more we shall endeavour, when the Indians are out of the river, to employ as trappers. Fort Langley now losing much of the original importance attached to it, a still greater reduction can perhaps be ventured upon when there is more appearance of security, & after the attack made upon Messrs Yale & Annance with their 10 men I was most anxious that the governor should be made acquainted with that affair in case he might have been led to think that all risks of this kind are now at an end at Fraser River.

On the subject of the salmon I cannot as yet speak from experience; all we had here last year was fall salmon and of course not too well calculated for foreign market, and of this season's we have as yet seen but few. Information on this head as well as our own necessities induced me, before the Establishment is curtailed and while the vessel is in the river, to send the two Gentlemen and 10 men up to the falls on Sunday last. They are now just returned but without any salmon in consequence of the high state of the water. I am nevertheless in hopes that towards the middle of next month there will be an abundance, and that a strong party once up the river will be secure in trading and salting a stock. With respect to our own labours in that way I should not like to build too much upon the slight knowledge of the chaps we have here who profess themselves fishermen. Still I think it most probable, under the wing of the fort, that a fishery well regulated would pay well. We shall at all events make the trial as far as our means go this season.

I will not take upon myself to point out any method by which we can communicate with each other in the fall in case it may be inconvenient on your part. We shall therefore continue to go on here best way we can, making the Beaver the first and grand object. The *Cadboro* now brings you 1,400 skins in 9 deal boxes and a pack including 400 ... so perfectly destitute are we at present of any tempting articles that would invite the Natives of the Sound our way in the face of opposition that I fear the ensuing part of the season will not be so productive. To add to the information this conveys, I send you a copy of our journal this spring.

Fort Langley, 14 September 1829

To John McLoughlin, Fort Vancouver

Since Lieut [Aemilius] Simpson's departure [Captain of the *Cadboro*] nothing of moment has occurred with us here – everything goes quietly, and the Beaver trade, notwithstanding the perfect blank from the southward, continues to keep pace at least with the Returns of last year. Our

Tariff still is from 2-2½ to 3 skins per Blanket according to circumstances, and hitherto we have got on with this distinction without giving material offence to the parties we deal with. A coasting vessel hung off Point Roberts a few days in July and returned towards de Fucas ... altho she did not pick up many skins. The evil tendency of her coming this way at all is sufficiently obvious, and can only be counteracted now by a profusion of property.

The salmon trade this year was also good, and it is much to be regretted that we are not in a better condition to make more of that branch of the trade, neither are we likely I fear, from the remoteness of our situation and the infrequent communication with us even from Columbia headquarters, to be for some time yet perfectly prepared to make the most of it. Salt and Barrels is the main want; all we had of both this season was applied at our very wharf from the 12th to 20th of August, and I have no doubt a great many could have been procured the last ten days of the month. After that period the salmon fell off and always will. However by establishing a detached salting camp during its force the chance might be doubled. The safest and I venture to say at long run the cheapest way would always be to trade the fish. In this case a suitable assortment of goods will, of course, be required.

As to casks, though we have no oak or any other hard wood for that purpose in this quarter, we have raised a quantity of white pine staves with which to make about 100 of 25 galln, the size recommended by Lieut Simpson as best adapted for land carriage, but unfortunately the cooper is wanting. After we had something to equal to fifty tierces [casks] salted, we got nearly as much dipped into brine for 48 hours, and then hung up and smoaked, which I am happy to find promises to keep in a good state of preservation, and might hereafter be found deserving of attention ...

We have in like manner turned our attention to boards and shingles; the former however by mere manual strength cannot be made a lucrative business, but I dare say few places are better adapted for shingles. Mill sites could be procured in the neighbourhood, but for an undertaking of that nature I apprehend we are also deficient without means of going on with the necessary expedition.

With respect to the people, as many of them as are not personally connected with the place [they] are not yet wholly reconciled to it. Faneant [François Piette] and [Étienne] Pépin ... are bent on being off, and those of them whose equipments were obtained last season think themselves specially required at Fort Vancouver. From some impression of the same kind I think that Mr Annance also is getting indifferent of Fort Langley and [Simon] Plamondon and Pierre Charles will be following his example. At this rate Fraser River cannot be supported, and to abandon it entirely as matters now go on is not the way to render the vicinity unworthy the notice of strangers. More, I do think, notwithstanding the many objections that begin to prevail against it, that tis well worth looking after. On the subject of supplies ... everything is scarce but Blankets, and they now are by no means overabundant. The 200 at present on hand will I hope be done long before the same time that the *Cadboro* visited us last season. Indeed if our first supply in that way be those now leaving England, the consequence must be felt as the coasters are again to be this way in the fall and no doubt early in the spring. My intention if possible is to visit the Sound soon, and there drop a few Blankets at an incomparable cheap rate, for dear fur is cheaper than no fur, and it may have the effect of disgusting the new visitors.

If anything is to be expected of Fraser River, a couple of cows and two or three draught animals, so as to reduce much of the heavy labours imposed upon the men that might otherwise be employed, ought to be sent. Our little crops are tolerable; of pease and wheat situated as we are we have quite enough, and potatoes, tho considerably reduced by the overflowing of the river, will not I hope be scarce. Grease there is none, for hitherto, on account of the Natives being in the way, we have failed with the elk, and in the winter the attention of our hunter shall be directed to the Beaver.

I was about writing something in this strain by two Indians from the southward not long ago, but thinking it unsafe I merely gave them a note that could do no harm even in the hands of the opposition, and now I give this a chance by the upper route in case it may reach Okanagan before the York Express passes. Should all be peace and quietness with us, I may possibly give you a call from the Sound, for I do think a personal communication at this juncture almost indispensable.

Fort Langley, 20 October 1829

To James M. Yale, Fort Langley

The business connected with this district and above all the evident want of goods rendering it necessary that I should make a trip to the Columbia this fall, you will take upon you the charge of the Establishment during my absence. The bulk of the Natives having withdrawn from the river, and those of the neighbourhood manifesting no hostility towards us, I think with the seven men and the boy that I leave with you out of our whole complement of 15 you will be perfectly secure until we return. Precaution and strict watch however is required. Tis needless to say more; your own long experience now, and perfect knowledge of Indians will suggest all that is necessary. The memorandum herewith handed will guide you in the event of the *Cadboro* coming this way before my return.

Memorandum for Mr Yale

Let the furs be shipped if you understand that the vessel that brings our Outfit in summer does now immediately return to the Columbia – if otherwise the step will be unnecessary. Let the salted and smoked salmon and boards and shingles be sent also in the following quantities if you learn that the vessel passes to the southward before we can see her again. viz:

25 Tierces salted, if you find as many pickle right

3,000 ... smoked made up in Bales ...

10,000 shingles in Bales

3,000 fwwt or 300 2 in plank

Fort Vancouver, 14 November 1829

To John McLoughlin, Fort Vancouver

Notwithstanding the risk and inconvenience with which I came this length to consult with you on the various points contained in my letter of September last, it is with great concern that I must now, in consequence of the non-arrival of the York Factory Express by which of course our measures must mainly be directed, return without arriving at a full understanding. However the vast deal of duty now to be attended to in this neighbourhood owing to the opposition induces me at once to come in to the suggestions of last summer by reducing my Establishment to a clerk, 12 men and two apprentice boys viz: Mr Annance, John Kennedy, &c &c; Yale and three others withdraw.

In reducing the complement, situated as we are, to this small force, it must be distinctly understood that our whole operations must be confined to the fort. Consequently every speculation in salmon, timber, extension of trade must be given up. At same time, could one of the above named men have been replaced by a cooper with a quantity of salt on the spot, it might so happen that a good stock of salmon could be secured. Another of them in like manner might be advantageously employed for the general depot as blacksmith, provided sea coals and efficient tools be sent with him. Let me observe however that in the event of a vessel being attached to the Establishment for the Gulf and Sound trade, we might still afford her some assistance in hands at a particular season.

It appearing an object of no great import to send the *Cadboro* this fall for the few boards, shingles and salmon now laid up there, I apprehend the trading goods will fall short before the month of April, especially as I propose reducing our Tariff to the standard of the Americans before they visit the Gulf next season. To send the schooner to Fraser River anytime before the Outfit arrives would hardly answer any purpose, unless she might be so employed to take the cattle &c hither, and return with our accounts before the departure of the York Factory Express. But here again we must be left in doubts ... Herewith is the requisition of the ensuing Outfit, made out under the impression that we shall have to contend with an opposition and introduce a system of liberality hitherto avoided in that quarter ...

Fort Langley, 30 January 1830

To Francis Noel Annance, Fort Langley

Our contracted knowledge still of the surrounding country requiring that we should make some effort in that way, it is my wish that with the six men just pointed out you proceed, after reaching the Goose Lake, on a land trip to the Flatheads into the country called the Oussaak.

We have sufficient proof of the few Indians in that inland part of the country killing many of the Beaver that come this way, but I fear from the eagerness with which skins are now carried to the southward, that we shall lose that hunt. Your object then will be to see the Indians, and to ascertain whether or not it be prudent & convenient to fix a small trading post among them there, or rather more to the southward and eastward, that would be the means of keeping a good deal of that part of the Sound trade from reaching the coast at all. As it will be impossible to carry Blankets, perhaps in the event of their having a few skins among them the Indians could be prevailed upon to accompany you to the fort ...

Fort Langley, 20 February 1830

To Governor and Council

... since the date of my letter of 22nd March [1829] nothing unpleasant has transpired in this part of the country. From that time however until the close of the season, the most vigilant eye over the motions of the Natives was necessary; exactly 25 days after the attack made upon our people, the Yewkaltas in double their former number again appeared in the mouth of the river where they butchered and took prisoners several of the Natives of this quarter[1] and then with marks of equal atrocity made the round of the Scadchad [Skagit] to the southward of us; since that time, except in numberless reports, I believe they have not been in this part of the country. The season was far advanced before we heard from the Columbia; the *Cadboro* did not enter the river before the 8th of July, nor had we the least information of the melancholy event in that quarter [the loss of the *William and Ann*] before then. This to us unaccountable delay, joined to a thorough knowledge of the Americans being all over within the Sound, kept us in very great anxiety, and when the Outfit at length did come, it was with equal concern we found that instead of increasing the order so as to meet the threatening evil, even the original requisition was incomplete. With such means we could not of course think of underselling the Rival, nor indeed would it have been good policy in us, when we had not the wherewith to satisfy them, to invite here Indians that received a Blanket at home for a Beaver skin, while with ourselves the same articles fetched two or three.

Notwithstanding this great drawback however on the Fraser River trade, it is with no small satisfaction that I can acquaint you with its continued increase. The strength of the Establishment I conceive is still thought extravagant – last summer we dismissed two more engagés, [bringing] the present number down to 15 men. It is possible however that 12 might do, yet from the various reasons assigned in the report herewith transmitted I am in hopes that for the present a further reduction is not insisted upon. In my humble opinion it is not when we are from circumstances compelled to encourage the free use of arms and ammunition among the Natives and to allow them generally a greater degree of latitude in and about the fort than heretofore that our force ought to be reduced to an extreme ...

The report in other respects, though not at very great length, touches upon all the essential points immediately connected with the Establishment. The journal with official correspondence is also prepared for your further information ... but having neither seen nor heard anything from the Columbia since I returned from a trip made there myself last November we are now ... obliged to try a packet by the upper Indians that will contain nothing but a few portable papers. We have plenty to eat and drink, our people are all reengaged and still a few Blankets to go on with the trade, besides the requisite stock of Powder & Ball for our own security.

[1] See Morag Maclachlan, ed., *The Fort Langley Journals, 1827-30* (Vancouver: UBC Press, 1998).

P.S. 4 March ... six days ago an Indian from the Sound handed me a budget of private letters that seemingly left Fort Vancouver middle of December, but brought me no information whatever connected with business ...

Fort Langley, 27 February 1830

To John McLoughlin, Fort Vancouver

Accompanying this is a duplicate of my letter to Gov & Council, the only document for that quarter that I conceive it of any avail at this late date to trust to Indians ... With this I in like manner send you the necessary notes relative to the accounts in case they may come to hand in time, & a requisition more enlarged than the one left with you last fall ... On last Outfit we did not expend in Blankets above 210 or 20 for close upon 1,500 skins in trade, but this might be no criterion now if we must have the Beaver.

I perceive the *Cadboro* is not likely to come this way soon. When she does I shall be sending you all the surplus salmon and in collecting for us all the surplus casks possible you can rely on those going from here for your own use, if it be too late to send them to market. I have Faneant now employed in that way until he leaves us and finding him disposed to overvalue himself as a cooper, we have commenced with Anawiscum [McDonald] also, whom I have no doubt will make a very good one in the course of no great time under an experienced tradesman. Attention to everything regarding salmon in the requisition would be most desirable. I also in official manner urge the necessity of making a stretch to accommodate our people in the shop this season; their order is herewith enclosed.

Chief Factor John McLoughlin, who took charge of the Columbia District in 1824. (BC Archives PDP00291)

Fort Langley, 5 March 1830

To Edward Ermatinger, St Thomas, Upper Canada

Tis needless to say the pleasure I had in receiving your very kind letter from London [Upper Canada, later Canada West, now Ontario], which in your own good-humoured way conveys me the leading incidents of your travels, although I shall anxiously look for a perusal of Frank's edition or rather your enlarged edition to him, which I am convinced must be interesting. On arrival in Canada I think among us all you'll have lots of Columbia news. The Clallam campaign[2] occupied our pages last year and so will the Clallams this – but in neither have I had myself the honour to carry arms. Frank however will be looking out for a medal. I see the result of the former campaign was known in London, & has affected the promotion of the Commander in Chief [A.R. McLeod]. This Gentleman has fallen off in the opinion of the Great considerably, since you left, perhaps unjustly. He & [Peter Skene] Ogden with large parties are now to the southward.[3]

What a melancholy case the fate of [Capt. John P.] Swan & the *William and Ann*. I heard nothing of it here before the middle of July & I dare say you knew of it much about that time in Lower Canada. At that period the Lieutenant [Aemilius Simpson] landed me my little family all well[4] & returned in a few days with 1,900 skins and his Princess; he was since to the northward but did little or nothing for want of [trading] goods ... This year we would have exceeded 2,000 [skins] had we only had the Blkts: but no, not a single one. Consequently were obliged to keep our Tariff to 2 or 3 skins while Jonathan [the Americans] & [Jean Baptiste] Ouvrie in the [Cowlitz] portage gave the Blkt for a solitary Beaver ... We now propose entering largely upon salmon curing which with the great progress already made in the timber may well be the means of covering much of the expenses. One half of my people are turned into coopers & assistant coopers. Your friend Anawiscum is my head man: what say you to that?

I suppose you would have heard of the attack made upon my staff by the Indians of the Gulf as they were returning home after leaving the packet at the Cowlitz last year, but they & their ten men got off with

[2] In June 1828 a party led by A.R. McLeod was dispatched by McLoughlin to avenge the murder of Alexander McKenzie, a clerk at Fort Vancouver, and four of his men by the Clallam near Puget Sound in January of that year. Frank Ermatinger's controversial journal of the expedition was critical of McLeod's leadership.
[3] That winter Ogden explored the regions south of Fort Vancouver as far as San Francisco.
[4] Jane and the three boys arrived at Fort Langley aboard the *Cadboro* in July.

flying colours. With the exception of these summer vagabonds we get
on pretty well with the other tribes & altogether friend, between you &
I, am not quite so unhappy as many think, & to be equally candid I take
no pains to deceive them. The little Archies are quite smart & Madam
has nothing about her to give additional encumbrance since you left us.
You have always her good wishes; every letter I begin she gives a peep
over my shoulder and asks if that is for le petit Amis. I say no; the reply
is then you'll be forgetting him, & saying you have no time when all the
others are served – this I do assure you is a true bill – and after all you
see what a pretty fist I am making of it. I never knew before what a bore
letter-writing is (you excepted of course), especially such long ones as I
invariably undertake. The irksomeness of the task now is increased by
the shortness of the time & the vast number of great men I am in correspondence with.

I returned to Vancouver myself last fall with Annance & 8 men after
the Indians were out of the river & was safely back in a month. There
I was disappointed; no Express till 4th Decr, 20 days too late for me.
Seemingly my Budget of private letters from York Factory was consigned
to the Indians on 16th and by some miracle or other found me out here
last of last month. This is all I know of the Express or any business whatever. It was accompanied by one of the Dr's short notes, & a letter from
poor [John] Work which he addressed me in Oct previous to the arrival
of my own, & previous to his own setting out for the Flatheads, and by
no other document from any man west side the R. Mountains. We all
seem in the dumps with each other since you left us.[5] At Vancouver I
remained 12 days & then was heartily glad to be off. Never was the poor
Dr half so much tormented in his life: [John Edward] Harriott who
came out of New Caledonia with a mad wife was his second & accomptant – Dr [Richard] Hamlyn, his trader & man of business among pork,
molasses &c and looking after the women – Squire [John Warren] Dease
a kind of volunteer that went down in poor health &, Fort Vancouver
being rather an unfinished garrison, dissatisfied with all the marks of
distinction shewn him as next senior officer of the Honbl Company –
and poor [James] McDougall had quite enough to do to look after his
crutches – this is a kind of picture of the scene. But when I tell you that
he & the first two were hardly on speaking terms & that something
worse existed between him & the third you will be astonished. Saying
this much to you I say more than I have said to many; I have nothing

[5] Edward Ermatinger left the Columbia in charge of the eastbound York Factory Express
in April 1828 and retired from the HBC later that year.

against the Dr, on the contrary we are the same good friends as heretofore, & I know he is harassed, but I also know Edwd that his temper
is become much ruffled & that he is himself the cause of much of his
trouble & unhappiness. He is still full of the [Simon] McGillivray business[6] & according to his notion of things is making fresh discoveries of
their fraud & imposition every day. He is to be with us until '32 & I
believe [William] Connolly then takes his place. Whatever people may
say of him & his bustle, his perseverence is the means of circulating
plenty in the Columbia.

Frank will be giving you a long story about Captain Hains[7] and other
occurrences in the Columbia last summer. I fear that buck will not make
Grieve's dispatch home, perhaps he may if out of Grog & that none be
had on this side of Land's End. If you continue with us you see the
prospect of accomptants in the service. So our friend [Robert Miles] is
Governor of York [Factory] at last and my cousin Donald Ross is Gov
at Split Lake. I presume [Robert] Cowie will be taking [James] Keith's
place & charge. The firm hand of the old codgers however is against a
great number of rapid promotions. Work, I know will be the next, some
say the Lieut [Aemilius Simpson], then you know the host of others. At
this rate we can't get up the hill neither. I think you are getting tired of
me & my parliamentary hand. I shall therefore conclude with my paper
& wish you every health, wealth & happiness ...

P.S. Three days ago I sent a few papers regarding accounts & duplicate of public letters to the Gov & Council by way of Puget Sound and
tomorrow Yale & eight men start with our regular packet by Thompson
River. All my accounts consist of list of furs, note of inventory and statement of men's accts according to last Tariff, for not a document, as I
have already said, came to me touching accounts or any other business.
Do write me a long letter and no reference to Frank for you see our
distance from each other. I cannot learn whether he is about getting a
successor to his Shuswap. You know my allusion.[8] Send me up old French

---

[6] McLoughlin harboured ill feelings towards McGillivray that harked back to the negotiations prior to the 1821 merger of the HBC and NWC, when the two formed a delegation to London to represent the views of the NWC wintering partners.

[7] L.J. Hayne, captain of the *Ganymede* when it arrived at Fort Vancouver in 1829, was
removed from his charge before he returned to England later the same year.

[8] Frank Ermatinger had an Okanagan woman known as Cleopatra living with him at
Thompson River. She bore him a son, Lawrence, and a daughter (who died in infancy)
but went off with another Native, causing Frank to take revenge by having her
paramour's ears cut off. Frank thus fell into disgrace among many of his fellow fur
traders, although McLoughlin defended his actions in a letter to Governor Simpson,
maintaining that 'if the Indian had not been punished, it would have lowered the

newspapers ... Late ones would answer just as well. I suppose you are full of politics by this time. How come you to allow them to consent to the *Grand Question.*

Fort Langley, 21 June 1830

To James M. Yale

Having communicated to you already the object of your present trip ... I shall simply observe here that you might ... before you enter the Sound satisfy yourself that the vessel is not within de Fucas Str – that even after reaching the portage, if information of her having sailed should come from any of our own people, you ought to return, but otherwise you will proceed to the Cowlitz and once there, whatever news ... continue your route to the fort and ... be back as speedily as possible.

Should you find our vessel still in the Columbia you can return by her or not, as Mr McLoughlin and you may find convenient; and in this case should hands be very scarce at the depot, [Simon] Plamondon, [Francis] Charpentier and Ossin can be left and you will embark in their stead such hands as I have applied for to Mr McLoughlin.

With your small force of six men, you ought not to throw yourself much in the way of Whidbey Island Indians or indeed any tribes along the Sound ...

Pray pay every attention to the wants of the place when at the depot. Wishing you a safe and speedy trip.

[Note in letter book]

No allusion is made in this letter to the Clallams but it was sufficiently understood that they should be visited & dealt with in the same manner as the other tribes without coming to any compromise or explanation whatever touching on old affairs.

Fort Langley, 1 August 1830

To Capt William Ryan, Schooner *Vancouver*

From the unfavourable weather you must have had since I left you for getting in to the river, and our great want of everything in the shape of goods here, I am induced to send down Mr Yale with two canoes, trusting that you will be able, though I am convinced with some difficulty, to let him have the package mentioned in his memorandum. I am the more compelled to give you this trouble as the present moment is very precious; the Beaver is coming in and the salmon trade about to begin.

Whites in their estimation, as among themselves they never allow such an offense to pass unpunished.'

You will be relieved of the pigs so as to give you more room upon deck, but the horned cattle of course must continue on board. Mr Annance you will keep if of any service; indeed I would not wish him on any account to leave you before you are fairly in the river.

Fort Langley, 18 August 1830

To John McLoughlin, Fort Vancouver

On the evening of the 30th ultimo Mr Yale arrived safely here & handed me your letter of the 7th with the various documents accompanying. It was the first intimation I had of this year's misfortune,[9] again in the mouth of the Columbia, though not attended with the same calamity as the former wreck ...

The following day I visited our friends at the mouth of the river and in conferring with Lieut Simpson, who had that evening but arrived ... found from their late arrival that it would be impossible for the *Eagle* to proceed up the river with the Outfit and afterwards make the trip to the northward with that expedition which her ultimate voyage required ... decided on leaving the *Vancouver* here, so as to return to the Columbia about the middle of September. On the 2nd Inst the coast cargo was removed and ours from the *Eagle* stored into her with some difficulty. On the morning of the 4th, the two Lieuts got under weigh and the same day I left the *Vancouver* placing Mr Annance on board to assist Captain Ryan. I was not so long at the fort when I apprehended that the vessel might take more time coming up than our short salmon season would well afford, & on 6th sent Mr Yale & 10 men down with 2 canoes for the indispensable articles of trade, which was very fortunate as she did not reach this before the 15th.

I am now, tho the time is extremely short, about dispatching her to make the round of the Sound with Mr Annance as trader. The Outfit solely for the use of this place, with the exception of guns, is very abundant, but did it not require to be so? A muskrat cannot now be obtained without a prime article. Before the arrival of the vessel we never gave a Blanket for less than 1-2 skins good fur, and I understood you thought it quite low enough, yet I was surprised on boarding the *Cadboro* to find that the Captain had already opened trade with all the Indians here by giving a Blkt for a Beaver or Otter indiscriminately. The expectancy of getting hold of all the skins we can along the coast without using much ceremony with each I truly admit, but the step in question was in my

---

[9] The supply ship *Isabella*, which replaced the *William and Ann*, was wrecked in May 1830 and the cargo lost, though all hands were saved.

opinion unnecessary and impolitic. If the Tariff was to be reduced to that standard we might at least be allowed the credit of doing it ourselves with our own Indians. From the southward I am not too sanguine of great Returns, however, the more we appear in that quarter the less influence & credit will the opposition acquire.

Mr Annance is directed to forward you this letter to the portage by Indians, and when the schooner finally leaves us she will in all probability drop him & his family and perhaps six others, near Point Partridge so as to make the best of their way across to the Cowlitz without any of them giving further trouble to Captain Ryan. This will be leaving me still with 10 men, a number by 2 or 3 that I would do without in dead of winter, and at the moment I regret that some kind of vessel is not employed in the Sound ...

I am sorry to inform you that our means of living in the article potatoes has failed this season; what the high waters left has since been entirely destroyed by a frightful pest of caterpillars that left nothing above ground but the little pease and wheat.

We have shipped on board the schooner now 13 Bales furs, 15 Tierces salmon, 15 Barrels ditto, & 10,000 shingles, as it is not my intention to drag her into here on her return unless we have a very successful fishery during her absence, & that I now much doubt, for hitherto we have hardly had daily rations & I fear much the things will fail altogether. I shall write you more fully by the return of the vessel but in case the time will be very short after she gets inside the Bar ...

Fort Langley, 18 August 8 o'c. P.M.

To John McLoughlin, Fort Vancouver

It is only 4 hours ago that I addressed you my letter & in which I calculated on having a certain number of men. Short as the time is, they are now I am sorry to say one less – poor [Pierre] Therrien was shot this evening from one of the guns of the schooner as she was getting under weigh, and did not survive above three hours. I stepped on board the vessel myself with my family for about 10 minutes a moment before the launch was timed. Captain Ryan came ashore with us as far as the gate & as he returned asked Mr Yale if his guns were ready and instantly embarked with Mr Annance. While they were heaving in the anchor he slipped down with him to the cabin, and about three minutes after the anchor was up he came up on deck & asked if all was clear; being answered in the affirmative he directed the man with the match to fire. Most of our people and a good many of the Natives were still about the beach. The load, made of top yarn, took the poor deceased in the right groin and shattered the whole thigh down to the knee. The Captain again instantly dropped anchor & came in shore & I must say for him that no man could possibly have evinced more grief and unhappiness than he did the few minutes he remained on shore, for the melancholy event in which he conceives himself instrumental; he is now a few miles down the river and I mean to send these few lines after him that they may be forwarded to you across the portage with my letter of today.

Fort Langley, 18 August 1830

To Francis Noel Annance, Fort Langley

Agreeable to certain arrangements with Lieut Simpson for employing the schooner *Vancouver* under the command of Capt Ryan on a trading excursion towards Puget Sound, you will embark with him in charge of the trading goods now put on board. I shall confine you to no particular Tariff; you know our sentiments already on that head and the Captain will endeavour to bring the vessel to such places as you may wish to gain the desired object, but in that he will of course guide himself by his instructions from the superintendent of the marine department.

With a copy of your journal I shall expect a detailed account of the disbursements of goods under three different heads; viz: for Beaver, for provisions, for ship's company and the various presents you may have occasion to make to the Chiefs or other deserving Indians.

While at that point which you conceive the most convenient for forwarding the packet addressed to Mr Chief Factor McLoughlin you will do it by means of Indians the length of the portage.

Fort Langley, 1 September 1830

To Captain Ryan, Schooner *Vancouver*

Should you arrive at the mouth of the river any time before the 10th you might by all means proceed up without delay at least as far as you can, for our fishery has turned out better than we apprehended when you sailed, with now ... more salmon than a Boat can take down.

To gain all chances possible of conveying you this information in time, I send down by the Natives several such notes.

Fort Langley, 9 September 1830

To Captain Ryan

As Mr Annance gives me to understand that you must now be in the river, I am most anxious to see you here. We have already close on 200 Barrels of salmon & if that is not sufficient to load you, I dare say we shall have more by the time you are up. Do not allow too many Indians about you; we have had some troubles with them of late. Indeed nothing short of their having killed one of our people in secret; this is the tenth day since he disappeared.

Mr Annance safely arrived four days ago. That we may know how you advance, write frequently by the various Indians coming up.

Fort Langley, 13 September 1830

To Captain Ryan

So anxious am I to see you up that I am daily sending down notes by the Indians to let you know of our situation here, but regret to say that we hear nothing of your progress. In these notes I have hinted to you the difficulties we have got into with the Natives and the necessity of your keeping a good lookout yourself while in the river. They will now be passing and repassing you in large bodies; do not however fire at any while they show no disposition to molest you. The Nanimoos [Nanaimos] of the large village below the fort have murdered one of our Owhyhees about 14 days ago and their conduct in other respects is not over good. It is therefore our determination to punish them if possible as soon as the vessel is here or rather on her way up when abreast of the village. For this purpose a party from the fort will slyly join you when near the upper end of the island, but if you are not there in a very few days I fear they will all be off and of course too late to affect anything.

Write me at length on what you think, such as the time this vessel may yet take to come up, the latest period you would like to sail from here, the quantity of salmon you can conveniently take on board with the cargo you already have, and any other matter that may occur to yourself, the time now becoming very short. Pray have you any knowledge of any of the [Sandwich] Islanders falling into fits on board your vessel coming to the Columbia; if so please let us know the particulars as I understand such was the case with the unfortunate Owhyhee in question.

P.S. 14 Sept. Your note ... just recd ... Thank God one happy & unlooked for event has very timely arrested further progress in the profession of armed war and the effusion of blood. The dead man in perfect life walked into the fort yesterday evening!! You shall know all about it when we have the pleasure of seeing you.

Fort Langley, 20 September 1830

To John McLoughlin, Fort Vancouver

... I am impatient to unfold to you an extraordinary occurrence that occupied our attention for 15 days & that almost involved us in trouble & difficulties that might have ended in the total ruin or abandonment of the Establishment. And as I conceive that any event of that tendency & magnitude ought not to be slighted or overlooked, I also conceive it my duty to give the fullest and clearest account of the whole affair which you will find on a separate sheet herewith transmitted as extracted from the journals. The man was absent 14 days & nights & during that time we had no tidings of him whatever except day after day one story more circumstantial than another confirming his murder in the most atrocious manner by the Natives, but fortunately his unexpected and miraculous appearance at the end of that time changed the picture of all that was before our eyes & to which we had made up our minds. The alarm however has been so serious & its occasion so recent that I do not think it a prudent step now to make that reduction in our force to what I was disposed in my last letter. Still Faneant and Plamondon are allowed to accompany Mr Annance & leave me with 4 Canadians, 5 Iroquois & Hlf Brulés [Métis] including the boy, & 5 Owhyhees …

Mr Annance returned to me on the 7th but Captain Ryan with the schooner did not get round Point Roberts & up here before the 18th. He had got out most of his ballast & made all the room possible in his hold, still I fear he cannot ship the whole of the salmon … I send you Mr Annance's report, which together with his own verbal information and that of the Captain is all we have to look for. The Outfit in prime woollen articles … was 250 skins at the present low Tariff here … This is fruitful enough at first sight but the skins, few as they are, will still pay for all, & that is so much out of the Returns of the opposition … As it is of the utmost importance that the trade within the Straits should be rendered more fruitless to [the Americans] than unfortunately it has been, & this not being very practicable but by a permanent vessel there & a popular trader … Mr Annance is arranged with for three years & ought to be sent back immediately with the [sloop] *Broughton* if neither of the schooners can be spared, and if you insist on it I shall return you Mr Yale for the Nass station, though I fear from the late troublesome disposition of the Natives that I am consenting to far too much. When things go on peaceably & well there appears but little to do here, but when otherwise our numbers are very insignificant …

The cargo now sent by the *Vancouver* as per invoice will I hope under existing circumstances be very satisfactory. The furs in all amount to close upon 1900 skins … Of the salmon, though it came late & of consequence is not of that prime quality we could wish, we made the most. It commenced slowly about the 20th of August and continued to the 10th Inst in which time we have cured about 15,000 − 60 Tierces − 140 Barrels & 10 half ditto at a cost something near 25 pounds, with the 33⅓ p.cent exclusive of the salt. This with 20 Tierces old stock gives us a grand total of 230 casks, that if immediately & direct from here were sent to market would I think take well. But if not, and that our own made casks to be tossed about from beach to beach and ship to ship, they will become utterly unfit for their purpose. Indeed in any case I would not undertake the like task again without a regular cooper & the necessary materials. The stave wood itself is none of the best & without iron, wood or a good tradesman to make the casks, with wooden ones it will all be lost labour. With the few iron hoops sent this summer we have secured the two ends ... best way we could, but still they are far from being efficient barrels.

By this result from the fishery, hopeless as it was in the beginning, I am satisfied it is sufficiently clear that more could be made of it hereafter, and as I am equally convinced of the advantage the coast trade within the Straits would give us, I cannot too strongly recommend its adoption, and in that case would pledge myself that with a couple of months assistance of the vessel up the river, which of course could well be afforded without any material detriment to the Beaver trade, we could turn out 500 Barrels of salmon & perhaps 2,000 skins. Without a connection of this kind we cannot now rely on above one-half of these Returns ... Besides, if the fishery is to be persevered in, I apprehend our staves must come from the Columbia or Puget Sound & this can only be done with the cooperation of the vessel.

This year ... our potato crop entirely failed; consequently salmon is of very little use to us, and I shall expect by the first conveyance that you will be so good as to send us a little grain & grease instead. Our people never want, still they far from enjoy good health or look well upon it. Meat is an article of food very precarious here, unless we expose ourselves for it more than is warranted by prudence. The same objection, situated as we are now, I would have to the working of a large farm at the distance of 5 or 6 miles from the Establishment; besides I begin to doubt the climate. The soil however appears excellent & the space of open ground is extensive enough ...

By the present conveyance I [send] the journal & official correspondence of last year and the men's detailed winter advances, which we did not think safe to trust to the Natives that carried in our spring packets for Hudson Bay.

[There follows an extract from the journal recounting the story of the disappearance and return of the Owhyhee employee, the comings and goings of Native war parties, and other activities of the Natives. See Morag Maclachlan, ed., *The Fort Langley Journals.*]

Fort Langley, 21 September 1830

To John McLoughlin, Fort Vancouver

I have closed my letter of yesterday and still have to report that the schooner crossed here from the Sound on the 18th, that on Monday morning the 20th they began to unload the first cargo put on board ... and that I now have the satisfaction to see her ready to proceed on her voyage to the Columbia with a full cargo. In affecting this business, it is by departing from the letter of your instructions (privilege I know we ought not to indulge in) for by returning her from here in time to be with you by the 15th of September she would have little or no salmon and the few skins collected in the face of the Americans would have been entirely lost. As it is I am sanguine enough to hope that Captain R. will be within the Bar by the end of the month or at all events the first week of October.

The various documents sent you this season will show what little time we lost in employing the schooner but I shall do that justice to the Captain to say that no perseverence is wanting on his part to push, tho their progress on these trips was very slow. Indeed at one time I apprehended much that the suspicious conduct of the Natives absolutely required the presence of the vessel latter period [sic], and even now appearances are far from being agreeable – nothing but scares, pother & commotion among themselves. This very morning no less than 44 war canoes left the river, as tis said to retaliate upon the Yewkaltas, & left all their families in this quarter till their return.

Maniso, the poor Islander that caused us so much anxiety lately, goes back on the vessel & in his room I keep one of those on board to make up the complement of 13 men ...

Fort Langley, 10 February 1831

To Governor and Council, Northern Department

The annual period is now arrived when I should do myself the honour of addressing you from this remote corner of the country ... to lay before you a brief relation of every occurrence worth your notice since the date of my last communication ... When I had the honour to address you in February last ... our stock of goods then was not for more than a very few weeks and our sole reliance in having it replenished was in the speedy arrival in the country of an English vessel. The unfortunate fate of that vessel is but too well known to you already, and I feel assured that no observations of mine is necessary to remark in the general disappointment it entailed upon us in this quarter, yet in point of immediate distress ... perhaps no place suffered more than Fort Langley!

Up to the 20th June we never heard a word good or bad from the Columbia, and the next days, though the Natives were beginning to assemble, we came to the resolution of dividing our party, and of sending Mr Yale and six men to Fort Vancouver, while Mr Annance and eight hands with myself guarded the Establishment. At length the last day of July brought the *Eagle* and the two schooners to the mouth of the river, but it was 15th of August before the *Vancouver* reached this fort. This entire stop to the trade for at least three months [left] the Natives, of course in possession of an unusual number of furs which Lieut Simpson, on their being proffered him as he arrived, picked up, knowing that the American traders were in his rear!

Among other disappointments occasioned by the last unfortunate wreck [the *Isabella*], might be estimated the impracticability of having one of the schooners solely appropriated for the use of this place, and the protection of the trade within de Fuca Straits ... The sacrifice at first sight might appear great for the actual quantity of furs she would collect, but the effectual opposition and annoyance she would give to the new adventurers would in the end be also a real advantage ... [American] perseverence I do not think at all likely, for exclusive of the collection made here by the *Cadboro,* our own Indian trade under every disadvantage does not fall 15 skins short of the returns of last year. It is unnecessary to say that the cost of this year's furs however is considerably dearer than heretofore!

Immediately on the receipt of our Outfit we reduced our Tariff here to very near the standard of the coasters ... the trader was authorized to even undersell [John] Dominis [Captain of the American brig *Owhyhee*] ... The Clallam trade, whatever it may have been, he completely monopolized for the last two years, and no doubt to suit his own views helped to keep up the difference which unhappily existed between that tribe & us. It therefore became an object to thwart him there, and of course to undeceive them without coming to anything like forgiveness or compromise touching old affairs, and with this view principally, the *Vancouver* was dispatched thither three days after her arrival here, and was back at the end of the month. Mr Annance, was put on board as trader ... and although the proceeds of the entire voyage did not much exceed 100 skins, I am satisfied that the very appearance of our people there was far from being encouraging to those whom we opposed.

In my last communication, I touched at some length on the prospect of curing salmon at this place as an additional source of Returns, and I have now the satisfaction to inform you that the experiment of the last season completely proved the theory. The fish it is true arrived late ...

but from the 15th August to the 15th of the next month we were fortunate enough to procure upwards of 15,000, enough to make up more than
200 Barrels, which in that very short space we contrived to do into nearly
that number of casks of our own making, with the means so imperfect
however that I fear from the sample that remained with ourselves the
first cargo will not stand the test of a foreign market, and trust by next
season we shall be provided with a good cooper, that will know something of fish curing. To bring the transactions of the year more completely under your view, I take the liberty of inserting here the cargo, as
shipped on board the *Vancouver* last Sept. Viz:

9 Bales no's 1-9 each 100 skins, part of Outfit 1829
9 Bales no's 10-18 each 100 skins, part of Outfit 1830
6 Bales kippered salmon 1829
20 Tierces salted salmon 1830
45 Tierces   "   "   1830
120 Barrels salted salmon 1830
10,000 dressed cedar shingles 1830

[The return of Annance to Fort Vancouver] reduced our complement to
4 Canadians, 5 Iroquois, boys and half breeds, and 3 raw Islanders besides
Mr Yale, a force that will not, I hope appear too extravagant ...

Canyon of the Fraser, Siwash Indians Catching Salmon, by F.M. Bell-Smith c. 1905.
(City of Toronto Archives A75-20)

Last spring, to satisfy ourselves as to the nature of Harrison River, Mr Yale with eight men was fitted out for the purpose of exploring it, and after having seen our Hudson's Bay packet in a fair way of reaching Kamloops he bent his course up that river until he reached that part of it in which Mr Francis Ermatinger fell when he visited it from Thompson River in the autumn of 1827, but holds out no prospect of drawing Beaver from that country so perfectly inaccessible with mountains! The river could be navigated just that length, but we know that the route again across from that point to Fraser River presents obstacles too formidable to entertain any notion of opening an easy communication with the Interior by the Lilliwhite [Lillooet] now called Harrison River ...

As to the Oussaak to which I also made some allusion last year, nothing has been done since Mr Annance attempted to ascend it. The quantity of woollens now required for a very moderate trade rendered a land communication with it impossible, and to gain its mouth along the coast would be attended with greater inconvenience than our contracted means at present will admit of. We have therefor resolved in giving such encouragement to the fort traders as will enable them to vie with the Sound Indians that draw the Beaver from there and barter with the vessels ... A few days ago we were visited for the first time since the formation of the Establishment, of a canoe of Chishalls [Sechelt] from the northward and although their trade did not exceed 20 skins, yet am in hopes that the encouragement they have met with will at least lead to further intercourse ...

In point of improvements I have little to say – last spring still with the hoe we prepared what might be considered an extensive crop for the use of the place, but an unusual high rise of the water did it great damage, and immediately on that subsiding what remained of the potatoes and all sort of vegetables was destroyed by a frightful pest of caterpillars. We however secured near 100 bushels of grain, which with our other resources make things go on sufficiently well notwithstanding. Our stock of pigs now, though by no means a rapid increase, is up to 20 head and the horned cattle received from the Columbia do very well. Our time at present is principally occupied about cooperage and the construction of wharves and other conveniences for the salmon business.

The death of John Kennedy which happened in April last, arising from a severe cold he sometime previously caught, I regret much, as he was likely to have become very useful in the capacity of interpreter; and I cannot too much deplore the unfortunate circumstances under which Pierre Therrien lost his life in the month of August by the wadding of a gun fired from the *Vancouver* giving a salute ...

Altogether I flatter myself that if the Fraser River does not come up to original expectations, we will find as much is done as circumstances will admit of, and considering the struggle made all around to deprive the place of much of its anticipated Returns, and the moderate scale on which the Establishment is now kept up, that its affairs present no object of very deep disappointment.

Fort Langley, 20 February 1831

To Edward Ermatinger, St Thomas

Although I do not commence this with the usual stale compliments ... allow me in one word to say that few letters ever came to my hands that afforded me more real pleasure & information than yours of 2nd April last from Montreal. It not only communicated all the ordinary occurrences met with in which you thought I might feel an interest, but gave me a faithful & feeling account of yourself & all that is dear to you ... I trust that long ere now you have my letter of last year, which will at least convince you that I do not wish to fall into arrears with a friend & correspondent I so highly value.

With regard to the Chats,[10] you will find by my last I anticipated so much from what Mr A. Stewart himself wrote me, & I really never thought the place an eligible one for you; but what surprises me most is the account you give of the arrangement for returning amongst ourselves again, & its failure.[11] I am very sorry for it, & could hardly believe you would have met with such a denial, the application to the Board being made at the instance of the great man himself. However, I recollect the case of our friend Leslie & I believe then with the sanction of our Governor it was decided that no clerk retiring at his own free will should be admitted again. But I do think your case ought to be considered an exception to the rule; if it was thought of am convinced you could have got leave of absence for a year when we were at York & would have been the safest way for you, & the most regular way to deal with their Honours. Look at the case of Chief Factor Alex R. McLeod, that appointment, once cancelled, there is no appeal to a higher tribunal.

As I am by this last remark inadvertently dragged into Columbia affairs, I shall ... say something of ourselves, although I ought to leave all occurrences south of the Cowlitz portage entirely to your Columbia

[10] HBC post on Lac des Chats, on the Ottawa River west of Chaudière Falls.

[11] After Edward Ermatinger resigned from the HBC in 1828 he paid a visit to England, where he discussed his future with his father. Apparently on his return to Montreal he applied for reappointment, but Simpson, although at first encouraging, in the end refused.

correspondents, as to myself they are only known by mere report. But the loss of another of the Honbl Company's brigs is too great an event to pass over in silence. Conceive this 2nd blow to the coasting business. Yet we are persevering. Immediately on the loss of the *Wm & Ann* being known in England, the *Isabella* & *Dryad* for the country & the *Eagle* for the homeward voyage, were dispatched. Here I was out of goods beginning of May ... & sent Yale with 4 men to the Columbia latter end of June. Last day of July he returned with the *Eagle, Cadboro* & *Vancouver* to the mouth of this river, followed by the two American vessels. The former had our Outfit on board with lots of horned cattle, pigs, horses, &c &c but the season being so far advanced, we thought it unwise to drag her up to the Establishment as she was intended to accompany the Commodore & the two schooners on the coast & to have a peep at Nass en passant. Accordingly her cargo was made over to the *Vancouver* & that vessel entirely detached from the squadron. On the 17th day of August she landed our supplies, & on the day following Annance with a small Outfit was put on board and sailed for Puget Sound & the Clallams where Dominis, with the *Owhyhee* had brought to, while Thompson with his [American] brig [the *Consort*] was up to this vicinity. The *Vancouver* in about a month's time, returned with about 110 skins; in mean time we had our hands full at the fort. Say that from the 25th Augt to 10th Sept we traded & cured 15,000 salmon, & on the 21st of that month shipped them in 200 barrels of our own making ... & 18 Bales Furs ...

I wish I had now time & paper to relate another extraordinary circumstance to you which happened also latter end of Augt. One of these poor new Islanders disappeared late in the eving & no trace could be found of him; in a few days we were credibly informed he was murdered by the Natives, & a day or two after that again his clothes was acknowledged to be in their possession. In short, one acct more circumstantial than another came day after day proving the fact. At length the vessel returned from the Sound & preparations were made for a war of extermination, when most opportunely the night before the contemplated attack the poor man issued out of the woods, after an absence of 14 days a complete skeleton, perfectly naked. Guess our astonishment and happiness at his miraculous appearance at such a critical moment. He went off in a state of derangement, met Indians in the woods who stripped him of his clothes & otherwise maltreated him. But the thing being not quite so bad as we first apprehended, we all became good friends again and the poor lunatic was provided a passage to the doctors. By this account you will perhaps think it a mere laughable affair, but it was more serious and had nearly proved more fatal than either the Clallam or the Clatsop expeditions. Thank God however everything is quiet & agreeable between them & the common enemy to the north, 'the Yewkaltas.' I must now bring you back to the Columbia again.

My budget of private letters were entrusted to [Jean Baptiste] Ouvrie about 10th Decr it would appear, but as usual passing thro the different tribes [via the Cowlitz] did not reach me here before the 15th Inst. The Dr & Ogden wrote me by which I understand my consignment per the *Vancouver* got safe to port, that the *Eagle* sailed for England latter end of October, that Lieut Simpson and Capt Ryan with their respective vessels were off to California & the Islands with deals and salmon, & that [Capt Thomas] Sinclair with the *Cadboro* was in port, all to be sent on the coast early in spring, & that the sloop *Broughton* with a Capt someone was to be put under the directions of McDonald about the Sound & Gulf.

You see my Columbia correspondents are not numerous in these days. Work is off to the Snake country in the room of Ogden & that accounts for him, but what think you of Frank – I have been most punctual in my communications with him ever since we parted, but with the exception of a long letter from him dated the fall I came here I have not seen the scratch of his pen. When Yale was in the Columbia last summer he made fifty apologies to him for this remissness, with which I was far from being satisfied. At that time it would appear he was not in his usual good spirits, but this ought not to prevent his giving part of his mind to an old friend; when might he do it more than when under pressure of a little disappointment. I will not go into the merits of the case; indeed I know very little. The Dr in his last tells me he was obliged to make greater changes in the appointments in the Columbia than perhaps I was aware of, that he sent Black to Kamloops, [George] Barnston to Walla Walla & Ermatinger with himself. That the cause of the change originated at Kamloops but that he'll take another opportunity of telling me all about it. I am very sorry Frank did not take my advice about that woman [Cleo] four years ago. The recommendation I gave to have him connected in high life has also failed, for which I am sorry on his account; a C.F. for a father-in-law to a rising clerk nowadays is a good support. James Douglas is at Vancouver & rising fast in favour.[12]

Of the other bucks there I hear nothing ... I understand our friend [Duncan] Finlayson is in nomination for a Factorship. This looks well.

12 James Douglas had taken Amelia Connolly, daughter of Chief Factor William Connolly, as his country wife.

[John Lee] Lewes has gained a feather also, but I believe he will be the only one of the original 12. There are three [Chief] Traders named also: the Lieut [Aemilius Simpson] is one & I believe Work the other, perhaps Dr [William] Todd the third; yet this would be too much of a good thing on our side [the Columbia]. The Gov and his Lady will now grace the fashionable circle at Red River – so will Squire [James] McMillan with his cousin.[13] Apropos, this kind of family alliance being now very fashionable, why don't you try something of the kind ...

The full acct you give of the McDonald & McDonell clan in the course of your peregrinations is very interesting to me. I know them all. So the Ex Gov [Miles Macdonell] is going to be a Yankee & poor Michael was at the stumps tooth & nail. You did not tell me of Rodk McKenzie's death, nor was I aware of poor Dease's when I wrote last year tho he was then in his grave 6 months. Monr Joe [McGillivray] is now strutting about in his top boots within the Arctic Circle & Simon [McGillivray Jr] on his way to the Columbia. [Francis] Heron came across to us 2 years ago but at the end of one winter was disposed to go back again because he did not like this side nor the ways of the great people in it!

Now two words about Jenny & the boys & then to a close ... be it known to you that she brought her 3rd son [Alexander] to this world on 18th Octr last & that she is become an excellent scholar. I already feel the beneficial effects of the Govr's & McTavish's marriages. She has picked up sense enough to infer from their having changed partners that the old ones were deficient in learning & that her own case may be the same when tis my turn to visit my Scottish cousins. Tool [Ranald][14] is a stout chap, reads his New Testament and began his Copy the other day as he got out of his 7th year. Now Angus is at it. Altogether my friend, few places in the country would afford me the same facility of teaching them myself. In the living way we do tolerably well also. I was thinking to send them across in fall '32 ...

[13] James McMillan had departed from the Columbia with Simpson in the spring of 1829, leaving behind his country wife Kilakotah and her children. While in Great Britain on furlough he married his Scottish cousin Eleanor McKinley and later brought her to Red River where he took charge of the HBC farm in 1830. That same year Governor George Simpson wed his English cousin, Frances Simpson, and Chief Factor John G. McTavish took as his bride a Scottish woman named Catherine Turner, both abandoning their mixed-blood partners in Rupert's Land.

[14] 'Tool,' or 'tol,' is the Chinook word for 'bird.' Ranald thought it meant 'boy.'

Fort Langley, 20 February 1831

To John McLeod

I have very great pleasure in acknowledging rect of your kind letter of July last from your old quarters [Norway House], which came only to hand five days ago via Puget Sound after a march of 11 weeks thro the different tribes between Vancouver & this: & when I tell you that my private letters alone furnished the whole of my news from Hudson Bay, you can guess at the avidity with which I glanced over two & thirty of them. It is with sincere regret I find by yours that you enjoyed but very indifferent health last season, a blessing as you say we never sufficiently appreciate when we have it, & when decay and sickness overtake us, few mortals present a more dismal & forlorn situation than an Indian trader, in a manner abandoned by the world and by himself. Thanks to the great Father of all blessings I have had little cause of complaint myself since I last had the pleasure of addressing you; yet I have had awful warnings about me. I have buried two of my men since – Jno Kennedy who was unwell but still walked about entered our kitchen one day in the month of April & dropped dead on the floor. In the month of August, another of them (Therrien) ran out of the fort in sound health and was brought back a corpse in a very few minutes – his case was an accident; shot by one of the guns of the *Vancouver*. I was very sorry indeed to hear of poor [Roderick] McKenzie's death, but noone told me how it happened. Finlayson says he died in June & you say it was January. When I wrote you last I was not aware of Mr Dease's fate; it would have been much better had he not returned to the Columbia.

I should now like to give you some of our west side news, & you know my itching in general for writing long letters, but really if I attempt it on this occasion it will be with great disadvantage, for almost the whole of the occurrences of any importance in this quarter are known to me but by mere report. There is lots of it however, & the loss of another brig is not the least important. Their Honours' liberality however in that way, by sending out two others beside, has saved our distance – one of them returned to England with the Returns and the other with the two schooners is cruising about … & the whole three of them on their return will proceed with Ogden's expedition to Nass[15] … He is succeeded in the Snake country by Work … Our friend Black is at Kamloops & our t'other friend [Heron] at Colvile … let us back again to Fort Langley,

---

[15] Peter Skene Ogden founded Fort Simpson (Nass) at the mouth of the Nass River in 1831.

where ... it is only myself that knows anything about it by having the field to myself. However, do not suppose that I impose upon you all when I say that in the face of two vessels our trade is not 150 skins less the great Returns of the year before, & that this deficiency is more than made up by 220 Barrels of salmon, & the Establishment now reduced to one clerk & 10 men besides 2 or 3 raw Owhyhees. If the Americans are off this year I hope things will be still better. Am now preparing from 2 to 300 Barrels to be at the salmon immediately on the commencement of the season; they say a cooper is come across for me, but we saw nothing of him as yet. In consequence of my casks of last season losing the pickle, the Dr sent nine of them to market, but sent his own & kept ours for home consumption, so the end is always answered, & perhaps this might at all times be the arrangement as the Columbia fish is acknowledged better than ours. Curious they are caught a week or two sooner at the Bridge than here; last season it was approaching the end of August before they appeared here.

I must now congratulate you all on the great acquisition to your society of late. The governor's residence at Red River must give a wonderful lustre to the state of affairs there & it is to be hoped his own health will also improve there. I see our grand Joint Stock Company [the Buffalo Wool Company] has fallen to the ground & an Experimental Farm substituted in its stead under the superintendence of my predecessor here [James McMillan]. So you see even rank N.Westers give a hand to promote the interest of poor Red River. By the bye, I had a letter from Mr [John] Halkett by the last conveyance. He was returned from the continent with Lady & family & even then living near London with Lady Isabella Douglas. Countess Selkirk was daily expected there with her two daughters from Scotland & Lord Selkirk was at Oxford, grown tall like his father, stout & in good health. What nonsense I do write to a man just returning from England. Never mind, I did not give it a thought at the moment that you was across the big water & I knew it would afford you pleasure to hear of the family.

Jenny & the boys are well. I think I forgot to tell you that her 3rd came into the world last October, quite enough to transport out of this rascally country ...

Fort Langley, 21 June 1831

To John McLoughlin, Fort Vancouver

Tis needless to enlarge upon the extent of our disappointment here this season for the want of goods, & I fear it is but too certain that the same disappointment is common to the whole Columbia. With the little inventory remaining with us 15th February, by keeping up the Tariff we contrived for some time to pick up the skins, but everything now is at an end & I dispatch Mr Yale & 6 men this evening for some certain information relative to the vessel and to what we are to expect ... [can] any other man, even an Islander, if unmarried, and another boy be sent? I shall of course expect a cooper in the room of Faneant ... in the article white blankets we have perhaps requested only absolute wants, but in everything like cloth, duffels, Guns, &c we are, I apprehend, under the mark – that is to say if we must have the Beaver.

I hope nothing will intervene to prevent our making the most of the salmon this season. Here itself with the very imperfect means we have had, we have contrived to put up 150 casks which with what I expect from the Columbia will I suppose suffice. The salt ought not to be later than the beginning of August ...

Fort Langley, 15 January 1832

To John McLeod, Labrador

... I have no doubt you will find your situation in the Labrador more cheerful and comfortable than at Jack River [Norway House], & it may perhaps, after all lead to greater renown. I am glad to hear you had so favourable an interview with the great folk of the concern at home, & one thing certain, these occasional visits to England can do a man no harm, especially when he can do it at his own expense & with becoming respectability ... Mr [Alexander] Stewart you must have found a very amiable man & I conceive you were very fortunate in your choice of a travelling companion. He wrote me a long letter from York & gave me some interesting news from Glenco-Appin & Fasnacloich.

... You will be glad to hear that I myself weathered over another year's campaign on the N.W. Coast, & thank God I can further say that I have experienced nothing very unpleasant either of a public or private nature since I last had the pleasure to address you, & what is more, when I add that with these blessings everything prospered, you will own that I have reason indeed to be satisfied, I should rather say thankful. Man's life now in the Columbia is become mere lottery. Your friend Joseph Moreau & 2 or 3 others were drowned at the Cascades last summer; a couple of men also perished below Alexandria in Fraser River, & ten to one there will be some lost in the Snake country. This with the natural deaths make the scene melancholy enough. Among the latter we have to lament the loss of poor Lieut Simpson who died on board his own vessel at Mr Ogden's Establishment [Nass] last Sept of a liver complaint after a few (13) days illness. In the course of the season he had seen the land party picketed in & secured, & then made a very successful cruise on the coast from which he was only returned 14 days when he was a corpse. Independent of his loss to the concern, I regret him very much as a private friend … A Mr [Charles] Kipling who came out with the last English vessel is now the commanding officer, & Capt Ryan who broke the *Isabella* went home in charge of the *Ganymede*. Sinclair & [Alexander] Duncan have the 2 Schooners. Nass you see is established, & with less risk & difficulty than was originally apprehended. [Donald] Manson writes me he did not find the Natives by one half so bad as those of Fraser River & the Gulf of Georgia. The spot chosen is not I believe very favourable for gardening, nor does it appear that Nass is the entrance of any considerable stream. The principal river thereabouts according to recent discovery made by the deceased is more to the northward. However, on acct of the shipping & other considerations, perhaps Fort Simpson [Nass] is just as well where it is, for in my opinion there is no river that will lead to an easy communication with the back settlements of N. Caledonia. There is Beaver in that quarter but the price is enormous. Still the Yankees stick to it & what is more strange they say they make something by their labour. Here we got rid of our opposition, a very fortunate circumstance. We are gaining by it in many respects, but in none more substantial than in a considerable increase of trade. Fort Langley this year is up from 1400 to 2500 Beaver – Tariff rose from one to two skins the 2½ pt Blkt which I trust will be found a good start for one year. Our salmon, for all the contempt entertained for anything out of the routine at York Factory, is close upon 300 Barrels, & I have descended to oil & blubber too, though not on your large scale. So that altogether, whatever others may think of Fraser River, I am well satisfied with its proceeds myself.

Late last fall after the Indians left the river I ventured on a trip to see the Dr & Mr [J.E.] Harriott [at Fort Vancouver]. There I had the pleasure to receive your kind letter, for Mr Finlayson was around a few days before me. At that time he & Harriott were below at old Fort George previous to the sailing of the London ship. Had I arrived with them a few days sooner tis probable I would have taken a passage in her to the Islands … Harriott goes out this spring with the accts. accompanied by Heron. Your last year's laws give me 15 years of the blessed country. Go who will McDonald can't budge. Therefore I begin to make myself as comfortable & happy as I can where I am. Our gardens increase in comfort in this way, & I have now 4 milch cows. We already killed 3 pigs this winter, & 3 more are fattening. This with country resources in abundance you will own ought to keep a little Establishment like mine in perfect affluence. What I regret most is the condition of the boys, for there is nothing like early education. However, I keep them at it, mother & all. My Chinook [Ranald] now reads pretty well & has commenced cyphering. Your children must soon afford you great pleasure & happiness. Mr James Douglas gave me a very flattering account of Flora, and her education ought to be followed up. Jenny returns the kind compliments of Charlotte [Pruden McLeod], sympathizes with her much in the melancholy loss her family met with lately ...

Fort Langley, 20 February 1833
To Edward Ermatinger, St Thomas, Upper Canada

I have great pleasure acknowledging rect of your long & very interesting letter of Decr 1831 from St Thomas which I received in the Columbia last fall ... If you wrote me the preceding year – on which by the bye you yourself seem doubtful – I did not receive the letter, & this being the case the high pride of a C.T. was so much up that I believe you will not find the Fort Langley govr on the list of your Columbia correspondents last year. No, my friend, these were not his feelings if he did not write. It was from a very different cause, which I explained to Frank & which I begged of him to make known to you ...

Frank I have not seen since the fall I parted with you, nor has he been much more regular in his communications with me that I complained to you of the year before. I must confess however that while at Vancouver last fall, I had one long letter from him which wiped off all scores and explained certain grievances of his own which put him entirely out of his usual good humour of letter writing. I do not think the Dr is his enemy – rather the reverse, yet he & I can never agree in the merits & demerits of that celebrated [Clallam expedition] Journal. It was mainly the cause of [A.R.] McLeod's disgrace, & of a mortal offense to his old colleagues. This displeasure of theirs in a certain degree recoiled upon the Dr who himself was not altogether free from blame from the informal & indecisive nature of the instructions. But Frank would ultimately have weathered over this storm, had he not by some mishap or other raised a second squall [at Kamloops] in the face of some of his old H.B. friends. This I think he will get over too, for the Dr at bottom is his friend ...

On condition of his being allowed [William] Kittson & Annance for his staff, Heron came back [to Colvile] again, so that Frank was allowed to rejoin the Dr, but being out in the plains in the fall [he] was not yet arrived when I left Vancouver beginning of Decr. I am in a few days again to set out for that quarter, & to leave this for good & all. The probability is that I shall be moved still further to the northward ...

The *Eagle* was with us in good time last spring. Soon after her arrival she went with Mr Finlayson to the Islands, then came here, & Capt [John C.] Grave being such a good jovial fellow I took a passage with him to the Columbia. Singular enough, off the Bar we fell in with Finlayson & the new brig from Oahoo [the *Lama*], and who was on board also but our old friend David [Douglas] after two years perambulation over the Californias. The two nights we were outside the Cape, depend upon it, there was no lack of news, but to the exploits of our friend & his man Johnson every other topic gave way. Bears, Bulls & Tigers had cause to rue the day they went there. Both brigs entered in company & the 3d with Capt [Alexander] Duncan we found ... ready for sea again to the northward. Sinclair with the *Cadboro* was still on the coast & the fate of the *Vancouver* you know already. She will, nevertheless, still make a nice little vessel. The *Lama* & her captain [William H. McNeil], also in our service now, was part of the American force on the coast for the last few years. Mr [Robert] Cowie of Montreal is now our head store-keeper & accompt. [James] Douglas goes out with the books this spring. [George] Allan & Anderson are the officiating characters in the lower grade. Tom [McKay] retires to the Wallamette with his old Jonathan friends, of whose migrations brother Frank no doubt will write you. [Pierre] Pambrun is at Walla Walla & his predecessor [Samuel Black] at T. River. Poor Work still continues wandering among the serpents [Snake country] & independent of their venom ... To the northward we find Manson & Dr [John] Kennedy ...

Jenny has now her 4th Boy [Allan], so that with herself and Tool [Ranald] at the head of the class I am in a fair way of having a thriving school, but this blasted coast business will now put an end to that agreeable & interesting pastime. They must all be moved on to Klyne [Jane's father, postmaster at Jasper] & thence to the Red River new Academy. I shall say nothing of the Dr & family ... wherever he goes he shall have my cordial support & good wishes, being amply due him for his liberal & polite conduct towards me for the last 8 years.

Before I blacken my sheet I must thank you for your fund of domestic news ... Do continue writing me on these home topics as regular as possible. I feel much interest in the fate of old acquaintances. I saw a few Upper Canada papers this fall, & St Thomas made no small figure in the Queenston *Advertiser.* Don't be surprised to see me yet bring to in your neighbourhood ...

Fort Langley, 20 February 1833

To John McLeod

... your kind letter of March last came duly to hand, and much grati-
fied was I to learn that you & yours were safely landed in one of His
Britanic Majesty's Canadian domains. That wing of the country however being rather new to us all in this part of the world you might have
said a little more about it. Chicoutimy – where is Chicoutimy? why, you
tell me tis near the seat of government [on the Saguenay River north of
Quebec City], but more out of the way of news than even Kamloops. If
this be the case, tis what classical characters would call a great anomaly.
But Master John, if the truth were known you have the Quebec *Mercury*
& Montreal *Herald* wet from the press the 2d & 3d morning after their
publication & of course have become brimful of Canadian politics – by
the bye to all appearances a most fertile subject of discussion these days,
so much so that, if he does not look sharp, His Majesty will ere long be
apt to lose his valuable domains this side of the Atlantic.

As to the King's Posts [on the lower St Lawrence east of the Saguenay River] – the Seignory and all that is great & good along that side
of the Gulf of St Lawrence is now ours. I hope we shall soon have a
flaming account of your profits in order to match up the full extent of
first expectations on our side. Do not however imagine that I insinuate
by this that we ourselves are making a losing business of it – on the contrary, west side the mountains last year cleared 20,000 pounds & this, I
expect, it will do just as good. Still, I would not be sorry that all the
Factors who have heretofore in snug corners distinguished themselves
for having made good & profitable Returns, were sent to the N.W. Coast
or Gulf of St Lawrence & then they would see the difficulty of making
out a shining balance. That here, this year, in the face of 3 American
vessels, we collected 2,000 skins; Nass in opposition to no less than 7
got as much besides 1,000 picked up by each of our vessels. But then
they cost dear – near 2 dollars per made Beaver – will your trade be
much cheaper? I presume not for I understand your Micmacs from the
opposite shore know how to value their Beaver & to teach the Natives
of the district a good lesson also ...

With respect to myself, I at the request of our great folk, took passage in the *Eagle* last fall from here, spent a month with them in the
Columbia, & found my way back to the family a few days before Christmas after spending some time in Puget Sound looking out for a place
fit for an Establishment [Nisqually] more suited for our purpose than
Fort Vancouver, which, you must understand, is, in this case to be

Mount Rainier from La Grande Prairie, Nisqually, September 1845, by Henry Warre.
(National Archives of Canada C26341)

abandoned. The Doctor & Mr Ogden I believe go out this spring. At
all events, I am directed to be at Vancouver early next month with bag
& baggage & whatever becomes of the baggage, goods & chattels, poor
things, tis more than probable I myself shall be sent to fill up a hole on
the coast. They say I cannot be off with less than 15 years of the Columbia
… Black is at our old place & Pambrun at Walla Walla. Work continues
to follow the freemen in one direction & Michael Laframboise in another.
Manson & Dr Kennedy compose Ogden's staff [at Fort Simpson]. Exclusive of all those in the Columbia proper, these sat at table when I was
at Vancouver last fall. Factors McL & Finlayson, Trader Cowie, Mr
David Douglas just returned from California via the Sandwich Islands,
Messrs James Douglas, Thomas McKay, Geo Allan & Wm Anderson,[16]
Captain Duncan of the *Vancouver* & Capt McNeill of the brig *Lama*
(lately bought at Oahoo by Mr Finlayson) & two or three mates besides
these. There were a Captain [Nathaniel] Wyeth & a Mr [John] Ball both
from Boston with a party of settlers to form a colony on the Wallamette;

[16] This could refer to Alexander Caulfield Anderson, who arrived in the Columbia in
1832.

of a great many that started on the expedition only nine arrived at the place of destination. The plans intended for the establishing of this colony you will see at full length described in all the American papers. To complete the catalogue of our Gentlemen in this quarter I should say that Capt [Charles] Kipling with the brig *Dryad* & 2 mates, & Capt [Thomas] Sinclair with the schooner *Cadboro* & 1 mate were then to the northward. Yale is with me here and takes charge when I leave the place; he will have 12 men, & 1 cooper as assistant – force in my opinion adequate to the security of the place, as another Establishment is to be formed in the Sound.

In one respect I regret leaving Langley. It is a snug comfortable place, but then I find it is high time for me to get my little boys in school. God bless them, I have no less than five of them, all in a promising way. Jenny is glad to hear of Charlotte's welfare & begs to be most kindly remembered to her ... If I succeed with my six men in reaching the Columbia safely I shall endeavour to write you a few lines on the envelope to say how I am likely to be disposed of ...

Cowlitz Portage, June 1833

To Dr William Fraser Tolmie[17]

... This will be handed you by Mr C.F. Heron, who, of course will relieve you of your charge at Nisqually, and as your professional attendance was the primary object of your being detained there, solely on my responsibility and contrary to your instructions from Mr C.F. McLoughlin, I have to acquaint you that, if you remain beyond the time you conceive your patient fairly in the way of recovery, it will be on Mr Heron's authority. Having lost your passage on the *Vancouver*, of course to return to the Columbia when disengaged is the plan to be adopted.

[17] See William Fraser Tolmie, *Physician and Fur Trader: The Journals of William Fraser Tolmie* (Vancouver: Mitchell, 1963).

PART 3

Fort Colvile,
1834-44

McDonald left Fort Langley in the care of James Murray Yale and set off for Fort Vancouver in March 1833. He was expecting to be reassigned to one of the posts on the Northwest Coast. Whatever his move, it would be temporary, as he had a long-awaited furlough coming up in 1834-35, and it was arranged that Jane and the four younger boys were to go to Jasper House to be with her parents, the Klynes, during his leave of absence. Ranald accompanied his father to Fort Vancouver, where he was enrolled in John Ball's new school.

Back in November McDonald had selected a site for the new Fort Nisqually to be built at the lower end of Puget Sound (near what is now Tacoma, Washington). On McLoughlin's orders he stopped there for twelve days en route south that spring to make a start on the buildings, leaving a small crew to continue the work when he went on to headquarters. He was accompanied to Fort Vancouver by David Douglas, his Scottish botanist friend whom he had encountered at Puget Sound.

After renewing old acquaintances and conferring with McLoughlin about future plans, McDonald set off on a short exploration of the Willamette River. The doctor [McLoughlin] had not yet decided where McDonald was to spend the months before he left for the east, but in the meantime he was to go back to Nisqually to consolidate the establishment there.

Returning to Fort Vancouver from the Willamette on 8 May he found a newly arrived young naturalist, Dr William Fraser Tolmie, about to set off for his posting at Fort McLoughlin. The schooner *Vancouver* was on hand to take them both northward. Much to Tolmie's delight, McDonald offered instead to accompany the young doctor on an overland journey so they could explore the interior region as far as Puget Sound, gathering plant specimens along the way. They travelled by canoe, with four Kanaka paddlers, down the Columbia to the Cowlitz River, which they followed until they came to the Cowlitz plain. There they took to horseback, accompanying a party of HBC men who had left Vancouver earlier with four oxen destined for the new fort at the Sound.

From 30 May to 21 June McDonald remained at Nisqually, marking out the locations of mills, a bridge, and a stockade, and supervising the building of a small house to add to the crude outbuildings that had gone up in his absence. When the schooner arrived with the Outfit of trade goods and supplies for the new post, McDonald decided that Tolmie should remain at Nisqually, where he was needed to care for an injured man, Pierre Charles, who was in danger of losing a limb from a severe axe wound. It was six months before Tolmie finally moved on to Fort McLoughlin.

As he travelled back to headquarters, McDonald encountered Chief Trader Francis Heron, who had been appointed to Fort Nisqually, and learned that he was to be given Heron's former command at Fort Colvile. Fort Colvile had become the key post on the Columbia River, the meeting place where brigades from the north and south met, accounts were completed, and preparations were finalized for the Express canoes heading east. Situated in a beautiful valley (now under the waters of Lake Roosevelt, flooded by the building of the Grand Coulee Dam in 1941), it was eminently suited to raising livestock and field crops. In the ten years he was to spend there McDonald built a large and thriving farming operation, at the same time supervising the fur trade among the nearby Kettle Falls and Spokane Natives and at the Flathead and Kootenais posts that came under his wing. He took over in late summer 1833 and, during the following winter, he spent many of the lonely evenings composing 'A short narrative and a few remarks and suggestions connected with the Colvile district' (BCA A.B.20 C72M), a document that summarizes the history and activities of the American traders in the region over the preceding years. This he appended to the letter book before departing with Duncan Finlayson (with young Ranald in tow, en route to the Red River Academy) and the eastbound Express in April. After attending the meeting of the Northern Council in July, he sailed from York Factory for England. There he reported to Hudson's Bay House in London before heading north to visit family and friends in Scotland.

Jane and the children went from Jasper House to Red River to enrol the older boys with Ranald in the school there. Young Allan and the new baby sister MaryAnne (born 3 February 1834 at Jasper House) stayed with their mother at the home of Reverend William Cockran, rector of St Andrew's parish. McDonald returned in time to attend the Northern Council in June 1825, and a gala celebration was held after the meeting ended when all adjourned to the rectory to witness the formal wedding vows of Jane Klyne and Archibald McDonald. A few days later they were on their way back west with the two youngest children, leaving Ranald and their three older boys at the academy.

The correspondence from Fort Colvile broadened to include many new acquaintances, along with the usual friends and colleagues. McDonald's visit to Scotland introduced him to a circle of scientists, including Professor William Jackson Hooker of Glasgow University, later keeper of Kew Gardens, London, for whom he collected specimens, as he had for the British Museum of Natural History. Roman Catholic priests from Quebec came to the Flathead region. American missionaries from New England, in the vanguard of settlement of the Oregon Territory, established a mission only sixty miles from Colvile. Both groups became dependent on McDonald for most of their needs, both social and practical. Scientific exploring parties and other travellers of all stripes passed their way. Letters to many of these are included here, providing a rounded picture of the diverse aspects of life on this 'remote outpost.'

Fort Colvile, 4 January 1834

To Mr François Payette

Now that you are unable to proceed by water you must with 5 men find your way by the plains to Walla Walla. When there, if you learn from below that the river, in consequence of a change in the weather, is free, you will take a Boat. Otherwise go down [to Fort Vancouver] by land with whatever assistance Mr [Pierre] Pambrun can afford ... Yourself & the rest of the party to follow with Mr Ermatinger's pieces in time to be at Spokane by the 4th where he himself will meet you. Should you ... not be there by that date, you will nevertheless, when you do come on, forward [Louis] Preveau [Proveau] & [Antoine] Plouffe with the pieces to the Coeur d'Alènes portage until further orders. You and the rest of the party will come on to this place.

Tis to be hoped that the horses you now take will be able to come back with the pieces in question without any great demand in that way upon Mr Pambrun especially if a large band is likely to be in a position for an early start to the plains from Walla Walla.

Fort Colvile, 1 March 1834

To Francis Ermatinger, Fort Colvile

The time is now arrived to begin another campaign in the Flathead district ... it is much to be regretted that we have not the benefit of Mr Chief Factor McLoughlin's conclusive opinion upon the plans submitted to him ... The letters [from McLoughlin] are not arrived, still we may yet reasonably calculate that by the 5th or 6th you [and Payette] will ... find yourselves [at Spokane]. Therefore let 7 men be dispatched with that part of your Outfit now here to the Pend d'Oreille bay, the mountain to all appearances being passable for horses, and meet you with the 2 Boats at the Coeur d'Alènes traverse on or about the 8th. Should you ... hear nothing from below by that time you will make the best arrangements you can to proceed with one Boat to close the Flathead trade and trust to the others to follow you as expeditiously as circumstances will admit of. On the supposition that you will be nowise disappointed from below, & that Mr [W.A.] Ferris is to be employed in the service, you will take with you the 5 Engagés now pointed out & equipt for the summer duty on the plains, & 6 that will return with the two Boats.

Once the spring trade in every description of property the Indians may have to dispose of is made & forwarded, you will again yourself accompany the Natives to the plains, & use your usual activity & judgement to secure from freemen & Indians of whatever denomination & character all the Beaver you possibly can. To good free American trappers that may be disposed to hunt for us give any reasonable encouragement as I believe it is the Company's determination to secure at any cost the trade it formerly had in your quarter. On your return in the summer, should no unforseen event prevent it, you may rely on receiving an ample supply of everything at the Flathead House about the middle of August. With the Outfit I would recommend a Gentleman to go up in the same manner as I did myself last year so as to guard against a disappointment that would arise from any accident happening to you ... at Spokane avail yourself of any communication made to me on the business of the district, should the letters from below arrive there before you pass.

I will only assure you that should another party set out from there this season, as far as it rests with me they shall be equipt here ... to prosecute the route proposed for Payette last year by the Blue Mountains & the Grand Rond, so as to follow either side of the main Snake River as circumstances & the nature of the information the person in charge receives may suggest. Of course, once in the vicinity of the Trois Butes you & he may meet, & can always communicate with each other in the course of the season. Were it possible, a letter from you on your prospects & on the state of affairs in general, sent down to Walla Walla prior to the return of the summer Brigade from Vancouver, would in my opinion be of great advantage to yourself & to the person at the head of affairs here.[1]

[Note in letter book] Mr Ermatinger left us on the 3rd – on the 4th Mr McL.'s Budget came to hand – that same evening a courier was sent after Mr E. to come back, which he did early on the 5th, & left us again in the A.M. of the 7th.

Fort Colvile, 6 March 1834

To Francis Ermatinger

By the communication just received from Mr C.F. McLoughlin you see we are not authorized to engage Mr Ferris; but we are at liberty to make over to him & Mr [Nicholas] Montour[2] an Outfit sent up for the purpose if we think it prudent under certain conditions; and as a judicious application of these goods in their hands among the American trappers is expected to supercede the necessity of our sending that far ourselves into the heart of the country frequented by the Americans, you will take forward the Outfit in question and deliver it to them ...

Of the 5 men you have for the plains, if you can afford a couple for the season at their own charge to Ferris & Montour, you can do it. Mr Payette will accompany you from Spokane to the Flatheads & as his services are not likely to be required in your quarter you will send him down in charge of the two Boats & the spring trade. The canoe need not be sent down, as it will always be found useful going & coming between the [Flathead] House & the horse plain. Should you find them in a condition for the trip, take on 10 of the W.W. horses from Spokane as tis more than probable some of your horses above met with misfortunes during the winter ...

Fort Colvile, 17 April 1834

To John McLoughlin, Fort Vancouver

With Mr Finlayson & Mr Cowie on the spot both preparing ample materials for you ... I will not myself go into those particulars connected with the district which I otherwise would have done. Suffice it to say I am well satisfied with the result of last year's trade. It is about 1,000

---

[1] McDonald was to leave Colvile in the spring for a year's furlough in Europe. Francis Heron was appointed to take charge in his absence.

[2] Ferris and Montour were American free traders.

Beaver ahead of the former Returns; & of the unusual heavy Outfit we had I am happy to say that more than eight hundred pounds worth of it is still on hand & now under way for another campaign into the plains. Neither do I think the two clerks & 25 men attached to the district last year an object of unusual extravagance ... Mr Heron is now here & will, I have no doubt, see all the arrangements in progress for another campaign carried to a successful issue ... Allow me however to add, before I take my leave of you, sir, & of the Columbia, to express my warmest acknowledgement for all the friendship, kindness & attention I have uniformly experienced at your hand for the past ten years ...

Fort Colvile, 18 April 1834

To Francis Ermatinger, Flathead House

Your various communications in the Flatheads & the plain business since you left this beginning of March came duly to hand & although there was no Beaver trade made this spring at the F.Hd. owing to the nonarrival of the Natives, I am happy to learn that matters in other respects was even more favourable than we apprehended.

Mr C.T. Heron now succeeds me here & to him I have made over your notes & otherwise freely communicated with him in every subject relative to your present expedition ... Plouffe leaves this in a few days with your horses.[3]

Edinburgh, 20 January 1835

To Professor William Jackson Hooker, Glasgow

When we parted I certainly did promise myself the pleasure of addressing you a few lines long ere now, but somehow or other once I got into the hands of my old Caledonian friends, writing letters became utterly impossible. Here I am now on my way back to the south again, & before I proceed any further I must, agreeable to your wish Sir, commit something to paper connected with our friend [David] Douglas in case it may assist in the design his friends have of laying something before the public prior to Mr Douglas' own return to England. It is very little I can say, beyond what is expressed in his own letters, but little as it is, I have

---

[3] McDonald left for the east with Duncan Finlayson, who had brought young Ranald from Fort Vancouver to travel with the party as far as Red River to join his half-brothers at school there. They arrived at Boat Encampment on 2 May, had a brief stopover at Jasper House, and arrived at York Factory in time to attend the meeting of the Northern Council in June. McDonald sailed from there for England on 12 September. He and Finlayson and Robert Miles, all enjoying leaves, were presented to the HBC London committee on 22 October.

thought it a good plan to accompany it with a rough topographical sketch of the country to which you can refer for the relative direction of places, but not a correct scale of distances.

On his arrival in the country May 1830, Mr Douglas ascended the Columbia for some distance – returned in Sept. & soon after took passage in one of our vessels to California. There he remained till Autumn '32; in Octr of that year he returned to Vancouver by way of the [Sandwich] Islands & spent the winter in that vicinity in the most advantageous way he could, principally in astronomical pursuits.

Beginning of March '33 he met me at Puget Sound & returned with me to Vancouver – 20th of that month he embarked with our people crossing over to Hudson Bay and landed at Okanagan. From there he continued with the cattle party to Thompson River – Alexandria and Upper Caledonia – at Stuart Lake he found one of the Company's officers preparing to set out on an exploring expedition down a river (Simpson River) which falls into the Pacific two or three degrees north of McKenzie's small river & was much disposed to accompany him, but fearing they could not reach the sea or any of our settlements on the coast & would in that case lose time & be disappointed in other projects he had in view he did not join the expedition. With his man Johnson he shipped himself in a small bark canoe down to Fort George [New Caledonia]. There he remained a day or two with Mr [Robert] Linton. His 2nd day down the stream he experienced the disaster he communicated in his letter to yourself. From Alexandria he got back to Thompson River & Okanagan by the same route he went & with the same means he had from our people in the spring.

At Okanagan he took two Indian canoes and half way down to Walla Walla he on the 14th July met Mr [William] Connolly of New Caledonia & myself on our way up with the supplies for the Interior. With Mr Pambrun at Walla Walla he continued some days, making journey occasionally to the Blue Mountains. Finally he attempted the ascent of Mount Hood & in Sept. '33 he wrote me he was on the eve of sailing again for the Islands.

I have now to acknowledge the kind & hospitable reception I met with in your family & do me the favour to make an offer of my very best respects to Mrs Hooker & all the young ones, not forgetting the old Gentleman ... Mr Finlayson was here yesterday & from him was happy to learn that you were all well.

I experienced much kindness from Messrs Graham & Neill & saw the McNabs also. Altogether few Hudson's Bay men home on their rotation have enjoyed their time better than I have. In ten days time I expect to be in Paris & in 7 weeks to be in New York, hence to Montreal & the Indian country, where I shall always in my humble way be ready to promote any object you may have in view in that quarter & I trust you will command me without hesitation ...

Fort Colvile, 1 April 1836
To Edward Ermatinger, St. Thomas, Upper Canada

When I did myself the pleasure of addressing you from the frozen bank of the Ottawa River last May [letter missing] I did not anticipate the idea of having Frank at my shoulder when penning you my next. What a wonderful creature is man & how little does he dream of the career he is deemed to run on this earth – lucky he does not. Trifling as the incident at first view may seem, yet, it leaves room for a great moral reflection: that little domestic comforts I had formerly in hand at this place & left unfinished as I thought on my part for ever and ever, it was in reserve for me that I should, after traversing much of Europe & America, retrace back my steps to Colvile a distance of several thousand miles & complete the work I commenced. One of the jobs in question was what you in Upper Canada call an American sledge which an early spring discouraged me from finishing & which my amiable successor [Francis Heron] as is often the case, condemned & mutilated to his heart's content, but which I, as I have just said, have since had the opportunity of finishing, & in company with my wife & little children have enjoyed myself with last winter, to *my heart's content.* This you will say is a strange preface to a letter coming so far, or rather going so far, but it suited the thought at the moment & as such you have it.

Our inland voyage last summer was very enjoyable, at least the two Factors [James Douglas and Duncan Finlayson] & I found it so. I will not undertake to say quite so much for our fellow travellers. Poor [John] Tod, I hear has made an unhappy selection – the lady's sanity did not at all improve coming up; at first it was even in contemplation to send her home to a proper place. That idea being relinquished he was not himself pressed to come this way, agreeable to appointment, but allowed to pass a year with her somewhere about Lake Winipic [Norway House].

Now as to myself, with so deplorable a case before my eyes, I thought the safest & least burthensome course for me to pursue was to close in with the old woman tout de bon & accordingly on the 9th of June after Council broke up [at Red River], the whole cortege appeared at the parsonage house before the chaplain [Rev William Cockran] & assistant chaplain [Rev David Jones] of the Honbl Company, where Archy & Jenny were joined in Holy wedlock & of course declared at full liberty to live together as man & wife & to increase & multiply as to them might seem fit. And I hope the validity of this ceremony is not to be questioned though it has not had the further advantage of a Newspaper Confirmation. All my colleagues are now about following the example, & it is my full conviction few of them can do better – the great mistake is in flattering themselves with a different notion too long; nothing is gained by procrastination, but much is lost by it. Some there are, as you know, who even do worse – despise, maltreat & neglect their partners when at the same time they cannot bring themselves to part with them. You are aware of your brother's *penchant* towards a connection of this kind. His *cher amie* [Mary Three Dresses, a Pend d'Oreille woman] is more desirable than the generality of her class in the country & with proper attention to her further improvement would, I have no doubt, make a good wife & is one that would make Frank perfectly happy. Indeed if he is not absolutely bent on quitting the country ... this is the very best I see he can form ... I think on all hands the sooner they are together now the better. I have the honour to be somewhat in the confidence of the old Gentleman [McLoughlin][4] on this subject, at least I was before I went out, & will probably ascertain his real sentiments this summer when I go down. Frank on this account is getting to be very impatient. In our convivial moments here last winter he used to exclaim after exhausting this subject & just as he was at the door with the candle in one hand & the latch in the other 'McDonald, by Gd all in this world I want are only two things, a C. Tradership & Ma.' I in my own way, as you may suppose, occasionally teased my friend on his extravagant wishes; that he counted as mere trifles the two most valuable prizes now in the mark. But joking apart, I am one of his staunchest advocates in both his pretensions.

On the subject of the Commission, I can only hint to you that at this moment the expectants are numerous while the vacancies are few. The great move in the Factors will be about '37. The *old* traders will I believe succeed them, but conditionally that they also will resign instantly to enjoin the ½ interest of that grade. By this measure few old hands will be in the country in 2 or 3 years hence. Of Frank however, I must say few in the country ... are now more entitled to consideration. They may however in one or two instances now go back to old deserving characters whom they leaped over before, but even at this he ought not to take the dudgeon. Before I parted with the Gov I had confidential conversation

[4] Frank Ermatinger tried unsuccessfully to get McLoughlin's permission to marry his daughter Maria. She later wed W.G. Rae.

with him about him & was authorized to tell him ... that his promotion was certain the moment changes in the country would admit of it.

As to myself, I am still an 85th man[5] – the bar against one step is against the other. Ogden is the only Factor made since '31. However the blank intended to be filled up in '37 by old C.T. will I dare say be making room for some of the juniors the year following, so that once that object is gained I certainly do not contemplate the idea of remaining much longer in this wilderness. Taking us altogether we are men of extraordinary ideas; a set of selfish drones, incapable of entertaining liberal or correct notions of human life. Our great password is a *handsome provision for our children;* but behold the end of this mighty provision. While we are amassing it like exiled slaves, the offspring is let loose upon the wide world while young, without guide or protection (but always brimful of his own importance) to spend money & contract habits at his own free will & pleasure. The melancholy examples resulting from this blind practice are I am sorry to say but too common. Much better to dream of less, to set ourselves down with them in time & to endeavour to bring them up in habits of industry, economy & morality, than aspire at all this visionary greatness for them. All the wealth of Rupert's Land will not make a *half breed* either a good Parson, a Shining Lawyer or an able physician if left to his own discretion while young. With this impression, I am myself for being off with them as soon as possible. Three of them are at present at the Red River Academy. Ranald [age 12], or if you will have it Tool, was removed there from Pritchard's last summer & now costs me 30 pounds a year. As I hinted to you before I am very anxious to send him down before me – by '38 I think he ought to be qualified enough to begin the world for himself. Will you then do me the favour to take him in hand – without flattery I feel confident he cannot be under a better guardian. You know their facility with the pen, & indeed their aptness altogether while young. He will not at the time I am speaking of be a learned lad but, with the help of what he can pick up with you, will have knowledge enough to develop what may be in him as a man. Bear in mind he is of a particular race & who knows but a kinsman of King Comcomly is ordained to make a great figure in the new world. As yet he bears an excellent character. Unless he takes it after his father and Prince Cassacas (I do not mention the princess) he won't have an itching for liquor. Be good enough next spring to write me your sentiments about him, & suggest the best way of getting him on in

[5] Chief traders held one eighty-fifth share in the HBC, while chief factors held two eighty-fifth shares.

summer '38 from the Sault Ste Marie by way of the Lakes. In a few years you may be looking out for Work & myself. Were it not for its too great bulk we would like to have your Book of Laws & other provincial regulations to pore over & digest here at our leisure before we appear on the great theatre of civilized life, for I suppose the least of our ambition will be to take a seat with Your Worship on the Magisterial Bench.

I see your House of Assembly business is by degrees falling into the hands of your reformers & democrats, but I trust they will never go the length of the proceedings of those of the Lower Canada Houses. Is Earl Canterbury likely to settle all & to the satisfaction of the deserving minority? I fear not – our friend the Dr [McLoughlin] on the other hand says they cannot concede too much to the poor [French] Canadians!

Frank gives me the perusal of all your letters & I must say the progress you are making reflects great credit on yourself. We all know the difficulty to be encountered in accumulating wealth anywhere, but from the stage you have already arrived at I can judge of your footing, and of the improving field that is before you. Your connection with the Burnham family is another judicious situation, especially as the Lady herself is so much to your taste. The old Gentlmns' place in particular attracted my attention when travelling that way in '16 & '17.[6]

April 10th – I have just heard that [Robert] Cowie is at the Grand rapid below. Squire Sam [Black] is also on the way. Of [Thomas] Dears & the Captain I know nothing yet. Perhaps the melancholy end of poor [Robert] Linton will be the means of keeping one of them in. That poor Gentleman with his interpreter Westrape, their 2 wives & 4 children were drowned in Fraser R. last Novr on their way down to [Alexander] Fisher's in two small bark canoes.

... This spring I have quite my hands full with only old [François] Rivet to assist. We have 3 ploughs under way since the beginning of last month & have already, including our *fall wheat*, got upwards of 140 bushels in the ground. We will require it all. You have no idea of the quantity of grain now consumed here & dragged to the other posts ...

17th – ... the Express from Vancouver ... brings us the pleasing intelligence of the arrival from England of a new ship called the *Columbia* & our famous steamer the *Beaver*. Lots of news from all parts of the world, even from Canada of latter end of July. Our two clergymen[7] on

---

[6] Edward Ermatinger married Achsah, daughter of Zacheus Burnham, of Cobourg, Upper Canada (now Ontario), sister of Reverend Mark Burnham, rector of the Anglican Church at St. Thomas.

[7] Reverend Herbert Beaver and his wife arrived at Fort Vancouver from England in the fall of 1836.

account of their ladies declined a Cape Horn voyage & will in all probability this spring be coming on by the Montreal canoes. Our chief farmer [William Capendale] & his however undertook & performed the arduous task; the lady is to conduct the dairy business & the education of the *young ladies at Vancouver*.

Of Frank, I heard this morning by our people just arrived from the F. Heads he was well on the 10th, preparing for the plains … Cowie, his assistant Benjamin McKenzie & our friend the Captain are with me for some days back; the two last will start for the east side on Tuesday but poor Cowie himself is in a very bad state of health & does not think it prudent or safe to attempt the mountains. Black sticks at Okanagan. I think you will own this is writing you with a vengeance. Now I am done. By the bye Dears & family go out by Peace River.[8] The Captain is waiting me to finish the flagon of wine we began at dinner, so adieu once more …

Columbia River, 15 April 1836

To Professor William Jackson Hooker, Glasgow

It was the day before I left London that the first account of our poor friend [David] Douglas' death[9] appeared in the newspapers. The manner in which that melancholy event was said to have taken place seemed to us all about the Hudson's Bay House so very improbable that we were unwilling to give the report implicit credence. It, however, I am sorry to say was but too true, & we have to lament the premature death of a man whom indefatigable perseverence in almost every species of danger, privation & hardship for the advancement of knowledge ought to render his name dear to the scientific world. Poor man, in his lifetime having experienced but little of the countenance & support of the great, tis the least tribute that can now be paid to his memory. I presume his unexpected death has put an end to your kind undertaking for the furtherance of his views & interest when I was in Glasgow, & I have no doubt Sir you regret the sad catastrophe which rendered unnecessary a further prosecution of that generous appeal to the public feeling on his behalf, more than any other in Great Britain.

Singular enough, the very Gentleman [Linton] who was in charge at Fort George on New Caledonia River, and to whose house Mr Douglas returned for a second canoe on the occasion of his shipwreck in '33 was

[8] Thomas Dears settled near St Thomas with his family and died there in 1840.
[9] Douglas was gored and trampled to death when he fell into a bullock pit trap in Hawaii on 12 July 1834.

himself, interpreter & six other persons drowned in a similar way last autumn and it was perhaps in the same place as none of the party escaped to tell the particulars of the distressing tale. We all in this quarter lament the loss of poor Douglas exceedingly. Since he left us we are a good deal frequented by American subjects on similar pursuits. Mr [Thomas] Nuttall[10] and a troop of Botanical, Ornithological & Clerical characters by way of the Missouri came in upon us last season. Some of them have proceeded to the Sandwich Islands and others of them are about return-ing to the U. States by the route they came.

My own progress hither from New York, which place I left middle of April, was to Montreal, Lake Superior, Red River Settlement – down to Hudson Bay, back to Lake Winipic – up the Saskatchewan River and across the Rocky Mountains by the *Mount Hooker* pass, thence down the Columbia River to the Pacific Ocean, which occupied us to the end of October. I have not yet seen Mr [W.F.] Tolmie but heard from him. Poor Dr [Meredith] Gairdner on account of bad health took a turn to the Islands before my arrival. I am sorry to say his case is dangerous. Your polar expedition Gents we met in July. Dr [Richard] King appeared much chagrined at his being from necessity compelled to leave the bulk of his Botanical & Mineralogical collection still within the Arctic region. Neither do we think the grand secret is much developed by their coast survey. It however, though a detached one, adds another link to that chain which will eventually prove America an island.

I need not say the pleasure it would afford me to have it in my power to repay in some shape your marked attention to me Sir when at Glas-gow. Do me the honour to be kindly remembered to the whole family & to Mr [Stewart] Murray[11] to whom I know our late friend was much attached ...

Fort Colvile, 18 April 1836

To James Hargrave, York Factory

A few days ago our friends from Vancouver joined me here, as well as Capt [Benjamin] McKenzie of New Caledonia. Down to that period the novelty west side was hardly sufficient to furnish matter even for an ordinary letter. The melancholy end of poor Linton & companions & the disastrous expedition of the leather party, of which no doubt you

---

[10] Thomas Nuttall, a Yorkshireman, spent many years botanizing in North America. Part of that time he taught at Harvard University. His *Genera of North American Plants* was published in Philadelphia in 1817.

[11] Stewart Murray, for whom David Douglas had been head gardener, was the superin-tendent of the Glasgow botanical gardens.

would have been informed in course of the winter from Fort des Prairies, were the material events of the season, until the arrival of the Columbia squadron the other day, which now gives additional lustre to the scene of action. It would appear both vessels [the *Columbia* & the *Beaver*] crossed the Bar about the day Mr Cowie left the Establishment, but it was only yesterday per an extraordinary packet that we received the news here. Lots of great doings going on there now of course. The fine ship will soon be in operation & our fortunes made – 40,000 pounds to start with on that spec is a mere bagatelle – and the bother about collecting your paltry Rats will soon become a useless pursuit altogether.

Our friend Mr Cowie I am sorry to say is not in sufficient good health to prosecute the journey from here; although his bodily strength has rather improved than suffered by the trip so far, seeing Mr Benjamin McKenzie on the spot & so very competent to undertake the duties of accomptant out, I certainly gave it as my opinion that he ought not to attempt the mountain in his present condition. The few memorandums I had prepared for him will now be made over to Mr McK. who will also attend to the little commission I was induced to throw upon your shoulders last season respecting my little things coming out in the ship of '35 … I hope the little supplies sent for last summer to go up for the boys in the fall were sent on this summer with Mr [Rev David] Jones' packages. I am rather troublesome to you all but I cannot help it. When tis my turn to do so much for your little ones, command me at pleasure …

As to our success here in the way of trade and everything else, I must refer you to official documents. Ermatinger left me for the plains a month ago. Tis from that quarter we look for our main Returns, but the swarm of American adventurers & vagrants all over the country now have deranged everything. My own principal avocation at present is the superintendence of a very large farm, to which our friend [W.G.] Rae last season did every justice.[12] Our own consumption in grain is very considerable & the call for the supply of other places is great & incessant. The failure of salmon made it particularly so last fall on the part of Ogden, Fisher & Black.

I do not expect a long letter from you in the summer, but by the winter packet I anticipate that pleasure as then you will have more time at command …

[12] William Glen Rae arrived in the Columbia in October 1834. He was sent from Fort Vancouver to Fort Colvile in February 1835 to take over from Francis Heron, and he remained there until McDonald returned late in October.

Fort Colvile, 15 August 1836

To Benjamin Harrison, Hudson's Bay House, London

A few months ago I had the honour to receive your very kind & obliging letter of August last per the arrival of our two new ships. They both safely entered the river in sufficient time to communicate that happy event to me here before the crossland Express for York Factory took its final departure hence the latter end of April, and I have no doubt ere many weeks are over the pleasing information will have reached the Honbl Board in London.

The routine of business here as in most other parts of the Indian country requiring our presence at the western depot, I am just returned from Vancouver. The trip thither was rendered particularly agreeable by the opportunity it afforded of seeing both the lately arrived vessels before they could have been got ready for sea again. The steam ship [the *Beaver*] in particular & a jaunt of about 60 miles in her for a trial, after the erection & complete adjustment of the machinery, was truly pleasing & yielded a novel & most interesting sight to all who beheld her. She sailed for the coast a few days after, & we are not without sanguine hopes she will prove an acquisition to our business in that quarter notwithstanding the unavoidable heavy expense with which she was got up.

I am extremely sorry to understand that none of the clergy ... could have been prevailed upon to undertake the Cape Horn voyage. As I anticipated when I had the honour of an interview with you in London, two or three American missionaries are now actually among us; & when at Red River last season on my way here I understood from the R.C. Bishop there that he also was about applying to the head of their church at Quebec for a couple of priests for a similar mission, and this being the case, I cannot but lament the nonappearance as yet of one or two divines of the Established Church on the scene of action. I may be a little selfish in this preference to the Episcopalian clergy, there being very few of us on this side of that persuasion, but I am confident the respect & general interest of the community at large are best secured by the presence of such characters patronized & supported as they would of course be by the Company.

Mr Capendale & wife I had the pleasure to see at Vancouver. They both seem very decent people, and always appear ready & willing to give the folk there, as far as they are able, every insight into the way of doing things as done in England. It must however be admitted that people from the Old Country in whatever station, accustomed to everything in perfection, view our doings in this obscure part of the world as

exceedingly lame & imperfect, without considering the means or inducement we have for conducting them in a different scale, and probably this
will be the first impression on the Capendales.

The introduction to the Columbia of families of moral, industrious
& civilized habits it is certain could not fail being of advantage to the
country & those in it. In justice to ourselves, however, I may be permitted to say that in the whole Indian country & in the Columbia especially, we by no means within the last ten years have been remiss in
greatly increasing our comforts & improving the condition of the country generally. Even at my place, 600 miles from the sea, our well cultivated & enclosed fields are not much under 200 acres, with a tolerably
good water mill, a stock of from 50 to 60 head of horned cattle, grunters
& other domestic animals in equal abundance. The same spirit for improvement prevails all the way from the Columbia River to the most
northern settlement in New Caledonia & the north west coast.

I will not trespass on your attention with any observations on the fur
trade. Much of our doings in that way in this district is to watch the
Americans & prevent as much as possible of the trade contended for by
both parties in the R. Mountains falling into their hands, in which I am
happy to say we have as yet been tolerably successful ...

Fort Colvile, 25 January 1837
To Edward Ermatinger, St Thomas, Upper Canada

Perhaps you will say tis premature in me dating my letter 25th January,
but I do not think so myself, for before I go a line further I conceive
the fund of things I have already to speak of will more than fill this sheet
& should anything interesting occur by the 20th of April we can give it
berth on another sheet as I believe our letters whether single or double
cost you the same thing. Then to make a familiar fireside story of it,
Frank happily joined me here from the plains 10th of last month & would
as usual have spent the holidays with us before starting on the trip for
below but the cold weather gave us the alarm & off he was with 2 Boats
& 15 men on the 22nd. On the 23rd I heard of his being icebound ½
way to the Spokane Forks. Immediately horses were sent to him & I was
glad to see him safe back again just in time for the roast beef & plum
pudding. As the stoppage was not attended with any of those disagreeable measures that usually follow similar events in the Indian country,
we made ourselves very happy and I was almost going to say very fu' on
the occasion. Little did we dream that he was still to be more effectually caught in frozen Rapids. After doing ourselves & about five & thirty
men all the justice that the profusion of good things at Colvile would

admit of, he & party again left us on the 9th, being informed & assured by the Indians at the *Cache* that the river was free, which we did not at all doubt from the mild weather that came on immediately after his return. But what was my chagrin & disappointment when 3 days ago one of the young Rivets entered with a note from poor Monsr François dated at the *Grosse Roche* above Okanagan, again stopp'd by some of the old ice. He was nevertheless in good spirits with full control over about 80 Bags of flour, pease, corn & gammon ... to enable them to stand it out fairly till a general breaking up of the river relieves them ...

It is now high time for me to acknowledge receipt of your very valuable letter of February last, & thank you very cordially for the trouble you took to write us so much useful information ... Above all, your own comfort & happiness, next to that your comparative greatness & fair prospects in the world gave us infinite pleasure. I say us because I speak not only for Francis but my wife also. Many were our plans here this winter, but all were to be subservient to a location at St Thomas. Our houses are already built, the very shape & size of the kitchens selected, indeed the happy imagination is carried so far that Frank actually disputes the palm with Work & I that his field of wheat is 25 percent better cultivated than ours! Joking apart, if God spares us, the day may come when something of this kind may be realized in the neighbourhood of St Thomas.

I wrote you last spring of all I knew respecting his probable speedy promotion, & he this fall himself had a very flattering letter from the Governor & Council – that is from Geordie [Governor George Simpson] himself, setting forth their high sense of Frank's talents & merit, & of course admitting his claim to preferment the moment circumstances will admit of it. There will be few or no promotions in either grade till the clause in the new [HBC] Constitution takes effect & compels resignations in '39. No less than ten Factors & invalided Traders are now absent in various ways from their duty in the country. Will these men retire when they can retain their full interest so cheaply? I do not know whether or not his matrimonial project will succeed. If he does not get a definitive answer on this trip I have advised him to drop the idea in that quarter for ever. When he left me he talked very earnestly of going out to see York. If so I think he will return a married man – lots of fine accomplished young ladies now on the other side & no gallants, Chief Factor's daughters too ...

I was at the sea last season with Ogden & Black. The home ship arrived early accompanied by a beautiful steamer for the N.W. coast trade. We had one delightful cruise in her round the mouth of the Wallamette, but as she passed the summer with Work I leave to him the task of describing her advantages and perfections in that quarter. I wrote him the other day & enclosed him the proceedings of the railroad meeting in St. Thomas. Christ, what an undertaking for Ned, he will exclaim, a railroad of 300 miles & 50,000 pounds!!! The project certainly is a magnificent one, & does great credit to the enterprising spirit of the projectors. Indeed the greatest objection I see to it is its vast extent when compared with the population & the means of the country. But as you say, foreign capital may soon complete it. Railroads seem now the order of the day. Ours, on the St. John communication [LaPrairie Railroad][13] I see is in operation & will I believe do pretty well if [Louis Joseph] Papineau & the House of Assembly would only leave us something near the original privileges. How are you all now coming on in political matters? Your Sir Francis [Bond] Head[14] seems an active off hand chap. I like his character much better than the one given the noble Lord below. Dalhousie was the fit man for the clique.

I am glad to find you notice the allusion I made to my young Chinook [Ranald, nearly 13], as in my last I have expressed myself still more serious as regards him. Indeed my mind is made up to send him down in '38 if your letter of '37 will not absolutely prevent me. I heard very favourable accounts of him this fall from Mr Jones, & who knows but he may turn out a rare exception to the race. I tell them to keep him at a jointer plane or Beauvet's sledge hammer when the younger boys are at play, & he will in reality be turned to one or the other should we unfortunately discover a leaning to unsuitable habits. Two of our other boys [Angus, age 10, and Archibald, age 8] are with Mr Jones also: a young one [Alexander, age 6] is there with the Klynes – another [Allan, age 4] & the young lady [MaryAnne, nearly 7] with ourselves. We lost the last boy eight days old [John died 26 April 1836]; something new is again on the way [another John was born 3 May 1837], so you see we don't dread poverty. At all events if we cannot make Gentlemen of them, I trust we

[13] McDonald invested in both the LaPrairie Railroad and the Montreal and Lachine Railroad.

[14] Sir Francis Bond Head was lieutenant-governor of Upper Canada from 1835 to 1838. This was a particularly volatile time, when the British government was attempting to follow a policy of conciliation between the established conservative regime and the reformers in Upper Canada. Bond Head's failure to follow instructions from the Colonial Office and his overt support of the Conservatives (the old Family Compact) was thought to have fuelled the fire of the more militant reformers, leading to the Rebellion of 1837 in Upper Canada. He resigned in September 1837 but remained in office until January 1838.

shall always have the wherewithal to set them up as humble unpretend-
ing farmers. At Colvile the wife & myself are in excellent practice. Her
butter, cheese, ham & bacon would shine in any ordinary market & I
think myself with 3,000 Bushels of wheat, 1,500 of Indian corn & 1,000
of other grains this year would pass with your Yankee neighbours as
rather a considerable sort of farmer.

April 8th – Five days ago I was much pleased to hear from Frank all
safe at Spokane. He tells me he wrote you from W.W. & may not perhaps this year again address you. His trip thence to Spokane was one of
10 days, & my horses that left this on the very same day (21st) would
have taken 20 to get to him. Such is the state of the snow here this
spring. Indeed the courier that brought me his letter met with the Outfit
on the 1st not yet half way. This being the case, we thought it advisable
to push off a strong horse ... with a few of the good things of Colvile,
as [they] were likely to be in short commons before the Brigade joined
him. I hope the worst of his campaign is over, still from the difficulty
attending the transport on this occasion, the trip up will not be the most
comfortable he has performed. The poor little boy [Frank's son Lawrence]
also gives him uneasiness but I expect the moment the last horse gets to
him he will be sending him off to us ... I regret much his not being able
to come to see us as usual after returning from below, & so does he himself. To make up in some shape for this mutual disappointment, he took
the trouble to write me three closely written sheets of folio on affairs
below ... He says he intends sending Lawrence down next year by way
of St Louis. Till then we shall endeavour to brush up a little the poor
fellow for the civilized world, for despite all their reformation & Christian improvement at the great Fort Vancouver, the young élèves [pupils]
are in a deplorable condition. The character of that Seminary is most
extraordinary.

Besides Frank's own interesting report, he was also the bearer of a
large Budget of letters for me from our friends along the coast. It would
appear, of the two Factors, Finlayson is the one going out, & will not I
dare say again in a hurry cross the mountains a third time to relieve the
Dr. He & [James] Douglas I shall be looking out for on the 11th, Parson [Henry Harmon] Spalding & Lady [Eliza] tomorrow, if Frank's
horses opened the track sufficiently for them. Black I do not expect &
I am very sorry for it ... but [Alexander] Fisher, tis said is, with his wife,
sister-in-law & four little ones ploughing the snow from Alexandria on
their way to cross by the *Batteaus* & ascend the Grand Côte this spring.
Before they are upon me, I congratulate myself on having closed all my
private correspondence. With such guests you know very little writing

can be done, & you know my own propensity for talking when I have about me any one decent to talk with.

Could you not send us something worth reading on the news & politics of the province – we will pay you well for it. The steamboat going to Sault Ste Marie might carry a small parcel to the care of the Honbl Company's representative there. As I must take a turn to see the progress making by four ploughs turned out this morning I shall conclude my letter with an offer of my most respectful compliments to Mrs Ermatinger, although I have not had the honour of her personal acquaintance, & for yourself ...

[Cross written over first page of this letter:]

21st – Since I blackened my envelope I had 2 Budgets from Frank, one from Spokane & another today from Flatheads dated 15th ... I am sorry he did not leave the boy with us for a year. From hints I have just collected here I am of opinion the negotiation he had below will not succeed. On the east side again, one of Mr C.'s [Chief Factor John Charles] daughters is gone & a youth from here on his way out from New Caledonia is likely to be the happy one for the next – a Mr John McLean lately from the Montreal district.[15] Mr Douglas returned from here in consequence of Benjamin McKenzie's ill health, to attend to the duties of storekeeper accomptant ... Finlayson, Black & McLean will be leaving us this evening ...

Fort Colvile, 25 January 1837

To John McLeod, Saint Maurice River, Lower Canada

... If I on my part take up the pen this early in the season tis not to say this is the latest date you will hear from us, no my friend, but as I am situated, some preliminary steps are necessary to make the winding up of my correspondence more sure & convenient [by] 20th of April when the more important & pressing affairs of the concern must be attended to. I am not assisted with the scrape of a pen by the clerks, as heretofore was the case; indeed I may almost say there is not a man in the district that can sign his own name. Fr Ermatinger, with the exception of a couple of weeks middle of December, I never see, his sojourn being constantly in the Fhead camp, & the Kootenais business is in charge of Big Charles & Antoine Felix. Old Rivet is the summer master & deputy governor of Colvile so you all cannot say that our Bal of expense to the clerks here is extravagant. I must own however that the Bal of

---

[15] Frank Ermatinger had at one time entertained the hope of marrying one of the daughters of Chief Factor John Charles.

wages nevertheless is heavy – we have 28 men & boys & most of them being old hands or otherwise useful their wages amount high. The trade also is on a more liberal scale than in our early days in the Columbia especially in the upper country, both with Indians and freemen, in consequence of the number of new adventurers now pouring in upon us from the American side of the mountains. Our profits however continue between 3 & 4 thousand. The farm at present is on an extensive scale – what think you this winter of upwards of 5,000 bushels of grain! – namely 3,000 of wheat, 1,000 of corn & more than 1,200 of other grain. Your three calves are up to 55 & your three grunters would have swarmed the country if we did not make it a point to keep them down to 150. With all this & its concomitant comforts I need not say that we live well. Last season, to complete our independence I had a handyman from the sea & in three months got us up a new mill & new stores, the best between Cape Disappointment & Fort Coulonge. With your two friends of old, Ogden & Black, I made the trip to the sea last summer accompanied by Cowie who discontinued here the intended voyage out. There we found the usual vessel from England & a very superb steam vessel intended for the coast. In this *Skokum* ship, as the Chinooks call her, the Isle a la Crosse Gents & myself were treated with a delightful cruise ... before her final departure for the coast with Finlayson, who superintended her first essay in these seas. By last account she reached her destination safe & proved well adapted for the project in view. She was to have returned by Johnson's Straits inside Vancouver Island & winter in Puget Sound ... Three other vessels are also employed in that trade & the occasional trips to California & the Islands. Work & Dr Kennedy are at new Fort Simpson substituted for Nass. [Donald] Manson & [Charles] Kipling ... at Fort McLoughlin, Yale at Langley & [William] Kittson at Nisqually in Puget Sound. This is the coast distribution & you cannot say there are supernumeraries. [James] Birnie again is at Fort George; Laframboise has the Umpqua dept; Payette the lower Snake district & Tom [McKay] the upper. Your friend [...] is a sort of go between the three last places, who I dare say will be writing you himself. Black & Pambrun are at their old places [Thompson River and Walla Walla]. So that if you should be at a loss to know where the deuce the superabundance of Gentlmn are, if there be any, look for them at Vancouver. Ogden, besides Squire Fisher, has seven clerks with him at the 7 ports, namely McLean, [Richard] Lane, McBean, Fraser, [A.C.] Anderson, [Archibald] McKinlay & McIntosh ...

On politics I could also dilate a little ... Our betters seem to have a wonderful attachment to the service; not one of them will budge, rather make the tour of Italy & the Holy Land on the advantageous terms of *full pay* than either retire or return to the country. I see the honest man your father-in-law [J.P. Pruden] is at length promoted & I believe has already resigned, at least he himself wrote me as much last fall. I do not know when or how all our expectant clerks are to be provided for, but they seem increasingly impatient at present. The last affair into which we were all lugged was to entail upon us advantages that I cannot for the life of me foresee; the general profits are annually decreasing & will continue to decrease.[16] Happy those who have their fortunes already made. But enough of this gloomy subject. I hope you continue to have pleasing accounts of the boys. My wife is anxious to know what family you & Charlotte [Pruden] have now. Flora must now be an age to demand the untying of your pursestrings. We have as yet but an only girl who with one boy is all the family we have here; the other four chaps are at R.R., three with Mr Jones & one with the grandfather [Michel Klyne] ... The traversing of the continent ... is now becoming more safe & familiar to our ear every day. I have now St. Louis cows & horses at Colvile. Two or three American clergymen with their families & household gear came across last season & are now settled, the one on the Wallamette, another in the Blue Mountains of Walla Walla, & a third at the Clearwater forks of the Nez Percés.[17] We also have an Episcopalian minister [Rev Herbert Beaver] of our own at headquarters, so you must own that the 'march of intellect' is making great progress in our part of the wilderness. Tis now almost an age since we saw one another, so much

[16] McDonald and other HBC officers in the 'Indian country' had invested in Pelly, Simpson and Company, a timber business trading in Norway, which proved to be a money-losing project and was closed down in 1843. Writing to McDonald on 1 April 1843, Sir John Pelly referred to 'the general stagnation of the trade' and informed him that shares would be valued at a loss of about 20 percent of the principal invested. McDonald replied: 'It is I suppose needless on the part of so many of us in this country ... to cavil on the subject at the 11th hour. The deed is done & seemingly there is no alternative ... True we Indian traders have but a very limited idea of the general commerce, but somehow ... we cannot reconcile to each other the two facts ... a profit of 8 to 10 percent accruing annually from the business up to the hour our interest in it commenced, [and] for the five years that connexion lasted [the investment] should not yield one shilling.' See McDonald to Pelly, 1 April 1844.

[17] Dr Marcus and Narcissa Whitman, and Reverend Henry Harmon Spalding and his wife Eliza, arrived at Fort Vancouver in September 1836 after a 3,000-mile overland journey from western New York. The Whitmans established their mission at Waiilatpu, near Walla Walla, and the Spaldings set up at Clearwater. Reverend Jason Lee, who came to the Columbia with Nathaniel Wyeth, established a mission on the Willamette River.

so indeed that you seem to forget the exact place. My memory is better:
it was the Forks of Spokane & not Okanagan. This recollection brings
on other melancholy reflections. Poor [John Warren] Dease is no more
& the fate of poor [David] Douglas still more appalling in the Sandwich
Islands. They were both our companions in the last parting glass. I have
a very long and interesting letter from Edwd Ermatinger at St Thomas
in U. Canada ... His brother joined me here middle of last month, left
us 9th inst. with 14 men & 1 Boat ... intended for Walla Walla and a
large party is to be fitted out from there in the spring ... We must now
absolutely make a bold stand on the frontiers; though not a lucrative
business, its prosecution will have its advantages. We are satisfied from
good information that the Americans attempting that trade make nothing of it. Indeed the equippers from St Louis sent up an agent last summer to secure from the traders & trappers all they could before these
Coureurs de Bois were declared insolvent. While the Outfits continue
from St Louis ... we shall always be able to compete with them, but the
moment an entrepot is formed by American subjects near the mouth of
the Columbia goodbye to our advantages.

   April 3rd – Two days ago Ermatinger sent me a Budget from Spokane
after his return from below – a vast deal of domestic news & upon the
whole nothing amiss all the way from Fort Simpson to the Umpqua.
Finlayson safely landed from the steamer in Puget Sound last fall. I expect
him here in a few days on his way out – also Douglas & Fisher, but
Black it would appear won't budge from Kamloops. McLeod got as far
as Cape Disappointment on a Monterey voyage but being 45 days wind-
bound there was recalled & succeeded by Birnie. He is now at Walla
Walla arranging affairs for the south expedition. We have had a very severe
winter here; would you believe that the horses which left us with the
FHead Outfit the 21st of last month are not yet at Spokane. It will be
some days yet before we can turn out our ploughs. Ermatinger took
upwards of six weeks going down the Columbia even by leaving his lading at Okanagan. I am anxious to close my private correspondence as a
very disagreeable task is just imposed upon me to collect evidence & make
out affidavits from our men here in the case of that unhappy man Heron.[18]

[18] Francis Heron was generally unpopular with his colleagues in the Columbia District.
   He had a reputation for 'intemperate habits,' and on more than one occasion he had
   been reluctant to fall in with McLoughlin's plans for him. At the meeting of the Northern Council in 1836 it was decided to investigate his behaviour. See W.K. Lamb's Introduction to *McLoughlin's Fort Vancouver Letters, First Series* (Toronto: Champlain Society,
   1941), xcix.

Fort Colvile, 10 April 1837

To Benjamin Harrison, Hudson's Bay House, London

Last season, by return of the Honbl Company's ship the *Columbia*, I had myself the honour of addressing you a short letter & would not again so soon have trespassed on your notice were it not for the occurrence of two events since the date of that letter, which I certainly at the time did not look out for so soon, namely, the arrival of Mr & Mrs Beaver & the return of the Capendales. By the unexpected arrival of the *Nereide*, I was exceedingly glad to hear that Your Honours at length succeeded in getting us out a Chaplain for Fort Vancouver. I have not yet had the pleasure of seeing that Gentleman, but by my letters from below in the course of the winter, it was with much pain I heard the reception Mr & Mrs Beaver met with was not of that cordial nature I ventured to anticipate when I had the honour of conversing with you in London on the subject. But as all my information on the disagreeable altercation between them & Mr Chief Factor McLoughlin is derived from correspondence only, I cannot venture to offer an opinion of my own on this much to be regretted misunderstanding. The abrupt departure of the poor Capendales however, might, I think have been avoided. If they were not strictly up to the train of this country, & at once prepared to rough through things as they could, they were I am certain the sort of people who were cheerfully disposed to accommodate themselves to circumstances, & would in the course of time with proper arrangements have made themselves sufficient useful. But in the cause of the rupture with them also, I am not prepared to speak from personal knowledge.

On the general business of this department, I will not presume to trouble you, Sir. Our annual reports as usual are just under way for the Seat of Council. I have however the satisfaction to say that that part of the Company's affairs entrusted to my own particular management is as productive & prosperous as I could reasonably expect ...

Fort Colvile, 2 February 1838

To Edward Ermatinger, St Thomas, Upper Canada

... The Express cast up 25th October & the circumstances of your letters for Frank & myself having been delivered by an old shipmate of ours of 20 years back – Charles Ross, alias the parson – certainly added to the sensation I felt on the occasion. The *Prince of Wales*, the voyage & the host of sanguine adventurers stepping ashore in Hudson Bay with high glee came across my thoughts with rather melancholy retrospect![19]

---

[19] McDonald was returning to the Red River Settlement on the *Prince of Wales* in the

Davidson died deaf – Williams went to his long home penniless – Brown stopped off in London – Loutted ended his days in a madhouse – poor McBean went for a grave in India – Sterne, it is true survives but miserably enough as a common labourer in the Highlands – the Major is low enough in the service & I cannot say the parson himself looks exceedingly hopeful. I have thus in 1838 gone out of my way for a picture of the prime in 1818, & in order to return to your very interesting letter, I shall leave the winding up of the moral to your more happy imagination.

Frank's letters I sent off to the FHds beginning of Novr & on the 2nd of next month he himself gave us a very agreeable surprise two days before we expected him. After 11 months separation occupied on both sides by all the scenes & vicissitudes of fortune peculiar to this blessed country, I need scarcely say time did not lack on our hands the first night. Were I not afraid some of your temperance friends might overhear you read this letter I would say good strong Beer, Port, Madeira & excellent Cognac gave increased stimulus to the conversation of the evening. We acknowledged in suitable terms the honour you did us in a drop of Brandy & water while concocting the Colvile letters, by drinking yours in a *bumper* with something like three times three. Nor were we like you too squeamish at returning to the charge. No, your wife & two little ones were thought of also, & perhaps even then the good things were not immediately stowed away. To guard against the possibility of a false impression going abroad however, I must assure you that this kind of manifestation of good fellowship does not often occur with us. What you say on that head with respect to yourself, I apply in its full force to my own self. In the first place, what I in days gone by conceived a glorious merrymaking I now look upon as beastly, & in the next place, were I unfortunately ever so much inclined, my constitutional frame would not endure it. When I do venture in a very moderate allowance, the system is painfully affected by it. So much for temperance, and it must be confessed that those who first proposed the erection of the great Community into Societies for its strict observance have as great a claim upon the gratitude of mankind as the projectors of the Railroads themselves.

How much soever I would delight in the company of your brother for the holidays, the miseries of last winter were too keenly felt to risk a repetition of them this ... off he went on the 20th with one Boat & 8 men & just as much of the good things of Colvile as would enable him

summer of 1818, after giving the HBC London committee his first-hand account of the events that occurred in the colony in 1815-16, when he met his fellow passengers, the Ermatinger brothers (who were en route to their first assignments as HBC clerks).

if necessary to pass a reasonably good Xmas on les Isles de Pierres & his New Year on Cape Horn; but I believe he would have managed it otherwise – the one with [Jean] Gingras & the other with friend Pambrun. We however took the precaution to show off something on the fantastic toe [a dance] at the Kettle Falls itself before his departure, in which our Belles exhibited a striking example of the march of improvement, though of course still far behind the fascinating assemblage of female elegance our friend Mr Dears so bewitchingly describes at St Thomas. Apropos of him, poor man, that he at all determined on leaving the Indian country so soon, he was particularly fortunate in falling into your hands, & in locating himself as judiciously without the loss of time or any of his little means. He will however I fear have a good deal to contend with unless his own constitutional vigour is still unimpaired. The unavoidable expense of servants is what I dread myself, & without outdoor & indoor servants too I foresee one cannot promise himself a very comfortable & a very productive Establishment back in the Canadas. Nor'westers, from their constant habit of commanding others, & that at times in great numbers, will not readily accommodate themselves to the uphill work of the indefatiguable and thriving backwoodsman. After all, this may be a mistaken idea, for when they come to see their own interest in acting like other people why not do it just as cheerfully there, as they often volunteer to endure *greater* privations & degradations too in this country from the very same motive. Do you, my friend, recollect that dismal night we passed in April '26 without fire, food or Blanket when our friend Annance was meeting the Commodore? Yet we looked upon it as but an ordinary occurrence in the life of an Indian trader.

Having got this far on my third page, methinks it's high time for me to congratulate yourself, Sir, on the comfort & happiness you seem to have arrived at. I might say in a limited sense, independence too, for with you the foundation is already securely laid … My own partial knowledge of the wages & means of getting on in the Colonies however will not allow me to subscribe to the very common idea that the moment a man commands a respectable appearance he is by the knowing ones pronounced a very opulent personage. In the present day U. Canada is not what it was in one respect – the 'march of intellect' now tempts every squatter to be his own merchant & this as a matter of course must curtail the chances of the real man of business. Frank speaks of going out to York [Factory] in the spring & if things don't suit his views there, of proceeding to Canada. Still he is not particularly bent upon either step, but on parting I told him to take a turn to the Bay & that for the season I would contrive to do here without another until his own return in the fall. A promotion is certain. The contemplated alliance [with McLoughlin's daughter] is at length finally dropped and this is another reason for my recommending him to visit Rupert's Land & to mix for a few days with the parents of some very fine young ladies at the R.R. Seminary. [John] McLean got Miss Charles & is now Governor of Fort Esquimaux. Little Lawrence no doubt long ere this must have joined you. We have had marvellous accts in the Columbia of the many hair breadth escapes he & his guardian [W.H.] Gray had in passing thro the Blkfoot country. We however heard of their having safely joined the St Louis Caravan at Rendezvous.

I am exceedingly obliged to you for the readiness with which you came into my views respecting my own boy [Ranald]. If Frank goes down he is to take him, but if not I will for a year or two yet have him at Mr Jones', which must finish all the education I intend for him. Were I certain of the time I can get down myself, I could with more ease say how I would like to have him begin the world. In short, my aim is to try how useful he can make himself to me in the first place, & in the next to acquire those habits of industry & good conduct that might at a future day be useful to himself. Upon the strength of your suggestion I have made up my mind to send my other two boys [now at school] at R.R. down to Toronto as soon as I can. While on the subject of Bois Brulés the late adventures of three of them below in '36 recurs to me, namely the sons of Factors [John] McLoughlin, [John] McBean & [A.R.] McLeod. If you did not hear of the young Captains themselves individually, I think you must have heard of their General [James] Dickson[20] & the motley army he embarked with at Buffalo that summer for the conquest of Texas. In certain exploits at Long Point & near Fort Gratiat McL. [John McLoughlin Jr.] was made Major of Brigade – at the Sault Lieut. Colonel. At Fond du Lac he & Capt [Charles] McB. had a quarrel with the Genl. Hence by different route the wreck of this extraordinary army (II) reached R.R. where ... ended the glory of this division of the heroes of Mexico. [John Jr.] McL[oughlin] came across to us last fall for the N.W. coast – the other two sons of Mars are sent to set nets in Athabasca & McKenzie River. What think you now of all that! and the melancholy satisfaction parents have in this way ...

... You say you don't dab much in politics. The active support you for six long days gave the unlucky candidate in the London hustings does

---

[20] An account of James Dickson's ill-fated expedition is given in Frances G. Halpenny and Jean Hamelin, eds., *Dictionary of Canadian Biography*, vol. 7 (Toronto: University of Toronto Press, 1988), 249-50.

not look like indifference … If you lost the race on that occasion it was some consolation that on the meeting of the new Senate you saw ⅔rds of its members range themselves on the right side of the House. For myself, I have never yet come to any fixed principle as to the proper mode of governing the American Colonies. So far, however, I am influenced by a kind of inherent love for everything that tends to the glory of Great Britain & the prosperity of its descendants & I do think that in furtherance of those laudable objects the cause of U. Canada cannot be in better hands than the present House of Assembly. They are however in the humour of drawing rather largely on the credit of the province, & will ere long, if they continue borrowing, exhibit a pretty respectable national debt. But your country is a growing one, & the loans, laid out as they are on productive improvements, hold out a more favourable prospect of redeeming the debt than in the case of poor John Bull with his 900,000,000. Your Sir Francis [Bond Head] has proved himself decidedly a clever fellow & tis to be hoped with the large majority he has now in the assembly that before the expiration of the undisturbed period of 4 years the members have secured themselves of the House, he & they will so far reconcile the … Radicals as to present a formidable barrier to the revolutionary doctrine of les enfants du sol.

By a paper or two that came my way from the lower province it would appear your grand western Railroad passes more to the westward than the vicinity of St Thomas … The rage for Railroads all over the world now, & deservedly too, is truly astonishing & I believe you American merchants & planters, by the universal adoption of them, will for your part enhance the value of the new world beyond the calculation of the most sanguine … Our LaPrairie [railway] affair will I think do, but so far they have divided us no dividend. Tis said a premium of 10 pounds per share is offered. As to affairs in the Indian country, suffice it to say they are much in statu quo. By dint of economy & good management those possessing the sheepskin [CFs and CTs] lay up a little annually, especially those holding a double one, & we of the second grade are most anxious to get rid of them, both on our own & junior friends' account, but the old codgers will not budge … all that remains for me to touch upon is something about Colvile & my own fireside. I have elsewhere said that the precise time I can get down myself is very uncertain. It is so, but I trust in God not very distant, for, the moment I can retire upon a full 85th my mind is made up. Till then it is some consolation that in no part of the pays de sauvage could I be quartered more to resemble the condition of a considerable sort of Canadian farmer than where I am; practice of every description in that way there is no want of, & of course it follows our domestic comforts are proportionately great. My Man [David] Flett is just come in now with word that the good wife & little ones have stepped into the sleigh waiting my company to prance off with the Blond [horse], so goodbye for the present.

My friend, it is now upwards of two months since I left you with the Blond & I need scarcely say I have had many pleasant turns out with him in that time. Within the last ten days however, the vehicle is changed for a wheeled carriage, something half way between a caleche & a gig. Since that time I have also had the pleasure of seeing your brother after a less disastrous trip to Vancouver than the one of the former year. I will of course leave him to tell his own story. He left me 22nd of last month, but in order to be back here before the departure of the Express. What is to be his destination then I cannot say. The moment it was discovered below that I could dispense with him for a season (on a brief visit to York) he was immediately pronounced a disposable hand, & forthwith named for the Bonaventura [California], but if I can I shall thwart that appointment. He may after all go out.

The only news of importance he brought us from below is the premature death of our Commodore [David] Home of the *Nereide*, who with four of his best seamen while crossing the Columbia in the Long Boat 26th January from the Red Bluff to Fort George unhappily met with a watery grave. He was bound for a voyage to the Islands & Monterey & was the same Gentleman who came out in command of the steamer. The accident occurred near the very spot where Messrs McTavish & Henry were drowned 24 years before & happened very much in the same manner. Five men in the prime of life added to the Columbia's precious Roll of Mortality.

Fort Colvile, 28 May 1838

To Peter Skene Ogden, Okanagan

Mr Black, on arrival here yesterday with 18 men, handed me yours of 25th touching on the delicate situation in which you say you are placed by Mr McLoughlin's total silence with you on matters connected with the general Brigade this summer. As regards the strength of the force to be employed, all I distinctly know of the arrangement is that my own presence was not required & that six Bouts & nine middlemen is the complement of hands I am directed to furnish. In other respects we have made more than ordinary efforts to provide Boats, Guns, Lodges, provisions &c &c for the trip; & I have no doubt Mr Black is prepared to furnish you with every particular as to what was proposed & finally settled upon between himself & Mr McLoughlin.

Mr B. left us this afternoon with 5 Boats, 37 men & 220 pieces, which we thought lading enough in the present high state of the water & I trust all will be safely delivered to you at Okanagan …

Fort Colvile, 22 September 1838

To the Gentlemen in charge York Factory Express

Our mountain Boat starts today with 8 men, two to remain building at the upper end of the second lake. Three of the others, namely Canote [Umphreville], [Pierre] Dubois & [Antoine] Duquette return immediately to join them with the canoe sent to the portage in the spring. Joe, Paul and the Fool await your arrival & in meantime work at the road. After Canote leaves them, there will still be four Bags of grain at the portage with 30 lbs grease & some little things for yourselves, say a piece of bacon, ½ doz tongues, some butter & a Bag of biscuits. Should you be in want of more at McKay's he has orders to supply you. For the other side there is a Bag of flour for Fraser, a gun & a small parcel to the address of Mr Charles, & a Bdle from ourselves for the spring Express. All well here & trusting to have the pleasure of seeing you with us soon.

Fort Colvile, 27 October 1838

To John McLoughlin Jr., near the Dalles des Morts

The two Indians arrived here this forenoon with the melancholy intelligence of what took place at the *Dalles des Morts*.[21] I lose no time in despatching you all the assistance possible. The moment Mr Tod got here on 19th his Boat with six men was sent back; he himself with the only other Boat here started the following day for Vancouver. The only craft of any kind now at the place is a *canoe de cliche* & with it LaCourse, our Boatbuilder, & three other hands are sent you with all possible despatch … LaCourse has with him the wherewith to make another cedar canoe. We in like manner send you all the provisions you are likely to require, namely: 3 Bags fine flour, 1 Bag coarse flour, 1 Bag gammon,

---

[21] John Tod had charge of a large party coming down from Boat Encampment when one of the boats capsized in the Dalles. Twelve of the twenty-six occupants drowned, including Robert Wallace (a visiting English botanist) and his bride Maria (George Simpson's daughter by Betsey Sinclair [who wed Robert Miles after Simpson deserted her at York Factory in 1822]); Peter Banks (another botanist); Pierre Leblanc (a carpenter); three other HBC servants (Kenneth McDonald, Fabien Vital, and Jean Baptiste Laliberté); and five children (three of Leblanc's and two of André Chalifoux's). The pilot, Chalifoux, with his wife and two other children, escaped. Leblanc's wife, who also survived, was the woman J.G. McTavish abandoned when he and Simpson brought their English wives back to Rupert's Land in 1830.

1 Bag biscuit, 1 Bag potatoes, 20 lbs grease, 50 lbs pork, 1 tonnel butter, 1 quarter veal, 6 Buffalo tongues, tea, sugar & 2 Gal kegs spirits.

You ought to endeavour to get the broken Boat down here at all events as without it you can scarcely get on to OK ... if LaCourse is able to put it in a condition to drift down even this far perhaps by that means you could convey here as many of the bodies as are found, but in this you can use your own discretion. With further reference to LaCourse ...

Fort Colvile, 27 October 1838

To James Douglas, Fort Vancouver

Another melancholy event on the Columbia river! No fewer than 12 souls perished below the *Dalles des Morts* on the 24th as you will see by Mr John McLoughlin's letter of the 27th herewith enclosed. Without a moment's delay we got off LaCourse, Preveau, Bessou & Jacques ... in order to lend all the assistance possible, & I enclose you a copy of what I have written to Mr McL. on this deplorable occasion ... on enquiring of the Indians I find the wreck & all the survivors had arrived [at McKay's] ... from what they say I think LaCourse will be able to make the Boat efficient.

Henry Warre painted this view of HBC men hauling their boat up the Dalles des Morts in 1845. Twelve people lost their lives when their boat capsized here en route to Fort Colvile in 1838. (BC Archives PDP00057)

As the delay which this lamentable event will unavoidably occasion to Mr McL. must create uneasiness below, I forward his note without delay by a courier to Walla Walla tho alas! the tidings it will convey are anything but cheering ...

Fort Colvile, 3 November 1838

To Samuel Black, Kamloops

Your will of course, in common with us all, lament the deplorable occurrence ... [repetition of arrangements]

So far from having received that efficient assistance so confidently expected & promised when Mr Ermatinger was withdrawn from us, it would appear we were not even thought of at York Factory [Northern Council]. I have however for the present claimed the services of a new apprentice clerk [Angus McDonald] for Vancouver ... as without something in the character of a Gentleman that could at least read & write, the business at the Flatheads this fall would be very lame indeed. Besides I am informed by Mr Ermatinger himself that we are likely to have opposition in the plains this winter, so you can see how we are situated ... The trade however ... must I suppose be conducted by [Antoine] Berland. Altogether, nothing could be more pitiful than the makeshift we are compelled to make, instead of exercising the mighty control & influence over our Indians the American Congress gives us the credit of possessing ...

Fort Colvile, 5 November 1838

To James Douglas, Fort Vancouver[22]

However unwilling to draw your attention to what is passing in this quarter ... I must advert to the exceedingly lame condition in which we are at length placed here. Even when Mr Ermatinger was with us, the propriety of having a rising young man of promise initiated into the business of this district, was repeatedly pointed out. He is now gone, without a provision being made at York Factory either to replace him or provide the young Gentleman in question. I have so far got through with makeshifts but most assuredly they will not answer long. A clever active young Gentleman with the mark of soon making himself master of sufficient French & Indian is absolutely required for the plains if we mean to secure strength & influence in that quarter. Poor Mr Angus McDonald, whom I took upon myself to detain here, is now up at the Flatheads, &

---

[22] James Douglas was in charge at headquarters when John McLoughlin Sr. was on furlough in 1838-39.

will I am certain do all that can be expected from a perfect novice, but that will fall far short of what is required. Mr Ferris, indeed from his knowledge of the French language & some experience as a trader, would, I thought, have answered much better, but he, I understood, was *specially* appointed for Fort Vancouver. [Hypolite] Brouillet goes out in the spring, and I am not very clear that Thomas Flett can be relied upon. There is not a word from either of them this fall yet.

As regards the call upon us for the Snake depot, I am satisfied you will consider the 23 Bags flour sent per Mr Tod's Boat, besides indispensable supplies for Thompson River, to be all that could be done under existing circumstances.

Owing to the late melancholy affair, our Boat work up the river is stopped. Wood for 5 is squared, but I think we must endeavour to have enough for a 6th, that an extra one may go to the mountain next spring ...

Fort Colvile, 1 February 1839

To Edward Ermatinger, St Thomas

In the usual way, I avail myself of the quietness we generally have at Colvile about this time to write some of my more distant friends before the bustle of the Express is upon our hands ... Your kind & very interesting letter of March 20th & P.S. of 6th April I had the pleasure to receive on the 20th Octr thro our mutual friend Mr John Tod. The progress of a certain detachment of that Gentleman's party from the R. Mountains to here I am sorry to say had been attended by one of the most appalling calamities we have ever experienced in the Columbia, fertile in disasters as it ever has been – no fewer than 12 individuals perished in that first Rapid below the *Dalles des Morts* on 22nd Oct: namely Mr Leblanc & three children, one of them McTavish's, two of Chalifoux's – this man again returned from Canada into the service – three of the common men, two Gentlemen botanists from England, & the wife of one of them, the daughter of another great man, poor Maria Miles. Our people as usual went up with the fall Boat, but Mr Tod & the new accomptant, young McLoughlin, finding the two Boatloads inadequate for all they had, divided the whole into three Boatloads & ran down with the two to a new Establishment I was just in the act of forming beyond the 2nd Lake. Thence they returned Chalifoux to the Boat Encampment with one & Mr T. himself with the other came on here & continued his route for Vancouver ...

The Dr [McLoughlin] left us on a trip to England last spring, & Mr [James] Douglas ever since is the acting man at the depot. Black, our

Chief Factor, is still stationary at Kamloops, where his talents in some measure are kept in play & rendered highly useful to the Honbl Company by the old jawing about Martens & dried salmon with his friend Squire Fisher. Ogden, the best of the three, takes great delight, as you may suppose, in keeping up this kind of party contention ... On the coast, the Gentlemen are exactly as they were last year with the character of an additional C.T. in the person of Mr Donald Manson, Commandant of Fort McLoughlin. [Michel] Laframboise is the Bonaventura [California] leader, assisted occasionally as supercargoes in the *Cadboro* by [John M.] McLeod and Charles Ross. I believe the only group of adventurers now to touch upon are the *Serpents*. Well it would appear people thought your brother & I had not enough to do in this quarter, or, that we were on too good terms together to be sufficiently useful, & off he was sent to second McLeod at Fort Hall, I believe much against his inclination. The Dr's palaver however, and the assurance of a positive promise ... of a commission next year ... overcame his scruples. As I know neither the one or the other came, & from sentiments he expressed to me on the subject before we parted, I am much inclined to think he will be going out ensuing spring ...

What a dreadful hullabuloo you Canadians have at length stirred up in the political world.[23] How all this will end must be a source of uneasiness to many, even to us poor Nor'westers whose life cord is as much in jeopardy by the machinations of Papineau as the interest of our other fellow subjects beyond the great water. If unfortunately we do lose ground below, it is one consolation it cannot be ascribed to a want of loyalty & attachment to the cause of our maiden Queen [eighteen-year-old Victoria came to the throne in 1837] on the part of [those of] British origin – a few, of course, excepted. I see my friends the Glengarry clans have already declared themselves in the most martial humour. I wonder what our friend Finan [McDonald] says to it, poor man; there was a day in which he would certainly have acted his part. Upon the whole, the open and early declaration made by McKenzie and Papineau of what they have but imperfectly matured, is perhaps the best turn the affair could possibly have taken. It at least shows where the danger lay'd, and gives time to the new congress at Quebec to adjust the new constitution, which it is to be hoped will afford satisfaction & ample security to all parties. What you say of brother Jonathan's cause in jobs & speculations

---

[23] The Canadas were in turmoil in 1837, when Louis Joseph Papineau (in Lower Canada) and William Lyon Mackenzie (in Upper Canada) led 'reformers' in rebellion against the government.

is strictly correct; they are a great & enterprising nation certainly, but with equal correctness.may it not be said that the moral & social virtues are lost sight of in the monstrous growth of the Confederation. Last fall I had the good luck to lay my fingers on a file of the N[ew] York *Albion* & of the Quebec *Gazette*, & what a picture of woe & despondency in the whole series. One can scarcely convince himself that they allude to that land of milk & honey which the rest of the world is called upon to take as an example of all that is glorious & happy under the sun. Much of their present confusion however will subside into its natural channels when proper bounds are put to their inordinate spirit of speculation.

As regards myself, the older I grow the more I am fixed on a settlement in Upper Canada, tho I doubt if this be the case with many of our west side friends. The Wallamette & Cowlitz is now getting to be too tempting for them, yet, I keep probing John Work as much as I can in every letter passing between. Should Frank go down this summer he will be taking Ranald along with him & indeed should he not, it is still my intention that the youngster should accompany someone to the *Sault*. I will enclose him a letter for you, suggesting what we will endeavour to make of him. He has a high character for application & good behaviour from Mr [John] McCallum [schoolmaster at Red River]. The other two, if they live, will be following in a couple of years, I think for the Toronto Seminary of learning; but how comes it about that in this country we know nothing of the nature & conditions of that institution. It would be nothing against the professors if they were to let us know their terms. I should like much to have something in that way before I finally determine with respect to my own boys. It will go very hard with me if I let any of them loose in this vile country, tho that nevertheless seems to be the lot of the entire rising generation. I am sorry to hear the good folk of St Thomas have had such a bad specimen of us in the person of Lawrence; he will however, I trust, improve. The bereavement in your own family, Sir, we were exceedingly sorry to hear[24] ... Poor unhappy Mrs Leblanc lost 4 of them in the short space of 20 days. It was a consolation to us however to hear that you & Mrs E. bore the loss with that Christian resignation becoming to us all. In this country you know how indifferent we are in general to the divine duties required of us; yet the awful warnings we have had in our small community begin to impress upon myself very forcibly the propriety of withdrawing very soon to a retired corner where we can have the benefit of those good moral lessons we are so long without in the wilderness. I must confess however that

[24] Two of Edward Ermatinger's children died the preceding year.

since your time great changes for the better have taken place in the Columbia. Within the last six months we have had no less than six ministers of the Gospel, two Roman C. & four New England Presbyterians – of the latter I am to have one here & another at Spokane. The other two join the old missionaries at Nez Percés & Walla Walla. Mr [Jason] Lee, the head of the Methodist mission in the Wallamette, went down last season by way of St Louis to return ensuing autumn with a strong reinforcement for that station, so you see the extent of the change. Poor Mr Beaver, I believe he is off, at least when he wrote me in the summer such was his determination.[25]

20th March – Mr [William G.] Rae arrived here yesterday by the plains [from Fort Vancouver], & in a day or two we shall be looking out for young McLoughlin & the Boats. He is to be the only outgoer this spring & I hope his coming will be more fortunate than the last. I had three or four letters from your brother since the 1st of February; his last acquaints me with the determination he came to of not stirring, which I by no means approve of. York Factory he ought absolutely to see, but it seems he believes from those who have an interest in keeping him in, that the commission is on the way. I wish it may, but I doubt it. One thing certain, it will come sometime by his remaining in the country … We have a vast number of expectants about as sanguine as Frank, & I dare say some of them with very fair promises too. They know very well *old* clerks & old Traders have a greater temptation for remaining than *young* ones …

This I hope will be handed you by my son, together with another letter entirely about himself, & I trust in God the poor fellow may be a credit to us both. I have written to Mr [Chief Factor Alexander] Christie [at Fort Garry] & to Mr [William] Nourse about him, also to Mr [James] Keith should it so happen he goes by way of Lachine. I hope there will be no difficulty about a passage for him as far as the Sault. Mr Christie

[25] Reverend Herbert Beaver, the Episcopalian clergyman sent out from England by the HBC, arrived with his wife at Fort Vancouver in September 1836. From the beginning of his stay he was critical of everything about his situation and the conditions and inhabitants in the fur country. The well documented feud between Beaver and John McLoughlin culminated in actual blows when McLoughlin attacked Beaver after learning that the missionary had written in insulting terms about his country wife, Marguerite Wadin McKay, in a report to the governor and committee. Beaver did not acknowledge the validity of country marriages, and McLoughlin, a Roman Catholic, refused to be married in a Church of England ceremony. Fortunately, McLoughlin left the Columbia on furlough a few days after the final blowup, and by the time he returned in 1839 the Beavers had departed. See *McLoughlin's Fort Vancouver Letters, First Series*, vol. 1 (Toronto: Champlain Society, 1941), cxvii-cxx.

is directed not to send him to Norway House if it is possible to meet the canoes at Bas de la Rivière direct from Red River.

We are all well here at present thank God. The wife is much flattered by your kind enquiries & begs to be very kindly remembered to you & Mrs E. tho we have not *yet* the pleasure of her acquaintance. There is no sister-in-law for you in the Columbia; perhaps tis just as well. The Lady [McLoughlin's stepdaughter, Maria] is now the mother of a young Rae ...

Fort Colvile, 10 March 1839

To Edward Ermatinger, St Thomas

This will be handed you by my son Ranald, of whom I have already made mention. Having seen nothing of him myself for the last four years, I am much at a loss how to speak of him to you now. All say he is a promising good-natured lad. Before he went to Red River in '34, I had him myself pretty well advanced in arithmetic, so that one would suppose he is now something of a scholar; yet I am aware boys of his age leaving school not infrequently are very deficient & that a little practical learning about that time brushes them up amazingly. I will just quote you a sentence about him from the Rev [William] Cockran's letter to me last fall [from Red River]. 'I preached at the upper church last Sunday & saw the boys – they were all well then. Angus (the little white-headed chap you [knew] crawling about at Okanagan House) still takes the lead,

Ranald MacDonald, photographed in 1891 at age sixty-seven, was the son of McDonald's first wife, Princess Raven, daughter of the Chinook chief Comcomly. Ranald grew up under Jane Klyne's care and attended the Red River Academy with his younger half-brothers. In 1848 he became known as the first teacher of English in Japan. He later spent many years in British Columbia and was a member of Robert Brown's Vancouver Island Exploring Expedition in 1864.

but Ranald has *certain indescribable qualities* which lead me to imagine that he will make the man that is best adapted for the world.' So far, good. Still I cannot divest myself of *certain indescribable fears* which you can conceive as well as I can; but in your hands, without flattery, I feel the grounds for those fears are considerably removed.

I should like to give him a trial in the way of business, & with this view have him bound to yourself, Sir, as an apprentice. By the spring of '40 you will be able to judge of his conduct & capacity, when I shall trouble you for a full exposé of all you think about him. My reply to that letter you will have in the fall of '41, which will either confirm all our plans of making a Gentleman tout de bon of him, or have him enter on a new apprenticeship of any trade he may select for himself. In either case, I will with great pleasure attend to all the little demands you may make on his account ...

You know the rock on which split all the hopes & fortunes of almost all the youth of the Indian country. Ranald, I hope, will have none of those fatal notions. His success in the world must solely depend on his own good conduct & exertions. He has a few letters his father & mother lately addressed him with the very best advice we could give situated as we are, which you will have the goodness to see that ... he will frequently peruse. Above all let him be a constant attendant at church. Had I known the name of your Episcopalian preacher I would certainly have taken the liberty to address him a few lines about the moral duties of my son, which I dare say the Reverend Gentleman would not take amiss. We had him vaccinated some years ago, but as the inflammation was scarcely perceptible there would be no harm in giving it him again.

Fort Colvile, 18 April 1839

To Rev Elkanah Walker, Tshimakain Mission[26]

Your last courier got here yesterday afternoon. I am happy to know the war upon the dogs has closed so satisfactorily; here, we too made a

---

[26] Reverend Elkanah Walker and his wife Mary, and Reverend Cushing Eells and his wife Myra, arrived in Oregon in the fall of 1838, sent by the American Board of Commissioners for Foreign Missions to join the Whitmans and Spaldings in their work in the 'Indian country.' Walker and Eells established their mission on the Tshimakain plain, about sixty miles south of Colvile, and the McDonald family welcomed their new neighbours enthusiastically when they arrived on the scene in March 1839. McDonald provided men, tools, and supplies from the fort to assist the men in building their new homes, and the two wives were invited to stay at Colvile until the mission buildings were made habitable, giving Jane Klyne her first intimate contact with women from 'the civilized world.' By the time Mary and Myra moved down to their

demonstration of hostilities in your favour when we heard your sentiments ... I am aware it would not yet do for them to annihilate the
whole race, for a few good ones for deer & bear they will find of infinite
service until they are entirely independent of the Chiuse [Cayouse], &
these they can very easily keep out of harm's way by tieing them up as
they usually do. I told the masters of the dogs here that they need never
expect any person to come to enlighten them while their dogs are so
numerous.

Agreeable to your wish, we send the seed grain, namely 2 Bushels
white wheat, which I think will answer you better than the red, & a
Bushel of pease.

As to the cows, there will be no necessity for your taking along your
milker when you come for the family, a trip you seem to have in contemplation much sooner than we anticipated. The Ladies themselves
write you by this convenience, & will of course express you their sentiments on the subject. Naturally enough they will both like to see you,
which you can both well do without taking them away. But you of course
regulate these things according to your own mutual inclinations.

I find your stupid man is off without advertising us of it so as our
notes must be sent after him I cannot write as much as I could wish ...

Fort Colvile, 14 May 1839

To Rev Elkanah Walker, Tshimakain Mission

A party of our people from Vancouver arrived here this morning, &
I am sorry they did not think of leaving in your neighborhood a separate packet of letters they had addressed to your mission. I now send it
back without delay by a young Indian of this place ... I believe a good
deal of the correspondence has reference to your things, just arrived at
Walla Walla ...

We shall be happy to hear that you all safely reached home. The
weather for one thing was much in your favour & I think you must have

---

mission in May, the three women had become friends, and on a number of occasions
in the ensuing years they made the overland journey on horseback with their children
to visit back and forth. Jane became a member of the Columbia Maternal Association, the first women's organization west of the Rocky Mountains, formed by Narcissa
Whitman to assist the missionary women 'in the right performance of our Maternal
duties.' See C.M. Drury, ed., *First White Women Over the Rockies*, vols. 1 and 2 (Glendale, CA: Arthur H. Clark, 1963); and *Nine Years with the Spokane Indians: The Diary,
1838-1848, of Elkanah Walker* (Glendale, CA: Arthur H. Clark, 1976); and Jean Murray
Cole, *Exile in the Wilderness* (Toronto/Seattle: Burns and MacEachern/University of
Washington Press, 1979).

found the roads good. Johnny often speaks of his friend Cyrus ... I have one London newspaper as late a date as the 14th October noticing slightly the Montreal & New York news of 9th & 14th September ... the appearance quiet & peaceable then throughout North America. Amongst the Mexicans however I believe there is some fighting going on. On the continent of Europe, Spain alone still had the credit of being in actual war. Don Carlo it is said is gaining ground fast.

The wife joins me in kind respects to you all ...

Fort Colvile, 12 August 1839

To Rev Elkanah Walker, Tshimakain Mission

Our friend the Bighead [Cornelius, the Lower Spokane chief] at length made his appearance, not however with a large bundle of Beaver ... Poor old man in self defence says that the few he actually at one time did possess again slipped thro his fingers in a manner he could not help. However, we met & part good friends & his gun is mended. He is one of the few not much captivated by the showey ceremony of the R.C. divine [Father Modeste Demers];[27] I believe he did not go near him. His account of the gardens your way is not very flattering, but if what he says of his own potatoes be true, methinks we must all look to him for next year's seed.

Here, notwithstanding our flourishing appearance when you left, we will not have a potato. True, even at that time the effects of the drought was beginning to be felt, & the total absence of rain or of even the ordinary dews ever since has completely destroyed the vital spark in everything, saving the wheat. Add to this a new plague in the shape of grasshoppers, or rather locusts, which has entailed upon us their own good share of mischief. They are exceedingly numerous at present and I am sorry to say are apparently dropping their eggs for a fresh brood next season. They must be peculiar to Colvile as I hear no mention of them elsewhere by any of my correspondents.

I am sorry ... the want of proper information should have led you to perform the trip to Walla Walla. To prevent another wild goose chase in the direction of Okanagan ... I have the pleasure to inform you that all [your things are] here. This being the case we anticipate the pleasure of

[27] Father Modeste Demers and Father Francis Norbert Blanchet, of the Roman Catholic Quebec mission, came to the Columbia with John Tod's ill-fated party in October 1838. They established missions in the Willamette area and, later, the Cowlitz, but they made visits and held conversion ceremonies among the Natives of Okanagan, Walla Walla, and Colvile.

seeing one of you soon ... previous to your setting out for the general meeting ... As for poor Mrs Eells, from the very severe attack she has had it cannot be expected that her recovery will be otherwise than exceedingly slow ... Is there anything we can do for her?[28]

Your report of affairs at Walla Walla gives me great concern. Whatever the fate of the scoundrel that has already ventured as far as to take away three of Mr. Pambrun's horses ... it is clear a feeling exists there sufficiently bad that may lead to very serious evil ...

The good wife's crisis is at length happily over, & as she was so long about it, thought it a good joke to favour me with a couple of boys at a time.[29] They are now three weeks old and so far promise to do well ... We have got an Indian woman to assist her in nursing them ... Cornelius is standing at my elbow all the time I am writing this, & most impatient to be off ...

Fort Colvile, 22 August 1839

To Samuel Black, Kamloops

As it was not finally decided upon when we parted whether or not you would let us have 20 or 12 young horses for the Flathead trade out of the band you are about sending off to the low country, I could wish that point was settled before we go to the trouble of getting them from elsewhere.

I also avail myself of this opportunity to inform you that we will not have a single potato here for next year's seed & of course must look to OK for that indispensable article. In case you may think I was serious in approving your proposal to send us Mr [William] Thew[30] for the Kootenais, I must remove that impression by giving it as my opinion that he will never answer our purpose. Mr Angus McDonald is here now. In the plains he did as well as could be expected for a porkeater [novice or newcomer], but the application, or rather the demand made for him

---

[28] According to Mary Walker's diary, Myra Eells had a severe attack of ague in August and, for a time, thought she was not going to recover.

[29] The McDonald twins, James and Donald, were born 23 July 1839.

[30] William Thew was a young clerk who had a short career with the HBC. According to Chief Factor John Rowand of Edmonton, he was 'exceedingly negligent and inefficient' and had neither 'the will nor the wish to make himself useful.' He was sent from the Saskatchewan to New Caledonia, where his reputation preceded him to the Columbia. When he was assigned to McDonald in 1841-42, his conduct was so bad that McDonald finally ordered him off the fort and he was dismissed from the Company.

from below renders it quite impossible for him to take any active part in
the duties we could otherwise have chalked out for him ... Berland made
the Kootenais summer trade consisting of 27 chevr[eaux] skins ...

Fort Colvile, 23 September 1839

To the Gentleman in Charge of York Factory Express

Our mountain Boat with 6 men is this moment about starting, accompanied by Mr Fisher & family, The lading is as follows viz: 3 Bags fine
flour, 3 Bags coarse, 2 of corn & 1 of pease, and a Bag biscuit, a Bale of
hams & bacon (45 lbs), 6 Buffalo tongues & 20 lbs dried meat for the
mess coming down. The people have for their own use to go up with 3
Bags grain & 50 lbs grease and a Bag of grain for the Boat. Mr Fisher
is supplied apart from all this ...

Fort Colvile, 10 October 1839

To Rev Elkanah Walker, Tshimakain Mission

Your last note per the Indian came to hand the day before yesterday
when Dr McLoughlin was here [returning from furlough]. That Gentleman cast up the night before & left yesterday with two Boats. Two more
are still on the way down and may be expected in 8 or 10 days. In all
the letters I saw for the mission, there was but the accompanying one
for you. Those for Messrs Spalding & Whitman went on to Walla Walla.

As yet there is no actual war between Great Britain & the U.S. tho
both parties seem to be preparing for something of the kind. The boundary line is the bone of contention, & upon such a frivolous point it is to
be hoped two such enlightened & powerful nations will not be fools
enough to plunge the civilized world into a ruinous & demoralising war.
Most assuredly if once declared, it will become a general one and perhaps a lasting one ... with little or no advantage to either.

Could not one of you come down to see us about the 18th, as I think
the war party will be here about that time. Mr Gray remained five days
with us. We got him straight on to the Piscahoes without going the way
of Okanagan at all ...

Fort Colvile, 31 October 1839

To Rev Elkanah Walker, Tshimakain Mission

Probably ere this reaches you, you will have heard that the Boats arrived
about four hours after you left. The wife was for sending after you, but
I thought it scarcely worthwhile ... They remained with us two nights
... I am sorry you had not the opportunity to be introduced to Mr
[Alexander] Simpson [cousin of George Simpson, brother of Thomas],

as his destination is the Sandwich Islands & he will of course mix with
your friends there.

... The wife desires to be very kindly remembered to Mrs Walker; we
found the cakes most delicious. She will next opportunity do herself the
pleasure of addressing her a few lines ... Mr Eells will give you all our
news. I believe he has got all he required ...

Fort Colvile, 12 December 1839

To Rev Elkanah Walker, Tshimakain Mission

Had there been an opportunity, I would ere this have acknowledged
receipt of your very kind letter of 24th of last month, but as I have just
observed in my note to Mr Eells, Simpleton went off without my knowledge when he found that I was not *simple* enough to pay him for his
trip in coming here. That disappointment however gives me no less concern now than to hear of your own late indisposition ... I do think you
fret yourself too much with that confounded Indian jargon. Your desire
of speedily acquiring a competent knowledge of a subject on which much
of your success depends is very laudable, but still I am clearly of opinion
the language must be studied by degrees, & the classification of the parts
of speech attempted only after a great deal of experience & common
observation made in your daily intercourse with the different tribes.

... I hear none of you are sufficiently well off in family comforts. Get
the Indians to procure you venison & make your houses warm for the
poor women & children ... The wife joins me in kindest regards to you
& Mrs W. & the children speak of Master Cyrus ...

Fort Colvile, Thursday morning [December 1839]

To Rev Elkanah Walker, Tshimakain Mission

Your courier came in very apropos, & I thank you for the diligence
used for pushing on our Budget from below. Mine for that quarter was
just made up about two hours before the Indian popped in and ... tomorrow Mr [Angus] McDonald will be off accompanied by Charles. This
youth having lost himself last summer is rather doubtful about his knowledge of the low road. Will you therefore have the goodness to recommend to them a young man that can lead them across the plains until
they fall in upon the Spokane track. But now that I think of it, I thinks
me you will be going yourself along with Mr McDonald instead of putting
off your trip to Walla Walla till the first week in February, especially with
such inviting weather. In this case you can both return together also, at
the same time that you can always benefit from Charles' knowledge of
the language.

I am glad to hear you were at home for Christmas, & doubly so on account of the Ladies, whom I should grieve to hear being without a good comfortable dinner on that occasion. A couple of Buffalo bosses for them were overlooked when you started, but are now sent on. Mr [Donald] McLean himself is writing you ... I think you may depend upon [a visit from him] before he returns to the upper country. What you say of the blackguards in the mountain is quite correct, but if you & I live long in the Columbia I am mistaken if this is [not] but the prelude to a great deal worse that we shall see in it. In haste ...

Fort Colvile, 10 January 1840

To John McLoughlin, Fort Vancouver

The mild state of the weather being sufficiently tempting to induce me to forward a packet the length of Walla Walla ... Mr Pambrun may find an opportunity of seeing it conveyed to Vancouver before the Express starts. Of the few things we require by that conveyance a list is herewith enclosed. Mr McLean & party safely arrived here [from Flatheads] as late as Xmas eve with a fair supply of everything. The cause of his keeping out so long was the great distance which the poor Natives were obliged to travel in search of cattle before they could load the horses. The collection of furs for the year from that quarter ... will exceed either of the two last years by about 250 Beaver, & might perhaps after all be made to keep up to something thereabouts for years to come yet, but I fear this we cannot do if Indians & freemen are not allowed something of the same inducement for exertion that is given elsewhere. The freemen in particular are disposed to avail themselves of the Fort Hall prices in both goods & furs, & we can scarcely maintain that in so doing they are unreasonable. It is certain however that the Company, at least in this district, gains nothing by seeing indebted freemen move off to other sections of the country where they will ... begin a new score & thus not only evade the payment of a just debt but relinquish hunting grounds that might be made available to the district they are in ...

Here itself I am in hopes we will not fall much short of the ordinary amount of Returns, & by the last accounts from Thomas Flett the Kootenais too will do something. Last fall, in order to relieve the upper Indians from the unnecessary trouble & loss of time in coming down to trade at the present House, it was made with them at the Tobacco plain 6 days march higher up on the river ... The contracts of a good few of our men being about expiring, & most of them determined on renewing their time under no other condition than that of being free at the expiration of one engagement more, it was with considerable difficulty I got five or six of them to renew for two & three years, without of course pledging myself to any condition of the kind ...

About the Boats ... we are now sawing the wood for four new ones which is all that can be depended on here for the ensuing season. Our most pressing work at present is in the barns. Felix is at the Big Plain with most of our horned cattle, where I think they will thrive well ...

Fort Colvile, 11 January 1840

To James Douglas, Fort Vancouver

I believe I addressed you a few hasty lines in the fall, merely to say that we were well. To have attempted amusing you with anything beyond that, at a time too I knew you would be overwhelmed with news of the world [McLoughlin had returned from furlough], would have been a very idle tale ... In the fall I understood Tod was to come up for N. Caledonia in the winter; if he did, I have neither seen nor heard anything of him.

The only document come my way since the doctor went down (which I believe was thro Dr Gray) was an envelope into which friend Work had thrust a Fort Simpson letter of his, just about as laconic as Caesar's, saying he had come there himself, saw you all & was about returning. How are the affairs of the new company[31] coming along? Bless me this 200,000 pound item is a most astounding sum even to think of! Still more so to devise ways & means for its profitable investment. The moment the freehold grant is obtained, I move that the Clallam district in a line from Hood's Canal to the Pacific be barred up & appropriated to the preservation of the poor expiring Beaver race, still leaving country enough for the ostensible objects of the Agricultural Company in rearing Merino sheep, horned cattle & all the rest of it ...

Fort Colvile, 25 March 1840

To Rev Elkanah Walker

... With us the last part of the winter [was] particularly severe, nor did the spring open upon us with the temperature & rapidity I at one

[31] The Puget's Sound Agricultural Company was organized as a separate enterprise under the auspices of the HBC in 1839, 'with a view to the production of wool, hides, tallow and other farm produce for the English and other markets.' The new enterprise was to be supervised by McLoughlin, who had enthusiastically supported the idea when he met with the London Committee that year when on furlough. The HBC transferred the Cowlitz Farm and Fort Nisqually to the Puget's Sound Agricultural Company 'at a fair valuation,' and McDonald and many of his fellow fur traders took up the offer to purchase shares. See E.E. Rich, ed., *McLoughlin's Fort Vancouver Letters*, Second Series, vol. 2 (Toronto: Champlain Society, 1943), 15-16.

time expected. We have not been able to do anything at the ground yet, but God willing tomorrow morning we shall make a commencement with 4 ploughs. The greatest drawback upon us will be the want of hay for so many horses, before we can have a blade of new grass, & at a time too that the poor animals are not over vigorous ...

Your friend Mr McLean left us on Monday, and would have come up to his people that night somewhere about the Fool's ... I rather suspect he must go round by the Coeur d'Alènes. In that case he will of course be with you a night, if not two, to compare notes on 'Tama' & all the rest of it ... Our friend the Bighead was not yet in, or any account of him, but tis said there was no lack of Buffalo or Blackfeet in the plains throughout the winter, & the story goes that the common enemy carried off no fewer than 170 horses from the Nez Percés. Should your homeguards bring in any quantity of dried meat, fat & tongues, I suppose you must pay well for it ... In the plains it is true we don't pay high for these things at first cost, but every day's journey made with them before the trade ... the price is increased ...

Your request with respect to the account I attend to as much as practicable; the actual cost of the different items can only be totalled after the accomptant is here, but ... I have struck out an approximation of the amount – 27 pounds ... Perhaps were one of you here about the middle of April when the accounts are making up it would have been more satisfactory to all parties ...

We were happy to hear all is well to the southward. Mrs Gray's letter was very acceptable. So poor Mrs Spalding has got a further increase to her little family. You did not say how Mrs Smith is. By the doctor's [Whitman] last letter she seemed to be very poorly. The wife desires to be very kindly remembered to Mrs Walker & so do the little ones to Master Cyrus. Our two young chaps are thriving ... keeping up with each other to a tee, their first, second & third teeth appeared with each the very same day ...

Fort Colvile, 1 April 1840

To Donald Ross, Norway House
... yours of 24th June last enclosing copy of a circular drawn up by a committee of management of the Chief Factors & Chief Traders assembled at Norway House last season ... I fully concur with the committee in all they have said in admiration of Governor Simpson's public spirit & private worth ... and trust the funds raised for this laudable purpose may afford to purchase a service of plate in quantity, quality, design

and execution commensurate with the merits of the distinguished character whose worth it is intended to commemorate. Herewith you will find a draft on the Honbl Company for 25 pounds as my share of the subscription ...

Fort Colvile, 2 April 1840

To Edward Ermatinger, St Thomas

Here am I once more at your service, & it is with great pleasure I acknowledge rct of your much esteemed favour of April last with the sundry & very acceptable packages of Newspapers which accompanied it. The bearer [John McLoughlin Sr.] was one I presume you would little expect from your passing remark that 'he was out of the Columbia at last.' He was so, but is back again, & I suppose for life. Our friend in his late travels discovered that there are quite enough great men already on both sides the Atlantic to give him any chance of excelling there, & in his wisdom is once more back at the helm of affairs to give a fair trial to his old hobby of planting a new Colony on the N.W. coast of America. To be serious, you are to understand that such a project is in contemplation under the auspices of the Honbl Company. A new association called the 'Puget's Sound Agricultural Company' is formed, with a capital stock of 200,000 pounds already taken up in *hard dollars* by the HB stockholders & the Gentlemen in this country in the proportion of interest they respectively hold in the fur trade. Certain shares are also allowed clerks of different grades, even to married men ... The license for exclusive trade was renewed by the home government for 21 years more, & another addition to the business is acquired by a recent contract with the Russians for the undisturbed possession of a good deal of their trade in that quarter for a period of ten years. So you see our perseverence to keep hold of a good thing as long as we can. Indeed were you only able to pacify Jonathan for us, the rising class of traders might still find a bone to pick in the wilderness.

I am in constant paper communication with your brother, but have not seen him since spring '38. The other day I had a sheet from him from Walla Walla on his way to Vancouver, when of course he will see the Chieftain & hear of present & prospective prospects. By the ship, he had the governor's permission to visit you next season, but being previously pledged to continue in the plains till '41 he was apprehensive he could not avail himself of the privilege till then however. Having mentioned the thing to the Dr *en passant* he told me that by all means *he could* if so inclined, and in other respects, whether he got the commission under way for him or not, seemed particularly anxious to serve him, even to a wife. His granddaughter, Miss [Catherine] Sinclair of Lac la Pluie, a very accomplished young lady from the Red River boarding school he has brought in with him to replace Maria with the old Lady [McLoughlin's wife]. But I dare say it will be her own fault, a failing by the bye that few of her sex can be charged with, if she does not soon follow the example of the charming aunt.

Friend Work was on a visit below last winter, and will no doubt give you a very interesting account of what is passing his way. I believe the Big Man himself accompanied him in the steamer to Fort Langley to take a survey of the coast & surrounding country for the intended operations of the new Company, & you know that honest John, if once fairly a partisan in the business, can talk & judge of such matters with as much propriety & philosophy as anyone. Do not however my friend suppose that I am myself smitten with this colonization mania of ours. That a large population may in course of time spring up over the country I do not at all doubt, but with one eye one can see the motley crew of which it must necessarily be composed: it will be of every cast & hue into which the naturalist has subdivided the three primary branches that first peopled mother earth, and God's mercy be upon the executive ruler that will have to keep them all good peaceable subjects long before they are half so numerous as the less discordant mixture you have at present in the Canadas; to which evil by the bye I see is now ascribed the radical cause of all your late troubles. On that topic I am much obliged to you for the means you have so kindly taken to make me acquainted with the state of affairs – indeed I was unusually fortunate last fall. Through the kindness of one friend or another I had the Quebec *Gazette*, Durham's *Report*, his appendix B & the admirable book of your own Sir Francis [Bond Head's, *A Narrative*]. So you may judge of my proficiency in Canadian politics, & what a clever fellow I shall make when honoured with the important privileges of a portly yeoman amongst you.

This step may not be so soon as I at one time anticipated, but I do sincerely trust many years will not pass over my head till I am free of this blessed country. It is a move however in which I do not expect to be followed by many of my west side colleagues ... I have my own views, but theirs may be different. Without your express desire to that effect, I have sent you Ranald & am satisfied you will do towards him all that one friend can consistently expect from another. After you have an opportunity of seeing the bent of his own inclinations, you will have the goodness to suggest to me what we can best do with him ... Without my saying it you can imagine the source of anxiety he is to me. I do not like this country for them, yet, how many of them have done well out of it! I am glad to hear the young nephew [Frank's son Lawrence] is likely to turn out better than was at one time expected. With them both it rests to develop the character of the *west sidians* & God send it may be a creditable one.

I perused the *Patriot* with very great interest. It is as you say rather violent, but I fancy the Caustic Editor knows the Am. character well, & most assuredly if they do come to crow in the present struggle it is not because Mr Thomas Dalton has not done his duty as a staunch Conservative writer. Within the province itself I see there is nothing serious to apprehend. Your senators upon the whole appear to be in tolerable good humour, especially as the great bone of contention – the interests of poor devoted church – is likely to be settled to the satisfaction of the opposition. Those papers I forwarded to Frank as Tod is otherwise well provided at headquarters, being as you must know now, farmer general at Cowlitz. He is however again I believe to return to New Caledonia. So is Charles Ross after a year's sojourn at Fort McLoughlin. Manson, whom he relieved, is at Vancouver on his way out in the spring. The dearly beloved cousin Sam [Black] is at liberty to do so also if inclined; Squire Fisher, bag & baggage took the lead this way in the fall & McLeod about the same time set sail by way of Cape Horn. Douglas, Rae, Jno McLoughlin Junr & a young [Roderick] Finlayson proceed to the Russian settlements early in the spring. There will still be enough at the Emporium, for the good man himself came in with 7 messmates, besides a host of Halfbreed apprentices from the R.R. Academy. Master David [McLoughlin] too, after finishing his education in France & England, is quartered in the *depense*, to qualify him at some future period for a distinguished part in the will-be new government. Tom [McKay] & Jos [McLoughlin] with young wives (Miss [Isabella] Montour & Miss [Victoire] McMillan [daughter of James McMillan and his country wife Kilakotah]) are already on their own bottom & the three young McKays are to return from the U.S. professional men in a year or two. So much for the Pacific British Settlement.

As to ourselves ... we continue in the enjoyment of all the blessings this country can afford. The wife is much flattered by your kind enquiries. She is doing all she can to raise young recruits for her maiden Queen, her 7th & 8th sons she presented me with at a birth in July last, both doing very well. Our missionary neighbours give us a call occasionally which helps to enliven the scene usually so very dull at an inland past. Gray with his lady from Ithaca also honoured us with a visit from W. Walla last fall. So far we have experienced nothing unpleasant as resulting directly from the bad feeling between the two nations on your side the continent, but I dare say the boundary line hubbub will in some shape or other bring us under the notice of the contending parties before the all-engrossing question is amicably settled ...

20th − My friend, I have given you such a long story already that I am almost ashamed to begin again, but the temptation is irresistable ... I have Manson & young [Dugald] McTavish with me here for the last ten days enjoying the good things of Colvile. They will I believe be off for the Grand Côte tomorrow. Our friend Tod they dropped at OK. Two days back the Dr's *ultimatum* of the 5th reached us by land ... I heard from your brother, but of course will avoid troubling you with what he says of himself. I am about sending him a boatload of Colvile grub to meet him at W.W. which will be accompanied by a kinsman of my own [Angus McDonald] I have had in training here since last fall and is to complete his education among the *Snakes*.

At Colvile itself we are pretty busy for the present, building Boats, grinding wheat, counting Beaver, making packs & giving ample employ-ment to 4 ploughs & as many harrows that commenced labour 25th ultimo & will continue till we leave this end of May. Our dairyman too (old Joachim) is hard at work scouring up his milk tureens, in order to meet our share of a very heavy demand in butter & cheese that is to be made upon all cattleholders in the Columbia for the fulfilment of our contract with the Russians to the tune of 200 firkins in the article butter alone. I hope however there will be no call upon me for *Buffalo tongues* as another item in the bargain. Black says that so far from his being able to give the 'premier' − he means the Dr − ten Kegs, he has not enough for himself!!

... I enclose you a short note for my son. Had you been obliged to pay a heavy postage, I would congratulate you on the speedy extension to Upper Canada of the Imperial Act lately passed reducing the postage of a letter to a *penny*. By the last English vessel that came in I got a good few numbers of the *Times* up to middle of Sept but cannot sit down to read them before the Express is off ... The Report & address to the Crown from your House of Assembly Select Committee I see in the *Times* − but enough of politics, I must be at Beaver & Rats. Adieu.

Fort Colvile, 15 April 1840

To Governor George Simpson, Lachine

I had the honour of receiving under your cover of 25th April last from Lachine, the circular and Prospectus issued by Messrs Pelly, Colvile & Simpson on the subject of a new association about being formed for carrying on extensive agricultural operations on the northwest coast of America [the Puget's Sound Agricultural Company], and after duly

considering the practicability of the plan set forth in the Prospectus have
thereunto affixed my signature. Two young Gentlemen with me have
done the same, the one for two shares, and the other for one, conformably
to the 'Memorandum of Appropriation arrangement' and I herewith
transmit with the Prospectus the various documents required by the circular. Trusting the success of the project in view may be commensurate
with the means thereon to be employed and the enterprising spirit of
the patrons of the undertaking ...

Fort Colvile, Thursday morning
To Rev Elkanah Walker, Tshimakain Mission
   Your Indian came in yesterday afternoon & handed me your communication sheet of 6th. He now returns with I believe all you require, namely
60 lbs fine flour & 60 coarse and a bushel of pease. The gun cock too
is repaired, *polished, glossed* & all. We wished the chap to rest his horses
today but he is clear for being off ...
   Both our Oahoo & English ships came in before the Express started.
No open war yet between America & England, & probably there will
be nothing of the kind. Commissions appointed by the two nations to
run the northern line boundary.

Fort Colvile, 25 April 1840
To John McLoughlin, Fort Vancouver
   I was duly favoured with yours of 19th ultimo per Mr McTavish &
will endeavour to attend to all its contents ... with respect to the second
Boat brought up, it appeared the first arrangement was changed & that
the duties assigned that Boat was merely to go to OK & thence the people to return here by land to help down the Brigade ... the seven Boats
can nevertheless be taken down in May, namely, the one in question, two
coming up from OK & four amaking here. To man them from Colvile
I think there will be no difficulty, but to judge of our means in that way
for nine Boats from OK I beg to submit for your consideration the following statement:

   Colvile – 15 men exclusive of Guide
   Vancouver – 5 men including Anawiscum (gone to portage)
   New Caledonia – 22 (the two doubtful are not gone out)
   Thompson River – 9
   Nine Boats at 6 men each – 54 – In foremen we seem to be deficient

... with steersmen we can manage yet, but appearances are much against
our being long in condition to do so. A most extraordinary craze to quit

the service has arisen one & all of our people this spring – four of them are still unsettled with – to wit P. Martineau, Dubois, Wacon [Pierre Umphreville] & Jacques, but all will go down [to Fort Vancouver] to see what conditions they can obtain below.

Mr McLean left us on 20th of last month for the plains, accompanied by four hands & as well equipped in other respects as we could wish, except indeed in tobacco. To obtain this essential article I wrote to Mr Pambrun on purpose to see that 2 Rolls might be brought on for us per the Express Boats, but much to my disappointment not an ounce came ... Next morning the man left by Mr McL[ean] for the sole purpose of following him with a Roll was dispatched with the little we had in reserve for Berland's spring trip to the Kootenais, which trip must of course be deferred until we can get some of Mr Ogden's stock at OK. I conveyed to Mr McLean your sentiments about our freemen prices. He wrote me from the Flatheads on 8th, in good spirits, but complains much of the quality of the Blkts from below last summer.

Mr Angus McDonald, agreeable to your desire, proceeds to W.W. to join Mr Ermatinger ... Herewith I forward letters from Messrs Ogden & Black, also our own requisition & a list of the distribution of our men for the season. You will ... be happy to see the result of our last year's campaign, the amount of Returns not only equal to what it was five years ago, but shows a profit of 7 or 8 hundred pounds more ...

Fort Colvile, 31 May 1840

To Rev Elkanah Walker, Tshimakain Mission

Here are we still; Messrs [Alexander Caulfield] Anderson and [Archibald] McKinlay of New Caledonia came on to us about the usual day, but the men from that quarter in the habit of assisting us down [to Fort Vancouver], being obliged to come down by water with 2 Boats, did not arrive till this morning, consequently cannot make a start before tomorrow. The wife ... is disposed to do herself the pleasure of a visit to her friends at Chimakaine with the children ... She proposes being there on 15th & I think it likely, God willing, that I shall be there myself about 18th. Let this be the arrangement as far as we are concerned, if agreeable to you. If otherwise, perhaps she would leave this on 15th June ... & come back with someone of our people that remain inland ...

By all means send for anything you stand in need of. I believe, without inconvenience we can at all times accommodate you. We wish you & Mrs W. much joy of the newcomer [daughter Abigail born to Mary Walker 24 May 1840]. I certainly give Dr Whitman & the whole of you great credit for the accuracy of your calculations in this case ...

Within the last four days we have had most delightful growing weather which made everything look green and blooming. God send it may continue favourable throughout the season. There are no signs of grasshoppers so far, but we are likely to have a few grubs. Look minutely at your Indian corn; it is the first thing they will attack. The wife joins me in best respects to you all ...

Walla Walla, 5 June 1840

To Samuel Black, Kamloops

On safely landing here this morning we were handed a packet from Mr McLoughlin of 13th ult containing with other papers the enclosed letter, by which you will see we all three anticipated him as to the summer arrangements; further remarks on this head are unnecessary. We thought it advisable to send back William Pion ... As it is likely you will be sending him to OK soon after his arrival, have the goodness to order Thomas Flett to make up 6 elk skins to take down for Mr Ogden. If there is no gum at Okanagan, Gingras ought to get a little ready for the Colvile Boats by the time they return, as we find Mr McL puts in requisition all I brought down this summer ...

... In the afternoon another packet cast up from the Dr announcing that Mr Lee & the Wallamette ship came in on 23rd. There is about 24 preachers & other subjects for that mission ... Tomorrow morning, God willing, we make a start. The water is remarkably high & not yet at its height.

Walla Walla, 9 July 1840

To Rev Elkanah Walker, Tshimakain Mission

On arrival here this morning at 5 A.M. ... I had the pleasure to receive your kind favour of the 3rd from Clearwater [Spalding's], by which I was most happy to hear you were all well in the Colvile region. I trust that for their mutual pleasure & felicity the Ladies contrived to meet & pass a couple of weeks together at Chimakaine during our absence. It would have afforded me much especial pleasure to pass by your way ... & assist my family home ... but my dear sir the thing is impossible. Mr Black awaits my arrival at Colvile & consequently I must conduct my own Boats hence ... My worthy friend Mr Ogden & self had a very [good] trip of it to headquarters, where we had the pleasure of meeting a great many of your friends & country folks, but until we have the happiness of meeting I will reserve all my news with respect to them. During our stay there another Newport vessel came in, a small brig of 99 tons with a crew of 12 persons whose sole object is the curing of salmon ...

Let us now to business – 21 pieces for the mission we contrived to ship at Vancouver & to land safely here, but I am sorry to say that beyond this we cannot take that portion of them for your station, as from the circumstance of our leaving one of our eight Boats here we not only find it impossible to embark yours, but are compelled to leave 10 pieces of our own. On leaving Vancouver, I suggested to Mr [George Traill] Allan to forward the mission invoice in duplicate, one of which we now transmit to you ... We start tomorrow morning ... at same time that three of my people for the harvest work, accompanied by Mr Demers, proceed by land. One of them is our little [David] Flett whom I send over to assist the wife & children to get home ...

Fort Colvile, 12 August 1840

To James Douglas, Fort Vancouver

Methinks tis high time to take the pen & score off the heavy arrears ... with respect to you in the way of letter writing ... Your esteemed favours of Feby March & April came to hand ... the first making the round of Whilatpu, Clearwater & Spokane, not before the middle of May. The one of 5th April with the overlooked document for east side & the parcel of newspapers reached us just in time for all good purposes ...

By the way however I can scarcely resist congratulating ourselves & the fur trade on the memorable success which has attended the exertions of our friends on the polar sea last season.[32] The existence of a Northwest passage is no longer problematical, it is proved by the clearest of all demonstrations: its actual survey making Boothia an island & King William's magnetic pole not on the continent of the New World. This is an achievement that will not only entail lasting honours on the names of the explorers, but will add another leaf to the annals of the British name in the catalogue of discoveries. To be sure, the thing is not yet brought to the utmost limits it is actually capable of, but tis certain our friends in power will now never relinquish the task they have so creditable to themselves proposed until one of their boats is made to gain open sea from Back's Montreal Island to somewhere in the Atlantic Ocean. Tho we have said this much in admiration of praiseworthy exertions of *one* corporate body in England – no doubt a little tainted with conservative feelings – yet I fear it will hardly go down with the advocates for torchlight

[32] Thomas Simpson, a cousin of the governor, and Peter Warren Dease, who had been with Sir John Franklin's second Arctic expedition, were co-commanders of an HBC Arctic exploration that was completed in October 1839.

meetings & the dissemination of O'Connor & Stephen's gratuitous advice to the Queen's liege subjects. But after all, one can discern that in matters immediately connected with our own dear selves we can view popular sway, universal suffrage & the like, when they come to work west side of the R. Mountains, quite a different thing to what it is fashionable to recommend as a good principle in the British Constitution.

As to the new speculation for farming & colonizing the country [Puget's Sound Agricultural Company], I wish it every success its most sanguine promoters could desire, tho I do not expect to see its good fruits realized in my time. That I have given the project the sanction of my name, for reasons best known to myself, is true enough, and after all with proper management, perhaps something of the kind is the best self defence the Honbl Company could set up in these [piping] hot days for new colonies and foreign plantations. You lost a grand sight in the exhibition we made below this summer. Our friend Monr Peter [Ogden], despite himself, showed off by turns more sanctity & elegance of manner than is that Gentleman's wont at times. Brother Sam [Black] says he very much regrets not being there, as he thinks his dancing school lessons at Aberdeen will still carry him through very well in promenades & close contact with the Ladies! especially if they be *bodies* that understand anything about geology.

On affairs in the interior I have scarcely anything out of the common routine to communicate ... You will find them set forth in my letter to the Dr that I mean to address to him before the return of Mr Demers. I got here myself by land from OK 25th & Mr Black with the Boats a few days after. I shall of course expect the pleasure of hearing from you at some length on the state of affairs to the northward; a most untoward event it would appear engaged your attention in the offset. Poor Yale I am certain felt all the pangs of a man of honour & responsibility on that unhappy occasion[33] ...

Fort Colvile, 17 August 1840

To Rev Elkanah Walker, Tshimakain Mission

On Friday, your very kind & communicative letter I had the pleasure to receive thro the hands of, I believe, some of the Bighead's family. By the way the big fellow talks he would have us believe that he is Cornelius'

---

[33] Fort Langley, which was the charge of James M. Yale, was burned to the ground on 11 April 1840, with the loss of all the buildings and 958 pounds worth of furs. Only some ammunition and trading goods were saved.

son, & that he expects some consideration [for the] horse given to my children. It certainly was & is my intention that the present should meet with an adequate acknowledgement but I do not like this direct application to that effect ... Independent of the horse, I am always disposed to recognize the Bighead with an indulgent eye, & his firm & disinterested behaviour in a late affair of ours down at the Barrier strengthens this feeling. My generosity however must be to himself, & not thro a third person as the present courier would imply it should be. I believe Flett sends him 3 feet of tobacco & a little ammunition en attendant.

I was glad to hear you were safe back & that affairs among our friends in the Walla Walla district are quiet & peaceable. The death of the marauder is not to be regretted. The Dr [Whitman] seems to give a flattering account of all about Whilatpu. His crop, despite the dry season, is it would appear a very bountiful one. Here it is by no means so, the drought if possible has been more intense than last season ... This moment a brisk shower is falling ... Even tho it may retard the harvest labour, it will greatly benefit the green crops ... by the 15th of next month I shall look out for some tidings from below ... It is said 3 or 4 R.C. priests are coming on by way of rendezvous so that I think amongst you all there will be no shortage of reapers in the Columbia before long.

The wife desires to be very kindly remembered to you all, & the Ladies in particular to be informed that one half her occupation now is in keeping her two little boys, who within the last ten days begin to run about the fort as alert as herself, a task that at the same time gives her great delight ...

Fort Colvile, 24 August 1840

To John McLoughlin, Fort Vancouver

I avail myself of Mr Demers return to give you a word of our doings in this part of the country since my return from headquarters. The trip up, once we left the Dalles, was sufficiently smooth and prosperous. At OK we found Mr Black ... who immediately embarked in the Boats, while I proceeded by land myself with as little delay as possible ... The very evening of my arrival (25th) Mr McLean too cast up. Early in the season he dispatched from Racine Amer [Bitter Root] Brouillet & Charles Lafentasie with the best share of the property under the wing of a camp going in our direction, himself joining another that took a more easterly course, accompanied by [Theodore] Leclair & young Lafentasie ... poor lad, soon after fell indisposed and continued getting worse until he died on his hands middle of July ... His trade on this interrupted trip was about 150 Beaver ... by his letter of 13th he says Brouillet had just joined him, but brought in nothing, having left the 4 packs he traded in the hands of Charles on the 10th at a place called Stinking River, kept company by a Mr [Pierre-Jean De]Smet, a R.C. priest of the Order of Jesuits sent out from St Louis & then awaiting the return of Mr McLean to see on what terms he could be supplied by the H.B. Co for establishing himself & others of his order in the upper country by the time they can be up next season ... Mr McLean with Brouillet, Pierre & Leclair pushed off immediately to see what could be done yet in the plains ... all the Indians having started in a great hurry for the camp at Stinking River. Edouard Berland whom I fitted out here for the Kootenais ... is also back with something rather better than the ordinary summer returns from that quarter, arising in some measure from the attempt we have made to meet the Natives at the nick of time up at the Tobacco plain ... our business there cannot I fear succeed long thro the individual exertions of an obscure coureur de bois, however willing & laborious ... Middle of July when our man got to the place of rendezvous, a small band of his Indians was just returned from east side the mountains carrying with them a note from an American three days march off ... the Indians add that he (Master J.B. Moncravier) is to cross to the Kootenais in the fall with the view of picking up all the leather &c &c he can lay his hands on. The other circumstance to show the avidity with which the trade of

Fort Colvile in August 1845, by Henry Warre. (American Antiquarian Society)

that poor country is now assailed from all quarters: as Berland arrived at the old trading place on his way down the other day, he there found a very large assemblage of Indians from the different tribes to the southward [who] had nearly succeeded in securing 22 Beaver from an Indian on the spot by previous appointment with Berland to whom ... they offered the three best horses in the band for the lot. This is a sort of traffic that has more or less been carried on for some time ... for the sake of the leather & the few Beaver they can pick up there to send to the southward for horses where the intermediate traders can get them. It is clear to me that unless some little responsibility is added to our business in that quarter, little as it is, certainly it will soon be entirely gone. Berland, I am about returning immediately to the Tobacco plain, to watch what is going on there with a small assortment of trading goods, the rest with the canoe as usual will be sent in charge of three common hands.

Will it not be possible to let us have a young Gentleman this fall to attend to these & other outdoor duties? In every respect one is much required. At a place like this where we have so many trips to make from one end of the year to the other, the necessity which compels us to trust everything without control to common men tends by no means to improve their own character & moral worth, no more than it does that of the Natives with whom they necessarily intermix. But should one be assigned us I hope it will be for a considerable time, as the mere stay for a winter with us is of no use whatever. Indeed, I am particularly anxious that we should have a smart active young Gentleman about the place now, since of late I find a strange falling off in the disposition of most of our people to do even the most ordinary work with cheerfulness & alacrity. [Louis] Brown you will hear is not going down & I am very sorry for it. To Mr Demers I must beg leave to refer you for further particulars regarding him.

When Mr Black left us he promised to have three men here 15th Sept for the mountain – even the conduct of that party I am certain would be the better of another leader besides Canote [Umphreville]; to him however it must be entrusted ...

On our way up we could obtain no certain information as to the practicability of a passage for cattle from the interior to Puget Sound, which I am nevertheless inclined to think could be accomplished; and when the thing is fairly ascertained the sooner the stock here is reduced the better. This autumn, say Sept & Octob, I think the best season for removing them. We could part with about 70 head including calves and still have enough for the place. Should their removal be deferred to next fall 100 might be calculated upon, with I suppose some from OK. Ours are not always sure of a sufficiently mild winter at the Big Prairie, where all but milch cows are at present.

I heard from Mr Ogden on his route in from Okanagan after passing the Forks – all well then … At Alexandria the means of living were very scarce indeed & the appearance of the crops did not hold out a very flattering prospect …

Fort Colvile, Tuesday forenoon [summer 1840]
To Rev Elkanah Walker, Tshimakain Mission

I am a little disappointed at not seeing any of you this way of late – I fear I did not express myself distinctly in one of my last notes when I said that we expected Mrs Eells; it is *Mrs. Walker* that promised the wife to favour us with a visit … I fear to this blunder of mine we have to ascribe her nonappearance so long. To us the pleasure of seeing either will always be equally agreeable, & as their quitting the establishment must of course depend upon their own convenience I hope Mrs W. will do us the favour to accompany you here in a few days. The Fool's son is now sitting alongside me while writing this, & says he will deliver it to you tomorrow. About the end of the week I shall be looking out for the Vancouver men as well as those coming from Mr Black for the mountain trip …

Should you have any of your wheat threshed I think you might as well bring a load or two that we shall grind it for you for your Xmas pancakes. The last of our own is in this morning & the very moment after we commence our Indian corn which will keep us occupied at least for 15 days. The potatoes, owing to the last rain, begin to improve very much.

As I expect the pleasure of seeing you soon to remain with us for some time, I will not enlarge on our domestic news. The wife and little ones thank God are in their usual good health. The good lady herself desires to be most kindly remembered to you all …

Fort Colvile, 18 September 1840
To the Gentleman in charge of the York Factory Express

Canote the Guide leaves this tomorrow morning with three Boats & 18 men including himself … the respective parties from Vancouver & T. River not having cast up before last night & the night before an earlier move was impossible. As it is however they are a few days in advance of the usual time, & being no wise encumbered with ladings, it is to be hoped they will be up by the 1st of Octr. The provisions entrusted to them is as per the enclosed list. The six Bags marked S will be forwarded

to Colin Fraser & as much more of the remaining 15 Bags as you think
you can dispense with. On the other hand, should you find yourself deficient, make free with any part of the aforementioned 6 Bags ...

Fort Colvile, 21 September 1840

To Peter Skene Ogden, Okanagan

Your favour of 22nd August with enclosed requisition came duly to
hand, but I regret to say cannot be complied with to the full extent, &
the threshed pease we have is 15 bushels & that Grégoire has gone with
1½ of corn, 3 Bags flour & 4 small grunters. There is no buckwheat &
our stock of turkeys is yet at a very low ebb but of pigeons Mr Tod can
have enough when he chooses. Your porkeaters we shall endeavour to
cross over from here with horses left by [Étienne] Grégoire for that purpose & others belonging to you here from W.W.

Fort Colvile, 22 September 1840

To John McLoughlin, Fort Vancouver

Your various communications of 2nd & 4th inst I had the pleasure to
receive on 17th. Mr Black's men being arrived the day previous we were
enabled to start the three Boats on the 19th ... Of the six men come up,
two – Igniace & the Islander – are laid up with the fever & ague; the
former however undertook the trip, being supplied here with a quantity
of quinine. I have also to regret the loss of one of my own men's service, tho certainly the absence of such a character himself is no loss to
any community. I mean that unprincipled villain Alexis Martineau, who
formed a league with the equally despicable Louis Brown & moved off
together to the plains. Brown gave his sister-in-law to Martineau & in
their conscience both are satisfied their conduct is in every way unim-
peachable, that the Red River marriage must be null & void. What
atrocious scoundrels! I have heard them say their first object is to find
Mr DeSmet.

Grégoire arrived here the other day from Alexandria for grunters & field
seed, & returned yesterday with the needful ... The discretionary power
you gave me with respect to the porkeaters is a great accommodation ...
as at this moment we have scarcely a barnman at the place, & not a grain
of threshed wheat will be on hand by the time the mill stops this fall.
As regards a Gentleman, I know you will do for us all that is possible ...

Private – It would appear that in the Snake country all went on
smoothly enough without the liquor & long may it continue to do so;
indeed could our business be equally & advantageously conducted without it all over, it would be a great blessing. Our friend however in that

quarter I am sorry to find seems not to conduct things according to the strict letter of his instructions, or perhaps himself with an overstock of discretion ... I have not heard a word from either himself or young [Angus] McDonald since they left Walla Walla ...

Fort Colvile, 20 October 1840

To John McLoughlin, Fort Vancouver

Having addressed you so very fully, both private & public not many weeks back, I shall trouble you with but little on this occasion ... I keep two of the porkeaters for the present, have also taken upon myself to detain a young postmaster of the party, conscious that in so doing I only anticipate your cordial assent to the measure. Mr [John] McPherson will soon I think become a very efficient hand with the Natives of this district wherever we may have occasion to employ him, & cannot be too soon initiated amongst them. The men for Messrs Black & Ogden cross direct from here in charge of Mr [Henry] Maxwell, but I fear our friend Mr Ogden will scarcely be pleased at seeing him arrive without the long-talked-of Blksmith. Little Igniace tho you did not direct me to do so, I have also sent that way ...

Fort Colvile, 2 November 1840

To Donald McLean, Kootenais

Till the very last moment I was in hopes of hearing from you in the usual way before the supplies were sent off, that we might as far as possible have the benefit of your own opinion on what is likely to be in most demand above ... There is neither rum nor sugar, because of these articles there has been already quite as much as the few freemen we have & the state of their finances will authorize. And should stragglers from the southward be tempted to come our way, it is not desirable that, while liquor in the Snake is entirely suppressed, we should display much of it on our side. Of tobacco you will find 3 Rolls ... The ammunition is 2 Kegs of powder ... & I think you will find the Blkts, shirts & Guns enough for a pretty decent trade. Although it is not my wish that anything fair & reasonable be withheld from either freemen or Indians, I must impress upon you the propriety of keeping everything together as much as possible, as we will have just enough to do to fit you out adequately next spring with what remains here.

This fall we send up but one Boat, which you will load with the furs, the tongues (as they won't keep without resalting), two or three Bales of meat & as much of the grease as you can. The surplus can remain till spring when we shall send up two Boats if necessary. It would be well to collect as much of the usual train as possible such as appechmts [buffalo hide saddle cloths], saddles, parflèches in case we may be called upon to furnish more of those things than is customary. I hope you will be able to procure us for our trade here a few Buffalo robes – an article greatly in demand ...

Accompanying the Boats is a young postmaster that came in this fall, whom I have ... detained here for the Kootenais in consequence of a threatening message from a man calling himself J.B. Moncravier ... It is the same note ... brought from east side by some of Berland's own Indians, but after all is I think but a mere bravado. However, get all the information you can on the subject & converse with & direct Mr McPherson accordingly ... he is directed to proceed forthwith ... & be back again to you with information & an account of the furs & goods now there. In this case he need not return for the winter if everything be quiet as usual with Berland, but if not you will send him back ...

Long ere this reaches you you will have seen the two blackguards, Brown & Martineau, that left this in Sept. Not the smallest countenance must be given to either. To add to the infamy of Martineau's conduct, his lawful wife is now here upon our hands in a situation deplorable enough. It would therefore in his case be making bad worse did we shut the door at forgiveness on the scoundrel if he is inclined to come back & look after his family, but otherwise let him be regarded as the greatest vagabond on the face of the earth.

I trust you have all so arranged that we need have no uneasiness about you in the Pendant d'Oreille mountain. Including your own, you will find 22 horses in the Bay.

Fort Colvile, 4 December 1840

To Rev Elkanah Walker, Tshimakain Mission

Many thanks for your kind & interesting favour per old Solomon. He came in yesterday accompanied by the Bighead's deputy & says he returns today. The rifle has been produced, but is I am sorry to say beyond our power to put in execution order. I am always ready & willing to help them with the repairs of their ordinary arms when not verging on all the defects ascribed to ... the arm in question. Moreover we find it necessary to discourage this foolish traffic of theirs in useless rifles that they can neither use nor keep in order as they ought, & I am glad you gave them no encouragement on the subject. Solomon has just been telling me he (the Bighead) has a few Beaver, & would like to have a gun sent him for them. Of course he has a right to expect that if he has the requisite number, but hearing that is not the case, however much I like my friend Cornelius, I am not disposed to advance him one on credit until at least our *old scores* are wiped off. Please tell him to be industrious in killing Martens to make up for the deficiency of Beaver and that he shall have the gun ... With respect to his expressed sentiments about yourselves, I have no reason to doubt they were not those of his heart. Upon the whole we always thought of him, for an Indian, a pretty fair character, & as I have said before, now that he has seen your firmness in everything it would be as well to show him some indulgence.

I am sorry to hear of the threatened rupture at Mr [Asa] Smith's place & of the revival of fresh troubles among the Walla Wallas & Cayouses, but with patience & firmness on the part of the Whites we may get over these troubles, though am far from thinking the aborigine of the wilderness is an animal that can be depended upon for a long time to come. Pity your first attempt at Bookmaking should fail; I fear you wanted to be too particular at the outset. In my opinion a parcel of sheets with legible letters & a few short significant sentences ought to suffice for a year or two yet, & then begin the *Book of Books*[34] ...

Should I find myself short of window glass, I will avail myself of the kind offer of the Gentlemen of Chimakaine. The house however is making but slow progress. True the frame is together, but as it must be erected on the site of the present dwelling everything connected with the new work must be finished before we take down the old fabric ...

All my *Albions* I sent per Mr Maxwell to Mr Ogden except one sheaf, which I believe is the one you was perusing here. Still I send it, & after you all glance over it have the goodness to send it back per first opportunity as I contemplate forwarding it to Mr Black ...

As to domestic news I have very little to say ... On Saturday last we were very fortunate in finishing the last of the largest fall ploughing we ever made at Colvile, say 25 acres under fall wheat & 40 of new ground. I begin to take the alarm, finding everyone in want but myself. At Thompson River & New Caledonia they are actually starving; within the last six weeks I had three parties here for grain. When the salmon fails in that quarter there is no other resource.

... the good folk below not only kept my English letters but wrote none of their own, thinking there would be no opportunity from W.W. Never mind, short as the time is since, I have got the start of them again

---

[34] Walker was increasingly frustrated in his attempts to produce a *Spokane Primer* in the Spokane language. Finally, 250 copies of the little sixteen-page booklet were printed on a press at the Lapwai mission (Clearwater) in December 1842. Walker himself set the type.

by the receipt of a packet three nights ago from Hudson Bay which left England beginning of June. All still quiet throughout the civilized world, or I should rather say no actual war yet, for in all conscience there is big talk enough everywhere. I have but one newspaper on *our Arctic* discoveries which goes down to Vancouver ...

Fort Colvile, 4 January 1841

To John McLoughlin, Fort Vancouver

... As regards the governor's route from Edmonton,[35] I suppose the one he proposes must be adopted, at least so far as it depends upon us I see no unsurmountable obstacle in the way ... I think they had better come by the Tobacco plain which is situated near the Kootenais House you see marked on the map, and once there ... they should come by the Flathead Ho ... Enough of provisions to answer all purposes was left up this fall in case they came that way. With respect to the required number of horses ... I would suggest they be procured at W.W. & marched on slowly in this direction ... Ours on the Flathead establishment would ... be too much fagged for the trip in question ...

Mr McLean returned from the plains with about 1,000 Beaver – this is short of last year's but above the trade of '38 ... we are not likely to derive much benefit from the Beaver hunters heretoforward. Last season their whole attention was taken up with the missionaries already amongst them & with the thoughts of those who in great numbers to come. A strong party of the young men started off with Mr DeSmet to escort him to Tully's Fort on the Yellowstone before Mr McLean could reach the main camp with his equipment ... McLean attached himself & little

---

[35] Simpson paid his third visit to the Columbia District on his trip around the world in 1841, arriving at Fort Colvile from the east on 18 August and stopping for only two days before going on to Fort Vancouver. There he spent the winter, taking excursions by ship to California and Hawaii as well as one up the coast to the northern posts and Sitka. In the spring he embarked again for Sitka and continued his journey to Russia and on across the continent to Great Britain. McDonald wrote many letters to Simpson, McLoughlin, Rowand, and others regarding the best route for the governor to follow through 'the mountains from Edmonton, and he made provision from Colvile for boats and horses covering several possibilities. He was ultimately pleased when, rather than taking the northern route via Jasper and Boat Encampment and then down the Colubmia, Simpson opted to follow his recommendation of coming overland from the Bow River Traverse on horseback by way of Grand Quête (Quoit) Lake (now Moyie Lake) and the Kootenais River Traverse to Kullespelm Lake, where McDonald's men had left a boat to take him and his companions down the Pend d'Oreille River to the Flathead plain. From there, they would ride over to Colvile.

party [to a group following them], near the head of the Musselshell River he had the good luck to fall in with Big [Joseph] Gervais & 7 or 8 of his associates, of whom he obtained a few Beaver & for rum, sugar & coffee; could have got more. Upon the Yellowstone itself they pulled up the escort who brought the enclosed note from the Reverend Gentleman. During this perambulation, which was occasionally in the vicinity of Buffalo, he lost two or three of his Indians in skirmishes with the Blkfeet that are an everyday occurrence in that dangerous & hostile country. The few freemen we have in the plains are about giving in too. Tis said they all move downwards in the way of the Wallamette next spring.

On affairs about the Kootenais, I am happy to say that so far we are exempt of the annoyance expected from the presence of 'Moncravier' but I regret to add that poor Berland himself ... met with a serious disaster in the month of Octr by the upsetting of his skin canoe coming down from the Tobacco plain. Of the property he actually lost four or five Bales of leather & 7 Beaver skins & very narrowly escaped with life himself ... His Beaver will I think be more than last year ...

With regard to the men ... exclusive of P. Martineau & Jacques, Bouts, three hands will leave us for below *early* in spring, & the Guide for the same direction with the Brigade, leaving but two Bouts for the district when at least six are required. In my last I informed you that Alexis Martineau had joined Brown, and since, that other hopeful youth, William Pion recommenced his old practices & is off to the Indian camp with his relations ever since 5th November ... To have to do with so many of these idle and unprincipled vagrants is truly provoking ...

For all the grain supposed to be accumulating at Colvile we are now, in consequence of the partial failure of the two last crops, reduced to a round year's consumption. This fall we had a considerable extent of new ground turned up, besides sowing of about 50 bushels of fall wheat ... Our dwelling house, you are aware, is going to pieces. We have now on the ground & in perfect readiness for a new one, all the wood that is required, but cannot think of pulling down the old one till we are sure of being in a condition without interruption to get up the one on the site of the other. [Pierre] Martineau, I should like much to remain with us for the summer for that purpose, which I think he would do. This is the *third* frame for a house at Colvile put together since 1827 ...

Fort Colvile, 7 January 1841

To Rev Elkanah Walker, Tshimakain Mission

... We have killed an ox about the holidays – the wife I see is making up two small pieces for your Ladies to taste of. As for yourselves,

Gentlemen, you must come here and take your share of it in potluck with us, which I hope will soon be the case ... We wish you all very happy returns of the season ...

Fort Colvile, 15 January 1841

To Rev Cushing Eells, Tshimakain Mission

Believe me when I say tis with heartfelt distress we heard of your late calamity. In any part of the world disasters by fire bring in their train numberless losses & inconvenience, but in your case, situated as you are & at so inclement a season, the bereavement is particularly distressing. The Indian came in last night with Mr Walker's letter, but I regret exceedingly your modesty should have prevented you from expressing what we could do for you ... I have resolved on sending you our carpenter & three hands to grapple on the instant with whatever work you may suggest in order to place you & poor Mrs Eells once more under shelter. The two young Gentlemen [McLean & McPherson] with me have also volunteered their services to give a hand. At all events they can set the Canadians more vigorously to work ... The people will have but a week's provision, but should you detain them for a longer period you must make shift to feed them and I shall replace the damage ...

I am requested by the wife to say that you must send Mrs E. here if she is in a condition to travel ... while here we could get some warm clothes made for her. Of course she can have the use of Mrs W. saddle – indeed at one time I thought of sending our sleigh for her, but I doubt the practicability of the road all the way to Chimakaine ...

Fort Colvile, 15 January 1841

To Rev Elkanah Walker, Tshimakain Mission

... The rapid progress of the fire in such a small confined place surprises me; but I suppose those confounded mats [lining the walls] very much tended to spread the flame – after all we do sincerely hope all that was in the front chamber was saved – and our packet, too, all the way from England was only saved by the presence of mind of Mr E ... I hope poor Mrs Eells will find herself in a condition sufficiently strong to travel to us here till she is better provided for at home ... Within the last four days the degree of cold with us has been exceedingly intense, but I have no thermometer to indicate the exact temperature. The depth of snow however is even under the ordinary fall, & most of our cattle being at the big plain I think little danger is to be apprehended on that score ...

I am glad to hear the Indians behaved so well on this calamitous event – there is no harm in allowing Bighead to indulge in his first impression, but I would not labour to impress it upon him beyond the fancy of his own mind …

Fort Colvile, 17 February 1841

To John McLoughlin, Fort Vancouver

Very unexpectedly & under the most painful circumstances I am this soon again called upon to address you: poor Mr Black is no more! He was most barbarously cut off from this world in his own house [Kamloops] on the evening of the 8th Inst by a single Indian belonging to the place. The melancholy news reached me here tonight thro [Jean] Gingras who had it from [Joachim] Lafleur. For the lamentable affair no direct cause can be assigned, unless it could be traced to the sudden death of one of their rascally Chiefs, Tranquille. This Indian in course of the summer applied to the deceased for a gun in the fort, which he said the owner, a North River Indian, had made over to him; a request that could not be complied with without a more convincing proof of the fact. In January he again applied, prior to his setting out for the Pavilion on Fraser River, with the same success, when I believe some angry words ensued. At the Pavilion he soon fell ill and died five days after. Pending his illness it was rumoured among the Indians & insidiously propagated by their vile conjurors that, if he did not recover his death must be ascribed to the base medicine of the whites & revenged. After the death of the vagabond, word came that much of the good feeling of the Indians would depend on the Whites to see him buried. Immediately on rect of the news from the Pavilion & of this message, poor Mr Black lost no time in sending two men, Edouard & [Michel] Fallardeau, to assist at the burying of him, & it would appear that the same morning, after passing the family encampment of Tranquille a few miles lower down, the murderer (his nephew) left it, & arrived at the fort about noon without any visible arms about him. He remained smoking in the hall the whole afternoon in company with two other young men from a different quarter. [Alexis] Laprade was that day occupied in the cellar under the hall flooring, overhauling some potatoes, & Mr B. frequently passed & repassed conversing with him from above. At length the two young men left the assassin, he telling them that it being too cold for him to go home, he proposed sleeping in the fort. About that time the deceased made another turn out, came in by a back door, walked thro the hall to get into his own room & while in the act of stepping in was shot by the villain from alongside the chimney not two yards off, behind which must have been secreted the fatal instrument. Laprade, still below, on hearing the report, called 'aux armes' but before any effectual assistance could appear the fellow was off. The Ball with a quantity of Beaver shot entered the small of the back & came out below the chest – poor unhappy man never spoke a word after! Laprade tho much excited and under great alarm put everything in the best posture he could & on the morning of the 10th sent off [Joachim] Lafleur.

It now remains for me to say what measures I am about taking myself in so calamitous a case. Messrs McLean & McPherson start immediately with 7 men by way of Okanagan & will I trust be with Laprade in about 10 days. Unfortunately there is a great deal of livestock & of one thing or another far too much at the mercy of the Indians should they be disposed to give further annoyance. My directions to Mr McLean are, in the first place to endeavour to pacify the Natives & smooth over any present difficulties that may be in the way, without pledging himself to a compromise ... And then in the customary way to set about removing everything to Okanagan except the horses & provisions that may be required for N. Caledonia. After that, I think Mr McPherson with the ten men belonging to the place can stand his ground till Mr Ogden is out. The moment Edouard would be back he was to be sent to Alexandria and as the Gentleman attached to the Chilkotin is I think wintering with Mr Tod, it is likely he will himself [Tod] come to Kamloops. In that case our people will be directed by him & I will take the liberty of suggesting to him, if need be, to remain there himself until further orders from you or Mr Ogden. Mr McLean with his people I direct to be back here if possible by the 20th March, the usual time for starting the plains expedition.

The body of our lamented friend will not be interred before our people or Mr Tod gets there. Nicolas & a few good staunch Indians had already rallied around Laprade, & I am in hopes, tho the case already is sufficiently distressing, nothing more of a serious nature will overtake us. P.S. The news has spread about here now among the Natives and is productive of considerable excitement, but I do not apprehend it will lead to anything serious in this quarter.

18 February 1841

To Donald McLean

After various consultations we have already had on the melancholy catastrophe at Thompson's River & the probable cause which led to it, I shall merely suggest for your guidance that, on arrival there with Mr McPherson & the 7 men now accompanying you hence, your first care will be to try & smooth over existing difficulties & ease the minds of the natives as much as you can, which on an occasion like the present must unavoidably be much excited: but let this be done in a manner so as not to pledge ourselves to any great sacrifice of compromise of the past. Then you will in the usual way set about removing the furs & live-stock to Okanakan, in a manner so as not to excite any great alarm, as, on account of New Caledonia it is necessary that the post should be kept up until Mr Ogden is *out safely*. And for this purpose, after you are satisfied that no serious danger is to be apprehended, Mr McPherson & the ten men attached to the Establishment will occupy it till then. The provisions & goods can be left with them in case Mr. O. may conceive it desirable to send them on to Alexandria.

It being in contemplation when Lafleur left Kamloops to send for Mr Tod, you will in all probability find that Gentleman there; if so, you will of course be guided by his directions, always bearing in mind the necessity for your being here with your people if possible by 20th March.

So many of our most efficient horses being now put in requisition, you will on return from OK bring along here 10 or 12 good ones. An inventory of course will be taken at Thompson on your arrival, & could it conveniently be done, an Indian ought to be sent to us express with an account of the state of affairs there. The New Caledonia packet will I think be out by the time you reach Kamloops: it & the accounts of the district itself, so far as you can find them above, might be sent us across from the OK forks, & the Gentlemen coming up with the Boats will bring on what will be necessary from Okanakan.

The following is a list of the Thompson's River men viz:

1. Laprade
2. Martineau
3. Gilbeault
4. l'Ecuyer
5. Fallardeau
6. Edouard
7. Robiard
8. Igniace
9. Baptiste, the porkeater
10. Martelle do [ditto]
11. Joyalle, Laprade's son
12. Lafleur – to return with you from OK

Wiliam Pion, one of the 7 from here [and] Baptiste, his brother, both go up to remain [there].

Besides this, Gobin will go up with you from OK – he, Laprade, Martineau and l'Ecuyer will come back with you, with the furs, horses &c

&c still leaving above, excluding the Pions, ten men … The family &
property of the deceased will come down in charge of Laprade. The pigs
& goats dispose of as you may think proper, that the people in the fort
may have nothing to look after but themselves & the defence of the
place. The New Caledonia horses and any others that it may be necessary to keep at hand will be best in charge of Nicolas at the Big Prairie.

Wishing you every safety & success.

[Numerous other references to Black's murder appear in the Fort
Colvile letter book, which continues with letters to Pambrun at Walla
Walla, to McPherson with instructions about the Flathead trade, to
McLoughlin, and to Walker. There is also a long official report on the
circumstances of Black's death. McPherson brought Black's widow and
three small children down to Colvile on 19 February.]

Fort Colvile, 5 March 1841

To Edward Ermatinger, St. Thomas, Upper Canada

… I would now endeavour to entertain you in the old way with the
little novelties of the Columbia, did not an occurrence at this moment
among us, & of a character I believe unparallelled in the annals of the
fur trade, preclude the possibility of my entering on lighter topics. Why,
my friend, tis nothing short of the deliberate murder of our old companion Mr Black in his own house at Thompson River on the evening
of 8th ultimo at the hands of a fiend of an Indian, without I believe the
shadow of a provocation. The only latent source to which could be traced
the semblance of a cause was the sudden death of one of their rascally
Chiefs, which the vile medicine men that surrounded him ascribed in
self-defence to the evil spirit of the *Whites*, too powerful for them to
counteract! …

When I last heard from your brother he was not yet arrived at W.W.
on his way down to headquarters, but his successor had already reached
Fort Hall. About the same time I had a letter from the doctor in which
he alluded to you … breathing sentiments of regard & great good feeling for you both, and insinuating to me a wish to prevail on Frank to
remain another year to see what may come up for him … He has not
only not yet got the parchment, but somehow or other has succeeded in
experiencing the frown of the big man. This however is not to that injurious extent to his interest your brother himself supposes … I am now
myself, my friend, getting to be somewhat dissatisfied at the mode of disposing of the good things. I hope in their wisdom the wiseacres on the
other side will this summer appoint Mr Chief Factor Donald Ross [CF
1840] to face the enemy at Kamloops in the room of his late colleague:

but No! it must be some poor devil not fit to show off at the *depot* &
with comparatively little importance attached to his services. It is said
the great man himself [Simpson] is coming in this season to put all to
rights; he will have much to do if he calculates on satisfying all the expectants without ousting from their bed of down all the old favourite Senators, worse still than the 'Family Compact.' With palaver & empty
compliments in abundance he may however after all do a great deal. In
course of the winter I had a packet from [Chief Factor John] Rowand
[Fort Edmonton] saying the he (the gov) would come in by the plains
& ordering guides, men, horses, provisions &c &c from here to meet the
cavalcade on Bow River. How all this can be accomplished with due
attention to all the troubles that threaten ourselves is more than I can
foresee ... I wish to goodness I was alongside of you at St Thomas, albeit
all I read & hear of Durhamites, agitators & incendiaries. Apropos, I
got all your *Patriots* & thank you kindly for the attention. I can now talk
on the merits & demerits of your great reunion question, responsible
government, clergy stipends, public improvements and all the rest of it
with the ease & facility of a Solon. You must I think my good Sir begin
to brush up, & with your fair stock of French meet the Jean Baptistes
in the united legislature.[36] It is a qualification I opine on which few of
your Toronto orators are calculated to shine, but I suppose on this head,
against all your safeguards to the new order of things, provided that
all that is said within the walls of the new assembly must be thundered
out in good plain *old English* ... To return to the *Patriots*, I sent them
all down to W.W. in the winter in order to meet your brother as he
came out, along with our Hudson Bay fall letters, but were very near
going for it in a fit element for all those who nowadays cover their igno-
miny with that honoured designation – the flames. The bearer [Donald

[36] McDonald's letters to Edward Ermatinger reveal his efforts to keep up with political
developments in the east. These efforts were prompted, no doubt, by his expectation
that he would eventually retire to that part of the country. His traditional conservative beliefs made him suspicious of the reform movement, especially when it turned
to outright armed rebellions in both Upper and Lower Canada in 1837, although he
disapproved of the Family Compact style of privilege. When Lord Durham produced
his two-volume *Report* in 1839, after his short sojourn as governor general of British
North America, McDonald sent for a copy and read it avidly. Durham's recommen-
dations led to the union of Upper and Lower Canada and a new form of responsible
government for the country. Edward Ermatinger had by this time become actively
involved in the local political scene; he was elected for Middlesex in 1844 but was
defeated in 1847. McDonald suggests here that Edward's experience speaking French
while involved in the fur trade would give him an advantage when making speeches
in the united legislature.

McLean] his second night from here 10th January, slept at the mission, & before next morning the manse unhappily burned to the ground. With exertions however, the Revd Gentleman himself (Mr Eells) saved the packet but very little of his own. This disastrous affair too occasioned a call on our humanity to see the poor hapless family once more under cover, when the thermometer was from 10 to 15 degrees below zero. So you see the variety of incidents we are now subject to.

About my son, I am truly at a loss what to say, & as it is probable your brother will be going down to see you I shall refrain from saying anything till I see him. I fear much the stupid fellow takes no right view of his new situation; he is now approaching the age of manhood & he must be given to understand that I cannot afford to make a Gentleman of him, nay, to put him even in the way of gaining a decent livelihood for himself without the proper exertion on his own part. What in the universe put the 'Army' in the head of the baby – does he forsooth think I am going to buy a Commission for him? Please have the goodness to tell him I am exceedingly displeased at his notions & that the sooner he drops them the better; otherwise, tho it galls me to say it, he must speedily shift for himself. My wife too is much concerned to hear of the little satisfaction he is likely to afford us.

21st April – From all you write about my son, I am placed in a very awkward situation, so much so that with the view of relieving my anxiety at once about him, I have resolved on trying the Indian country again, & to this end have written Gov Simpson & Mr [Duncan] Finlayson to R.R. My letter to Ranald himself is enclosed to the latter who will add a postscript to it according to the answer his Excellency may give. April '42 is the ordinary time he could embark at Lachine, but I have suggested that probably they could employ him at some one of the near hand posts for some months prior to that date by way of initiation, & thus avoid further encumbrance to you & Mrs E. to whom I am much indebted for her kindness. Herewith I enclose you a Bill in the Company for 35 pounds sterling & any further claim you may have, let me know it & I shall attend to it cheerfully. Should plan of mine with respect to Ranald be acceded to, you know how to assist in the execution of it. My paper is done, but all I could say to you, not one half.

P.S. I see young [James] Tod here on his way to you in charge of Dr Tolmie. I do not know how he may turn out, but so far he bears a very excellent character for sedateness & correctness of conduct. He will not pester you much for a Commission in Her Majesty's Army. Whether Ranald leaves you immediately on receipt of this or hangs about you till spring, have the goodness to drive out of his head his new notions of greatness. Even for the few months he was with you I can see he very much improved in his hand of writing & business appearance altogether. In case my application now may not be conceded to the full extent of my wishes, I shall after the governor is [here] renew the charge & write you acct by our fall Express, which generally reaches Lachine end of March or beginning of April; so that I hope you will have an eye upon the youngster until we can fairly dispose of him in a comme il faut manner. The eldest of my boys at R.R. [Angus, age 15] I am concerned to say is in a very precarious state of health & deranges the plan I had in view of sending him & younger brother [Archibald] to England this season. He is to come this way to ourselves & the other to remain where he is for the present. Here, my dear sir, commences the cares & anxieties of this world on the shoulders of a parent with a large family & far removed from them.

Fort Colvile, 18 March 1841

To Rev Elkanah Walker, Tshimakain Mission

Charlie came in late last night & handed me your obliging favour of 15th ... As regards your contemplated trip to the plains. I confess tis a subject on which I am unwilling to offer an opinion. You, Gentlemen, are come to the country to judge for yourselves & to promote the laudable objects of the mission you are upon best way you can, in which you are sure to meet no impediment on our part. On the contrary, I am certain you may always rely on our good wishes. But in extending direct support we are most anxious to save appearances, & to avoid everything like a participation in what may be termed party opinions, which in the present state of the country & of what the plains in particular ere long is likely to become, I fear would scarcely be consistent with my concurrence in the *mode* of campaigning as you propose. Without going into a long story here, I am certain your own experience & good sound sense will bear me out in this opinion situated as I am. However, by having your own lodge, horses, attendants &c &c and moving or encamping when you please, I see nothing to prevent your making a trip to the plains to see the Indians, & to be within reach of our people as much as may suit your own convenience. There is but one Boat going up this spring which will be pretty deeply laden; besides Mr McLean & family and three men exclusive of the crew ... but I dare say for all that you could be accommodated. A Bag biscuit & a little bacon we could send for you to the Bay should you decide on going, & at the Flatheads Mr McL. could supply all you may require in the rough & tumble way of the country till you get to Buffalo ...

I congratulate you on your prospects of having a more commodious manse. Mr Gray, if he takes it in hand, is just the man to make a good job of it. You cannot however be in earnest when you speak of me getting boards sawn for you at this particular crisis. I never was more pinched for help myself than I am at this moment. The ground here is now about clear of snow & the moment the frost will admit of it our ploughs, God willing, will be in the ground.

[James] Goudie having finished your riding spur, I send it on by the bearer ...

Fort Colvile, 8 April 1841

To John Rowand, Fort Edmonton

... Should [this letter] have the good fortune to reach you before [1st May] ... I have my doubts as it will be confided entirely to the hands of Indians. Poor Antoine Auger reached here morning of 29th and next day betook himself to bed with sore bones & muscles from head to foot & is scarcely able to move out of doors since. The Indian that came with him from Berland will therefore be the bearer of this as far as he will be good-natured enough to carry it himself before consigning it to the hands of others. The only other paper besides this that I mean entrusting him with will be my private letter addressed to you a few days back & which I believe touches more or less on everything worth mentioning hereabouts. More I do not like to send, in case all may fall into the hands of the Yankees hovering about east side the mountains.

Last night about ½ past nine Mr [George] Allan & two men joined me from below. There will be *no early Express.* Judge for yourself now what to do. The Boats won't be here before 13th or 14th nor can they leave this at the very earliest before 22nd. The doctor does not say one single syllable to me on the subject of this unexpected delay. The London dispatch must have reached him yesterday or today – the English ship came in the middle of February and the *Columbia* from California with Mr Douglas middle of last month. The *Cadboro* too, lately from Puget Sound & Gulf of Georgia, but no other arrival from the Northwest coast ... before Mr Allan came off. Mr Douglas, previous to his leaving California, got under way Messrs [Tom] McKay, [James] Steel & Laframboise & a strong party with some cattle & about 2,700 head of sheep, & will be expected some time in course of the summer – 250 of the sheep broke their necks over a precipice their first or second day's march. Poor Mr Alexander Simpson went home by the Vancouver from the Islands on hearing of the death of his brother [Thomas] ... Dr Tolmie is coming up with the Boats & Messrs. Ermatinger & McKinlay accompany him as far as Okanagan on their way to Thompson River. The latter to remain there & the former to return to resume the charge in the Snake country, when he sees the state of the place there. I apprehend no danger for the present ...

As to the governor's order of march,[37] the doctor writes me 'In regards to the governor's route I write him & recommend his coming up by the plains & send 30 horses to you, & as you have more correct sources of information about the country through which the gov is to come you will take the necessary measures & write to the governor what you intend to do.' Now, my most correct source of information, Berland, is not yet here, but will I hope be before the Expr starts & then my arrangements on the subject communicated to his Excellency ... you may rely on meeting horses either at the Tobacco plain, Rivière la Biche or Thomp Lake – to make that route however our future line of communication with east side is, I fancy, a hopeless business.

Two Boats go up this spring, in case they may possibly be required in August, and on the other hand I direct some provision for the party to be made at Flatheads.

P.S. Poor Antoine [Auger] expressing great desire to return to you himself this way, even in his present infirm condition, I have consented to his undertaking the trip, & in order to get him a good horse & otherwise prepared this Budget does not leave me before tomorrow morning, and Antoine's going emboldens me to send you a duplicate of my report to the Gov & Council as I do not see the possibility of their having any other news at Red River from the Columbia before middle of June even should Mr Allan follow you, and on this account my worthy brother-in-law [Antoine Auger was married to Jane Klyne's sister Madeleine Marie Klyne] is exceedingly anxious to be of service to you.

Fort Colvile, 7/8 April 1841

To Rev Elkanah Walker, Tshimakain Mission

Our friend Mr Eells is about taking his departure ... he brings you a couple of whipsaw files ... [Regarding your plains expedition] I am happy to find you readily coincided with me in the reasons I gave you, & let me now add that *under all circumstances* I think you are as usefully and agreeably to yourself employed in getting up snug comfortable lodgings for yourself & Mrs W. as anywhere else, & by way of varying the scene for you & partaking in other invigorating recreations, do me the favour

[37] Rowand was to accompany Simpson from Fort Edmonton.

to take a turn this way end of May & go down with us to Okanagan or Walla Walla as may suit you ...

Fort Colvile, 15 April 1841

To Governor George Simpson, Red River Settlement (Private)

A very uncommon thing with me, at this moment I find myself in the honourable position of being your debtor by three long sheets, namely the one of March across the Atlantic that came to hand in due time, & that of Dec '39 & August '40 by Cape Horn which reached me *together* here the other day ...

... I wish I could on the present occasion infuse into my sheet something of that gay & buoyant spirits you generally allowed me so much credit for ... but what awful instances of the uncertainty of human life, even without a moment's warning, have we not had since you favoured me with your last. Within the short space of 40 days tidings of the two lamentable events I allude to reached me here. The fate of your meritorious but unhappy cousin [Thomas Simpson] will be extensively [regretted] on many accounts, and I am certain the tragical end of our poor old friend Mr Black will not affect you much less. They are blows to the fur trade as little looked for as they will prove serious in their consequences ...

... [Regarding] the project of getting you in by the plains ... I told Mr Rowand, so far as we are concerned, his route would be adopted and preparations made to the extent he suggested ... Were I allowed to give an opinion I think with the necessary precautions with the Blackfeet I would recommend you coming by the plains instead of the Athabasca Portage & the Upper Columbia; either way however you can be accommodated as far as depends on us.

There is a great deal adoing nowadays west side ... but I suppose the best plan is to put off [further news] until we have the pleasure of the promised confab on the banks of the Columbia ... The affair of the parson [Herbert Beaver] was I thought at one time about being amicably settled ... however well meant the compliment of the Reverend Gentleman, I fancy the solitary distinction he is pleased to make in my favour is rather *a misfortune to me*. Be this as it may, I cannot reproach myself with any glaring indiscretion ... in the little marks of civility I might safely extend to the Beavers while on our forlorn coast ... As they were found disagreeable members of society, & I am willing to allow they had faults, I regret they were not got rid of with a little better grace ... They both wrote us ... their correspondence however we are not very anxious to cultivate ... we can be indulged in that way to our hearts content much nearer home. Priests, Methodists, Congregationalists & Independents are now become the order of the day on the Oregon waters, and I find the doctor's old & favourite friends the Jesuits, so shamefully used under the vile British rule of the Canadas, will soon be paramount. Their Vicar-General [Father DeSmet] came up from St Louis last season for the express purpose of selecting in the Flathead plains a suitable place for their college, so that upon the whole I think their Honour's Chaplain [Herbert Beaver] made a very timely & lucky escape.

... The trade I am sorry to say is certainly falling off, not only in the Colvile district but all over the country. Outfit '40 just closed is from 3 to 400 Beaver short of the preceding one, but rather above the one of '38, & I am in hopes we will this season again recover surplus, though I once more labour under the disadvantage of a change of trader in the plains. McLean being now in the temporary charge of Thompson River my only other recourse was young McPherson, who left me 20th of last month to see how he and the Vicar-General will agree on the propriety of employing Natives to kill Beaver instead of learning their Pater Noster. We may get on with them, but most assuredly this new crusade will derange matters much. The Finlays [freemen] & all the other Halfbreeds in that quarter are just now on their way down to this blessed Wallamette of ours. I am happy to say our farming operations are ... far advanced ... The Mill, Boatbuilding & other indispensable labour go on much in the usual way ...

[comments on news from home re various acquaintances] ... As for all the Douglases [Selkirk] in the upper society, I certainly wish them well too, but I think my debt of gratitude is paid them with interest long ago, including even their boon to me in the *Buffalo Wool Company* ... [however I] accept her commission with the most profound respect, & [agree] to exercise all my conchalogistical & ornithological talents in her Ladyship's service.

On family & money matters I will make bold to trouble you a little. My eldest son at Red River I am concerned to find is but in a very poor state of health & what to do with him at this distance is very difficult for me to decide on. If riding would not be against his complaint, perhaps he could accompany the cavalcade, at least as far as the Saskatchewan where the fall folks could pick him up. My son that went to Canada two years ago is still unsettled in the world, & I foresee that that sort of thing cannot even be attempted without much outlay in the first place, & doubtful success after all when so far removed from the eye of a parent. I have resolved in relinquishing all projects on his behalf in that quarter. Mr E. Ermatinger speaks very well indeed of his temper, good behaviour & close application, but does not say quite so much of his education & aptitude for business in that part of the world. Now, this is quite as much as I could expect to hear in favour of my son for the time he has been *in business*. I therefore take upon myself to recommend him for a trial in the Indian country on the footing you may consider he deserves. He will be 18 February '42 & in April of that year he might embark at Lachine if such be your pleasure ... My little pecuniary transactions in the hands of His Honour the Judge [Samuel Gale] are as yet as much unexplained as they were; all may be right enough but it would be still more satisfactory did one know something of the nature of the investment & the accumulation on the sum &c. As for the Norway business ... I would as soon that my interest in it be limited to the 500 pounds already paid up as go the full length of the 1,500 pounds, seeing that all I can realize for years to come must be absorbed in that way.

Fort Colvile, 24 April 1841

To Governor George Simpson, Red River Settlement

Edouard Berland is now here and has furnished all the necessary information on the subject of the land route to this place ... The round by the Tobacco plain and Flatheads he condemns in toto, as you will see by the enclosed sketch of the country, he proposes to leave the Kootenais River at McDonald's stream & cut straight through the country until you again fall upon that river at the Traverse. There is a regular Indian track ... [Berland] will be at the aforesaid little stream end of June with 25 horses, and at Thompson's House on the Columbia Lakes 10th July ... he will meet you at the Bow River traverse a day's ride above the old fort on or before 25th ... From Bow River old fort/four days from Edmonton/to Colvile have marked out 14 encampments & I have no doubt in the 15 days the distance can be performed ... Berland himself you will find very useful & intelligent on all points connected with the route &c &c ... The Columbia, after consulting the most experienced watermen in this country, I entirely disapprove of ...

Fort Colvile, 24 April 1841

To John Rowand, Fort Edmonton

... This forenoon the answer to your London Budget & the coast papers arrived from below, having left Vancouver as late as the 12th. Our Chief seems entirely in favour of the plains for his Excellency. Berland is now here & has undertaken to lead you all from the Bow River Traverse to here in 15 easy days riding without going by the Tobacco plain or Flatheads at all. He leaves this in a few days with 25 horses ... I have been very explicit on everything with the great man himself, and sent him a rule of thumb sketch of the country and all the encampments ...

Everyone is so sanguine about this land trip for the governor (mind we are not so as regards a general pass that way) we sent but *one* Boat to the mountain ... In truth all the most celebrated boatmen in this country condemn the idea of attempting the Upper Columbia before September ...

I shall be looking out for you all here by the 10th August ...

Fort Colvile, 26 April 1841

To John McLoughlin, Fort Vancouver

... Mr Allan left us about noon yesterday ... Sylvester leaves for W.W. tomorrow & by him that far I send the paper trunk, in case a safe conveyance thence for Vancouver may offer before the Brigade goes down ... Mr McPherson's people from the Flatheads came in today ... All the Finlays, [Antoine] Plante, Fivelle & Brown are on their way down here to proceed to the low country. Edouard Berland too will be leaving me in a day or two & the best explanation I can give of his mission is the copy herewith sent of my communication with Governor Simpson. Copy of my letter too to Mr Rowand ...

In reference to the R.C. Mission in the plains, I think the best thing I can do is to forward Mr DeSmet your letter entire, as it wholly repects himself. Those here are quite reconciled to the answer I gave in their case & nowise disposed to construe it into an act of unkindness. Mr Walker, being more desirous of a change of air & scenery than anything else, I have offered him a passage in our Boats to Okanagan & Walla Walla if he chooses to avail himself of it ...

Not a man here ... can be relied on as a future Boatbuilder ... please be explicit as to Canote and son. [Pierre] Martineau I have settled with ... & remains inland to put up the house on the site of the old one now tumbling about our ears ...

Fort Colvile, 26 May 1841

To Governor George Simpson, Red River Settlement

... The last news from the Gents gone out is of the 10th ... and came safe to hand six days ago ... Two days previous to their return [Joseph] Monique & 4 other Bouts joined me from Vancouver for assisting down our craft. On the 23rd also cast up Mr McLean from Thompson River, & yesterday was followed by Messrs McKinlay & Maxwell with 26 men

from Okanagan detached thence by Mr Ogden – all for the purpose
of lending a hand down with our six Boats ... To complete the happy
assemblage here within the week from the four cardinal points, parson
Walker popped in upon us this afternoon for a passage down to attend
what they call their annual meeting, this year to be held at Dr. Whitman's [Waiilatpu], and tomorrow God willing we make a move ...
Berland left this with 28 horses at the appointed time ...

... After Mr Tod left Kamloops (8th March) and before [Frank] Ermatinger and McKinlay arrived (about 18th April) McLean's people had
two bloodless shots at the murderer. Not many days after, he himself
came up with the villain again, but not I believe altogether bloodless.
Since then no further attempts have been made on the life of the fiend
... The place [Kamloops] at present is, in the usual way for the summer,
in charge of Lolo [Leolo, guide and interpreter] ...

It is with much concern I have to inform you that poor Mr Pambrun
... [had] a very serious fall from his horse ... Dr Whitman of the near-
est missionary station who was immediately sent for writes me of 12th
thus: 'The cord slipped out of the horse's mouth, Mr P. rose in his stir-
rups to bring the rope up to the horse's throat & in this act he got a
very serious bruise from the saddle & afterwards fell to the ground with
great violence ... all the lower extremities suffer much ... nothing can be
told yet as to the probable result of the case.'

Walla Walla, 31 May 1841

To John McLoughlin, Fort Vancouver
On arrival here this morning in company with Messrs Ogden &
McKinlay, it was with feelings of very great distress we heard of another
melancholy death in the list of our friends & associates. The arrange-
ments you propose in yours of 19th for providing a successor to poor old
Pambrun I immediately set about affecting ...

Fort Colvile, Tuesday morning, 15 June 1841

To the Ladies & Gentlemen at Tshimakain
Madame Goudie going your way, I am irresistably impelled to say
something, especially to the female part of the community to cheer them
up in their present interval of solitude. Mr McLean I fancy encamped
near you the second day after he left this, & of course gave you the news
here. Probably he brought his little girl with him; be this as it may, he
certainly did another thing I don't approve of, the taking back of the
woman after we all thought it was to be a final separation; but there is

no accounting for these things. I think he would have reached Walla
Walla before the good folks from Whilatpu [Dr and Mrs Whitman]
would have left it ...

The nipping frost of the night of 4th June we had to the southward
did not do much injury here tho all did not entirely escape. So far, ever
since my return the season has been most glorious; but I fear the
grasshoppers – this soft weather has animated myriads of them.

There is no want of salmon now at the falls, & had the lazy hounds
offered such a blessing been only half so industrious as they ought they
might have lain up a good standby before the time they say their creed
will allow them to commune. Instead of showing any energy of the
kind, the idle drones are off with the forlorn hope, the women, to see
them dig up roots. The Bay is I believe the great field for this harvest
at present. Our salmon Chief has located himself in the mountains to
the north of us, masticating deer's meat to his heart's content, & sends
word from time to time to his less fortunate dupes on no account to go
near the falls, or trespass on the established law until it be his will &
pleasure to say the *thing is very good*. Two or three however have shown
sense enough to break thro the law & by means of the dart [spear] furnish their own starving families & us with a fish occasionally. I think

Tshimakain.

The Tshimakain Mission in 1844, sketched by visiting botanist Charles Geyer.
Walkers' second house is on the left. Eells' second house at centre with two
original cabins attached. (Washington State University Libraries 70-0401)

the wife is about sending you a piece of the last that came in – but will it keep? I had it weighed this morning as it came in, & proved to be within 3 lbs. of the heaviest I ever saw or heard of in the Columbia – bodily it weighed 40 lbs. And this is the godsend the silly creatures are so scrupulous about touching in what they call *out of season*. Nay, there is more in it – sheer laziness. To fix the Basket now would subject them to the necessity of shifting it out and or in, according to the state of the water, & this is what they cannot be *fashed* [bothered] *with* as they sometimes say in my country. The rule then is to do nothing till the water is stationary, or next thing to it! It is now I believe at its height & nothing more than the medium of our high waters. In one respect this is lucky, that is for the craft in the river, but the Colvile farm has heretofore gained more than it lost by the highest water. Our little boy James is rather indisposed at the present. The rest of the family are, thank God, in their usual good health. The wife herself desires to be kindly remembered to you all …

Thursday morning – Since I had the pleasure of addressing you … we have had great varieties, of which you are of course in part aware. The Commodore [Lieut Robert E. Johnson][38] & travelling companion came in late last night after passing a most uncomfortable night half way [from Tshimakain] under the canopy of heaven in rain, thunder and lightning; but they are young men still, calculated to endure that sort of thing, & it is but right that all travellers should have something marvellous to talk of … I believe they will again be back your way in three or four days & it might not be improper to observe that a guide might be on view for them in case they go by Clearwater …

Fort Colvile, 19 June 1841

To Donald McLean, Walla Walla

This will be handed you by Lieut Johnson of the U. States Exploring Expedition, who with his party is travelling in this part of the country on scientific pursuits. You will see his letters of credit & introduction from the Company's office in Puget Sound & I have only to add my own special desire that the party meet with every accommodation & attention while in your quarter. I send back by them four of the horses I have with me from Walla Walla. Lieut Johnson is still uncertain whether he returns to the ships by land or descends the Columbia …

[38] Lieutenant Robert E. Johnson was a member of a US government expedition of four ships led by Captain Charles Wilkes. This expedition was sent to the Columbia to explore the coastal regions; several parties were sent into the interior, and Johnson and his companions visited Colvile and Tshimakain.

Fort Colvile, 20 June 1841

To Governor George Simpson, en route west

Here I am once more, after a hasty trip of ten days of it by Okanagan & Walla Walla & back by the plains. The cause of this unexpected
return is the death of poor Mr Pambrun, who survived but three days
after the date of Dr Whitman's letter to me. It was not till the morning
of the day of his death those about him wrote to Vancouver. On receipt
of the melancholy news there, which held but little or no hope for his
recovery, Mr McLoughlin wrote Ogden to leave McKinlay at W.W. and
to me to return immediately by land & send down McLean to relieve
him, as I believe he is so far the person intended to succeed Mr Black
at Thompson River ... First of June I commenced my journey back &
the same morning my colleague drifted down the stream alone with nine
Boats. True he had with him passengers, Mr [Cornelius] Rogers [who
had accompanied the Walkers and Eells party to the Oregon Territory]
& the family of the deceased. This man it is said is to become the
guardian of the family & the husband of the daughter in virtue of a previous arrangement to that effect with the father. His Will was made
out & signed the day of the poor man's death. Mr McLoughlin & Mr
Douglas are the executors ... One thing allowed on all hands, Rogers is
a keen, stirring intelligent fellow, but the young lady herself is I believe
less inclined to the match than the mother.

By this last dispatch from headquarters we had very little good news.
I did hear however that Rae is off by way of Oahoo to take up his residence in California & that Wood accompanied him to be the assistant
of our chief at Honolooloo. The *Wave* which brought the last consignment from England for those two places is now in the Columbia in the
pay of the American government, employed from the Islands as their
store ship by the commander of the Exploring Expedition [Wilkes]. Of
the present condition & employment of that squadron itself, I have
lately had the most authentic information of any, before my eyes here
for the last four days in the presence of a detachment from it of a Lieut
[Johnson], a surgeon, a purser, a botanist & an officer of Marine. The
four vessels consisting of the *Vincennes* Capt Wilkes, the *Peacock* Capt
Hudson, the *Porpoise* Lieut Goldring, & the *Flying Fish* Lieut Knox,
entered the Sound between 10th & 15th May. On 17th the Commodore
himself proceeded by land on a visit to Vancouver & the same day the
inland exploring party commenced their undertaking by Mount Ranier
across to the Columbia River, which they made about half way between
OK & W.W. after 15 days hard toiling with horses & guides from
Nisqually; from OK they came on here by the ordinary land route, &

one by one dropped in on us on the 15th & 16th. They left us yesterday afternoon after taking the meridian Alt, to make the round of the different missionary stations and sweep in again upon W.W. From that place Lieut Johnson is yet uncertain whether he recrosses the Mount Ranier range to gain the ships in the Sound or goes down by water to Vancouver.

There being no time to hear from Mr McLoughlin before they started, the only credentials they brought are from Mr Anderson at the request of the Commodore. Their object, tis said, is entirely scientific. They of course stood in want of our assistance which they received & acknowledged with apparent gratitude, besides the tender of good bills on the government & altogether seemed pleased with their reception – the time allowed them from the squadron is two months. One of the vessels was I believe to have come round for Capt Wilkes & the purser of the flagship that accompanied him to Vancouver. Mr [George] Pelly it would appear had a hand in sending in this vessel, being himself at a loss how to set about disposing of the cargo she brought … Another vessel called the *Thomas Perkin* from New England is in the river for some time back, on a salmon speculation: the Dr I hear has bought them out & undertaken to lead them himself with the needful.

I cannot say the destination of our own vessels this summer – one I suppose goes with Rae and Wood. The steamer was in the Sound getting her boilers repaired when Lieut Johnson left. He says had they found her in working trim they would have pushed hard to get the use of her for a few weeks to complete their survey in that quarter. Their schooner the *Flying Fish*, with six Boats well manned, was off towards Fraser River and Johnson Straits. In July last they had a Lieutenant & a midshipman killed in one of the s. sea islands which brought on a destructive war with the Natives that ended in the death of 60 or 70 of them – the chief instigator they have on board the flagship. Capt Croker of the British Navy too fell a victim to savage ferocity in those islands about the same time.

On affairs here itself, I have nothing thank God unfavourable to report, unless indeed it be the effects of a nipping frost we had the night of the 4th & the promising appearance of another destructive generation of my old friends the grasshoppers. The very favourable turn however which the season has lately taken may yet destroy them. Young Masoville left the place with 30 loads of grain the day before my return, & was back again with the strangers to pass the summer with us until the Brigade is up … He was taken out by his Bourgeois with the intention of returning him from Thompson River with livestock but owing to some altercation with the Natives as they came along between that place & Alexandria,

Mr Ogden did not think it prudent to send him back until they all go in together. About the middle of next month I shall myself be obliged to go down to OK for the Boats coming up to this place, & I don't well see how we can manage to work up all that are required if the Dr does not send up a good few extra hands. For yourself Sir, there will be at least 2 Boats required & perhaps as many for the mountains in the fall. Now our whole number in the river is but 14 hands & four effective summer men here.

Wacon [Pierre Umphreville] leaves tomorrow with a Kootenais guide & will be with Berland by the appointed time at McDonald River; thence they move on to Thompson's House where they leave the horses & meet you on the Bow River Traverse about 15th July. They will have in all 30 horses.

The Columbia is still rising – a very uncommon thing ...

Fort Colvile, 7 July 1841

To Rev Elkanah Walker, Tshimakain Mission

... The weather for the last few days has been exceedingly warm here, the thermometer often in the shade from 95 to blood heat. Our crops yet look pretty well, but should this heat & drought continue I fear everything will wither ... the failing already perceptible in our potatoes. The main river began to fall about 25th and the Indians have thought it a wise plan to stop further [delaying] in the business of the salmon; the Basket is made and the fish jump in to their heart's content. So you see [their] prayers in that way avail as much as mine for rain ...

Fort Okanagan, 19 July 1841

To John McLoughlin, Fort Vancouver

On meeting with Mr Ogden here the night before last I had the pleasure of receiving your communication ... The measures recommended to my attention with respect to the governor we shall of course as far as practicable attend, but the dilemma in which the uncertainty of his movements & the inadequate means furnished for meeting them place me, & at a moment when so much is to be done on the place itself, will be very great indeed ... In short, to follow up all the arrangements proposed, the duties of the place must be entirely neglected. Instead of being in a position to reinforce Mr McPherson with two active hands in addition to the two boys now with him, he cannot get even *one* of any description. My intention was to throw ample supplies into the plains this summer, but without adequate means to do so & the necessary protection to the property, the execution of the project must be very lame ...

21 July 1841

To Peter S. Ogden, Grosse Roche

I met your people this morning on their way home, after safely deposit-
ing my 80 pieces, for which accommodation I thank you much. The
Boats with the 15 pcs in had great difficulty in the Dalles; the Guide
was very near going for it, being forced out into the stream by the action
of a tremendous whirlpool, the line was unable to hold it & down it
went, but miraculously without dashing on any rocks or bouillons [rapids]
below ...

Fort Colvile, 1 August 1841

To Governor George Simpson, en route westward

... Yesterday forenoon I thought the best arrangements I could make
were made, but before the day was over entered the Indian that guided
Wacon with word that on joining Berland at the Lakes ... they found him
seriously disabled in one of his legs & totally incapable of continuing
the route with the other lad to Bow River as contemplated in the spring
... I am much concerned ... I now despatch William Pion with another
Indian to go on without pulling bridle till he meets you ... Wherever
that meeting may take place, it would ease my mind much and otherwise
greatly tend to facilitate future operations could the Indian be returned
immediately with such fresh orders as you may conceive necessary in so
complicated an affair.

... The Outfit & horses for the plains trade I send off tomorrow in
charge of Indians and four common hands, quite uncertain ... whether
McPherson will be on time or not to meet them at the House and load
the Boat. Canote will be accompanied to the end of the Kootenais portage by old Charlo and both will proceed to the Traverse, carrying with
them for Berland the supplies intended for the summer trade at that place.

Here itself we are all now in the press of our work ... the gathering
[of our grain] will I much fear be a tedious and a losing process with so
many sick, lame & blind as we have to depend upon for that duty ...

Fort Colvile, 19 August 1841

To John McLoughlin, Fort Vancouver

It is now ½ past ten & Sir George Simpson[39] having just retired I avail
myself of a moment's relaxation ... to address you a few lines, as he proposes to start with the peep of day tomorrow. By a very happy conjunction of good arrangements we were the night before last advertised of

[39] Governor George Simpson was knighted by Queen Victoria in 1841.

his approach: the plan suggested to him in my last communication ... succeeded to admiration & the Boat accordingly was back to me on the evening of 17th with his Excellency's note of 11th dated 'Grand Quoit Lac' [now Moyie Lake, BC] in the heart of the Kootenais country. The Boat, as promised, they found on Coeur d'Alènes Lake & horses in abundance at the Pendant d'Oreille Bay. The governor's opportune arrival among us starts up new operations with respect to the Boat Encampment: a craft down of no less than eight Boats will be required this fall, say 5 for the Red River settlers that they are themselves to build at the portage under the direction of Mr James Sinclair & to be guided down by Monique, & 3 Columbia River Boats for the porkeaters, including the one now going up guided by Joseph Anawasan.

... From the Kootenais very little is expected this summer. About an hour ago one of our Flathead men came in with Mr McPherson's news; his trade is but very indifferent, say 300 Beaver. He saw Mr Ermatinger who was then about closing a bargain with Mr [James] Bridger [American trader] to the tune of 1,500 Beaver ...

Fort Colvile, 25 August 1841

To Rev Elkanah Walker, Tshimakain Mission

... I have been quite on the run here; goes & comers almost every hour in the 24. But the appearance of our governor (now Sir George Simpson) amongst us is the greatest event of all ... He got here about noon of 18th & left us early on 20th. His party consisted of Chief Trader [John] Rowand & his son [Alexander] a young physician, a Russian gentleman from Petersburgh [Nicolas Von Freymann] on his way to Sitka on the N.W. coast & himself & secretary [Edward Hopkins]. They came by my route thro the Kootenais, left Red River 3rd July, Montreal 10th May & England beginning of April. Was accompanied from Canada to Red River by two young Lords, one the son of the Marquis of Normanby, Viceroy of Ireland & the other the son of the Marquis of Sligo; so you see great folks take a fancy for a turn to the Indian country too ...

I suppose you have heard thro other channels of the misfortune which befell the *Peacock* sloop of war, Captain [William] Hudson [Wilkes Expedition], in the mouth of the Columbia 17th of last month – a total wreck – no lives lost but everything private & public went to the bottom save the charts, journals & instruments ... On Monday our mountain boat for the 2nd time left me, its object this time, instead of going for the governor, is the descent of 130 settlers young & old from Red River, coming to try their fortune in Oregon ...

Our Flathead people are back; they found Mr McPherson at the house after making his round with the Natives as far as Pierre's Hole. The priests he did not see, but was told three of them had arrived at rendezvous on their way to the Bitter Root plains. My trader from the Kootenais is also in, but our collection altogether is very poor. The harvest is far more promising than the Beaver trade, & will no doubt ere long become the grand consideration everywhere west side the R. Mountains as well as on the Atlantic board. Our whole grain will I think be cut tomorrow night, & the carters are close on the heel of the cradlers ...

The wife joins me in kind regards to yourselves & the Ladies − trust the young stranger is doing well [a son Edwin was born to the Eells on July 27] ...

Fort Colvile, 27 August 1841

To Archibald McKinlay, Walla Walla
... Antoine Felix starts today with the cattle. They are as follows viz:

52 Cows including 4 heifers of last season
28 calves of this season
1 Bull
30 Oxen including 8 of one year old
Total 111 Head

Felix & his 2 Indians it is expected will return here after the cattle are delivered to you & the people for Vancouver ...

Fort Colvile, Thursday afternoon (September 1841)

To Rev Elkanah Walker, Tshimakain Mission
This moment after I returned from escorting our friends [Rev Henry and Eliza Spalding] from Clearwater (I forget your official name for it) [Lapwai Mission] I received your note of yesterday together with the spectacle case ... As you said, their appearance so unexpectedly gave us a little surprise, but did not diminish, I hope, the cordiality of the reception. I am most concerned altogether at the position of our worthy friends in the hands of those uncouth raskals they have to do with. But I hope with patience & a little sacrifice of personal feeling the brutes will relent & see into the egregious folly of quarreling with their best friends. I think one of you, the moment your own pressing avocations will admit of it, ought to take a turn to Clearwater. If it does no good it can do no harm ...

... a considerable change in the movements of our emigrants from east side. Instead of coming by water from the mountain where I have Boats

& Guides awaiting them, they are beating their way over the governor's track & will I expect be at Spokane about the 25th. We sent horses & provisions off to meet them ...

Fort Colvile, 10 September 1841

To Archibald McKinlay, Walla Walla

Very unexpectedly, young Joseph Klyne [brother of Jane Klyne McDonald], one of Mr [James] Sinclair's party, cast in upon us late last night with a note from that gentleman announcing his advance after all *by land*. The note is dated 30th August from 'Red Rock near Columbia River' which I understand to be the place where our horses met Governor Simpson. At Edmonton the party set their face against coming *by water*, & accordingly left that place on the 4th, Jamie Jack guiding them to Bow River, got to Red Rock 27th. There one of the wives brought an increase to the party, already 120 souls. Garber & family remained at Fort des Prairies. Mr S. says they had then but 10 days' provisions which would scarcely take them to the Kootenais Traverse. Their horses were still pretty vigorous but fast falling off in flesh. To prevent any misunderstanding as to what I am about doing for these people & the assistance they will still require before they can arrive at Vancouver, I herein transcribe the material part of my letter to Mr Sinclair, and I think you ought to send it down to headquarters without delay.

... you know best what assistance in horses you can afford to give, one thing very certain, 20 or 30 would be a great relief to them & in no small degree tend to pass them thro upon a less expenditure of provisions than slower marching would necessarily require. My Indian that now carries you this could on his return bring on the horses ...

Fort Colvile, 10 September 1841

To James Sinclair

By the arrival here last night of Joseph Klyne ... it is with no small surprise & some disappointment I heard that after all you were coming *by land*. That you ... will be ere this reaches you out of the worst part of the journey, we must see how you & the party are to prosecute the remainder of the trip to Vancouver. Herewith, I enclose you a rule of thumb sketch of the country you will have to pass for attaining Walla Walla, being now your only plan and only route, for to make for this place in the existing state of things would be a perfect waste of time & labour as at Colvile a single Boat is not at my disposal. Instead therefore of coming on to the Pendant d'Oreille Bay you will cross the river at what is called the Spokane Traverse, between the Lake and the Chute,

& thence push right on for old Spokane Fort; except for the first 10 or 12 miles the whole distance is a perfect prairie and excellent pasturage for your animals. Taking it for granted that by the time Klyne reaches the aforesaid traverse you will be thereabouts & by means of the provisions he carries will have 10 days rations with which to commence the W.W. trip ... Joseph & the young man with him leave this tomorrow with 16 horses to help you on to Spokane, and I will write to Mr McKinlay at W.W. to send on to meet you all the assistance he can in that way too ...

A Boat with one of our Guides & 4 other Bouts left this on 24th of last month to meet you at the Boat Encampment where it was expected they would find you well on with the construction of the craft for the descent from there. Of course they must now remain till the fall party comes on ...

Fort Colvile, 19 September 1841

To Archibald McKinlay, Walla Walla

Your old friend Mr Sinclair will be upon you a few days sooner than I led you to expect. For various reasons I am anxious that the party should go down without delay and with this in view have accommodated them with about 20 horses that will go on till they meet yours. Should William Pion be obliged to continue the route to Walla Walla our horses will not immediately on their return be in a fit condition to commence another trip & yet another & a much more arduous one is in contemplation the moment Mr Manson arrives here requiring at least 15 horses. It is an expedition to Thompson River [to hunt down Black's murderer] ... do endeavour to send by Pion 10 good horses & charge them either to this place or Thompson River. Arms, ammunition, tobacco &c &c being necessarily required for such a turn out I direct my 2 men if they go so far to bring on the 5 pieces at your place – say a case of Guns, a Roll tobacco, 1 Keg powder & two Bags Ball ...

Fort Colvile, 19 September 1841

To Sir George Simpson, Fort Vancouver

On return of our two men from Vancouver four days ago ... happy I was to hear that the trip down was as agreeable as it was prompt, being I believe in this latter respect the quickest in our Columbia Log. By the doctor's letters ... I see something is in contemplation to retrieve our affairs at Thompson River, & on my part nothing shall be wanting that I possibly can contribute to the attainment of so desirable an object.

Our Red River friends after all came by the Kootenais & now that they are safely out of the embarras I do not know upon the whole but it was the best plan – true it will be a disappointment to the men sent to the mountains ...

... By the bye, not many days ago I had Mr Spalding & family driven from their establishment on the Nez Percés River by the Natives: that is they in one half hour poisoned his two choice milch cows and manifested much ill feelings in other respects. The poor people however returned, but the issue of all this annoyance is very doubtful ...

Fort Colvile, 30 September 1841

To John McLoughlin, Fort Vancouver

Late last night Edouard Montignis [Montigny] came in with letters from New Caledonia & Thompson River ... Seemingly the murderer having taken the alarm, the success of the contemplated coup at Thompson River, at least for some time, is likely to be more doubtful than we could wish. This recent information however will not influence us in the task chalked out for Mr Manson unless directions to the contrary are here by 25th Octr ...

Fort Colvile, 30 September 1841

To Sir George Simpson

... The arrival here ... of a Budget from my northern neighbours renders another courier necessary. Mr Ogden gives me the substance of his official report to you ... and I agree with him as to the impracticability of his having been able to have done much, situated as he was, to secure the murderer en passant. But the part of it which relates to the cause of the calamity & the folly of *sending* for salmon when it could be procured *at the house*, I do not so readily agree with. He or no other ever yet supported nor can support such an Establishment as that necessarily kept up at Thompson River *without sending* for salmon, and the people of New Caledonia are the last that ought to disapprove of the system of collecting it out of doors from the Natives, as I believe, with very few exeptions, every year since my last [there] they were in the habit of getting more or less of their staff of life from Thompson River. For all this, I am not an advocate of frequent [excursions] to the Natives for salmon could they be avoided, and the only way in which we could get rid of that great evil is by having good gardens. With a small summer establishment – a thing never yet allowed at T.R. – I am certain the bulk of their livelihood in some kind or another could be procured in that way.

Such a round as Mr O. speaks of, that is down Thompson River & up Fraser River to the canoe by 2 Gentlemen & 25 men would I think

have a very good effect. Even if they were not lucky enough to fall in
with the murderer, it might be the means of speedily surrendering him
dead or alive & would always produce some terror in the different camps.
The abundance of salmon this winter offers a very favourable time for
this scouring & as the two fruitless attempts lately made must now alarm
the object of them to an extent that it renders it very improbable he will
in a hurry quit his lurking places, I could wish Mr Manson had fresh
instructions and was differently arranged before he left this ...

Fort Colvile, 1 October 1841

To John Tod, Kamloops

Montignis made a good trip of it here & delivered me your various
favours both public & private from the northward. The persevering
struggle of the d—d scoundrel we are in search of to keep out of the way
is very mortifying. As you say, the winter, when he cannot so adroitly
elude our vigilence, will I hope bring him to bay. By all I can learn from
below they will be stretching a point to reinforce the party at Thompson River this fall; and to this end it would be desirable that you send
in the least suspicious way possible some help in horses to meet them.
[Joachim] Lafleur I understand is on very bad terms with [Alexis] Laprade
& doing nothing; I therefore direct Edouard to take him on with him
(single of course) and once up at Kamloops you know what arrangement
you can afford to make in order to be of service to those going in. Probably the safest plan is to send Nicolas with at least 20 horses; he could
worm his way on slowly so as to fall in with the party if not in the first
mountains, next to the Forks on our track, at least somewhere this side
of *Rivière au Thé* ... I trust when the roving commission arrives [Mr
Manson] will be permitted to take double the number [of horses]; if not
the confounded Russian otters will be the cause for they must be shipped
to the coast by a certain day ...

Fort Colvile, 7 October 1841

To Rev Elkanah Walker, Tshimakain Mission

I am sorry to say your apprehensions of bad news from Walla Walla
were perfectly well founded. The whole establishment went for it the
morning of 5th. The most of what was in the stores within the square
they saved, but all in the back houses fell a sacrifice to the devouring
element, in which quarter I understand was some missionary property,
the flour, saddles & appèchements of the Snake country. To us however
the establishment was everything. It took 5 & 20 years to make it what
it was. No doubt they will now turn their attention to either stone or

dobies [adobe]. It would have been a very serious loss at any time, but in the present conjunction of affairs all over, it is especially so. It has driven me to turn our three ploughs tomorrow; all the threshed wheat we have will be thro the mill end of this week, say 800 bushels, but will I find be all too little to meet all the demands likely to be made upon me, tho more than we ever before had ground at one time ...

The fire it would appear took in the pickets behind the new milk house from a spark, likely from one of the men's houses. It soon communicated with that building & then to the dwellings immediately adjoining. Seemingly the Dr [Whitman] was soon on the ground & in his own generous way made an offer of all at his disposal, of which no doubt proper advantage will be taken until we are again in a position to recover ourselves ...

Fort Colvile, 13 October 1841

To Archibald McKinlay, Walla Walla

Most sorry I am to hear of the lamentable occurrence your letter of the 6th announces. We are all it is true liable to the dreadful devastation of fire, but the Fort of Walla Walla seems always particularly exposed to it ... What in the world are we to do?... Perhaps the expedition intended for T.R. will now be directed your way if we cannot meet both emergencies at the same time. I do feel, viewed in any light, we are placed in a most awkward dilemma at this moment. By the Boats we can send you three Bales appèchements but no saddles. Grain also will go down by every convenient opportunity, but the Snake folks and indeed all others we have to do with in that way must bear in mind our stock here is not inexhaustible. Of grease we will not have a pound by the time the Boat is back from the Flathead, but we shall send you down a Keg of butter to be at your disposal together with 8 more for Vancouver, & if you absolutely require more of the kind I think Mr McLoughlin under the circumstances ... will make no difficulty about one of the 8 also.

The Pelouse Indian tells me that the one who gave him the letters met Tatie near W.W. with his horse much the worse of the journey ... Those frequent couriers will no doubt be a heavy bill of expense but ... we ought to be thankful that they so well answer our purpose with cheerfulness & punctuality. The present Indian is not entirely settled with, partly because I thought it probable that they were paid already & partly with the view of inducing him to go your length now ... He has been kindly treated, & tis as well that *should be so with the whole of them* in our present untoward position. I see the missionaries all over are beginning to have their own troubles with them ...

Fort Colvile, Monday morning, October 1841

To Rev Elkanah Walker, Tshimakain Mission

The Bighead has now paid us a pretty respectable visit & is on the eve of returning. We had long conversations & to me he still appears the same upright character ... observed that upon the whole I was happy to find he was disposed to support the good opinion I had of him when I recommended him to you as a good Indian. He is going to the low country, that is as far as the Dalles, to collect salmon & make some trade in horses in connection with the other big fellow – a speculation they will no doubt make something of.

He is settled with in full on acct of Mr Johnson & seems quite pleased. He has moreover a Gun & a Blanket from me: the former for his Beaver & the latter a reward for recovering me three horses lost in the plains when the settlers passed ...

... Please tell the Ladies Mrs McD. & the youngsters are blessed with perfect health. She is now thank God again as active as a girl of 18 & were the weather not so cold would be very much disposed to pop in upon you one of these days with the whole brood! [Jane's ninth son, Samuel, was born 28 September 1841] ...

Fort Colvile, 15 October 1841

To Father J.P. DeSmet, Flathead camp

Herewith I enclose you a packet just received from Mr McLoughlin ... 4 Cows with their calves, a heifer & a Bull are now here in reserve for you ... You will however oblige me by not employing to come for them any of our runaway servants as I hear thru Indians was in contemplation. I mean Louis Brown & Antoine Duquette. Charles Lafentasie is now on a distant trip & will not be back before beginning of next month. His time being out in the spring he will then as a matter of course be at liberty to join your mission ... we never before ourselves were so much at a loss for hands in the Upper Columbia ... you may rely on field seed from us & any other little accommodation at our command in the way of domestic comforts ... I shall write Mr McPherson to do as much as will be correspondent with his means in that way also ...

Fort Colvile, 15 October 1841

To John McPherson, Flathead camp

... Along with [this] are letters for Mr DeSmet, whose acquaintance you have of course made before now. It is Mr McLoughlin's desire that he & associates should meet with every attention at our hands ... in the way of supplies you will be good enough to go as far as your limited means will admit without stinting yourself in the primary object of your perambulation. We are exceedingly harassed in these parts at present, & to mend the matter ... our Walla Walla establishment was burned to the ground the other day, with of course the loss of much property. A war party is in contemplation for Thompson River when the Express is arrived, but tis more than probable those doughty champions from Montreal will now be employed in the reconstruction of a new Fort for Mr McKinlay ... It was with some difficulty I got off the Kootenais canoe this morning ...

Fort Colvile, 21 October 1841

To John McLoughlin, Fort Vancouver

... Mr Tod's account of the death of the murderer reached me here two hours before the arrival of the Express, & to that Gentleman's letter as well as the verbal information of Joseph Mouselle, one of the capturing party, I beg leave to refer you for the particulars of the scene attending his destruction.

Messrs [Richard] Grant & [George] Allan leave today with 3 Boats & 42 men who, together with the encumbrance of their own & the packs, take down 15 pieces for W.W. Should Mr Manson be directed down the 4th Boat will be entirely loaded with supplies for that place ...

Fort Colvile, 21 October 1841

To Sir George Simpson, en route

Our east side friends are just arrived, all safe ... it appears to me in the present state of affairs the arrangement ought now to be different to what it was end of August. On the one hand the murderer is now annihilated & to all appearances the Natives, from the active part they took in securing him, are better disposed. On the other, the disastrous event at Walla Walla requires labour and attention that could not be foreseen ... detain Mr Manson till the 25th ... then he will with eight men proceed to take his stand permanently at Thompson River ... If anything of consequence is to be undertaken for the reestablishment of Walla Walla, Mr Manson clearly is the fittest person I could recommend for the duty.

Our poor boy [Angus, age 16, sent home from the Red River school severely ill] has just joined us & I regret to find the nature & present aspect of his case is such as hold out no hopes of his recovery ...

Fort Colvile, 31 October 1841

To Patrick McKenzie

You already know my views with respect to your occupation for the winter ... Had you been with us earlier in the season your station would have been the Kootenais, & even now you proceed to Berland at the Tobacco plain via the Flatheads. There you will remain a couple of weeks & make yourself as intimately acquainted as possible with the affairs of that place as it is more than probable there will be your future field of action. The language above all things you ought to direct your attention to, to acquire an intimate association with the Indians, the number of men in the different bands, the best disposed & the best hunters &c &c. You will take an account of everything at the Tobacco plain for our information here & then return to the Flatheads where you will pass the winter. Old Pierre will keep charge there till your return, and sometime in December we shall expect to hear a full account from you of all that is going on above ...

Fort Colvile, 1 November 1841

To John Tod, Kamloops

Yours of 10th Octr per Lafleur & 19th per Edouard I duly received – both these men now return with Mr Manson & party ... Mr C. Factor McLoughlin's last communication from below ... authorizes little deviation from his original plan with respect to Thompson River affairs ...

Fort Colvile, 9 November 1841

To Rev Elkanah Walker, Tshimakain Mission

... McPherson arrived on 1st with a fair trade in furs, but woefully short of other good things, above all grease for the men. Those confounded priests will now monopolise everything in that way, although so far it has been our own fault. I wrote up to Mr McP. to give them what little help he could in the way of provisions & this was construed to be *all they wanted* & ourselves to go without. However I know it will not be so another year. Indeed they have nothing to trade with & are to trust entirely to what we choose to give. DeSmet was with me three days & left with nothing but field seeds & a little flour. The vaunting of the Indians about their locality is all falderall. McPherson was at their place & thinks very little of it. They will evidently be exposed to the inroads of hostile Indians & by no means free from the importunities of lots of beggarly Indians that will feign to be their friends while they have anything to give. However docile the red man west of the R. Mountains may seem to the philanthropists at first sight, I am much mistaken or there are greater difficulties in converting him to the habits of civilized life than is generally supposed. Mr Blanchet and Mr DeSmet found them apparently well disposed & most tractable beings upon such cursory visits, did they expect to find them otherwise? The Indian is too good a politician to say no, you must not come here, but when we have you if you don't come up to our expectations in liberality we know how to serve you. They are fond of them because they obtain their wants from them, but he that gives most Blankets is the favourite & the priest that gives most tobacco will be the favourite too ...

Governor Simpson made a very expeditious trip of it to the Russian settlement – he was back in 45 days & visited all our trading establishments on the coast. He is now off to the Islands & California & writes me that he expects to be back to the Columbia in April ...

Fort Colvile, 20 November 1841

To Samuel Gale, Montreal

I have much pleasure in acknowledging recpt of your kind communication of May last & thank you very sincerely for the interest you so cheerfully take in all that concerns me in the great world of Canada. As regards the proceeds of the Bill of Exchange you was good enough to negotiate for me in 1834 & its management down to this date, I could wish much to relieve you of further trouble & responsibility in the business did I know how to set about it. When Governor Simpson passed me here three months ago we had a talk on the subject. He assured me all would be perfectly to my satisfaction in your hands Sir, at same time suggested that from the multiplicity of your honour's official duties now it might perhaps be as well to transfer the charge to some other hand & pointed out Mr [Hugh] Taylor. I will therefore, should Sir George himself pass this way next spring, endeavour to ascertain from him how to go to work. Meantime, with your permission we shall allow things to remain in statu quo.

It is very kind in Your Honour to make allusion to the 'Major' [John Fletcher] and our fracus of olden times about Lake Superior[40] ...

---

[40] In the autumn of 1816 Samuel Gale, Lord Selkirk's legal advisor, accompanied the Royal Commission led by William Coltman and John Fletcher as they travelled west from Montreal to Lake Superior to investigate the disturbances at Selkirk's Red River Colony. At the same time, McDonald, who had left the settlement to spend the summer in England, reporting on events to Selkirk's people there, got back to Montreal in time to take charge of a group of former de Meurons soldier settlers and their wives en route to Red River. Fletcher, who had been imbibing rather too freely of liquor, apprehended the party at Sault Ste Marie, claiming they were a military force, and forbade them to continue the journey. He took McDonald into custody, and it took all Gale's and McDonald's rhetorical skills to convince the commissioner that he was in error. See Cole, *Exile in the Wilderness.*

Those were strange times – a retrospective glance at them now would make one almost persuade himself twas all a dream ...

Fort Colvile, 30 November 1841

To Hugh Taylor, Montreal

Unwilling to trouble Mr Justice Gale any longer with the charge of my little money matters in Canada, I am recommended to you Sir for doing the needful, and unacquainted as I am at present with the proper form of power of attorney I hope in meantime this will answer every purpose. The money transactions in the hands of His Honour commenced in the fall of 1834 by a Bill of Exchange on London for the sum of one thousand pounds sterling, to which I added the following spring the further sum of one hundred & fifty dollars. On receipt of this you will therefore please compare notes with the Judge and assume management of the said amounts with accumulations thereon till further notice ...

Private to Taylor, same date

I fear you will think it intrusive in me on so slight an acquaintance to address you the annexed letter, but from your well-known commiseration for all us poor N'Westers ... I flatter myself I am not mistaken in the favour I solicit.

... I believe I have something to do with the LaPrairie Railroad & from all that can be gleaned from the public prints seems to be doing well enough. The present patriotic spirit for public improvements in the United province would lead one to expect good interest from money so invested. Should you therefore discover a promising spec in that way or indeed in any other way such as mortgages ... I think by the time I can hear from you I could place at your disposal 500 pounds more & perhaps be able to continue it for some years to the tune of three or four hundred pounds annually.

Fort Colvile, 2 January 1842

To Donald Manson, Thompson River

... glad to hear things were restored to so favourable a condition at Thompson River. [Cameron] now returns with the felling axes, pitsaw files, the barley, butter & other little wants that constituted his errand ...

Fort Colvile, 7 January 1842

To Gentlemen in charge of Districts and Posts on the communication from Vancouver to Red River Settlement

On the 28th of last month Mr Sinclair left this place ... for east side ... but on account of the unusual depth of snow already on the ground

... was reluctantly compelled to relinquish all hopes of getting thro the journey and accordingly was back here again his fifth day. Still we are about making a second attempt with nothing but Sir George Simpson's packet in charge of two men as little encumbered as possible, trusting they may reach some of the Cree camps near the height of land before the end of the month ...

Fort Colvile, 18 January 1842

To James Douglas, Fort Vancouver

It is now about the time I usually make up our winter communication for you below & most cheerfully would I do so now did I see the prospect of a canoe getting to W.W. The snow early in the winter set in hereabouts exceedingly severe. Mr Sinclair joined us 17th of last month, after taking seven days to do the 55 miles from the [Tshimakain] mission to here. On 28th he recommenced his journey as well arranged as it was possible to be, accompanied by LaGraisse, his own Indian & another from here ... even with the help of three extra Indians, [their progress] became exceedingly slow & indeed the journey altogether hopeless ... at the end of the fifth day were again back to us ...

... I had official orders to send [LaGraisse] off from here in the spring with 35 or 40 *of our horses* for the height of land that would ultimately be driven on to Edmonton. Now as regards the horses, I wish it to be definitely understood that we have no such bands at our disposal here, & that I very much fear from the loss already sustained scarcely enough will live to see the spring for our own indispensable duties ...

We had Mr Cameron also with us for a few days from T.R. He left that place with 2,000 salmon for OK about 7th Decr & arrived here 27th after a very tedious & harassing trip of it ... sometime with horses, then by water & finally on snowshoes ...

Mr McPherson with the Flathead people was lucky enough to get home before the snow was too deep. His collection in furs, considering everything, is pretty fair: the Beaver are within *a few* to the number of last year & the amount of all the furs from that quarter rather better, notwithstanding the loss on freemen's hunt ... In grease ... woefully short ... [because of supplying] the new missionaries ... His two men Brouillet & Leclair go out, as they are refused their *freedom*, Lafentasie, Wacon & Pion *take it*. Neither is little Pierre yet settled with, & Joachim & old Pierre are fairly done up; Canote however thinks himself able enough to serve another year. You will therefore have the goodness, as far as possible, to place 4 or 5 good hands at my disposal by the Express Boats ...

... Mr DeSmet, who was down to us for supplies in the month of

Novr wished our requisition to include the value of 30 pieces for them, but however willing we may be to accommodate those good people in ordinary matters, I distinctly say that so far as depends upon myself, I do not wish to have anything to do with their supplies, & this I candidly told the Rev Gentleman himself. We loaded 14 horses for him here, principally in provisions & field seed & he left us 400 dollars in Specie to meet that & future demands. He speaks of being down this way again about the middle of April to proceed to Vancouver by the first conveyance that may then offer.

Enclosed is a list of the few things we absolutely require per the Express Boats ... I shall expect to be allowed one Boat exclusively for the conveyance of a threshing mill this way next summer ...

Fort Colvile, 18 January 1842

To Sir George Simpson, Fort Vancouver (Private)

We are all again under deep obligation to you for the Budget of November & the best account we ever had of affairs on the Northwest coast ... reached me beginning of December ...

Poor Mr Sinclair very much against his own inclination, is upon our hands ... will I suppose favour us with his company till spring.

Mr Rowand writes me very pressingly about horses, in lieu of those brought across by the settlers & for some other undefined purposes about the height of land in July. As regards horses being replaced from here, the thing is out of the question ... no insurmountable impediment to our mounting enough between this place & Walla Walla to go *to the height of land* in July if required. Our friend [Rowand], it is clear to me, though in such good company & making quite a gala of it among Generalissimos, Excellencies & even Majesty itself, has his eye to the old Fort des Prairies [Fort Edmonton].

Were it not an uncharitable feeling in one to envy the happy lot of another, I should say such were mine in reference to those enjoying the present delightful trip round by California & the royal city of Honolooloo. Nor do I think, did my years & corpulency admit of so arduous an undertaking, I would relish the rest of the voyage to the very Siberian jaunt [Ogden accompanied Simpson to Siberia].

... I shall reserve a long yarn till in the inscrutable nature of things we are placed further apart ...

Fort Colvile, 19 January 1842

To Rev Elkanah Walker, Tshimakain Mission

Spokane Garry came in with [your letter] this forenoon just as we were preparing to start Atatie for Walla Walla, which they now do together on Friday as far as Spokane. Seemingly the snow is as great your way as it is hereabouts – poor Mr Sinclair had a tough job of it getting here ... by the bye, did both your horses get back? for you only speak of one ... they could not be found at all the morning of the day Mr S. got here ... The furnishing of them is another item in the catalogue of your kind offices ...

Until Garry came in Mr Sinclair & self had it in contemplation to pay you all a visit, but the undertaking I find would be too formidable, especially for a man of my corporation. I shall speak to Garry on the propriety of becoming one of your communicants. He & Atatie will of course pass your way ...

Fort Colvile, 18 February 1842

To Rev Elkanah Walker, Tshimakain Mission

Many thanks for your kind attentions in the post office department. The last Indian came in yesterday with Tatie's news, which is not exceedingly cheering ... The box [your Indian] carries from here will hold the package for your place ... which you will please see and nail up the box as before. He & Tatie start together for the cache ... we send him shoes & a little ammunition & tobacco & I think you may as well let him have the use of Bighead's gun ...

... I am sorry to hear things continue so critically with them at Whilatpu. The very same sensation you speak of seizes myself the moment I see a letter from that quarter, for assuredly I do not feel easy on their account all over.[41]

And again, the big man of the Stoney Islands is a d—d rascal whose influence will very little mend the manners of our men – all I hear of their pranks below I perfectly believe ... Probably Dr W. when he comes may find that he can spare us a few days here. If so, tell him we shall be most happy to see him. I suppose his Lady won't come out in such a dreary season of the year ... Our great men that went to sea, great & privileged as they were, could not make their peace with the mighty monarch of the deep, for three whole weeks detained in Baker's Bay.

... Everything to the northward of us looks bleak & dreary – not a biped moving & but I believe very few quadrapeds. Let us know anything you or the families may be in want of, without reserve ...

[41] McDonald repeatedly expressed his concern about the safety of the Whitmans and the unpredictability of the Cayouse in the neighbourhood of the Waiilatpu mission. His fears were borne out in 1847 when Marcus and Narcissa Whitman and eleven others at their mission were murdered by the Cayouse.

Fort Colvile, 1 March 1842

To Mr DeSmet, Flathead district

... In order that we may be sure of enough [grease] by the spring Boat, I hope you will direct the Indians coming out from the plains to proceed at once with all they may have to the Horse plain or little house for Mr McPherson ...

Fort Colvile, 14 March 1842

To Rev Elkanah Walker, Tshimakain Mission

... Will you have the goodness to tell the doctor that we would much wish to have from Mrs Gray the age of our children – a strange request is it not? The fact is, the two little chaps, when the mother was indisposed last season, took a wonderful liking to books & pictures & behold the leaf with the names in the prayer book disappeared. In the case of Alexander & Allan [at Red River] we would like to have it at once, as the poor little fellows are about taking a trip to Europe this spring & it looks awkward not to have their ages to a day, which we think Mrs Gray took down in her pocket book when here from W.W. ...

I have again spoken to Garry on the propriety of his attaching himself closely to the mission, which I think he is disposed to do.

Fort Colvile, 22 March 1842

To Patrick McKenzie, Flathead House

... Of your original destination for the Kootenais ... you make not even so much as a single allusion in your note to that place or to the trip you was to have made there yourself. This is not the way in which we can get on together. I chalk out duties for you & you chalk out for me the duties I ought to give you. Mr McKenzie this won't do; but as matters now stand & trusting to more useful exertions from you in future, I have decided on employing you for the early part of the season watching a very useful band of Indians conducted by the chief called Fruse and to that effect have given directions to Mr McPherson so to employ you en attendant.

Fort Colvile, 22 March 1842

To John McPherson, Flathead House

You are again about setting out in charge of the Flathead and plains Outfit and having already had a year's experience very little more is necessary than reference to my last instructions ... Your party will consist of Martin, McLeod & old Pierre & Mr Patrick McKenzie also will be placed under your orders ...

Wacon and the horsekeeper accompany you to the Boat and the directions you will there give them with respect to the horses must altogether depend on where you meet the Boat and the state of the snow ... I am not aware that the Racine Amer [Bitter Root] Mission will be making any demand on you that will put you to much inconvenience. Mr DeSmet I understand is going down for his own supplies & you are only furnished with the goods necessary for the trade ...

Fort Colvile, 30 March 1842

To Edward Ermatinger, St Thomas, Upper Canada

... Your very kind & communicative favour of 25th March came duly to hand. What a pity a few of us eloquent & patriotic Northwesters were not alongside of you when you took the field in the last honourable campaign.[42] By Jove those Radical Parkes [Thomas Parke] and Clenches [Joseph Clench] would have to take it, & if no other road to success could be found we might be tempted to *clench them* ... But what in the world is all this electioneering turmoil to end in! I'll be hanged, after reading files of your Canada papers of both creeds, if I even can make out who is a Whig or who is a Tory, who is for doing good from who is bent on doing evil, much less who is to win or who is to lose. All seems to be a new order of things, regulated by a love or hatred to the Governor General [Charles Poulett Thomson, Lord Sydenham] – a reunion or no reunion, & I believe a something too pending place or pension. Amongst you all in goodness' name let good care be taken of the Queen's American dominions. I thank you very kindly for the few Nos of the *Patriot* – poor Thomas Dalton [founder of the *Patriot*], the champion of the constitutional cause, I see has gone the way of all flesh. Confound that fellow [Francis] Hincks,[43] could he not have been kept out of the pool of honour. But who is he, this new court satellite that very nearly ousted our beloved cousin Sir Allan [MacNab]?[44] Unfortunately am no politician, still I have my eye on your movements & would I think have become a violent partisan in the good cause had my lot been cast among you.

I am ordering up from Lachine the new monthly *Review* announced

---

[42] In his unsuccessful campaign to become member for Middlesex in the Legislative Assembly of the United Provinces in 1841, Ermatinger was opposed by Thomas Parke (the winner) and Joseph Clench. Ermatinger was elected in 1844 and served until 1847.
[43] Francis Hincks, a reformer, was editor of the Toronto weekly *Examiner* and member of the Legislative Assembly.
[44] MacNab, who ran as a Conservative in Hamilton riding in 1841, defeated Samuel B. Harrison, a protégé of the governor general Lord Sydenham. Harrison was elected that same year in another election in Kingston. MacNab became Speaker of the House in 1844.

by John Wandby. Will it give anything like a fair statement of the opinions of parties in the united Legislature? I shall be most happy to hear
that our friend Colin R[obertson][45] has distinguished himself as a Senator more than his old colleagues are willing to allow he did as Indian
trader. How nicely he walked over the cause in opposition to such able
men as [C.J.] Forbes & McCord. I find John George [McTavish], [John]
McBean & Pheris only aspire to the dignity of grand Jurors. Your friend
the Cavalry Captain does more – he edified the Queen's lieges on the
noble science of bark canoe steering, with I suppose a voyageur song,
tho the regatta notice does not say so. Happy fellows altogether, instead
of being immured & shut up from society beyond the R. Mountain barrier as we luckless beings are.

   This season however there has been some novelty west side itself.
Sir George & suite along would at any time be a treat; add to this our
other distinguished visitor Commodore [Capt Charles] Wilkes with his
squadron of 5 ships & countless number of scientific men exploring the
country far & wide in their respective departments, & a place so famed
as Colvile for its beautiful sceneries, & as some say its domestic comforts, you may be sure was not a dead blank on their carte de route. Of
course the kettle of fish they made of it on our Columbia bar with one
of their splendid sloops of war is known to the world before now. The
greatest treasure they had on board – several tons of earth from the new
Antarctic continent with which to ornament the Washington promenades – is now singular enough intermixed with Oregon soils! & this
fact will no doubt be made use of to strengthen their future claim to the
country – that is this country. Another memorable event is the migration this way of some of the Red River settlers under the conduct of Mr
James Sinclair. Frank will tell you of two other caravans from the U.S.
[Elijah White party] on the same scent, namely to locate themselves in
the Umpqua & California. Hur-ra for the 'far' west.

   The Jesuit College too is in rapid progress under the superintendence of Father DeSmet, a Belgian. Father [Nicholas] Point ... & Mr

---

[45] Colin Robertson was elected to the Legislative Assembly in 1841 as member for Deux
   Montagnes. He and McDonald first met at Jack River in July 1815, after the destruction of the Red River Settlement by a group of Métis led by NWC men. McDonald,
   who had brought the colonists to seek refuge at Jack River (Norway House), decided
   to return to England to give a first-hand report of the troubles at the settlement. He
   put the colonists in charge of Robertson, who led them back to Red River to rebuild
   their homes. Robertson was an influential figure in the discussions leading up to the
   merger of the HBC and NWC in 1821. He died less than a year after his election, on
   3 February 1842, when he was thrown from his sleigh. See Cole, *Exile in the Wilderness*.

Belgamini [Fr Gregorio Mengarini], a young ecclesiastic red hot from the Vatican anvil ... DeSmet was down here for his wants in the month of November. The next event of importance with us is the arrival last summer of two droves of sheep & cattle from California, the one of 3,000 head & the other of 500.

... Poor Pambrun you will be sorry to hear followed Black in the month of May ... & poor [William] Kittson followed his voltigeur brother officer in the month of December. They say tis a bad wind that blows nobody good. Those two vacant commissions [Pambrun and Black] are, I believe, to fall to the share of your brother & myself, at least I have it from the *very best* authority that this is to be the disposition of them for Outfit '42 ... [Frank] has again changed quarters; he is now off to the southward [California] & consequently you cannot expect to see him down before fall '43. Then indeed, if so inclined, I think he can take a holiday, but probably this matrimonial alliance he is still in pursuit of may influence him even then. He is very close with me on the subject, & indeed every other subject since I last had the pleasure of addressing you. The truth is, Frank in many of his ways is somewhat changeable & finding us all, that is his old cronies, disapprove of any passion or policy of his that would subject him to a *second refusal* in the Big House,[46] (the fair one's individual merits always excepted) makes him now perhaps less pleased with himself & I dare say less disposed to be communicative with his friends ...

... [The governor] left [here] 20th & their sixth day landed at Vancouver. On 1st Sept, joined by James Douglas, the party was off to Puget Sound, there embarked in the steamer for Sitka & the intermediate posts & was back 22nd Octr. His Excellency is since away in one of the sailing vessels accompanied this time by the big doctor for Oahoo & California, to be back early in April with the view of sailing again for Sitka & thence in a Russian vessel for Siberia, finally cross the old world by land to Petersburgh & thus show to the world that as a traveller his Knighthood is not undeservedly bestowed. Rowand was taken ill by the fever & ague & remained at Stikine till the return of the steamer attended by three halfbreed doctors – his son, John Kennedy & John McLoughlin Jr. He passes the winter at Vancouver under the care of Dr [Forbes] Barclay & is I believe doing well. He would have given his two 85ths on this current year that he was back at his favourite Fort des Prairies. It was exactly a month after Sir George's arrival here that James Sinclair

---

[46] Frank was courting McLoughlin's step-granddaughter Catherine Sinclair, whom he later married.

& the new migration of Red River settlers consisting of 130 souls cast up by the same route, as I have already said. Strange enough many of them are the children & grandchildren of Governors [Thomas] Thomas, [James] Bird, [W.H.] Cook, [James] Sutherland &c &c. I hear the Canadian half of them, or rather the half professing the R.C. creed, are located on the Cowlitz farm to raise tithe for the priests, & the heretic half on Whidbey's Island in the Sound to be the hewers of wood & carriers of water. I will not pretend to say what this new colony of ours may come to, but upon my word in my own mind's eye at present I fear with such settlers it will be long before our stock rates at a premium.

In reference to my son, seemingly it would be a waste of time to say much. I believe I told you last year of the application I was about making in his behalf to return to the hopeful Indian country, & of course would have seen Finlayson's note from R.R. ... the governor himself has since informed me that to meet my views he had forwarded my son's name to Fenchurch Street [Hudson's Bay Company headquarters in London] before he left Red River & thought it probable notice of his appointment would reach St Thomas early in the spring. He may or may not make good use of this opening made for him. One advantage he will have by receiving the appointment thro Their Honours is of being placed on the footing of apprentice *clerk*, instead of *apprentice*, as is the case with all those received into the service from the country. Unwilling to lose this chance & to make assurance doubly sure, I by the Cape Horn vessel enclosed Mr Secty [William] Smith my own application direct to the Board, for him to present in the event of his finding the governor's recommendation overlooked or mislaid. And this is all I can do for the benefit of the Gentleman. You will however, as I have no doubt either the one or the other application will be attended to, have the goodness to continue your kind offices to him & keep him about you till you hear from London ... & look to me for a discharge of the bill of expense ...

... Your very just & pious allusion to the journey still before us to the Elysian encampment impeded with neither pas d'ours [snowshoes] or marrons [unbroken horses] I shall endeavour to make practical use of. In this way however it will please you much to hear that our Columbia morals within the last few years are manifestly improving; still if we say we have no sin we deceive ourselves & truth is not in us.

I am at fault in writing this far without once alluding to Mrs E. & the young lady. Ranald too gives us a very interesting acct of both, & by way of raising the character of Miss Maria says her birthday differs but a few hours from that of the Princess Royal of England – what a propitious day!! With my whole brood of ten I think I cannot in one instance come within weeks to any one of the numerous progeny of good George the Third. Our last, another boy [Samuel], is now about 6 months old. His twin brothers are very fine little fellows, now that they begin to speak becoming exceedingly interesting. In features, voices, height & colour of hair they are so alike as scarcely to know the difference & to mend the matter their mother, to a thread, keeps them in the same kind of garb. Were you at this moment to see them, assisted by an older brother [John] going five years who thinks himself amazingly wise with tables, chairs, sofas, cushions, tongs, broomsticks, cats, dogs & all other imaginable things they can lay their hands on strewed around me, you would say 'twas a delightful confusion, & then exclaim 'McDonald, how the deuce can you write with such a racket about you.' So much for the nursery, & did I not know that I was addressing himself an indulgent Father I would not presume to dwell quite so long on the subject. The good wife herself Thank God is very well & always grateful for your very kind remembrance of her. Allow us the honour of tendering you & Mrs E. our united respects & good wishes, & to the young Miss a kiss in our name, trusting the day may yet come when we can do all this personally, despite all you hear in praise of Oregon, the P.S.A. Co., priests, deacons & all the rest of it. Assuredly, unless my mind is *very much* changed, I am not for perpetuating my own exile in the wilderness from a mere romantic notion of founding colonies for future generations. Tell my good old companions in misery Mr Angus McKay & Lady,[47] first time you see them that I am much flattered by their kind remembrances. Angus decidedly was always the most correct & efficient man in my squad in

[47] Angus McKay and his wife Jean, both aged twenty, were among the party of Selkirk settlers brought from Scotland by McDonald to Churchill in the fall of 1813. In April 1814, they and forty-nine of the group formed an advance party that preceded the rest of the colonists to the settlement. Led by McDonald, they walked 150 miles along the trail from Churchill to York Factory; from there, they travelled by boat and on foot up the Hayes River to Lake Winnipeg, arriving at the Forks of the Red and Assiniboine rivers on 22 June. Along the way, just seven days from Churchill, Jean collapsed after falling on the ice, and McDonald's medical training was called into use when he discovered she was four months pregnant and in danger of miscarrying. After her treatment and two days of rest, the main group of settlers continued on to York Factory, leaving the McKays and several other stragglers to stay behind with one of the Native hunters accompanying the party. They rested and awaited McDonald's return to rejoin their fellows at the factory and to continue their journey. Jean McKay's son John was born on 23 August 1814 at the Red River Settlement; he was baptised by McDonald in a ceremony recorded on the first page of the register of St John's Church (now St John's Cathedral, Winnipeg). The McKays later went east and settled near St Thomas. See Cole, *Exile in the Wilderness*.

'13 & '14, and please intimate from me not only to Mr McKay but to all my old friends about Aldborough (in my time I believe called 'Long Point' but Angus was then near Newmarket on Yonge Street) that, until I go down myself to claim their suffrages as good loyal citizens … it is my earnest desire they support one who has already done so much & whose sole aim would be to do still more without fee or reward, for the prosperity of the county of Middlesex … That Gentleman, need I say, is Mr Justice Ermatinger of St. Thomas … don't forget my admonition to the Churchill pilgrims.

16th April – Up to this date I am without seeing anyone from the low country. My letters however by the plains intimate Mr [Alexander Caulfield] Anderson's departure from W.W. on 1st with two Boats, & ought I think to be here tonight. This young Gentleman's father is one of your U.C. citizens, Capt Anderson about Lake Simcoe. The youth is now James Birnie's son-in-law; his lady is to pass the summer with us here till his return from York Factory … Mr Allan, the last accomptant, is now at the Islands, the associate of our [George] Pelly & Squire Rae is the man of business in connection with them in California.

I have just received a long brotherly letter from our worthy & most esteemed mortal friend John Work … Poor man, like us all he is rapidly on the decline. The New Caledonia accounts reached me some days ago. Our other friend in that quarter [Tod] favoured me with a sheet too & from him in like manner I see to your address a good budget as well as to the host of other Tods now about you. He made a short sojourn at T.R. & certainly acquitted himself well in the critical situation he was placed, whether they give him credit for it or not. Manson is now the champion of that district. That Gentleman passed ten days with us here in the fall, his wife was below, he broke out in a case that might be called double adultery, the vixen at the end of 4 months brought about an abortion, & this creditable case is the first in which I have been called upon to preside as one of Her Majesty's justices of the peace for the Indian Territories. In my Magisterial capacity I wrote him the other day; he came down to OK to meet his lawful family. Perhaps I'll hear from him by Anderson.

While writing you this I am much bothered with a new race of men come on my hands: all the freemen about Jasper's Ho. They are come across to settle at the Racine Amer alongside my new priests & as habitants, depend upon it, they are in want of enough! But among their besoins [needs] not one has yet mentioned the words 'Beaver Trap.' What a change in the world –

… To conclude, I shall once more revert to my son. For God's sake don't lose sight of him until he is fairly embarked in that concern which I believe is the most suitable for every mother's son of them, bad as it has proved for many ...

Fort Colvile, 19 April 1842

To James Douglas, Fort Vancouver

... Mr Anderson with two Boats arrived here the day before yesterday. The supply of goods sent up is very handsome & seems to have come in most opportunely for all the Jasper House freemen dropped down here with Berland the other day to have themselves equipped for a settlement on the Racine Amer, and this moment people from Mr DeSmet too presented themselves for a large supply in ammunition, tobacco, Blankets &c &c for that quarter. I believe I have already noticed the manner in which we happened to fall short of grease last fall. In March I wrote up to the mission to beg that the Indians gone to the cattle might be allowed to pass on with that article to meet our Boats at the little house middle of this month. The Rev Gentleman now writes me as follows from the horse plain: 'I have the honour to acknowledge the receipt of your two letters of March. The winter has been very severe on the Racine Amer & famine & starvation was at our very door, with consequence spent all our provisions & ammunition to feed the needy & destitute Indians.' Now it is clear that at this rate we can no longer depend on the Indians for grease ... I am aware it is a sort of grievance that is not likely to excite much commiseration but it is nevertheless a most serious one to us, & one that must speedily be adjusted some way or other. My next object of distress is sacking, & the real object of the courier. Grain is called for from I may say every point of the compass, & I leave yourselves to judge how far a couple of pieces [of cloth for sacks] will enable me to meet the demand. Of the stock of last year 15 yards of the Osnaburgh is all that is on hand & of the sheeting not a foot. Chev'x skins too, which are occasionally turned to some account in that way, have entirely failed. So that altogether unless some stuff for Bags is here by 25th May the Boats must go down *light*.

LaGraisse was not back to the Kootenais till three days after Berland's departure. He however cast up here yesterday, the bearer of what is called the HB northern winter packet, which I forward without delay. We have now here three of Mr Rowand's men & three Indians that accompanied LaGraisse awaiting his orders ... With respect to the men, nothing decisive can yet be said, but if we can judge from the strong feeling there is among them to cross, it is my opinion the same number of Bouts & middlemen as last year ought to come up for the Brigade. The present courier is directed to bring on for us the 30 horses you are good enough to order us from W.W. as we stand much in need of them ...

To Sir George Simpson

I was much honoured by rect this morning of your very obliging favour of 12th March thru royal city of Honolooloo, & almost as much delighted to hear of the gay life the Columbians enjoyed on their recent cruise to California & the Islands as if I were of the party myself. Mr Anderson has been here for some time ... and now the only delay is in closing up of the business ... The collection of Beaver on this Outfit certainly does not appear to have improved on that of the former, but I think the amt of the general returns will be found very handsome, say close upon 45,000 pounds. Of this sum perhaps 20,000 pounds will go to cover expenses & I am not aware that as yet in any one year you much surpassed 25,000 on the Columbia. With myself here the Beaver are about 100 less, but the amt of our furs is above 300 pounds more than Outfit '40 and consequently profits proportionately better. We might still make something of it in this region were we perfectly quiet & the Natives left undisturbed, but it is evident everything must be deranged by the presence of so many new faces. The priests with all the riff-raff gathering about them have already plunged us into considerable distress. My people just returned from that quarter bring me not an ounce of grease for the consumption of the Establishment ...

Another evil that is gaining ground on us that is likely ere long to prove very serious is the reluctance of the servants to renew their engagements. No fewer than five and thirty of the most efficient men in the country go out this spring, most of them with the avowed intention of returning free & independent by some defile of the R. Mountains. We could do without *them*, but the example is likely to be followed by others & the move become general ... My own two half breed aides are also for being off – McPherson pleads hard to be released from serving the last two years of his five, and Patrick McKenzie has just sent me down a very peremptory notice of his being out next spring & of his intention to quit the service. Indeed it is my opinion but few of those young men in these days of idle speculation & foolery will be reconciled to the service on the footing they find themselves placed. One thing very certain, in the peculiar duty the man with me has to perform, it is not a fickle or a casual comer & goer I ought to have, but a rising man fixed to the service that will see it in his interest to qualify himself for the general good & act accordingly. A smart European apprentice of two or three years standing would be the man for our plains business at present.

As regards my poor organ, I am extremely sorry that I should quite inadvertantly be the cause of so much loss to the Company in getting out such an article. The truth of the matter is, Mr Manson on his way home the other year kindly offered his services in England for us; an organ was talked of in preference to a musical box. I immediately drew out a Bill for 10 pounds. Everyone present pronounced anything of the kind for that money a paltry affair; I destroyed that Bill & made out one for 20 pounds. On leaving England, Manson, it would appear, placed the order in the hands of Pelly, Simpson & Co and this very morning also I received Sir John Pelly's bill of parcel sent with the article, something in cost & charges to thirty-two Guineas, & thus my musical box has at length extended ... when most assuredly any sound contained within [a smaller] compass ... would have charmed my ear all the same. So that if I have sinned in this way it is very innocently – evidently the purchase was a stupid one. Now however that the thing is in the country, I suppose we won't be sending it back, but I won't incur further displeasure by attempting in any shape to get it up this way without special license for so doing.

The Fort des Prairies Chieftain [Rowand] I expect by the end of May. He is still very boisterous about horses. Unfortunately the greater part of ours died last winter from its excessive severity ... I allude more particularly to Mr Douglas' clear & flattering statement on the affairs of the [Puget's Sound] Agricultural Society. I have just filled up the power of attorney required of me in connexion with that association ... as well as the one required of me in behalf of the Norway [Pelly & Company lumber] business and I trust that in both cases our expectations sometime or other may be completely realized.

Fort Colvile, 26 April 1842

To John McLoughlin

I had the pleasure of receiving your various communications of the 8th three days ago & was most happy to hear of your safe & speedy return to us again.

The other day on discovering the want of sheeting [to make flour bags] I lost no time in advertising you all of the fact & the serious disappointment it would lead to if not speedily supplied. The deficiency in boat nails too I find more extensive than I was then aware of but the most alarming case of all is the total want of grease. A man sent off to meet the Boat to bring us immediate relief is just back with the astounding intelligence that not one ounce is come down in the Boat nor is anywhere else in prospect for us before the month of Decr.

With the little butter we had in, contrived to serve out the people till now, and the remainder of it supplies the Express men tomorrow. It will scarcely be credited that not a pound could be had this morning with which to mix the grain for the Boats. This I hope is quite enough to give you an adequate idea of the difficulties we have fallen into, & I must say all arising out of the stretch made last fall to accommodate the Racine Amer mission with no less than 28 Bales mixed meat & fat, in the belief that a good haul would have reached us at the Flathead House this spring. The case unfortunately is seen to be otherwise. If any remained at the Racine Amer, seemingly it is for the missionaries themselves as they sent down to me for ammunition & tobacco to secure it.

... Until we have some relief from below by the two men now sent down, our people here must have the wherewith to season their grain from the pork & ham intended for New Caledonia. Before the scanty supply of last fall came to hand they actually refused to work on grain alone.

Wacon takes down agres for six horses which it is expected he can find at W.W. and I write Mr McKinlay that the smart plan would be to let them have that number down to the Dalles to whip up at once whatever might be sent by them.

Fort Colvile, 27 April 1842

To James Hargrave, York Factory

... I have a boy [Archy Jr.] at Red River going home this fall & it would confer great favour on me to see that he is looked after while at York Factory & provided with a suitable passage home in the special care of the Captain should none of our old N. West friends be making a holiday of it across the big water in the same ship. Mr Finlayson is to direct his movements from R.R. to York & Mr Secty Smith is to do the rest.[48]

... I could wish you to recommend me some good snuff at York – they absolutely starve me in this way at Vancouver.

[48] James Hargrave was in charge at York Factory, the port on Hudson Bay where he supervised the disposition of cargoes of incoming and outgoing ships. Far-flung HBC colleagues depended on him to look after their personal needs. These included not only special orders of material things, but also, as in this case, the welfare of their young children who were being sent to school in England.

Fort Colvile, 26 May 1842

To Sir George Simpson, Hudson's Bay House, London

... I cannot allow Mr Secretary [Edward Hopkins] to start from the far west direct for England without troubling you again with a few lines. He & our most esteemed friend the Fort des Prairies Chief joined us here some days ago where, I am happy to say, all their wants are now completely made up. The two horses mentioned for Red River are added to the band & the best of the kind at my disposal. The party will I fear, owing to high waters have a very harassing trip of it, but from the certainty of there being snow in the mountains till well advanced in the season they can afford to march slowly ...

I was much edified by a perusal of the able exposé of the state of affairs along the Pacific submitted to us by Mr Hopkins, & I dare say all the changes & improvements in contemplation in the existing state of the country are the very best that could have been adopted, although it is very clear we cannot now anywhere get on half so well as when pure Beaver was the order of the day.

... Mr Ogden's men have not yet made their appearance to assist us down with our Boats. All goes on well enough with us at Colvile with the exception of one thing, the total want of grease. When our own exertions in this way proved a failure owing to the monopoly of the priests & their new congregation about the Racine Amer, I immediately sent off to Vancouver but I am sorry to say that this morning my people were sent back to me without one ounce of the needful. So much for the vexations of one where the means of getting on are no longer within his own control ...

Fort Colvile, 30 May 1842

To Messrs Ogden & Manson, Okanagan

... [received] yours of 25th announcing your safe arrival that day at Okanagan. Mr Cameron & party got here Saturday forenoon & had we been favoured with a note from the Forks we might possibly have got them off the same day. I notice what you say of Boats; we managed to finish [building] the last of 5 on Thursday evening & it was then too late to begin a sixth when it was only on that very day the nails arrived from Vancouver. However we have six good ones for you notwithstanding that will this moment be under weigh with 250 pieces as per enclosed disposition list, besides families.

... Mr Cameron & the two Guides will I hope conduct all in safety to the Grosse Roche where I understand they will be met with horses from Okanagan. The number of men from here is 14, including Wacon & Lafentasie, of the Vancouver men 5, of yours 29 ...

With respect to the wants of this district, I suppose tis as well to pass them at once under the notice of Mr C.F. McLoughlin ... I am grateful for the few pounds of grease sent up because it is more than I [got] from headquarters after a trip of 1,000 miles for it. We however killed a horse the other day which after boiling down the meat yielded about enough of oil to prepare grain for the Boats. In making up the ladings below I trust you will not overlook that indispensable article for us, as without grease at Colvile one may say he is without men ...

I have in like manner to beg that in passing Walla Walla you will have the goodness to acquaint Mr McKinlay that it is my intention in a few days to send to him for the 30 horses Mr Douglas wrote me I could have to replace the 33 (besides the 20 from W.W.) Mr Rowand left this with the other day.

As to men, I suppose I must trust to chance as usual. Three of our best Canadians went out this spring, & three of our Native engagés will be independent tomorrow. That famous man William Pion is at length free, now in possession of a stock of horned cattle obtained from the Red River settlers & a precious scoundrel he will make. He this moment came in to me to ask a passage to the Wallamette which I knew to be a mere fetch in order to get his family to Okanagan.

The arrangement you propose with respect to the T.R. supplies from here is a settled point. Saddles & appèchements are kept for that purpose, but no wrappers, cords or palettes. Mr Cameron can take the boar & the bull too if he chooses, which we the more cheerfully give as there is neither beef, pork or bacon.

This man Monique with his clique of associates gives me a great deal of annoyance when here. I wish they could be informed from the proper authorities below that while with me they are liable to work & subject to my orders ...

Fort Colvile, 30 May 1842

To John McLoughlin, Fort Vancouver

By return of our two men from Vancouver on Thursday last I was handed yours of 10th inst but much to my disappointment without an ounce of grease. There are a good many points which I thought might very advantageously be talked over together by us this summer & which I foresee no paper communication can obviate.

Six of our men left us this spring, besides Joachim, Philippe Lajoie &

Duquette whom I hope it is intended to replace with hands equal to the arduous duties the Colvile men have to perform.

... Herewith I also send down the district accounts with separate statements of the Flathead and Kootenais trade ... I have given old Philippe & Joachim with his family a passage down in the Boats, also Lajoie's wife & the wife of A. Martineau. Peter Grant too with his family goes down as far as Okanagan. It is quite a mistake to suppose that so many useless hands can be maintained at Colvile without feeling it & had there been fewer of that description our effective men might have fared today better than they do. Our grain of last year is now in a fair way to becoming very low. Three hundred bushels of seed is now in the ground but the question is how to secure the harvest should providence prosper the crops ...

Fort Colvile, 8 June 1842

To John McLoughlin, Fort Vancouver

Yesterday morning a confused report thru Indians reached us of the melancholy fate of our poor people, which but too truly was confirmed by authentic accounts from OK this morning.[49] It is a most lamentable case, & apart from what we must all feel as fellow men, one that is likely to have the effect of increasing our difficulties here. By a glance at the names of the men equipped for this district last year, they will now be found 13 less [including those assigned elsewhere], namely: Canote Umphreville, P. Martineau, D. Flett, H. Brouillet, C. Robiard, T. LeClair, W. Pion, C. Lafentasie, Wacon Umphreville, P. Lajoie, Ant. Duquette, Joachim Hubert, Philippe Desgrais ...

Fort Colvile, 8 June 1842

To Archibald McKinlay, Walla Walla

Having notified to Mr Ogden for your information my intention of sending for the horses as soon as I could, young Canote and our Indian courier now leave me for that purpose. Thirty of the best you can muster are expected ... The two lads leave me a few days sooner than I intended ... with the view of carrying to you in time a second report I am obliged to make in consequence of the painful affair at the OK Dalles, which it is highly expedient should reach Vancouver as early as possible ...

[49] Five men drowned when one of the boats in the brigade was swamped in the Dalles above Okanagan. They were Canote Umphreville (the guide), Pierre Martineau, David Flett, Louison Boucher, and André Areuhoniante.

Excuse me if I don't say more on this occasion. The lamentable tale you will have heard of has thrown me into a painful state of mind – My Guide [Canote Umphreville], my Miller [Pierre Martineau] & my own servant [David Flett] all gone!!! What a sad blow poor Martineau's wife has sustained within the short space of the same three days – on the 3rd of the month, three days after she lost her father, her husband, and nearly her brother, her only boy of six years old was killed here on the spot by the rolling down upon him of one of our fence boullins while in the act of climbing over it ...

Fort Colvile, June 1842

To Rev Elkanah Walker, Tshimakain Mission
    ... The Calamity you allude to has certainly been a severe blow to our Establishment – three of my principal & most trustworthy servants. 'When we are in life we are in the midst of death' – Another most painful occurrence amongst us came to my knowledge on Monday: the death of John McLoughlin Junr who was shot on the spot at Fort Stikine

Les Dalles, Columbia River, painted by Henry Warre in August 1845. It was here, 'in the overwhelming whirlpools,' that three of the Colvile men drowned in the summer of 1842 when their boat capsized en route from the fort to Fort Vancouver. 'My Guide, my Miller & my own servant all gone!!!' McDonald lamented. (National Archives of Canada C41437)

northwest coast middle of April by one of his own men. The assassin is carried to Sitka by Gov Simpson to be tried for his life, the crime having been committed within Russian jurisdiction. Mr Manson is now off to take charge of that Establishment. So you see what ups & downs we have in this world & the uncertainties of all human affairs ...

... My son who went down with the Boats may possibly come back with them, & from W.W. by land. His case is pronounced by the doctor less alarming than we apprehended, but he strongly commends the climate of the upper country to that of Vancouver ...

Fort Colvile, 16 June 1842

To John McLoughlin, Fort Vancouver

... Mr Patrick McKenzie quite unexpectedly joined me here last night from the plains, with anything but cheering news from that quarter so far as the essential articles go – furs & grease – as can be seen by Mr McPherson's letter herewith enclosed. The same demand however for supplies seems to be kept up, more especially in the article tobacco ... The Indians it is clear will not now leave the root grounds for furs or anything else if they can help it.

With respect to Mr McKenzie himself, I think if placed on a proper footing he would become trustworthy & make himself useful & it is on that account I now send him down in order to have the necessary understanding with yourself, & to be returned immediately permanently attached to this district as one of his description is absolutely required. He is even now without an engt & I cannot comprehend how anyone thrown on my hands in the loose way he was last fall could be expected to show any lively interest in the cause we are engaged in. Perhaps it is intended to pawn Mr Thew upon us. If so I beg to be excused for anything is better than him ...

Fort Colvile, 30 June 1842

To John McLoughlin, Fort Vancouver

Yours of 20th Inst was handed me as early as 27th by return from W.W. of the Indian sent down with Mr McKenzie. The perusal of that communication gave me truly the most unspeakable pain & most feelingly do I sympathize with yourself Sir in the severe family calamity you have thus sustained.[50] Good God! What awful visitations of providence have we not had of late years far and near.

---

[50] McLoughlin's son, John McLoughlin Jr., was murdered at Stikine by one of his own men on the night of 20/21 April 1842. Governor Simpson, en route to Russia on his

With reference to the melancholy occurrence in the OK Dalles, I see that it is your opinion that the accident might have been prevented by the presence of an *officer* – possibly it might; that you was also disappointed I did not go down to Okanagan ... there was a standing order of late years that Colvile should not be left without a Gentleman, & to that order in the absence of any other arrangement I adhered, finding that Mr Manson did not come up to relieve me ... it may not be irrelevent to notice that I was not a little influenced by the letter which I received the very day Mr C[ameron] was with me from Mr C.F. Rowand, copy of which is already transmitted, apprising me of the impropriety of ever leaving my Establishment in charge of such a man as William Thew ... Under the circumstances, had I gone down & reached OK in safety of course there would be no more said on that part of the subject, but if unhappily anything serious had taken place at Colvile during my absence, I think I might with greater justice be found fault with than for the case in which I now very innocently find my name mixed up ...

It is not enough for me to be subject to the troubles & vexations which really belong to the charge I have; I must be placed in a situation to receive every annoyance from an insolent useless fellow, incapable of appreciating common kindness & common attention even to himself: I mean that celebrated Gentleman Master W. Thew whose arrogance & insufferable behaviour after insulting myself and family before he was 12 days under our roof obliged me to forbid him my house & discontinue all further intercourse with him. Really with the general character throughout the country which this youngster bears I cannot look upon his being quartered upon me, merely to suit his own idle & unambitious disposition, for four long months as at all a compliment. He is however still provided for three times a day at a separate mess by my wife & family, on whom I believe it is well known necessarily devolves the kitchen duties at Colvile during the summer months ...

P.S. Master Thew's open declaration of war against us commenced with a refusal to let him have Ferris's daughter [Charlotte] to help while away the tedium of his lonesome hours while here, when he found himself in every other respect far too comfortable, & which purpose the gentleman ultimately threatened to accomplish despite anyone who dared to

---

round-the-world tour, arrived at the post four days later. Simpson's investigation of the event blamed young McLoughlin for the debauchery of the men under his command, and he referred to him as 'a man lost to Liquor.' McLoughlin Sr. never forgave Simpson, and, in subsequent years, he conducted a campaign to reopen the investigation in a vain attempt to clear his son's name.

oppose him. Most unaccountable, to say the least of him, how such a useless character could be so long tolerated in this country. He has just sent me word that his tea is not sweet enough nor his butter in quantum suffite, & that his candles for night study in the month of June that he may sleep till ten in the morning, are far too short! Judge of the graceless task we have in being obliged to provide for such a guest.

Same date (Private) – I have to thank you for the trouble you took to address me so fully on that tragical affair at Stikine, but though that melancholy intelligence was conveyed under an official cover you will excuse me if beyond the brief notice of it in my other sheet I take this method of giving my opinion more at large on the painful subject. In whichever way we view the unhappy event, such a horrible occurrence among ourselves is lamentable to think of. One thing pretty evident, with so many scoundrels congregated together within one fort like Stikine the Establishment ought to have been with officers ... In fact all over the country we are far too lame in Gentlemen which must give a footing to men & Indians to become saucy & flippant. [Urbain] Heroux must be a profligate wretch & Pierre [Kanaquassi] very little better, but between ourselves I fear the conduct of the poor deceased gave them all but too great a handle, of which depend upon it a learned counsel before a British Criminal Court would make the most in mitigation of punishment, and all things considered perhaps the verdict of an English jury would go no further than 'justifiable homicide.' The prosecution you propose against Pierre will I apprehend fall to the ground. True, the villain at a most improper hour & most wantonly as the case is stated rang the gate bell & let go a shot when [François] Presse approached him but hurt no one. Nor can it perhaps be clearly proved that he fired with intent to murder or do bodily harm to any particular individual ... The subsequent flogging he had ... he most richly deserved ... I hope you will excuse me for giving my opinion this freely. I know you must feel the atrocity of the deed with the becoming feeling of a parent, but however painful the result we must resign ourselves to it & endeavour to discriminate what is right & what is wrong between man & man. I can say Mr Manson with an eye to the Journal will be able to sift things more thoroughly than Sir George had time to do & without a good interpreter which I suppose he was at the time ...

Fort Colvile, 8 August 1842

To John McLoughlin, Fort Vancouver
    Though I did not do myself the pleasure of addressing you from OK per Monique it was not because I had nothing to say. It must have been

well known to you all that the 12 men made over to me there fell far short of the means of getting up an Outfit of 130 pieces; 26 of them I was compelled to leave there, 52 I put into each of the 2 Boats I could man, a stretch of ambition ... I had cause to regret before I got here. In the Stoney Island Rapids my own Boat filled & sank. Lost the greater part of the powder, salt & sugar, including Mr Rowand's Keg & I am sorry to say materially damaged the delicate contents of Governor Simpson's cassette before it could be got out of the water ...

While there drying the property had a misunderstanding with the Natives, the worst disposed set on the Columbia from one end to the other. Next day, on ascending the rapid on the line with half loads, the quarrel became more serious; they let their arrows go at the Boats & gave myself on the shore the most uncouth reception with their brandished knives & arrows. It was an ugly affair as it was, but had very nearly gone the length of something more disastrous in the helpless condition we were in with our property exposed along the rapid, & worse still with not a man of the party able to speak two words of the language to bring us to a better understanding. I mention this last circumstance seeing so little is made of the young linguists brought up in the district, all now I understand ordered away as a useless burden on the Establishment. Let the maxim be never lost sight of among Indians that much mischief can be prevented by a timely & proper understanding of existing difficulties, which in the absence of such simple explanations it might take years of main strength to correct, & then after all in nine cases out of ten we only come off second best. Interpreters are a necessary evil.

... Berland I have sent to the Piegan lands with a 2 gallon Keg of rum to see if he cannot get a little grease for us ... all our grain is now overripe & scarcely a man that worked in the river is in fit condition to put his hand to any efficient labour yet. In short *nothing* can be more distressing than our present plight with so much to do with means so limited *be it believed* or not − Of Mr Thew I have written already. During my absence he took incredible airs upon himself here ... On the evening of Saturday last he beset myself at the gate with exceeding violence which nothing could tolerate but a studied wish to avoid an open rupture with him. Yesterday afternoon (Sunday) the scoundrel followed me to the fields with a table knife in his pocket, provoked me with the most insufferable language till we reached the fort gate when I was irresistably compelled to knock him down, after which he exhibited the knife & confessed to my wife & Mrs Anderson that it was intended for me. Today I am about getting him off to W.W. (having refused to sojourn at OK for the few remaining weeks he has in the country) where he must remain till Monique & the mountain men come up. I must say the conduct of this young man altogether has been the most outrageous & unaccountable, & that too from a worthless fellow without house or home ...

Fort Colvile, 9 August 1842

To Peter Skene Ogden

At your earliest convenience have the goodness to communicate to me officially what the character & conduct of Mr William Thew had been while under your orders, as it turned out that for the few weeks he has been with me as a mere guest the whole turn of his behaviour has been that of a madman more than anything else ...

Fort Colvile, 15 August 1842

To John McLoughlin, Fort Vancouver

Without any direct orders from you on the subject another detachment of our people leaves me today for the Wallamette. Since ... the date of my last we have been unable to do anything at the harvest from incessant rains, a loss that has at least the advantage of giving our invalids time to regain their wonted strength, but alas the grain is going for it.

Please have the goodness let me [have] five good men from the Express, four of them we are actually short of our ordinary complement & let their wages be charged to the district; the fifth I should like to have in readiness for the plains next spring to replace three going out ... besides old Pierre who will be free in April to attach himself to the mission. The Rev Gentlemen have not yet sent for their cattle & I do not know how they will survive the winter, the big plains Establishment having necessarily been broken up & no means in the ordinary way of getting hay made even for ourselves. Fall ploughing is a thing that must absolutely be attended to, as no other grain now gives much satisfaction here ...

Fort Colvile, 22 September 1842

To Rev Elkanah Walker, Tshimakain Mission

... [Yesterday] evening Atatie cast up with his party giving us the doleful account of Thew's disappearance & this mishap ... threw us into another dilemma, so much so that I was this morning on the eve of getting off Wacon with the aforesaid two Indians to hunt for him in the plains when very opportunely the Gentleman made his appearance in the plight you saw him ... acknowledge the cheerful assistance you rendered, as well now as on every other occasion requiring expedition ...

Fort Colvile, 23 September 1842

To the Chief Factors & Chief Traders HBC

... [details of William Thew's behaviour] Mr C.F. McLoughlin on the same subject addressed me 12 days ago in these words, 'It would be well you send a narrative of this affair across the mountains so as Gentlemen might know how to act towards him' ...

Fort Colvile, 29 September 1842

To Frank Ermatinger (Private)

... In much you say about poor Mr John [McLoughlin Jr.] I perfectly agree & that the manner of communicating a tale so melancholy distressed the unhappy father about as much as the deed itself. I do not however readily admit that Gov Simpson, be his strictness in matters of business what it may, is the man *wantonly* to wound the feelings of a fellow creature ... & I dare say did you see it, his private letter has made some amends for the astringent style of his public one. If the information he obtained at Stikine be incorrect, we are in Christian charity bound to believe it was from no intentional design of his. Mr McLoughlin seems to think private character unnecessarily dwelt upon in the depositions, but depend upon it evidence of that nature in such cases has great insight in a court of justice & however sanguine we may be to bring the criminal to punishment we ought always be prepared to hear all that the law will admit in his defense – certainly it was wrong to have left the deceased alone & in my opinion not very judicious to have given him the principal charge there at all so soon. In common with all others that will hear of the lamentable occurrence, I most feelingly sympathize with the worthy old gentleman himself ...

Fort Colvile, 18 October 1842

To Rev Elkanah Walker, Tshimakain Mission

... Although the absence of the Dr [Whitman] for a season[51] must make considerable diminution in your already reduced numbers, yet under the circumstances of the case I think it is the easiest resolution you could have come to. And I am in hopes the inconvenience that will attend his absence will be more than compensated by the good his trip will secure the mission. If he does however bring you more secular

[51] Marcus Whitman went east in October 1842, partly to conduct mission business and partly to urge the US government to assert its jurisdiction over the Oregon Territory. He returned the following summer with the first large emigration of Oregon settlers, an estimated 120 covered wagons carrying about 1,000 men, women, and children to the far west.

characters I think they ought to be something more than volunteers serving only while it suits their own convenience ...

The letter for you from Mr McLean is herewith sent. He wrote me
also but does not say a syllable about his little daughter [Elisa, living
with the Walkers]. His mother [Jane McDonald] desires me to say she
could not well spare Angus [age 16] as fort hunters are rather scarce at
present! They all desire to be kindly remembered to you, Mrs W. & the
children ...

Fort Colvile, 10 November 1842

To Rev Elkanah Walker

... In case Solomon may be returning whence he came I send a packet
for W.W. – if he is not and that no other opportunity arises in the direction of the Pelouse let it remain in your own hands for the present, even
till Dr Whitman's guide returns next month ... The present budget is
part of a letter box ... containing principally servants' letters &c &c come
out to York by the last ships. Our regular winter Express had not yet
passed thro the country when the Gentlemen at Edmonton forwarded
two men with the packet in question in order at the same time to be of
some service to Mr Rowand himself should they meet him on his way
home ...

Without waiting for the father's answer, I think little Elisa [McLean]
ought to be sent to Mrs Spalding per first safe opportunity ...

Fort Colvile, Thursday morning [December 1842]

To Rev Elkanah Walker, Tshimakain Mission

Our annual winter courier for Walla Walla, Atatie, is about starting
& will probably sleep with you his third night even should he arrive early
that day, which will give you an opportunity to write by him. The snow,
by what we hear from Garry, is not quite so deep your way as here ...
do not apprehend insurmountable difficulties on the way ... What a sad
misfortune is the burning of the Dr's mill [at Waiilatpu] & as things
now stand I fear a new one will not be got up in a hurry. Is there no
one there at all? Your Book [the Flathead primer] really does you credit,
that is for a first edition ...

Since McPherson's arrival I had a communication from Mr McKenzie from the Kootenais where all was well ... Only one canoe got fast
by ice in the fall. No H.B. packet had yet arrived there when our man
left there 15 Dec. Neither has there been anyone on the move from Mr
Ogden's quarter. The miserable Indians already begin to feel the severity of the winter – not a deer has come their way yet ...

Fort Colvile, 2 March 1843

To Rev Elkanah Walker, Tshimakain Mission

... I hear nothing of the present condition of Whilatpu. It is said there is a good deal of snow in that quarter this winter ... Here I believe I never saw more; our horses in consequence begin to suffer severely. The snow at present is a solid mass perfectly impervious to the rays of the sun while the north wind continues.

Fort Colvile, 15 March 1843

To Edward Ermatinger, St Thomas, Canada West

Dear friend, I am still, thank God, in the land of the living to acknowledge rect of your highly interesting favour of last season & to thank you for that & all other obliging turns it had been your aim to confer upon me & mine. From Master Ranald himself I also heard by a few lines dated in March from London [near St Thomas, Canada West, now Ontario]. As matters have now turned out, I am not at all sorry that the young buck is made to look more to himself, but I fear from what you say of his thoughtless & indolent disposition that Mr John Clair's store has too many tempting cordials in it to be a fit nursery for the young Gents of the far west. Never mind, my friend, we have done our duty & things must now be allowed to take their course. If he can only keep out of egregious acts of impropriety till we can once more have him back to the Indian country I shall consider it a great point gained that the experiment with him was made & tested so early in life. Here for all I shall ever do for him again he may just crawl thro life as the Black Bear does − lick his paws. Edward, we are all most unfortunate parents. Instance the awful shock of mind our old friend the Dr lately experienced from the irregular & inveterate habits of his unhappy son John, after spending 2,000 pounds on his education in foreign lands too.

The blind policy followed up by one & all of us Indian traders − forsooth the accumulation of *money* for what we are pleased to call the lasting benefit of our offspring, is in its consequences but too lamentably verified all over the country. This vile passion for the darling 'competency' I altogether ascribe to the abominable stand in the gap our Seniors were allowed to make for the last 22 years, which selfish, I would almost say iniquitous, policy has not only at the long run rendered most of themselves unhappy, but worse still intruded upon every poor devil under them, gaping up for an opening from the very first rung of the ladder for a whole quarter of a century, the cause of similar misery without the satisfaction of acquiring a share of the accursed competency. I am now myself it is true a Factor after 30 years vagary & exile in the wilderness,[52] but this does not change my opinion of the system allowed to prevail. Would you believe that to this very day we continue indulging those same precious old Senators in 4s & 5s every year with furloughs, leaves of absence, prolongation of leaves & as many other plans for hanging on as you can easily imagine, at the expense of – Oh you can easily guess that too. As I told you last year, your brother & I owe our promotions to two singularly rare chances: a savage Indian & a vicious horse. On the footing we now stand, neither of us, without a departure from the rules of the last *deed poll* can leave the service before the expiration of 4 years. Thank God one of them is now over & it is to be hoped thro His same infinite mercies we may live to glide through the other three without experiencing any great misfortune. When I last heard from Frank end of Novr ... he left me to infer that he would be going down this season. That being the case I know you will excuse me for not entering on local news with my usual prolixity.

I must once again thank you for the fund of information you never fail to give on the political struggle going on your way & you are pleased to be rather complimentary in the knowledge you admit I already possess on that all-engrossing subject. I have certainly of late years been as assiduous as perhaps any of my brother traders west of Portage du Rat (our chief politician the big doctor excepted, who will never acknowledge things rightly done till he sees his friend patriot [Louis Joseph] Papineau reinstated) to lay up into my own noddle the best picture I can of all your doings below. I had not however a correct topographical idea of the country, which you know to a man thrust into an obscure hole west side the R. Mountains is much against the necessary acquaintance with the scenes of action. What did I do? Why, one day with all the confidence in the world I took my sheet of cartridge paper, ruler & compasses & in a trice sketched off what I call a very good picture that would not disgrace the mathematical talents of the Honbl Surveyor General [Thomas] Parke himself, of every county from Essex to Grenville with their cities & privileged boroughs & gave each a member or members according to circumstances. Kent & one of the ridings of York I then found unoccupied, but since see them confirmed in favour of [Joseph] Woods [Kent] & the defeated candidate at Terrebonne, the nominee of

[52] McDonald got his long awaited promotion to chief factor, thus doubling his salary, at the Northern Council meeting in 1841. At the same time Frank Ermatinger was made a chief trader.

the celebrated Dr [Robert] Baldwin & the old McKenzie clique.[53] My next effort in the fine art was to colour out my new map with your municipal districts, seats of the courts, the Wardens, Clerks, Councillors & all with their respective salaries. I then puzzled my brain to see the range of operation I could assign the prominent & seemingly indispensable characters called Executive Councillors & leading office holders. With this my beautiful panorama I suppose I must now endeavour to tutor myself into the best knowledge I can of the workings of your new constitution [the union of Upper and Lower Canada in 1841] & follow the progress for good or evil of your new men brought into notice as you say by the execrable policy of the defunct Lord [Sydenham]. My mentor however, old John Neilson of Quebec [owner of the Quebec *Gazette*] & the only one I can consult as honest Thomas Dalton is no more, is not I confess to my liking. Now my good sir, I dare say you ... will smile at this got up Child's Horn Book of mine as a means of making myself a man of the world!! N'importe, if it do me no good it can do no harm, & as a further clue to the story I have just ordered up the best printed report of the proceedings of the first united parliament of the Canadas. You must know that at present there is very serious talk with us of forming Colony No.2 under the auspices of the Honbl Company on the shores of the Pacific, & you also know in that case how proper it would be that the young legislators (Frank & myself for instance two of them) should begin with good wholesome laws & regulation. But to return to Canada: –

How is your Sir Charles [Bagot][54] likely to turn out? He at least has the advantage of having been reared up in the right school, but my friend, young as we are compared with Magna Carta, we see that what it would have been madness to suggest as a good measure even 20 years ago will nowadays be scarcely accepted: the Wellingtons & Peels of '32 cannot be recognised as the same men in '42, & I dare say their representatives in the Colonies must at least keep pace with concessions in the Mother Country. What is Lord Ashburton [the London banker sent by Peel as special commissioner to Washington] about? It is all very well that efforts should be made to put things to right with Jonathan, but I fear in the hands of this merchant Lord more than National honour will be

[53] This probably refers to James H. Price, who represented York South in the Legislative Assembly from 1841 to 1851. A Reformer, though not active in the 1837 Rebellion, he was commissioner of Crown lands in the second Baldwin-Lafontaine administration.

[54] Sir Robert Peel's Conservative administration in Great Britain appointed Sir Charles Bagot governor general of British North America in 1841 on the death of Lord Sydenham. He served, in failing health, until his successor Sir Charles Metcalfe arrived in March 1843.

consulted. True, the unhappy posture of our affairs in the east is not too well calculated to maintain a line of defiance with the sovereign people & perhaps upon the whole the princely bankers in their present financial difficulties, can do with them what no other could. In this part of the world, tho in all conscience anything but shrewd politicians, we ought not to be indifferent to what is going on for assuredly in the sacrifice that will be made for the sake of peace *our interest* will be a conspicuous item, and this ought to be another good reason for quitting the field speedily. Even now the dividends are miserable enough & daily going from bad to worse. I perfectly agree with you as to what might be your brother's prospects & usefulness below. He is still, comparatively speaking, a young man & not at all without abilities, certainly that kind of buck of all others that turn to best account in the rough & tumble doings of a backwoods settlement. And now that I think of it, perhaps if he should extend his jaunt to England he could negotiate a sale or terms of retirement at Fenchurch St., for your old Niagara acquaintance Alex Simpson effected a settlement of this nature his 2nd year holding a parchment. But peradventure our friend's late matrimonial alliance[55] will now have some influence on his future arrangements ... Factor Ogden I expect here in a few days on his way to have a glimpse at civilized life too, & a report says Factor McDonald is to be his successor [in New Caledonia]. I have however taken a rule of exception to this contemplated appointment on what I conceive two very good tangible grounds: the one that I am well & sufficiently useful where I am without any ambition to rise higher; the other that within the district itself (for N.C. & T.R. are now but one) they have an officer of equal efficiency better acquainted with its local affairs entitled to a field that may lead to advancement & not encumbered with a *wife* & *ten children*. What think ye of that please for backing out! Manson is again on the coast. Last summer we, the Worshipful Bench, furnished him with a commission to inquire, or rather reinquire, into the unfortunate affair of young McLoughlin at Stikine, which it was supposed Sir George on his trip for Siberia left incomplete. Work writes me our learned deputy has made a sweeping business of it: upon very slight evidence made every white man at the Estabt 13 in number, prisoners. I fear we have got ourselves into a hobble & that it will turn out we are more *au fait* in our humble occupation of Indian trader than in dispensing of Her Majesty's criminal law ...

21st April – Up to yesterday we saw nothing of the Express & your

---

[55] Frank Ermatinger married sixteen-year-old Catherine Sinclair, daughter of William Sinclair Jr., granddaughter of Mrs John McLoughlin, on 10 August 1842.

brother is yet bringing up the rear with the Dr's *ultimatum*. He does not go out himself, on the contrary he is now to ... [have charge of the Cowlitz Farm] & I verily believe the best they could have hit upon, that Monsieur Peter [Ogden] himself is about leaving us for a season. This last named Gentleman joined me here exactly this day month. A few days before he left his own headquarters [Fort St James] another melancholy occurrence took place on the Babines: his postmaster William Morwick was shot dead by an Indian. Of this circumstance the Dr is not yet aware ... We are in a vast deal of difficulties my friend. Your brother will inform you of the endless work the unfortunate affair at Stikine has given those of us adroit in drawing up depositions. The further we advance the more complicated & perplexing becomes the case ...

As I believe I have exhausted your patience with my long scrawl, I shall conclude with our united respects & best wishes for yourself, Mrs E. & the little ones − you see I use the plural number. I judge from myself. Our Joseph (you know the numbered rank of that one in the patriarchal family) is now a month old & but 4 years younger than the oldest of three older brothers ...

27th − Our accomptant, the *only* cabin passenger, is just on the eve of starting with his 18 men. [Ogden changed his plans and went on down to Fort Vancouver.] By your brother's note you see the arrangement we have come about: it puts me in mind of the drill sergeant's command 'As you were again − March back double quick to your quarters.' ...

Fort Colvile, 21 March 1843

To James Hargrave, York Factory

... yesterday I expected to have had the pleasure of seeing the outgoers, namely Monsieur Peter from the land of privation & misery & your worthy brother-in-law [Dugald McTavish, brother of Letitia Hargrave] from the gay world below; in both cases however I am so far disappointed ...

No doubt long before you see this or any of the aforesaid party you will have heard of our material wants in these parts ... The unfortunate affair at Stikine is of course one that will distress you all & the further loss in the river is much to be lamented. [Edward] Hopkins would have put you in possession of a great deal of news highly interesting not only from the Columbia but also from California & the Islands ...

I spoke to Hopkins about our boys. The other two chaps I alluded to we are unwilling to part with until we hear how Archy got home.[56] On

[56] Fourteen-year-old Archibald Jr. was sent from the Red River Academy to a school near Clairmont, Surrey, England, in the fall of 1842.

the score of politics, you are so very selfish with the newspapers that I hardly know anything of what is going on in the great world. I must however record my dissent from your view of the Income Tax & even the proposed one on funded property: both in my opinion are quite fair when the urgent wants of the State require it. Speaking as individuals, to whom my friend can we look in the days of need but the British government? Tomorrow tis perfectly possible a John Bull squadron may be in the N.W. Coast to protect our lives & property, & could we in the same breath that we solicit this support tell the Right Honble the Chancellor of the Exchequer that to replenish his coffers he must draw on the Manchester weavers & the Birmingham knife-makers? No, No, Gents. If you will be political advocates for the British operatives let it be in practice & not in theory only.

Since I turned the sheet Mr Ogden is in upon me, all strong, hale & healthy after a wintry march of nine weeks. Unfortunately he is the bearer of news which adds one more name to our black list: poor William Morwick was one of the best men I ever saw in the country. The Returns from New Caledonia & Thompson River are low in Beaver but in Martens & other small furs they are still pretty successful. As to myself here, by dint of great exertion on the plains we manage to keep up to something upon the trade of the last three years. Young McPherson with 7 men leaves me tomorrow on a campaign of 8 months of it in the direction of the Missouri where I understand he is to meet with a formidable opposition from St Louis this season. My good Sir, believe it or not ... we do contribute towards the grand heaps, & I fear little as was formerly thought of the Columbia, we shall miss that department of our resources when it is no longer ours. Nay, I find you all throw cold water on every other laudable exertion we make to find you substitutes for Beaver, & yet the universal cry is that the H.B. gold dust is gone forever. What say you to the whale fishery? As you will most likely be at Red River this spring [for the annual meeting of the Northern Council] and will have something to say in the distribution of the Canada newspapers I hope you will think of us. Strange not one of us as individuals can be allowed a single paper by the Lachine canoes ...

Fort Colvile, 2 April 1843
To Sir William Jackson Hooker, Kew, London, England

By our last Cape Horn vessel I was honoured in receiving your kind letter of Novr '41 [from] the Royal Botanical Gardens at Kew. Nothing in the world can give me greater pleasure than to write to you Sir in the little I can do in that department. Your obliging favour however reached me in the interior of the Columbia so late in the season that I could do very little in that way beyond the collecting of a few common cones, but I have since made some arrangement with the people under me that range more about the country than I do myself & I trust something in the way you wish will be forthcoming by & bye. These same agents of mine, Whites as well as Indians, despite faithful promises are so unaccountably careless & indifferent in matters of science that I am always prepared to get many blanks & pieces from them!

Our friend Mr Tolmie so far as I know is not yet returned to us, but is daily expected, & as I visit headquarters myself this summer I look to the pleasure of finding him there, where we shall compare notes & on my part acquire from his better knowledge of things a further insight into the task we have in hand. Whatever I may have shall in October be handed over to him for transmission to England in his own way by the ship of the season.

This vessel will also be carrying home from us a considerable collection of stuffed animals for the British Museum which, through H.B. House, we are called upon to contribute by Mr [J.E.] Gray, the keeper of that splendid establishment. There is no doubt [that] many of us in this wide unexplored country with the opportunities we have, though confessedly below mediocrity in our knowledge of the great world, might with a little exertion, as if by accident, stumble upon various objects of interest & curiosity to the professors of general science. But I believe Sir you sufficiently know our limited ideas in this way & worse still, we want that confidence in ourselves which with a little practice & perseverence might lead to a greater title to the study.

I believe I have somewhere read of a small monument being in contemplation to commemorate the name of our late friend David Douglas. If such be really the case anywhere I would most cheerfully contribute my mite. The fate of poor Messrs Banks & Wallace was unhappily followed last summer in the overwhelming whirlpools of the Columbia by the disappearance of my old Guide of 30 years experience in these waters & four others. These mighty vortexes are of such a nature that one Boat is swallowed down when others a few minutes after pass in perfect safety, as was the case in this instance. In other respects we struggle with the world in the usual way. Brother Jonathan making rapid strides towards us for the formation of a new state in the 'far west,' and as for sectarian doctors they are already become thick as blackberries, in some instances doing good, in others causing confusion worse confused ...

Fort Colvile, 27 April 1843

To Sir George Simpson, Lachine

... I could wish that of the general feature of affairs with us west side it were possible to speak more favourably. The unfortunate occurrence at Stikine of itself has caused more writing & botheration than all our other doings put together. The pile upon pile of papers the unhappy father has laboured to fill up upon this harassing question to prove his son to have been what in my opinion he was not is truly astonishing. That it was natural for him to receive the news with the painful feelings of a parent everyone will admit, but I believe few will admit that in all this oral credence ... he is supporting the character of a good correct man, the circumstances of his death be proved as they may. Immediately on receipt of the fatal news he opened a correspondence with me here, but on receiving my answer under *private cover* it speedily ceased. I cannot however disguise my dread of the attack that will be made upon me this summer if I go down [to Fort Vancouver] to bring me into his own way of thinking, as I believe is his habitual practice with everyone with whom he comes in contact. Altogether I lament exceedingly the spirit of opposition which of late seems to govern [him] ...

Besides our own ordinary troubles it is said that this season a new source of annoyance is to drop in upon us in the shape of American troops. We have so far seen but one Yankee wearing or pretending to wear official authority;[57] in all conscience if those coming are only to be half so meddling we shall have no comfortable life of it.

In the way of business, for all our grumbling we still continue to make something of the trade. I think the interior taking it altogether is fully equal to last year; I am myself upwards of 100 pounds *more*, though my profits are a few pounds less owing to particular causes, & should we not be seriously disturbed in the plains this season I am in hopes the incoming will do as well ...

I must not conclude this brief epistle without acknowledging the great satisfaction I had the other day in receiving the second sheepskin, & many thanks to all those who had a hand sheaving it my way ...

[57] Dr Elijah White, a former member of the Oregon Methodist Mission, returned to the Columbia in the fall of 1842, with a party of settlers for the Willamette and an appointment as a 'sub-Indian agent' for the US government. He caused a stir amongst the Nez Percés and the Cayouse by allegedly threatening to 'take their lands from them.'

Fort Colvile, 20 October 1843

To Sir William Jackson Hooker, Royal Botanical Gardens, Kew

... I was much honoured by receipt of your favour of October last per the Company's chartered ship the *Diamond* ... This summer too I [received] a note from our respected friend Mr [John] Halkett enclosing a few copies of the printed instructions from the 'Director of the Royal Botanical Gardens, Kew' – I fear Gentlemen I shall fall far short of reaching your high expectations from my botanical researches in the Columbia. I however flatter myself I at least have the *wish* to be useful, and shall continue of that disposition to serve you while it is my lot to sojourn west side of the Rocky Mountains, though I cannot promise much ...

There is at present a small box to your address which will leave this for Vancouver per the Boats hourly expected from York Factory. The contents have been collected within the last few days which I hope will give them a better chance of reaching England in a sound condition by the vessel leaving the mouth of the river the moment the Boats are arrived. Besides, I write a few lines to Capt [William] Brotchie recommending special attention as well to this small package as to my more bulky one for the British Museum.[58]

The cones I do not attempt to describe in any manner & I fear some of them will be found with no seed at all; there are four or five parcels of last year but I believe their fellows are in the collection of this fall also. The bulbs & tubers will I hope prove good specimens. The Bitter Root or spadlum I made some exertion to get & next season I shall certainly endeavour to procure some of the seed; it is a very pretty vernal flower rising but little above the ground, generally found on sandy hillocks & volcanic rocks slightly covered with earth. Some years ago I sent a small parcel of the seed in a mature state home to Mr Halkett which perhaps became productive somewhere in the vicinity of Richmond. The cactuses of Mr Douglas I am apprehensive we cannot stumble upon; I often heard the poor man express his disappointment at missing the seed

---

[58] Dr J.E. Gray, keeper of the British Museum, recorded a box, received on 28 November 1843, containing two rare pronghorn, or 'jumping,' deer with horns spanning fifteen to seventeen and a half inches; a small six-foot-by-four-foot buffalo skin; a reindeer; a wolverine; a black bear; an eagle; and a number of smaller mammals. The following year he received another twenty-five good specimens from McDonald, including six reindeer, a wolverine, a bear, a porcupine, otters, hares, squirrels, and other rodents. However, the 1845 shipment arrived in poor condition; the skins were decayed and only the skulls were salvageable. Some of these are still in the teaching collection of the British Museum of Natural History.

of a plant he saw in the Walla Walla Blue Mountains. Smith's *Introduction* I have consulted but my limited acquaintance with the science does not enable me to trace out *thus* the character of the plant.

I am extremely sorry to have to report that with the single exception of our mutual friend Mr Tolmie, the Gents of west side are very averse to dab in anything connected with the vegetable or animal kingdoms. I have however worked hard this summer to enrol into our service two or three of the N. Caledonia clerks to whom I sent one of the printed papers for their information & a lucky circumstance having now brought one of them this way I am enabled to get them at least to promise to act the part of cheerful contributors. There is a young Gentleman in that department, a Mr Alex C. Anderson, of considerable abilities, to whom I have intimated my intention of recommending him to you Sir as a valuable correspondent in that quarter.

I think it would be worthwhile if Mr Tolmie had at his disposal a little brown paper to hand about to those Gentlemen at distant parts. If they did nothing the loss of the paper would not be great; & the having a few sheets would be a stimulus for them to fill them up. Would you believe it, there was scarcely a flower in the interior of the Columbia this summer, owing to excessive drought. From the middle of April to this date we had but a few showers third week of June & an occasional one since the beginning of this month. Indeed so injurious was this unusual suppression of all rain that our Colvile crops failed. The enclosed rough memorandum is all I can give on the roots & bulbs now forwarded. Trusting they may give you some satisfaction ...

Fort Colvile, 5 November 1843

To Sir George Simpson, London

I need scarcely say the pleasure it afforded me to hear from you by the party which dropped in upon us here last night, and still more in learning thro my other correspondents that you have in every respect vastly improved by the Siberia trip.

As I see you are again next year to visit the Indian country my writing now is proformed ... Meantime however I take the precaution to have a few lines reach England per the Cape Horn ship in case unforseen causes may detain you on the other side of the water next season. It is Sir in reference to myself & a passage in Mr Finlayson's letter: our friend says 'In regard to your crossing in the fall, no answer can at present be given, unless you would send the family to pass the winter at or near Edmonton and you could in that case follow them the ensuing spring.' Now Sir, in all this I can see no accommodation whatever beyond the ordinary means of getting out, which really at my years of life, and with the tremendous burden now on my shoulders, one would suppose is uncommonly strict. Not one of my ten little ones is able to look after another, & worse still, the poor wife herself is lately fallen into a very precarious state of health by a weakness that has attacked her in the extremities, more especially about the wrists and fingers. I therefore trust sir that on due consideration you will direct the arrangement, per return of the vessel, to be otherwise. As for permission to cross en baggage fall '45 I shall look most sanguinely. My children, the greatest treasure I have, are now losing every day they remain in this blessed wilderness ...

P.S. There is a very fine 8-month-old black bear here which I intend sending down in the Boats to be consigned to Beaver House, London.

Fort Colvile, 22 March 1844

To James Hargrave, York Factory

Tho I am not one of those who like to refer their correspondents to the verbal information of passants ... yet I believe that on the present occasion it would have been presumption in me to go beyond mere complimentary sayings. Dugald [McTavish] & Squire [Francis] Ermatinger I shall be looking out for here every day [en route east] & shall defy the whole Indian country to produce better samples for enlightening others on all that is new & interesting in their respective departments, and ... you have Monsieur Peter [Ogden], this time tout de bon, to complete the grand picture ... Rowand will have it that twas I with my beer, roast beef & plum puddings that was the cause of his not going out last season! But with so many expected your way this season & that too of our most efficient hands, including Rae by the bye, how came it about that we got but a solitary apprentice clerk last fall?... really at the rate we are going on with respect to this indispensable class of servants, I fear the business here ere long will be completely at a standstill, or many more of us in the bottom of the Columbia. My *only one* here I could depend upon I lost last fall on the mountain trip from sheer exhaustion of animal strength after toiling in these rivers summer & winter for the last eight & twenty years.

By your kind & very obliging favour of July I am sorry to perceive that doings on east side are not likely to make up for our annual falling off in the west ... Jonathan is already in full form in the field & it will not be his fault if we are not speedily very much circumscribed in the extent of our operations here. With such a diminution year after year in the amount of exports is it not surprising that they cannot make more of what we do send them. The wiseacres write me that I labour under a mistake in expecting such a consequence from short returns, that the fewer the furs the lower the prices, because the furriers have betaken themselves to other [materials] that please the public quite as well as the Castor, hence the great éclat given silk hats. Poor Mr [William] Smith [HBC secretary in London died in January 1843] was my authority for this doctrine. What an awfully sudden end the honest man has had! I believe our D[onald Smith] here is a nephew of his … For my own part, low as my means are, I am clearly for a retreat. My health of late is a good deal impaired & when I think of my years [54] & my encumbrances this notion is very much strengthened. The difficulty is in getting out of my long imprisonment. Despite all you hear of the charms of Oregon I am by no means disposed to become a citizen of that will-be new section of the great American Republic. And yet one is sure to be, if not actually under a democratic government, at least under one rapidly verging towards it. Instance the present state of the Canadas, now under the entire sway of the most prominent rebels of '37 & '38. By the bye I have to thank you for the paper you was kind enough to enclose me, for but few gifts of the kind reach me – a whole file of … *The Church* was addressed me

Alexander MacDonald (seated at right), the third son of Archibald McDonald and Jane Klyne, was one of the chief factors of the HBC photographed by William Notman in 1871. Others in this portrait are (left to right) Lawrence Clarke, Donald A. Smith, James Bissett, Peter Warren Bell, George S. McTavish, and Colin F. Rankin. (National Archives of Canada PA143226)

by Mr [Reverend A.N.] Bethune [the editor] but seemingly miscarried, as indeed did all the papers I ever laboured to get from that quarter. I suppose to save freight!!! So much for accommodation at Lachine ...

                                                              Fort Colvile, 22 March 1844
To Edward Ermatinger, St Thomas, Upper Canada
    ... I must premise that I am just out of a bed of sickness which I find has made a vast alteration in the free use of the pen, but never mind, the buoyant spirit is still in the old place. My ailing was nothing more than rheumatic pains that confined me to the house however for some weeks, but now the fine weather is coming on & I expect soon to be myself again. Your obliging favour of 2nd April with its supplement reached me about the usual time. It is pleasing to find that amidst so much business, political strife & speechification one is not unmindful of his old friends in this country ...

    The case of unfortunate Ranald certainly gave me great pain. As it is clear however that the bent of his inclination was anything but what we could wish perhaps the step he has taken is the very best that could have happened. As for the service, in the case of these chaps I never looked upon it but as a mere apology to keep them out of harm's way, & that in all probability is as effectually done on the wide ocean as in the lost obscure corner of the Indian country, & all I hope is that he may stick to the ship *Tuskeny*.[59] His miserable scrawl does not enable us to say whenever he sailed but that is immaterial; it is enough that we know he was yet in existence, contrary to other rumours that reached the country from Canada. Both Sir George & Mr Smith wrote me about him, the latter Gentm a few days before his death ...

    My other boy that was indisposed here [Angus], it was the will of providence to take out of the miseries of this world in April last, & my third [Archy Jr.] is for the last two years in England at a school near

---

[59] The *Tuscany*, purchased in 1842 by John Budd of Sag Harbour, New York, sailed that year on a whaling voyage to Crozet Island, southeast of Madagascar, returning on 26 February 1845. Ranald wrote to his father from London, Canada West, in March 1842, telling him he had left Ermatinger's home in nearby St Thomas. Apparently McDonald had received another letter from his son after he signed on the whaling ship. According to Ranald, late in 1845 he again sailed from Sag Harbour on a whaling voyage, this time on board the *Plymouth* bound for the Sandwich Islands, where he hoped to find a ship to take him to the 'Japan seas' and fulfil his dream of visiting the then 'forbidden kingdom.' Ranald's subsequent adventures and his experience teaching English to Japanese officials are described in his memoir. See W.S. Lewis and Naojiro Murakami, eds., *Ranald MacDonald: The Narrative of His Early Life* (Spokane, WA: Eastern Washington State Historical Society, 1923).

Clairmont in Surrey. We still have seven & the young Lady [MaryAnne] about us, but the oldest – one 14 & the other 12 [Alexander and Allan] – I am just about sending down to Montreal [from the Red River school] in charge of Mr Ogden to be placed at a good school in Vermont, should your Canada seminaries be still short of what people could wish. This step you will say looks like one towards a general move that way & such my friend is now my firm intention, God willing, as there is little inducement to prolong our stay in the wilderness. One may as well lay himself on the shelf with eight 85ths in the shape of a retired interest while it is worth having as to do so at a more remote period when to all appearances it will not be much. I fear however I cannot be off before Ogden & your brother return, if return they do, but I shall put every iron in the fire, formidable as is the task, to be in Canada fall '46 ... In this case, for at least a couple of seasons we [Frank and self] shall once more be compagnons de voyage in the river, which would not at all be exceedingly disagreeable were things as you saw them.

Our men of every description have degenerated & above all among our superannuated *Bouts* but few efficient ones. Last season going down [to Vancouver] we had a Boat with all hands swamped in the middle of the *portage neuf.* The Judge [Ogden] was ashore, but Frank & myself being afloat with the craft, all hands were saved as well as the packs. Coming up we were less fortunate in the Dalles; by a Boat engulfed in one of the boiling whirlpools we lost one man & 4/5ths of the lading. We get no Iroquois up now & all the old ones are either gone or dehors le service. The Yankees too are now too near us & of consequence the Bourgeois' authority must be exercised with less rigour or he will be told the line of demarcation is not far off! In short, as I have said already, things are very much altered for the worse. Senator [Lewis Fields] Linn's military colonists sure enough made their appearance last season & with them another swarm of Jesuits, now as thick as blackberries in this district. One of their attaches all the way from the capital of Saxony on botanical pursuits is now quartered with me here.[60]

You can scarcely form an idea of the various characters from all nations

[60] Charles A. (Karl) Geyer was a German botanist who toured about from St Louis, Missouri, for several years before coming to the Oregon country in 1843. He joined a group with Sir William Drummond Stewart, who, when they parted at the Wind River Mountains, provided him with a letter of reference to McLoughlin. Geyer turned up at Fort Colvile in a near-destitute condition. McDonald took him in and encouraged him in his botanical pursuits. He later returned to London on one of the HBC ships, and Hooker published his record of his journey in the *London Journal of Botany*, vol. 4 (London: H. Bailliere, 1845).

now strolling to the far west but all find themselves disappointed. Of the 17 Methodist preachers we at one time had in Oregon there are not at present in the field above, I believe, three or four. All back to Jonathan land again. Those sent out by the A.B.C.F.M. still hold on but literally do nothing. The Jesuits & your Canada priests will succeed better – they have what they call themselves *un bon poteau* in the personal countenance of the Dr.

My strictures on your Canadian politics I believe I shall drop. Your eloquent & conclusive speech of 18th April last in defence of constitutional rights & privileges I perused with unspeakable delight; apart from its sound reasoning, it conveyed to us in this country historical facts we could not equally appreciate coming from any other orator. I see you are not the only old N.W. that is making himself conspicuous in the haranguing line. At Williamstown, the Montreal *Herald* does not give the exact words of Capt Finan McDonell on the occasion of his moving for a vote of censure on the judgement of his Excellency the Gov General for not making the Beauharnois Canal on the *Glengarry* side of the river. I am at liberty to conclude that the gallant captain must have been very fierce. Nay, more, that were the right Honbl Bart within arm's length to him he might share no better fate at his hands than did the Fort des Prairies Buffalo bull[61] & many a savage Blackfoot before that eventful day – what strange vicissitudes in man's life! No.16 of the London *Herald* I had no opportunity of forwarding to Tod yet, but the others I sent to your brother & now tis high time to thank you for them. Mr Bethune's Cobourg *Church* I am sorry to say miscarried, or rather that staid Gentlm at Lachine suppressed it to avoid the expense of freight to the Honbl Compy. I was more fortunate with the packet sent for me by Mr Advocate [Hugh] Taylor including Boz's *Notes*.

Honest Work I have not seen since I saw you, but hear from him regularly. His ever removing en baggage from west side is I think now doubtful, or indeed any other of them with encumbrance. Tod however will & speaks of '46, tho a leetle *encumbrance* begins to spring up in that quarter too.[62] Our friend, between you & me, is far from being popular with high or low. I hear from [Robert] Miles his aim is now Moose, with of

---

[61] In June 1827 Finan McDonald, a colourful former Nor'wester, was travelling with a party that included Edward Ermatinger when he was gored by a buffalo in a legendary encounter on the banks of the Saskatchewan River. This is an oft-told tale in the annals of the fur trade.

[62] Tod took as his second wife Sophia Lolo, daughter of a mixed-blood guide at Kamloops. He remained in the Columbia and settled on Vancouver Island after his retirement.

course the other step. Cowie is there already & has expectations also. At all events it will scarcely answer to have them together. [John Lee] Lewes is looking to the St Lawrence, tho he still speaks of Australia! Rowand is only waiting to see his son-in-law [J.E. Harriott] promoted to the first rank to be his successor ...

16th April – Here are our Red River friends still, instead of leaving this on 4th as originally contemplated. McTavish did not join us till yesterday & Payette with 2 Boats & 30 men the day before. Manson is still expected by the plains with the prisoners of Stikine & the necessary witnesses, amounting in all I believe to 20 men more. Your brother it would appear remains; he did not write me. Ogden did not go out by Tête Jaune's Cache. On 26th he dropped in upon us here. The outgoers in all will be about 60 persons & 4 Boats to the portage. Manson it seems is the man for N.C. ...

Fort Colvile, 1 April 1844

To Sir John Pelly, London

I had the honour to receive your favour of 3rd April 1843 accompanying your official sheet of same date in character of trustees for the final closing up of our connexion with the Borriguard Establishment [Pelly & Company of Norway], and I am *truly sorry* to find *on many* accounts that this last mentioned document is anything but cheering to those concerned. It is however, I suppose, needless on the part of so many of us in this country by our own simplicity so fearfully involved in this unhappy affair to cavil on the subject at the 11th hour. The deed is done & seemingly there is no alternative, unless it be found in the faint hopes still held out of ameliorating our condition in the shape of a liberal price for what is called our share of the stock ... True, we Indian traders unfortunately have but a very limited idea of the general commerce, but somehow or other we cannot very well bring ourselves to reconcile to each other the two facts as stated: of a profit of from 8 to 10 per cent accruing annually from the business ... up to the hour our interest in it commenced, & that for ... the five years that connexion lasted on a more enlarged & improved scale it should not yield one shilling.

I hope Sir you will excuse me for expressing myself thus freely. If others of my fellow sufferers do not make their sentiments known with equal candour, assuredly it is not because they feel their unexpected loss with less chagrin & disappointment,[63] and even anything calculated to

[63] McDonald wasn't alone in his anger. On 19 June 1842 Duncan Finlayson wrote to James Hargrave: 'As regards the Norway business ... public men and men of business

increase the pain with which one loses his money, in this instance it is the *manner* in which we were induced, as if even blindfolded, to stake, some of us, near our all in a speculation we knew nothing at all about. Altogether Sir it is my humble opinion as matters have turned out that our case, by taking a liberal view of it, is not one that ought to be strictly measured by the common commercial rule of D[ollars] & C[ents], and that a plan after all could be fallen upon by the present proprietors of the concern, not exceedingly burthen to themselves, that might still secure to us or our heirs something equal to what we are brought in for as losses.

As to the disposal of whatever it may be thought our due to receive of the investment in question, I do not know how far my other friends on this side the Atlantic may be disposed to leave it *at interest* in the business still going on, but for my own part, now bordering on old age, after a pilgrimage of near ⅔rds of my life in the wilderness, I shall require it all to set me up a small hut somewhere very soon in which with a very large helpless family to eke out the downhill of life, and with this view it will have to pass thro the hands of Mr William G. Smith of the H.B. House, who together with his late father, held my power of attorney in reference to my share in the winding up of the co-partnership.

Fort Colvile, 20 April 1844

To Governor and Council

You are probably through Mr Chief Factor McLoughlin made acquainted with my present indisposition, & with my wish expressed to him some time ago of being permitted to withdraw from the Columbia when most convenient to all parties. Allow me to say now that this desire, from the seriously impaired state of my health of late, is become paramount over all other consideration ... my mind, God willing, is made up to see if I cannot, with the little vigour I have, manage to recross the Rocky Mountains this fall with the horses returning from the Boat Encampment, after three campaigns of four & twenty years of it west side ...

---

may gloss over their actions as they choose, but in this case I do not think we have been fairly dealt with. We knew nothing of the business in which we were strongly advised to embark ... we came forward with our money with confidence in the parties to whom it was entrusted ... they were ... in equity honour bound to refund every shilling of it; instead we are it appears losers of about one-fifth of the principal ... I can very ill afford to lose 400 pounds sterling in this way, but I do not look so much to the loss of the money as to the manner it has been taken from me.' G.P. de T., ed., *The Hargrave Correspondence, 1821-1843* (Toronto: Champlain Society, 1938).

Fort Colvile, 20 April 1844

To Sir George Simpson

[Received] ... your obliging favour of 27th June from Red River ... I am sorry to report that I am myself at present far from being in my usual good spirits for writing. My general health is sadly broken in upon since the middle of January. Before that time all the inconvenience I felt was from an old standing complaint in the left foot that was gradually gaining upon me & is now I fear connected with a recent attack of the spine. My first relief in the winter was thro the kindness of Dr Whitman, but I must say my friends below, the moment they heard of my indisposition, lost no time in doing for me all they possibly could. Since the fine weather came on I am considerably recovered, but my appetite having failed, my strength too is gone. My being able to go down the river this summer is still doubtful, tho in consequence of Mr Ogden's absence, that Gentleman being now here with us once more on his way out this time in right earnest, I suppose I must make the attempt. At all events, my services for another year cannot be depended upon, as, God willing, my mind is made up to see if I cannot manage to recross the mountains this fall, a trip Sir I confidently rely on your usual consideration to sanction & provide for ...

I see that in every attempt I have made to strengthen my connexion with the fur trade, since the day I began with the raw youth you saw in Belleville 15 years ago, I have failed. Well Sir, I don't blame you for those unsuccessful efforts. The last failure however pains me on more accounts than one, as I reproach myself in some measure for having used language to the young man [Ranald] after I heard of his having left Ermatinger that very likely led to the step he eventually took. Our poor unhappy son [Angus] that came this way from Red River is gone, and I am sure I need not say how much we have been distressed by his case & the afflicting circumstances attending it. Of the boy in England [Archy] I dare say you have heard thro Mr Hopkins who kindly took charge of him home. So far there is nothing cheering in my domestic labours, yet to lighten our burden with the view of getting off from here, we shall in a day or two be reluctantly compelled to part with two more of our little fellows to launch out on the wide world without I may say friend or protector. In short, view my own situation now as I will, I see no time is to be lost in setting about the formation of some sort of a home that hereafter may become a kind of rallying point for the numerous progeny depending on my support, come of myself what may. But more of this if we both live to meet once more.

With respect to the unfortunate affair at Stikine, I dare say the turn it has now taken will be as unexpected to you all on east side as it is to us here ... The old Gentleman, on hearing of the arrival of the party in the Sound, wrote us up here a few hasty rather confused lines on the unaccountable indifference he thought the Sitka authorities had shown in the business & thinks they were influenced by first impression. In any view of the perplexing affair it is now high time it should be got rid of some way or other, and I expect the sending the case to Montreal will lead to more talk than a patient & serious investigation of it.

In every other respect it will be pleasing to hear that doings on west side during the last campaign, considering all we had to contend with, have told well ... It is very cheering to hear too that recent changes made in the management of affairs at Puget Sound have led to an improved state of things in that department also, and it is to be hoped that should the speculation answer no other good purpose our position there as individual members may have some influence on the decision about being come to on the boundary question. The first division of Senator Linn's settlers sure enough found their way to us last season, conducted by an homme de guerre. Lieut [John Charles] Fremont with his field piece & troop of mounted militias is since back with his report to the States via the Clamet [Klamath] and California. I believe neither he nor the new colonists found our Multnomah [Willamette] district to answer their expectations & I am certain they will be still less taken up with the charms of the Clamet country, now given out as the Eldorado of the west! Under the wing of the colonial caravan across the desert came more Jesuits & worse still more Indian traders, who together took up their station in the very centre of this district. Fremont is the son-in-law of the great democratic [Senator Thomas H.] Benton of St Louis, is attached to the topographical department, was summer '39 in the vicinity of Pembina with his Chief Mr [J.N.] Nicollet, accompanied by a third person, a Mr [Charles A. (Karl)] Geyer all the way from the capital of Saxony exploring the vegetable kingdom. This last mentioned person became unemployed when Nicollet's labours closed & was sent this way under the patronage of the renowned Captain Sir William Stewart, & is now on our hands here apparently without any great means.

The affair of the organ we shall now drop. I am very fortunate in getting my money, cost & charges back & I wish I could with the same composure banish from my mind some of my other dealings with the same source whence that bright bargain was sent me. But I suppose this is enough in reference to the unlucky affair I allude to. Sir John's official communication of last season I have just acknowledged with the best grace the case can well admit of ...

To Sir William Jackson Hooker, Kew Gardens, London

Until this moment I was rather angry that my letter & small package of last year was too late at the mouth of the river for the Cape Horn vessel of the season. By that communication it could not be inferred that I was myself speedily quitting the Columbia, but I fear the state of my health now will oblige me to rise camp and once more recross the R. Mountains. I have however succeeded in constituting in my stead a very good correspondent, Mr Alexander Anderson of New Caledonia. By a letter I lately had from this Gentleman he seemed delicate about intruding himself upon your notice Sir until he had heard from you, scruples I soon removed directing him by all means to write forthwith with the very first collection he could make himself, or get in from the young Gentlemen whom I commissioned myself.

Another Gentleman whom I dare say you have heard of by now, a certain Mr Charles Geyer, native of Dresden, favoured me with a visit here for the last five weeks. He is, I believe, well-known in the northern states of the N. American Union for his having largely contributed to the botanical knowledge of that part of the new world, but poor man, however laudable the object of his pursuits, it is evident that he is but ill provided for the work he has undertaken into this remote corner of the world without I may say a single letter of credit or recommendation. He crossed this way last season under the wing of a Jesuit Mission coming to Oregon. This much however he told me, that the fruits of all his labours the moment he reached Europe should be placed at the disposal of Sir W. Hooker, and two days ago I fitted out my new Saxony friend with little trifles of my own to enable him to move about a little in this tempting season in the region of the Flatheads & Coeur d'Alènes. What he intends to do afterwards I believe he himself at present is as ignorant of as I am. He speaks of a Sir William Drummond Stewart ... having pushed him this way & says he had a letter from him which I have not seen.

Geyer knows the cactuses you spoke of to a hair, and gave me a very correct drawing of one I described to him which I found on the banks of the Columbia in flower end of May '37, & which I made over to Dr Tolmie at Vancouver the same season; of all things in the world taking away the prickles & placing a sort of bonnet on the top whence the red blossom issued, it resembled an ordinary Sired Melon. He says he picked up two himself last Sept in the Snake country ... So much for what our voyageurs call *crapaud verd* & in our opinion the most worthless class of the vegetable Kingdom!

Lower Columbia River, 29 September 1844

To James Douglas, Fort Vancouver[64]

Some days before I left Colvile I addressed you briefly on the subject of a certain ore we talked of; at same time made up a goodly package of the mineral to go home by the ship for testing in England. I have now to inform you that I myself since visited that interesting spot & certainly found it pregnant with all that might induce a speedy attempt at working the ore if any other than mere lead.

Finding the Columbia waters almost impossible to surmount from a recent freshet, I thought it would be no great loss of time to delay to the mouth of the Kootenais River a few days while I, with a couple of our men & two Indians with their two small canoes should make a quick trip to the Kootenais Lake. This, by leaving the men at the head of the bad navigation & going on the rest of the route with the Indians only, I effected in three days & a half. The place in question is *not* into an inlet of the Arcplat Lake, but in one end of the Bow itself, thus (see sketch [HBCA A.11/70.Fp.86d]).

The ore is picked up in the two [illegible] of the Presque Isle at A, about 100 feet high. There is something of a crater at top, & tis from the debris heaving up of old, covering the land side of the conical hill that the ore is found in loose lumps among the earth.

It was after twilight when I arrived; by peep of day was at work but the weather becoming threatening & being completely debarred from returning to my people by the least puff of wind, my day was very short. I have numbered the few specimens I collected on the spot & in the vicinity & will leave them here with more of the ore to be taken down & afterwards disposed of as Mr McLoughlin & you may think fit. [Specimens numbered] From 1 to 13 on the opposite shore of the Lake, 19 & 20 the protruding rocks in the Kootenais River.

The Presque Isle is very remarkable. It is the only elevated spot along the whole of the east side shore from opposite the discharge of the lake as far northward as I could see, as indicated by my adjoining rough sketch, and would seem as if thrown by some violent concussion of nature from the opposite shore. The land behind it appeared a smooth

[64] McDonald went down to headquarters in charge of the brigade, assisted by Donald Manson, arriving at Fort Vancouver on 4 June 1844. He left there on 29 June to return to Colvile. After farewell visits back and forth with the Tshimakain missionaries, the McDonald family – Archy, Jane, MaryAnne (age 10), John (age 6), twins Donald and James (age 5), Samuel (age 3), Joseph (age 18 months), and Charlotte Ferris (a 'young relative' of Jane's who was to assist with the children) – left Fort Colvile on 21 September 1844 en route to retirement in the east.

surface limestone, receding back with a very gentle slope & scarcely any wood on it for some distance up. The west shore from on top presents one of the most splendid views in nature & the size of the geological wavy strata bold, clear & distinct, & I am much mistaken or they are indeed indications of a very rich mineral country.

By the light of a blazing fire which warmed myself and my two naked companions for the night, I cut my initials on a large tree along side of us to commemorate my own dear name, as no nook or corner could be spared me on the recently explored Hyperborean shore, and I do not know but I may yet claim the Kootenais as *my own*. On voirera.

Pray excuse this hasty scrawl & the very awkward position I am placed in to write it[65] ...

Boat Encampment, 11 October 1844

To Rev Elkanah Walker, Tshimakain Mission

Agreeable to promise & knowing the anxiety of yourselves & families about us until you are acquainted with our safe arrival here, I hasten to inform you of the happy accomplishment of that stage of the arduous journey still before us. The water was unusually high. To allow it to subside a little we laid by on various occasions to the extent of 5 days, which with 15 days work spun out the journey to 20, having arrived here but late yesterday. Thank God we all enjoyed good health & upon the whole had an agreeable trip of it. The weather was charming & the Indians kept us in fresh grub with bears, mountain sheep, chevreaux & reindeer.

The Gentleman whom I expected to find here, Mr Bourke of London, did actually appear at the place with his two men on 26th Sept but getting short of provisions & despairing of seeing us before his two days stock of eatables was done the silly man rose camp & returned to the east side to meet the Express ... two days before our arrival ... It is quite uncertain how long we may be here yet; so far there is no reason to apprehend a *very very late* arrival of the Express ... The mountains around us are covered with snow but at the altitude usually assigned it is perpetual. Over a very small portion of that elevation we shall have to pass our 4th day from here & of course on old snow about as hard as ice. Upon that there is usually two feet of *new* snow end of Octob, to encounter all which we are prepared. Our Colvile men return with one Boat tomorrow. The Vancouver hands as usual await the arrival of the

---

[65] By the end of the century, mining operations were being conducted at this site on the east shore of Kootenay Lake. The Bluebell Mine at Riondel was later taken over by Consolidated Mining and Smelting Limited.

east side party with three Boats ... Our baggage, winter provisions, &c &c will require at least 12 horses. Besides Mrs McLean & family we have to provide for three invalids.

As tis not likely I shall have time to say anything after Mr McTavish is arrived I shall leave you to pick up particulars of us from the passants & begging the favour of a few lines from you next spring & with our united cordial remembrances to you all ...

Boat Encampment, 12 October 1844

To Sir William Jackson Hooker, Kew Gardens, London

I fear, for one who has so little of importance to say, you will pronounce me rather a bothersome correspondent, but when I think of the long connexion you have with us & with the far west in particular I flatter myself this hasty epistle from the Boat Encampment will not be altogether unacceptable. Our mutual friend Mr Bourke I was much disappointed at not finding here. He left the ground but a few hours before my arrival, owing as I find by the note he left me, to his having been on short commons. But how could this be when master of half a dozen good fat horses, & my Lord Derby & the British government at his back to pay the damages!! Instead, as I said, of having the pleasure

The Rocky Mountains from the Boat Encampment on the Columbia River, 1846, by Henry Warre. (National Archives of Canada C26348)

of demolishing a choice glass of Maderia with him at the foot of Mount Hooker, my only consolation was to pitch my tent on the very site of *his* & kindle my fire on his very embers yet warm, & then in my turn in dreary solitude meditate on what was to be … Two Indians I sent on ahead to advertise him of my approach were just in time to capture a huge wolverine that had already commenced its ravages on the collection of Sir William & my Noble Lord with great impunity, and my regret was that the fellows had skinned it before I could preserve it for the British Museum. The carcass was by no means bad eating & next morning the same unerring hands furnished our breakfast table with two very magnificent Beaver. So much for eating when Mr B. starved …

This moment the vanguard of the Express made its appearance. They met Mr B. three days ago, about joining the main party, & as all will likely be here tomorrow I hasten to finish the little correspondence I have to make from the Boat Encampment without having the pleasure of saying I have yet seen our friend.

On my way up now I went four days with an Indian canoe out of my way to see the location of the ore I sent home a sample of last year. I am curious to know its worth. I see Mr B. is provided with crow bars & pickaxes to explore the bowels of the earth too.

Mr Geyer left me by land for Vancouver a few days before my departure from Colvile, & I shall now give directions to have his collections brought down in the Boats en passant. He was clearly of opinion that Mr Bourke would make a good harvest of it on the Snake River & towards the Enta or Great Salt Lake by being there *early* in the spring, as no botanist had yet explored that region so early in the season …

PART 4

Envoi, 1845-49

Delayed by bad weather and encumbered with six young children and a pregnant wife, the members of McDonald's party struggled through the mountains on foot and on horseback until they were able to take to canoes again when they reached the Athabasca River, still hoping to reach Fort Assiniboine and get to Red River before winter set in. By late November 1844, when they paused near what is now Whitecourt, Alberta, for the birth of Jane's eleventh son, Benjamin, ice was already forming on the river. McDonald decided to head south to Edmonton House, where Simpson had suggested they might spend the winter.

The following letters recount the poignant events of their stay at Edmonton: the illnesses through the winter months, culminating in the death of three of the little boys in May. In June the greatly saddened family resumed its journey east, arriving in Montreal in late fall, after stopping en route to visit the Edward Ermatingers in St Thomas and the John D. Camerons in Grafton.

After some difficulties and a prolonged stay in Montreal while he searched for a suitable country property, McDonald settled on his estate, Glencoe, on the shores of Lake of Two Mountains near St Andrews East. There all the children were gathered together, including the newest baby Angus, born on 27 November 1846; Archy Jr, who had returned from school in England; and Alexander and Allan, who had lived with the Anglican rector at Chambly for a year after leaving the Red River

Academy. Archy and Alexander were soon both apprenticed to surveyor/ engineers, Allan helped on the farm, and the younger children attended the village school.

McDonald continued to correspond with old friends and colleagues, giving a picture of his life in retirement: he spoke of the family's activities, of his visits with old associates, and of his dabbling in politics (he was made a justice of the peace for Argenteuil parish). He was invited to Government House to dine with Governor General Cathcart and to tell tales about life in the far west. 'So engrossing is the subject now become that my very lap dog from Oregon was hailed here as a perfect wonder,' he told Donald Ross.

The final letter included here takes McDonald back to the Columbia. Writing in April 1849 in reply to A.C. Anderson, who had recently explored sections of the British Columbia interior that McDonald had passed through on his journey down the Fraser River in 1828, he reminisced: 'I have just read over my old notes ... touching on the descent from Kamloops to Langley.' And he offered his views on the difficulties of 'opening a new communication with the interior via the Fraser River,' a project that was again being proposed by the HBC. His interest in all around him never waned. He regained his good health and was enjoying his new role as country squire when he died suddenly of pneumonia, after a few days illness, on 15 January 1853. Jane Klyne McDonald lived on at St Andrews until her death in December 1879.

Edmonton House, 12 May 1845

To Sir George Simpson, Red River

I am sorry, very sorry indeed, that ... I am deprived of seeing you at Red River. Many untoward circumstances have contributed to defeat this much desired interview. Indeed, my whole progress hither from the very first day I left Colvile was, I may say, but a tissue of troubles, vexations & reverses ... The early part of the season we passed here agreeably enough, but in the month of February myself, my little daughter & my servant man became violently attacked with a relapse of our Columbia fever & ague, which still sticks to myself ... But to me the most painful part of the chapter is to come – our own sudden & alarming family afflictions. The scarlet fever in a mild form was for some weeks back in the fort. Five days ago it got among my poor helpless group in a more malignant shape. The oldest boy with me but one, ie the elder of my dear little interesting twins, is at this moment at the point of death & all the others but very little better.

Under these painful circumstances & my own weakness to boot, I am compelled dear Sir George to forego all idea of seeing Red River this spring. I must therefore leave to your own kind & usual consideration all I should like to urge on my own behalf on the subject of getting down to Canada this summer with as much ease and security as is consistent with the nature of the voyage. Two canoes for ourselves is as little as we can possibly manage to stow ourselves into, and I need not say that the sooner we could get off the better.

Mr [Dugald] McTavish joined us today, all safe, and to that Gentleman in particular I have communicated my private views to an extent I cannot very well think of troubling you with on paper ... I am sure you will excuse my coming so hastily to a conclusion ...

Fort Alexander, 2 August 1845

To Sir George Simpson, Red River

... God knows I had endured troubles & privations enough before, without being doomed to experience a renewal of them on reaching the shores of Lake Winipic. Besides the boy you heard of that was buried 14th of May [Donald], a second [James] was committed to the same grave ([five-year-old] twin brothers) the 18th, and a third [Joseph, age 2] the 21st. Two others of them were at the time exceedingly low, indeed so much so that on the craft leaving two days after I could not venture to move them into a Boat; consequently we were compelled to remain behind. Mr Harriott however kindly left me three homeward bound European servants with which to make a move when able, at same time suggesting that for the safety of Norway House & the people of the different Brigades passing & repassing there it might be as well for me to proceed on to Red River from the Grand Rapid.

Our melancholy departure from Edmonton took place on 5th June. At Carlton, one of our surviving boys, from the unfavourable state of the weather, had a serious relapse which detained us there three days. The afternoon of the day we left the Pas my poor wife, already sufficiently borne down with sorrow & fatigue, was attacked with the fatal contagion, a circumstance which at once decided on my making for R.R. from the Grand Rapid. In the Lake 22nd of the month we nearly perished in a terrific storm of that afternoon (proofs of its violence are now visible enough in this house – our mutual friend the Major I just hear telling his Bourgeois that the breaking of so many panes of glass was produced by the enormous hailstones of said storm, which he maintains were the size of turkey eggs – one he could not get into a glass tumbler!). Per the schooner that I met near the mouth of the river I made Mr [Donald] Ross [at Norway House] acquainted with the fact of my arrival there & with my intention to be here to meet the canoes end of July. He ... made answer that the impression on his mind was that there would be no accommodations whatever *for me* in the canoes, and I regret to find that in every communication from him since the same tone ... is maintained. Here however I made it a point to present myself, but Mr Finlayson, who arrived yesterday, informed me that Mr Ross has already 18 passengers on his hands to go down in the only three disposable canoes he has ... Altogether I believe it will be admitted that my disappointment, suffering & losses are of more than common occurrence.

On money matters I have briefly written to Mr [Hugh] Taylor & took the liberty of saying that I know you will willingly afford him the benefit of your advice ... Tis more than likely that I shall be selling my funded property [in England] to reconvert it in Canada. The disappointment I feel in being deprived of the pleasure & advantage of meeting you soon, words cannot express. I am myself now getting frail (tho at present decidedly better that I have been for some months), bordering on old age, with my family & means scattered over the wide world, and what is very discouraging, my most anxious desire to have all under one view presents more difficulties today than when I seriously commenced working for that end two years ago ...

[The preceding letter was enclosed with the following letter and sent to Simpson from St Thomas in October 1845.]

St Thomas, Canada West, 7 October 1845

To Sir George Simpson, Lachine

I confess I ought before now to have reported myself as having safely arrived on the waters of the St Lawrence. The canoe I dare say is long ere this at Lachine with my letter from the Sault to Mr Finlayson stating the reasons which obliged me to pass by the Lakes.

From Sault Ste Marie via Mackina I had a speedy run to Detroit, but the *London* having left Windsor immediately as the *Missouri* arrived from Lake Huron, I could not have availed myself of her before I got my children vaccinated, hearing that many cases of the smallpox was about Lake Erie. Bad weather prevented the *London* returning till the eighth day (3rd). On 4th I came up here from Port Stanley [on Lake Erie, near St Thomas] to see Mr Ermatinger about my son that was off round Cape Horn & the north Pacific for the last three years [Ranald] & who I understood was back to Buffalo the other day. The *London* on her next downward trip will leave Port Stanley on the 9th & by her I mean to embark for Buffalo & thence onwards best way I can. My means of course are going for it but cannot be helped – expense was in reserve for

me whichever route I took. Perhaps I ought to have advised Mr Finlayson of the Bill I drew upon him at the Sault Ste Marie, & of another
for 117 dollars I had from the Messrs Dougald of Windsor ...

Chambly, Canada East, 1 April 1846

To Sir George Simpson, Lachine

Although the term of my furlough is now nearly expired, I regret to
say that in consequence of indisposition in my family and other causes
I have not yet succeeded in settling them and putting my affairs in this
country on such a footing as to enable me, with ease of mind, to return
to my duties in the service this spring. I have therefore come to the determination, with the Governor & Committee's permission, of retiring from
the service, providing I get leave of absence for the ensuing Outfit, say
up to 1 June 1847, and an extension thereof for Outfit 1847/48, whereby
my retired interest would commence with Outfit 1848, and when it is
considered that I have now been upwards of twenty-five years in the
Company's service and have only been absent from the country for one
winter during that period, I trust that the indulgence I request may not
be considered unreasonable ...

Chambly, 1 May 1846

To Donald Ross, Norway House

... Here I am on the first of May unable to remove out of my present
domicile to wend my way en baggage to my own future residence for a
year in the City [Montreal], or to give place to my successor in the present house – how exceedingly awkward. This dilemma is occasioned by
the measles having got into the family yesterday. Fortunately it is of rather
a mild character and the season is favourable. Our two boys [Alexander
and Allan] with the Rector next door to us are just getting out of it.
We have also to regret the indisposition of our son Archy who joined us
from England in course of the winter. His complaint is a violent inflammation of the eyes requiring the immediate application of a dozen of
leeches. This occurrence is particularly unfortunate as a recent appointment required that he should start this very day for Lake Superior to
join his Bourgeois, a Gentleman lately placed at the head of certain mining operations going on there on the British shore. He will however be
off the moment he can do so with safety.

Most likely you will have heard ... that we safely got down last season, though by no means without running many hairbreadth escapes from
drowning and the endurance of a vast amount of vexation and misery that
with a better defined arrangement and more agreeable companions could

well have been avoided. On this once to me exceedingly unpleasant
subject I at one time intended to have reported to you some of the facts
& occurrences, but I believe tis now scarcely worth while – I may get
over it …

It is unneccessary here to debate on the causes & conditions that led
to my own continuance in Canada this season. My leave of absence must
as a matter of course come before the Council. Neither can I go into a
lengthened story about our N.W. friends in this part of the world.
[William] Connolly is a great man. Allan, Dease & Fisher take their
ease; even [John] Clarke, tho straitened in circumstances looks well –
his son is a young Barrister & his daughter is the belle of the Montreal
General Assembly. [John] McBean I see occasionally, [J.G.] McTavish
often. The two Robertsons with their families are very snug; they are
even wealthy, proprietors of 4 or 5 good houses each that yield them
upwards of 200 pounds per family. McPherson is a grocer in partnership
with another, poor James McDougald is an exception to all. John McLean
I saw three days ago after his return from visiting U. Canada with the
view of settling in business there; he has decided on nothing yet. On
our way down ourselves we spent three nights at St Thomas with Ermatinger, & as many with [John D.] Cameron near Cobourg [Grafton],
but saw neither [Thomas] McMurray nor [Cuthbert] Cumming. [Jacob]
Corrigle's family we did.[1] The Member for Middlesex [Edward Erma-
tinger] is himself in Montreal now attending his parliamentary duties;
his seat for the two last Sessions has been disputed, but I believe & hope
unavailingly.

It was on account of our two boys here before that we ourselves came
to Chambly last fall. We took a small cottage for 6 months that cost 10
pounds. Food & firewood cost rather less than in Montreal, but all these
advantages had other drawbacks. The annual rent of a good house & a
small garden I have taken in town [on St Urbain Street] is 60 pounds;
the children must be at education there.

What think you of the War Cry! Has not Oregon made noise at last?
So engrossing is that subject now become that my very lap dog from
Oregon was hailed here as a perfect wonder. What then would not give
the Queen's high subjects for 5 minutes conversation with a man of my
own volubility of speech after a residence of 24 years in that memorable
country!! Even the Right Hon Earl [Governor General Cathcart] now

[1] Many of the old colleagues mentioned in this letter were among the original partners
of either the HBC or the NWC at the time of the merger in 1821. Cameron, McMurray, Cumming, and Corrigal all settled near Cobourg after their retirement.

at the head of the government of these provinces was not satisfied with less than two long interviews with me at the Government House, closing with an invitation to ... dine with Lady Cathcart – what think ye of that man? Before the head of the Engineer department too I was called upon to give semi-official information on the most tenable points of defence in the disputed territory. By the Washington papers of today we see that the President at his own discretion is to give notice of the discontinuance of the joint occupancy by the abrogation of the Convention of '27, that the attention of the Govt of both countries may be the more easily directed to the adoption of all proper measures for the speedy and *amiable* adjustment of the difficulties & disputes in respect to said territory. This does not look so bad as 'the whole or none.'

I saw young McVicar in town the other day. He came down from his Uncle John's, from St Andrews ... All the Red River settlers that came to Canada are doing remarkably well. George McBeath has a son with Colonel Talbot that is a great favourite. In the winter I was up to Glengarry seeing the N.Westers & Highlanders in that part of the world. Donald McIntosh is dead & [James] Hughes is very infirm. Dr [Alexander] Rowand is in good practice, it extended to the two last mentioned Gentlemen. I wrote a long letter to his father ...

Montreal, 10 December 1846

To Edward Ermatinger, St Thomas

Were I in Oregon itself, & you at St Thomas I think our interchange of letters should have been more frequent than as we now stand ... How can this strange fact be accounted for? I believe N.Westers after they come to the civilized world are the worst correspondents in the world. The day before yesterday I in Notre Dame Street met with your gallant cousin the Knight of the Golden Fleece, who told me he lately had a note from you accompanying one for myself & begged the favour of my calling at his office next day on the subject of Lawrence [Frank's son]. This of course I did. Your worthy nephew was sent for. He soon appeared in what was truly a very respectable style, namely in the cidevant costume of the Chief Magistrate of Police himself, before whom he then stood.[2] When I spoke to him the poor creature had not the least recollection of me – of Ranald he had. The Colonel is utterly at a loss what to do with him ... As he himself told me, when the fellow first made up to him on the street, in tatters as he was ... he had him clothed as

[2] Colonel F. William Ermatinger, son of C.O. Ermatinger of Sault Ste Marie, cousin of Edward, was superintendent of police in Montreal from 1843 to 1855.

above noticed [in his own castoffs] & lodged at 2½ dollars a week until he heard more about him. The interview yesterday was with the view of having the benefit of my opinion … his appearance and manners are exceedingly sloven & unprepossessing. At your cousin's request I gave him a very severe lecture … He does not like work. He says he did drink at one time when he had money about Kingston, but now that he merely drinks Beer at dinner! He says he was robbed, or rather that everything he had was stolen from him, Bible, prayer book & all; in short he is a miserable wretch. The Colonel wrote to his brother[3] to see if he could take him under his command, but the Captain, & I believe properly, declined it, as it would soon go abroad that favouritism was more attended to than efficient service … My own advice was to lop off *his Beer,* to place him at some retired house near town at a smaller expense & there keep him until the arrival of his father[4] whom I would recommend to have his son bundled off to Oregon …

… You knew I have myself made an arrangement about not returning to active duty. I am now with all my family about me in Montreal. My eldest son [Archibald Jr.] that was an amateur geologist up at Lake Superior last season is now bound for 4 years to a Civil Engineer here. All the others are at school except Benjamin [born en route to Edmonton, 23 November 1844] and the little fellow that came into the world the other day, for whom I am now at a loss for a name [Angus, born 27 November 1846] …

On the politics of Canada it would be too tedious & even dangerous for me to attempt discanting upon … we shall be seeing you down at the opening of the session. The new Governor General [Lord Elgin] is not yet arrived … Poor Cathcart is fairly on the shelf, living in private lodgings at Daley's Hotel. Our St Andrews turnout was there the other day when we had the honour of enjoying the company of three members of your Executive Council, not including the Honbl Francis Hincks … Next in importance to your House is the great Municipal Council of Montreal, & they if anything are more at loggerheads than yourselves … It is truly lamentable to see affairs of such importance in the hands of so many worthless & unprincipled characters. Do not however infer from these remarks that I am myself envious of becoming a City Councillor …

[3] Charles Oakes Ermatinger Jr., elder brother of Frederick Ermatinger, was chief of police in Montreal.
[4] Frank Ermatinger was on furlough in Great Britain.

Glencoe Cottage, the house on Lake of Two Mountains, near Montreal, where the McDonald family lived after Archibald retired from the HBC. (National Archives of Canada PA143229)

Montreal, 24 December 1847

To William G. Smith, London, England

I arrived from Glencoe[5] late last night after a journey of 42 miles in my own sleigh on very bad roads; singular enough one half the vehicles I met with in the middle of a Canadian winter were wheel carriages. The English mail from Canada (via Quebec & New Brunswick) is about being made up this evening & I have very little time to look about me for the Sale of a Bill of Exchange ... have put the thing in the hands of a broker ... My Bill is for 400 pounds St @ 30 days sight which in any shape I feel confident you will meet when due either from my resources or your own ...

Montreal, 22 January 1848

To William G. Smith, London, England

... I was happy to learn that I did not greatly exceed the funds of mine at your disposal from Outfits '44 & '45 when I drew 400 pounds ... on

---

[5] In June 1847 McDonald purchased a large farm on Carillon Bay, Lake of Two Mountains, near St Andrews East, in Argenteuil County, Quebec. The following spring, when improvements on the house were completed, the family moved to the property he called Glencoe.

the 24th of last month ... That money ... enabled me to pay for my farm ... The 200 pounds on a former occasion went to pay up my scores with the Lachine Railroad Co ... eighth instalment. So you see I don't exactly spend all I receive, but still there are unavoidable calls upon me for family purposes & other outlays in connection with my small property ... and I suppose H.B. stock is our only resort. You will therefore ... at any sacrifice, see and turn two hundred of it into cash to meet a call for 400 pounds more I shall be making upon you ...

Montreal, 3 February 1848

To William G. Smith, London
    ... When I [last] wrote I was not aware that with close shaving & the help of the semi-annual dividend paid us here about that time, I could without much inconvenience defer the drawing of any Bill on you until ... I had heard from you on the subject. In any case however I cannot put off the negotiation of the H.B. stock ... beyond the month of March ... payable about the middle of May ... I am myself unable to get to the country. Slight fall of snow we had two days ago scarcely yet covered the ground. Is that not most extraordinary for a Canadian winter?
    Our late electioneering excitement all over the two provinces is now about over & a pretty kettle of fish we conservatives made of it. The reformers (or rather the Rebels & Radicals) in the next House of Assembly will be two to one – so much for good sound Constitutional law & a lasting connexion with the Mother Country. The Arch Traitor Papineau tis said they will choose as their Speaker!! The last ministry has not resigned, but it is said they will do so before the House meets. Mr Secretary [Dominick] Daley 2 days ago did me the honour to enclose me a Commission of the Peace for the district [Parish of Argenteuil, County of the Two Mountains] before he does go out ...

Montreal, 2 March 1848

[confirming business transactions, power of attorney, etc.] ...
To William G. Smith, London
    From what you say of the ready sale of the Musquash at what must be acknowledged very fair prices & the increased demand for Beaver, I think we may look up to better times. If your London winter be unseasonable for the benefit of the fur trade, ours in Canada is doubly so. No one in Montreal, if they had not had them before, would take the trouble to think of a fur cap. Apropos your finely dressed & dyed Beaver sent to this country – they were certainly very black, smooth & glossy to look at, but, except for the fair sex, far too fine & short in the down for the

gents of Canada. I believe they are not all yet sold. Your prices too folks found rather high to treat their better half with.

Glencoe, Carillon Bay, 12 April 1849

To Alex C. Anderson, Fort Colvile

Your very kind & highly valued communication of last season came duly to hand & I thank you most sincerely for the fund of information it conveyed ... I am, now that the days have lengthened & the weather become fine, about turning out to oversee the little doings that must be attended to about Glencoe. You already have a topographical history of my location – six acres in front and a mile back is quite large enough for a *Gentleman* Habitant to work. Our domestics consist of a man, a boy & 2 girls at 6, 2, 2, 2 pounds respectively per month, yet the poor wife herself is obliged to work hard too. At present she is in the sugar bush making a pretty fine harvest of it – there is upwards of 1,000 tins [sap buckets] clear of underwood, the boiling booth is not 120 yds from the kitchen door. Two days' collection of sap the other day – 360 Gals – made a good Brasse [brew] of 134 lbs.

I gave up the idea of building a new house upon a new site, as by so doing I would be sacrificing the whole of the old premises. An addition to the present dwelling is what I now propose. Most of the materials are on the ground. My little crops of last year turned out very well – a rare thing in this country now, *all* our potatoes were sound. Has the prevailing disease in them yet reached you in Oregon? The children are all with us except Archy who continues at Montreal and Alexander up the Ottawa River, now articled to a Land Surveyor. Our daughter returned home at Xmas from the 'Sacred Heart' nunnery where she made considerable progress – her mother is quite pleased with her proficiency on the piano. I have not been able to get our school in the vicinity under way yet. Johnny at times goes to the village school.

Your very ... intelligible account of the progress made in opening a new communication with the interior via F. River I perused with much interest, & *did really* 'recall old recollections.' I have just read over my own old notes, that I happen still to have by me of 7, 8, 9, & 10th of Octr 1828, touching the descent from Kamloops to Langley.[6] What you say of the existence of certain ravines for portages behind the masses of

---

[6] See Malcolm McLeod, ed., *Peace River: A Canoe Voyage from Hudson's Bay to the Pacific by the Late Sir George Simpson in 1828. Journal of the late Chief Factor Archibald McDonald ... who accompanied him* (Ottawa: Durie and Son, 1872). Anderson had recently carried out an exploration of the region McDonald had passed through with Governor Simpson in 1828.

This family group photographed at Three Rivers about 1870 shows Jane Klyne McDonald with two of her sons, Samuel (rear left) and Benjamin (rear right), along with Mrs Edmund (Catherine) Antrobus and her four daughters. Kate Antrobus (front right) was the widow of Archibald McDonald Jr. (National Archives of Canada PA143227)

rock, detached from above & unperceived by us from the water I readily admit may be the case. We did however land at the head of the portage
you describe at the Fall, with the view of carrying the canoes, but our
Bouts preferred running. Again, lower down on the same side, they actually did carry the bark canoes, but I ran with the Boat. From Langley
to the falls can always be managed with time, & the difficulties of the
other 15 miles by water to your Kequeloose Station may I think, during
low water, be overcome also, but I fear the depth of snow in the mountain till late will not admit of your availing yourselves of the good water
before the regular freshets come on. Columbia Boats in my opinion are
preferable to Bateaux at all events to begin with. Suitable pasture for the
horses I am doubtful of for the first 3 or 4 days from below. Of course
the good will of the Natives must be secured. I shall be most anxious to
hear how the first attempt succeeded last season. One thing very certain:
to continue the navigation of the Columbia, subject to the laws, ordi-
nances & restrictions of the Oregon Legislature is impossible. We have
it here that a negotiation is on foot to transfer over to themselves all the
Company's posts south of 49' for the consideration of a million dollars.
In goodness' name let them have them.

   As you are now I presume on the high road to headquarters and in
the way of getting both verbal & newspaper information, anything I can
say in this sheet cannot interest much. Commercial & money matters
in Canada are far from being in a flourishing state. All the Banking institutions are much depressed; one of them, the Provident's Saving sus-
pended payment. The City Bank very little better. Our Railroads too are
not overprosperous, at least the Lachine[7] one. For all that, Railroads long
& short, more ship canals, even bridging of the St Lawrence, are projects the public are most intent upon – indeed we seem a good deal like
an individual on the eve of bankrupcy. We are to borrow the money from
poor John Bull & pay him if we can before we turn Yankees! – a con-
summation to all appearance we are now rapidly approaching. This time
the flare up will begin by the Loyalists because they see that to be Rebels
& the promoters of Rebellion is the sure path to reward & distinction
from the Sovereign. To their being taxed for the payment of the loans
sustained by the last Rebels they never will submit. Even the arch Traitor
Mackenzie the present ministry have whitewashed, & is soon to walk
into a very fat office. There is Responsible Government for you!!

---

[7] McDonald had invested in the Montreal and Lachine Railroad and the LaPrairie
   Railroad.

But what think you of the recent wonderful rush to California & of the attraction which produces it? Can we believe ¹/₁₀th of what we hear of the richness & abundance of the gold? Here, as all over the world, the story is gaining more credence every day. In fact the great City of Montreal will ere long be visibly diminished in population by the swarms of adventurers taking flight to the gold region. Are you aware that at one time I & a few other choice spirits on west side were within an ace of possessing that locality in free & common stockage – what nuncopups we were that we did not forthwith close the bargain with the wretched California govern't. But is it true indications of gold in Vancouver's Island too are discovered? We see that with the sanction of the Imperial Govt you are going to colonize it at all events, & a gold mine then in connection with the coal one would I think answer the 20-acre settler very well.

The folks at Lachine I have the honour of seeing occasionally. Finlayson and his wife went home in the fall & were followed by Miss Simpson accompanied by Miss Barnston.[8] The Knight himself is still quite brisk upon it; he goes up [to Red River] this year again to initiate his successor Eden Colvile into the government of affairs in the north. Paul Fraser is down with us this winter making a figure among the great that is creditable to Indian traders … His brother distinguished himself in the Upper House by recording his protest against the abominable indemnification Bill. Oh! apropos, do you know that I myself in some measure have figured in that business at the head of a delegation sent to His Excellency with a petition signed by 1,400 of the good & loyal citizens of Argenteuil. Poor Bruce [James Bruce, Lord Elgin] was courteous & condescending enough but could not express his compliance with the (request) prayer of the petitioners.

Should Messrs Eells & Walker with their ladies be still in the neighbourhood of Colvile do us the favour to be remembered to them most kindly. We deeply lament the tragical end of our poor late friends at Whilatpu.[9] Mrs McDonald in a special manner desires the expression of her warmest regard to the ladies & their children.

… accept for yourself, Mrs Anderson [Elizabeth Birnie] & the family the tender of our united best wishes for your Success, health & happiness at Colvile …

[8] One of the daughters of HBC colleague George Barnston, later a sister-in-law of McDonald's only daughter MaryAnne.
[9] The Cayouse massacre of the Whitmans and twelve others at their Waiilatpu mission took place on 29 November 1847.

AFTERWORD

Archibald McDonald died suddenly of pneumonia at home on 15 January 1853 after a few days illness. Jane Klyne McDonald, then still in her late forties, stayed on at Glencoe, running the farm with the help of Allan, age twenty-one, her eldest son still at home. After his marriage in 1869 she moved to a small cottage in the village of St Andrews East, where she lived until her death on 15 December 1879.

Ranald MacDonald, who in 1842 left his job with Edward Ermatinger and 'ran away to sea,' had been reported dead to his family sometime after his departure from St Thomas (see Jo Ann Roe, *Ranald MacDonald: Pacific Rim Adventurer*). He appeared unexpectedly at Glencoe not long after his father's death, much to the surprise of his stepmother and the rest of the family, whom he regaled with tales of his experiences on whaling ships in the South Seas, in Japan, in the goldfields of Australia, and on his travels in Europe and Great Britain. He remained around St Andrews for several years but went west to the Caribou gold region with Allan around 1857. There the brothers, later joined by young Benjamin, engaged in a variety of entrepreneurial activities: prospecting, ranching, and running pack trains. From 1859 to 1861 Ranald ran a ferry across the Fraser River at Lillooet. Allan returned to Montreal in 1862, and in 1864 Ranald joined Robert Brown's Vancouver Island Exploring Expedition (see John Hayman, *Robert Brown and the Vancouver Island Exploring Expedition*). After many years in British Columbia Ranald moved down to Fort Colvile (about twenty miles below the Canada-US border) in the 1880s, where a distant cousin, Donald McDonald (son of Chief Trader Angus McDonald), was living. He spent his last years on property he claimed there. He died near Toroda, Washington, on 24 August 1894.

Archy Junior became a civil engineer and architect in the Ottawa-Montreal area. He married Kate Antrobus, daughter of a prominent Three Rivers family (her father, Edmund William Romer Antrobus, who died in 1852, was overseer of highways for Quebec and served as aide-de-camp to the governors of Canada, including Lord Elgin), and they lived in St Andrews. Their only son died at age five in 1867. Archibald MacDonald Junior died at age forty, when his sleigh went through the ice in the Ottawa River in February 1868.

Alexander MacDonald (all the sons adopted the 'Mac' spelling of their name after their father's death in 1853) served an apprenticeship with a surveyor on the Ottawa River before joining the HBC in 1850. He surveyed HBC lands at Sault Ste Marie, Fort William, and around Lake Superior and Lake Huron during 1854-56. He later served at Eastmain,

Albany, and Whale River. He was named chief trader in 1866 and chief factor in 1872. He died at Moose Factory in July 1875 at age forty-four. Alexander shared his father's interest in botany, and on his travels he collected specimens for the National Herbarium and the McGill University Herbarium.

Allan MacDonald went west to the Caribou goldfields in 1857. He was joined by Ranald, and the two operated a ranch near Bonaparte; they also prospected and ran pack trains in the area. In 1862, shortly after Benjamin joined them in their enterprises, Allan sold his interests and returned to St Andrews, where he ran the farm with his mother until his marriage in 1869 (at which time Jane moved into the village). Allan married Harriet Robertson, daughter of Dr William Robertson of St Andrews and niece of Colin Robertson (an old fur trade friend of his father's). Allan was an officer in the local Argenteuil Rangers and went west to Red River with Colonel Garnet Wolseley's volunteer army in 1870. Sometime after this he sold the farm (his father's will left the farm to Allan providing that it remained for Jane's 'enjoyment and possession' during her lifetime) and returned to the west. He became the Indian agent at Qu'Appelle in the late 1870s, moving to the Indian Commissioner's Office in Winnipeg about ten years later. He died in Winnipeg in 1901 at age sixty-nine.

Archibald MacDonald Jr., second son of Archibald and Jane, was a surveyor who drowned when his sleigh went through the ice in the Ottawa River in February 1868. He married Kate Antrobus, daughter of E.W.R. Antrobus of Three Rivers, Quebec. (National Archives of Canada C49177)

Alexander MacDonald was HBC chief factor at Moose Factory on James Bay when he died there in 1875. (National Archives of Canada PA143223)

Samuel MacDonald, born at Fort Colvile in 1841, became a notary in Montreal. He married Emily Elizabeth Roberts, daughter of Professor George Roberts of Fredericton, New Brunswick. Samuel died in Montreal in 1891. (Eastern Washington State Historical Society)

Benjamin MacDonald was born between Jasper House and Fort Edmonton when the McDonald family was en route east to retirement in 1844. He married Elizabeth Pyke, daughter of Reverend James Pyke of Hudson Heights, Quebec, and later moved back to the west. He died in Los Angeles, California, in 1918. (National Archives of Canada PA143224)

Jane Klyne is shown here with her sons, Angus Michel (the youngest, born in Montreal in November 1846) and John (born at Fort Colvile in May 1837). Angus died at age twenty at home at St Andrews, and John died at age twenty-seven at the HBC post at Fort Shepherd, British Columbia. (National Archives of Canada C49179)

In 1857, at age twenty-three, MaryAnne MacDonald married Dr James Barnston, eldest son of another old friend of her father's, Chief Factor George Barnston. Dr Barnston had been sent to Scotland for his medical training and, on his return, became the first professor of botany at McGill University. He died in May 1858, and, less than two years later, MaryAnne and their infant daughter followed. As a teenager, in July 1850, MaryAnne rescued two young boys from the waters of Lake of Two Mountains near Glencoe when their boat capsized in a storm. She was awarded the Royal Humane Society medal for bravery in April 1852 and was presented with a silver tea service in recognition of her courage.

In his twentieth year John MacDonald went to St Thomas to apprentice with Edward Ermatinger in his Bank of Elgin. About four years later he joined the HBC. He died at Fort Shepherd, British Columbia, on 20 December 1864 at age twenty-seven.

Samuel MacDonald, who was born in 1841 at Fort Colvile, was eleven when his father died. He attended school in St Andrews and college in Montreal, where he became a notary. He married Emily Elizabeth Roberts of Fredericton, New Brunswick, sister of Reverend Goodridge Roberts (canon of Christ Church Cathedral Fredericton) and aunt of Charles G.D. Roberts. Emily died less than a year after the birth of their fourth child in 1883. Samuel died in Montreal in 1891 at age fifty.

MaryAnne, the only daughter of Archibald and Jane, born at Rocky Mountain House on 3 February 1834, married Dr James Barnston of Montreal (son of Chief Factor George Barnston). She and their infant daughter died less than two years after James's death in May 1858. (National Archives of Canada C49180)

Benjamin, the eleventh son, born en route from Fort Colvile to Fort Edmonton in November 1844, went west in 1862 to join his brothers ranching and running pack trains near Lillooet. Over the next few years he engaged in various entrepreneurial activities in the goldfields and in Washington State, where, for a time, he was part owner of the *Forty-Nine*, the first steamboat built on the Columbia River. He later returned east and, in 1872, married Elizabeth Pyke, daughter of Reverend James Pyke of Hudson Heights (near Montreal) and granddaughter of yet another fur trade figure, Chief Factor J.G. McTavish. They had three children (a fourth was born in 1883) when they moved to Denver, Colorado. Benjamin operated businesses in Colorado and Montana. He died in Los Angeles, California, in 1918 at age seventy-four.

Angus Michel, the twelfth and youngest son, was born in Montreal in 1846, shortly before the McDonald family moved to Glencoe, their retirement home on 'La Baie' on Lake of Two Mountains. He attended school in St Andrews and remained on the farm with his mother until his early death in 1867 at age twenty.

Appendix

Friends, colleagues, HBC officials, employees, and others mentioned in Archibald McDonald's letters.
* denotes correspondents.

Allan, George T. (HBC clerk 1830), to Columbia 1831, accountant Fort Vancouver 1834-42; to Honolulu 1842-47; chief trader 1845; retired to Oregon 1849.

America (NWC, HBC 1821), Sandwich Islander, 1821-30 middleman in Columbia District; on *William and Ann* at Fort George 1825; on Umpqua expedition; to Hawaii 1831.

Anawasan, Joseph, Columbia River guide 1840s.

Anderson, Alexander Caulfield* (HBC clerk 1831), to Columbia 1832; with Donald Manson to Milbanke Sound to build Fort McLoughlin; 1835-40 and 1842-48 in New Caledonia; 1840-41 in charge at Fort Nisqually; 1841-42 and 1851-54 at Fort Vancouver; 1848-51 in charge at Fort Colvile; retired 1854; to Vancouver Island 1858.

Annance, Francis Noel* (NWC 1820, HBC clerk and interpreter 1821), to Columbia with Governor Simpson's party in 1824; explored Fraser River with James McMillan 1824; Thompson River under McLeod; in charge Okanagan 1825-26; with McDonald at Kamloops 1826-27; helped to establish Fort Langley 1827-28; 1833-34 Mackenzie River (Fort Simpson); to Montreal 1834; returned to his Abenaki village, St Francis, in 1845.

Arquoite, Amable (HBC 1825), Fort Vancouver 1826-27, 1830-36; middleman at Fort Langley 1827-29; retired to Willamette 1836.

Atatie (Tatie), Fort Colvile courier 1840s.

Auger, Antoine, Fort Edmonton, to Columbia with Simpson party 1841; his wife was Madeline Klyne, sister of Jane Klyne McDonald.

Auger, Nicholas, middleman, New Caledonia 1829-31; Walla Walla 1831-32; Fort Simpson (Nass) 1832-53; retired to Victoria.

Banks, Peter, English botanist drowned at Dalles des Morts on the Columbia River in October 1838 when the Express canoe capsized.

Barclay, Archibald, HBC secretary in London 1843-55, succeeding William Smith.

Barnston, George (NWC 1820), HBC clerk York Factory 1821; to Columbia 1826; 1827 with McMillan to establish Fort Langley; 1830-31 in charge Walla Walla (Nez Percés); resigned 1831 and reengaged 1832; to Albany District; chief trader 1840; in charge King's Posts at Tadoussac 1844-49; chief factor 1847; Norway House 1851-58; Michipicoten 1859-62; retired in 1863; died 1883; son Dr James Barnston married McDonald's only daughter MaryAnne.

Berland, Edouard, Fort Colvile (Kootenais) c. 1830-53.

Big Charles, trading in Kootenais region mid-1830s.

Bird, James (HBC), in charge of Saskatchewan District 1810; chief factor in 1821; retired to Red River Settlement 1824; died there 1856.

Birnie, James (NWC 1818), NWC clerk at Fort George 1820-21; Spokane House 1822-23; Okanagan 1824-25; established post at the Dalles 1829; Fort Simpson, New Caledonia 1834-37; Fort George on the Columbia River 1839-46; retired 1846 to Cathlamet; died 1864; daughter Elizabeth married A.C. Anderson.

Black, Samuel* (NWC) to HBC 1823, chief trader 1824; chief factor 1837; Kamloops 1830-41; killed by Native at Kamloops 1841.

Blanchet, Father F.N., Roman Catholic missionary, came with Father Demers from Montreal to Oregon in 1839.

Boisvert, Louis, Fort Langley 1827-30; Snake expeditions; settled in Willamette Valley.

Bourdignon, Antoine (NWC 1818, HBC 1821), middleman, Okanagan 1822; horsekeeper at Kamloops 1826-28, Fort Colvile 1829-30.

Brotchie, Captain William, HBC shipmaster; commander of the *Cadboro* until he took over the *Nereide* after Captain Home and crew capsized in 1838; captain of the *Cowlitz* 1841, to Hawaii and California.

Brouillet, Hypolite, Fort Simpson 1831-33; Fort Colvile 1833-42 (Kootenais c. 1840); blacksmith.

Brown, Louis, Fort George 1822, on *William and Ann* 1825; Fort Colvile 1837-41; joined DeSmet's Racine Amer mission.

Cadotte, Pierre (NWC 1810, HBC 1821), canoeman and guide.

Cameron, John Dugald (NWC), HBC chief factor 1821, to Columbia with McDonald in fall 1821; to London with Chief Factor John Haldane 1822; settled in Grafton, near Cobourg, Upper Canada (Ontario).

Cassacas, 'Prince,' son of Comcomly, Chinook chief.

Chalifoux, André (NWC 1813), 1822 at Fort George, steersman; at Fort Colvile from 1826; two of his children drowned along with ten others in accident at Dalles des Morts in October 1838; died 1851 at St Paul, Oregon.

Charles, Pierre (NWC 1816, HBC 1817), middleman, at Fort George 1822; on Snake River expeditions 1825 and 1826; Fort Langley 1827-29, 1836-37; with McDonald and W.F. Tolmie at Nisqually 1833; settled in Cowlitz Valley.

Charpentier, Francis (HBC 1817), middleman and interpreter Fort Vancouver 1827-28; Walla Walla (Nez Percés) 1829-32; died in Snake country 1834.

Cockran, Reverend William, founder of St Andrew's parish, Red River.

Colvile, Andrew (Wedderburn)*, HBC London Committee from 1810; deputy governor 1839-52; brother-in-law of Lord Selkirk.

Comcomly, Columbia River Chinook chief, father of Princess Raven.

Connolly, William* (NWC 1801), HBC chief trader 1821 Lesser Slave Lake; Chief factor in charge of New Caledonia District 1824-31; left the Columbia to take charge of King's Posts on the St Lawrence River 1832-40; retired 1843; died in Montreal 1849.

Cornelius, 'Bighead,' Lower Spokane chief; friend of McDonald.

Cowie, Robert, chief trader, accountant Fort Vancouver 1830s; left the Columbia 1838; died 1859.

Cox, John (NWC 1814, HBC 1821), Sandwich Islander, engaged in maritime fur trade from 1810; Fort George 1814-22; on board *William and Ann* 1825; died 1850 at Fort Vancouver.

Dears, Thomas (HBC clerk 1817), to Columbia District in 1823; Fort Colvile 1825; Snake expedition with Ogden 1825; Thompson River 1825-29; on Clallam expedition with A.N. McLeod in 1828; New Caledonia 1830-36.

Dease, John Warren* (NWC 1814, HBC chief trader 1821); 1822 to Columbia; in charge at Walla Walla (Nez Percés) 1822-25, Spokane House 1825; established Fort Colvile 1826; Flathead House 1826-29; died January 1830.

Dease, Peter Warren (XY Company 1801, NWC, HBC chief trader 1821), chief factor 1828; with John Franklin's arctic expedition 1826-27; New Caledonia 1830-36; commanded arctic exploring expedition with Thomas Simpson 1836-39; to Athabasca District 1840; retired to Montreal 1842; died 1863.

Degrais, Pierre Philippe (NWC 1793), HBC Fort George 1822; Colvile 1826-42, middleman, blacksmith; retired to Willamette Valley 1842; died 1847.

Demers, Father Modeste, Roman Catholic missionary came to Oregon with Father Blanchet in 1839.

Deslard, Joseph (NWC 1813, HBC 1821), steersman, Fort George; Kamloops 1827; settled in Willamette Valley; died 1869.

DeSmet, Father Pierre Jean*, Jesuit missionary from St Louis, established mission in Bitter Root Valley (Racine Amer) near Fort Colvile's Flathead House 1840.

Douglas, David, Scottish botanist, arrived in Columbia District in April 1825 aboard the HBC ship *William and Ann;* collected plant specimens while accompanying HBC men on their travels; returned to Great Britain in fall of 1827; back in Columbia 1832-33; went from there to Hawaii, where he was trampled to death in a bull pit in July 1834.

Douglas, James* (NWC apprentice clerk 1819, HBC 1821), to Columbia with McLoughlin 1824; New Caledonia 1825-28; Fort Vancouver 1828-49; chief trader 1835; chief factor 1839; 1840 to Stikine to take over from Russian American Company; with Governor Simpson to Sitka in 1841; founded Fort Victoria on Vancouver Island 1843; on HBC Board of Management for Columbia District 1846; headquarters moved from Fort Vancouver to Victoria 1849; became governor of Vancouver Island 1850; retired from HBC to become first governor of the Crown Colony of British Columbia 1858; knighted by Queen Victoria 1863; died at Victoria 1877.

Dubois, Pierre (HBC 1825), middleman, Fort Colvile 1830s; settled in the Willamette Valley 1845.

Dubreuille, Jean Baptiste (NWC 1806, Pacific Fur Company 1810, HBC 1821), at Fort George 1822; on board *William and Ann* 1825; Snake River expeditions; retired to Willamette Valley 1842; died in California 1849.

Duquette, Antoine (HBC 1835), middleman, served at Colvile 1837-51.

Eells, Reverend Cushing*, ABCFM (American Board of Commissioners for Foreign Missions) missionary at Tshimakain.

Ermatinger, Edward* (HBC 1818), clerk/accountant, to Fort Vancouver 1825; conducted eastbound spring Express in 1827 and 1828; retired 1828; settled in St Thomas, Upper Canada (Ontario) where he became a merchant, banker, politician; preserved his private correspondence with McDonald and other former colleagues in the Columbia, including John Tod and John Work.

Ermatinger, Francis* (HBC clerk 1818), to Columbia 1825; 1826-30 Thompson River District; Fort Colvile (Flathead House) 1831-38; Snake expeditions 1838-41; Bonaventura (California) expedition 1842; left the Columbia in 1846; in charge Athabasca District 1847-50; retired from HBC 1853; settled near his brother Edward at St Thomas; died 1858.

Fallardou (Fallardeau), Michel (HBC), middleman 1827; served at Thompson River; New Caledonia 1836-44; died Victoria 1873.

Faneant, François (François Piette) (NWC 1817), middleman, HBC Fort George 1822; carpenter/cooper at Fort Langley c. 1827-30; retired to Cowlitz region 1842.

Felix, Antoine (HBC 1823), steersman, 1826-45 at Fort Colvile (Kootenais) except for 1842-44 at Thompson River; settled in Willamette Valley 1845.

Ferris, W.A., American free trader in Flathead region.

Finlay family, free traders in Rocky Mountains.

Finlayson, Duncan (HBC 1815), chief trader 1828; chief factor 1831; to Columbia District 1831; Fort Vancouver 1831-37 (on furlough in Europe 1834-35); married Isobel Simpson, elder sister of Frances Simpson; Governor of Assiniboia at Fort Garry 1839-44; HBC agent at Lachine 1844-55. and 1859; died in London 1862.

Finlayson, Roderick, to Columbia in 1839; ran mill at Fort Vancouver; to Stikine in 1840; Fort Simpson with John Work 1842; to Fort Victoria 1843; took charge when Charles Ross retired in 1844; chief trader 1850; chief factor 1859; retired 1872; died at Victoria 1892.

Fisher, Alexander (NWC 1815), HBC chief trader 1823; in charge Montreal department; in charge New Caledonia 1829-39; to York Factory 1840; retired 1845; died 1847.

Flett, David, Orkneyman, 1836-42 personal servant to Archibald McDonald at Colvile; drowned in the OK Dalles June 1842.

Flett, Thomas (HBC 1833), Fort Colvile 1834-51 (Kootenais 1837-39); retired near Fort Colvile 1851.

Fraser, Colin, piper, hired by Governor Simpson in 1827; to the Columbia with Simpson party in late summer 1828; steward at York Factory 1829-30; postmaster at Jasper House 1836-50; Fort Assiniboine 1853; Lesser Slave Lake until 1862; Lac Ste Anne 1862; died 1867.

Fremont, John Charles, American explorer, brought settlers to the Oregon Territory in 1844.

Gairdner, Dr Meredith, to the Columbia with W.F. Tolmie fall 1832; surgeon at Fort Vancouver; died in Oahu 1836.

Gale, Samuel*, represented Lord Selkirk at Sault Ste Marie with McDonald in 1817; lawyer and later judge in Montreal.

Gervais, Joseph (Pacific Fur Company 1810), HBC Fort George 1822; trapper, settled in Willamette Valley; died 1861.

Geyer, Charles A. (Karl), travelling botanist, visited Colvile 1844.

Gingras, Jean, (NWC 1820) HBC middleman, interpreter Kamloops 1827; settled in Willamette Valley 1841; died 1856.

Goudie, James, blacksmith, miller; at Colvile 1830-51; died in Victoria 1887.

Grant, Peter (HBC 1825), served in New Caledonia 1825-42; Colvile 1842-44.

Grant, Richard (NWC 1816), HBC Edmonton House 1822-23 and 1828-30; chief trader

1826; to Columbia 1841; Fort Vancouver 1841-42; Fort Hall 1842-51; retired in 1853; settled in Idaho; died 1862.

Gray, J.E., London, keeper of natural history collections, British Museum.

Gray, W.H., came west with Tshimikain missionaries.

Grégoire, Étienne (NWC 1813), voyageur Fort George 1822; Kamloops 1827; died in St Louis, Oregon, 1867.

Halkett, John, for many years a member of the HBC London Committee; brother-in-law of Lord Selkirk; plant collector.

Hamlyn, Dr Richard, HBC surgeon at Red River 1824-28; to Columbia with Simpson and McDonald in fall 1828; left spring 1830 for Red River; returned to England 1831.

Hanwell, Captain Henry* (HBC), commander of the *William and Ann* 1824.

Hargrave, James* (NWC 1820, HBC 1821), most of his career spent at York Factory; to Sault Ste Marie 1851; chief trader 1833; chief factor 1844; retired 1859; died at Brockville, Ontario, 1865.

Harriott, J.E. (HBC 1809) Columbia District 1828-32; chief trader 1829, to Bow River; chief factor 1846; Saskatchewan District 1832-54; son-in-law of John Rowand; retired to Red River 1855; died in Montreal 1866.

Harrison, Benjamin*, HBC London Committee 1807-54; deputy-governor 1835-38; cousin and brother-in-law of Sir John Pelly.

Hayne, Captain Leonard J., commander of the HBC ship *Ganymede* 1829; fired by McLoughlin, who disapproved of his drinking habits.

Heron, Francis (HBC 1812), chief trader 1828; served in Saskatchewan District, Mackenzie River, and Fort Garry; to Columbia 1829; Fort Colvile 1829-35; Nisqually; retired 1839; died 1840.

Heroux, Urbain (HBC 1833), to Fort Vancouver 1837; charged with murder of John McLoughlin Jr. at Fort Stikine in 1841; charges later dropped.

Home, Commander David, drowned with four seamen when his ship, the *Nereide*, capsized off Fort George in January 1838.

Hooker, Dr. William J.*, professor of botany Glasgow University, 1821-41; keeper of Kew Gardens 1841-65; sponsor of David Douglas; knighted in 1836.

Hopkins, Edward, secretary to Sir George Simpson, husband of artist Frances Hopkins; accompanied the governor to the Columbia in the summer of 1841; visited Fort Colvile; took McDonald's son Archy from Red River Academy to school in England; died in England in 1893.

Hubert, Joaquim (HBC 1822), Spokane House; Fort Colvile 1826-42; retired to Willamette Valley; died at French Prairie c. 1873.

Johnson, Lieutenant Robert, with Captain Charles Wilkes 1841 exploring expedition; visited Fort Colvile 1841.

Jones, Reverend David, minister and teacher at Red River Settlement; assistant to Reverend William Cockran; taught McDonald boys.

Kakarro (NWC 1817), Sandwich Islander; on *William and Ann* at Fort George 1825; died at Fort Vancouver 1830.

Kanaquassi, Pierre (HBC 1833), Iroquois; to Fort Vancouver 1839; involved in the murder of John McLoughlin Jr. at Fort Stikine in 1841.

Karonhitihigo (Karonhitchego), Laurent (NWC 1815), Iroquois boute at Fort George 1822; Thompson River foreman 1827-29; Fort Vancouver 1831; died at St Paul, Oregon, 1851.

Keith, James (NWC partner in the Columbia 1813-21, HBC chief factor 1821); Severn

District 1822-26; HBC superintendent at Lachine 1827-35 and financial advisor to some of the officers; retired 1843; died in Aberdeen 1851.

Kennedy, Alexander (HBC 1798), HBC chief factor at Fort George 1821-25; returned east with Governor Simpson 1825; retired 1829; died in London, England, 1832.

Kennedy, John (NWC 1814), 1821 in Columbia; Snake expeditions; Fort Langley from 1827; died there suddenly April 1830.

Kennedy, Dr John (HBC 1829), son of Chief Factor Alexander Kennedy; surgeon and clerk at Fort Vancouver 1830-31; Fort Simpson (Nass) 1831-32; chief trader 1847; retired to Victoria 1856; died 1859.

Kipling, Captain Charles, master of the schooner *Vancouver*.

Kittson, William (NWC 1817, HBC 1821), Spokane House 1820-22, Snake expedition with Peter Skene Ogden 1824-25; in charge of Kootenais and Flathead posts 1826-34; manager of Nisqually farm 1834-40; died 1841.

Klyne, Joseph, Jane Klyne's younger brother Joseph, born 1816, who was referred to in the Fort Langley Journals in March 1830 as 'little Joseph Klyne,' served in the Columbia District until 1835. He returned to Red River and married Louise Braconnier (born 1820). 'Young Joseph Klyne' who brought a message to Colvile from the Sinclair party of settlers en route from Red River to the Cowlitz Valley in 1841 was the same man. According to Bruce M. Watson, Joseph Klyne reappears in the Columbia records (1841-44) as a member of the South party. He settled in the Willamette Valley and died in California c. 1849.

Klyne, Michel (NWC 1798, HBC 1821), father of Jane Klyne McDonald; was with the NWC from 1798 to 1801 at Lake Superior and Nipigon; later served at Lesser Slave Lake, where Jane was born; postmaster at Jasper House 1824-34; retired to Red River in 1835.

LaCourse, Pierre (NWC 1810), boat builder; with McDonald at Thompson River (Kamloops); Fort Colvile 1827-40; died at St Paul, Oregon 1864.

Lafantasie (Lafentasie), Charles (HBC 1834), son of Jacques Lafantasie; Fort Colvile 1834-42; settled in the Willamette Valley in 1842; died c. 1861.

Lafantasie (Lafentasie), Jacques (NWC 1802, HBC 1821), Fort George 1822; interpreter at Kamloops 1827; died at Thompson River in 1827.

Lafleur, Joachim (HBC 1827), middleman at Kamloops 1830; killed in 1860s near Walla Walla (Nez Percés).

Laframboise, Michel (Pacific Fur Company 1810, NWC 1813, HBC 1821), overseer and interpreter at Fort George from 1822; with A.R. McLeod on Clallam expedition to avenge the murder of Alexander McKenzie party in January 1828; settled in Willamette Valley about 1841; died 1865.

Lajoie, Jean Baptiste, middleman Fort Colvile 1828-42; died in St Paul, Oregon 1846.

Laprade, Alexis, Fort George 1822; Thompson River 1827-43; at Kamloops when Samuel Black shot by Native in February 1841; died in St Louis, Oregon 1871.

Leblanc, Pierre (NWC 1810, HBC 1821), York Factory; married Nancy McKenzie, the country wife of Chief Factor J.G. McTavish 1831, after McTavish and Governor Simpson brought their new English brides to Red River in 1830; to Columbia 1838; drowned with their three children near Dalles des Morts 22 October 1838.

Leclair, Theodore, middleman, Fort Colvile 1840-42.

Lee, Reverend Jason, Methodist missionary, came to Willamette Valley in 1834.

Leolo (Lolo), interpreter and guide, New Caledonia and Thompson River; daughter became fourth wife of Chief Trader John Tod.

Lewes, John Lee (HBC chief trader), to Fort George in 1821; to Cumberland District 1823; 1845 returned to Columbia, in charge at Fort Colvile 1845-47; Cumberland 1849-51; retired 1852.

Linton, Robert (NWC 1818, HBC 1821), New Caledonia 1831-35; killed above Alexandria November 1835.

McCallum, John, schoolmaster at the Red River Academy in 1830s.

McDonald, Anawiscum (HBC 1824), middleman, cooper, carpenter; Fort Vancouver 1826-27; Fort Langley 1827-34 and 1840-42; Nisqually 1834-40 and 1843-46; settled in Cowlitz area about 1846.

McDonald, Angus (HBC 1838), great-nephew of Archibald McDonald; to Colvile as clerk 1839; Snake country 1840-44 and 1846; Flathead House 1845, 1848-50; Fort Colvile 1851-72; chief trader 1856; resigned 1872; died in Montana 1889.

McDonald, Finan (NWC 1805, HBC 1821), with David Thompson 1807-12; Snake expedition with Ogden 1824; served in the Columbia until he retired to Upper Canada 1827; died in Glengarry County 1851.

McDougall, George* (HBC 1815), clerk in New Caledonia 1820-30; Lesser Slave Lake 1831-49.

McGillivray, Joseph* (NWC in the Columbia 1813-17), son of NWC partner and superintendent William McGillivray; HBC chief trader 1821; New Caledonia 1826-28; died 1832.

McGillivray, Simon Jr. (NWC 1813, HBC 1821), HBC chief trader Athabasca District 1821; Walla Walla 1831-32; Colvile 1833; to New Caledonia; retired 1834; re-employed in Esquimaux District 1836-38; died 1840.

McKay, Thomas (NWC 1814, HBC 1821), stepson of John McLoughlin (son of Marguerite Wadin McKay); Snake country expeditions with Peter S. Ogden 1826-28 and 1835-38; 1837-38 at Fort Hall; retired to Willamette Valley about 1839; died 1850.

McKenzie, Alexander (NWC 1812), 1821 clerk Fort George; murdered with four companions by the Clallam at Hood Canal in January 1828.

McKenzie, Patrick*, clerk at Colvile, Flathead House, listed as apprentice postmaster 1841-44, postmaster 1844, interpreter 1851-53; at Thompson River 1844-46.

McKinlay, Archibald* (HBC 1832), to New Caledonia 1835; Walla Walla 1841-46; chief trader 1846; Oregon City 1846-49; married Sarah Julia, daughter of Peter S. Ogden; retired to Lac la Hache, British Columbia; died 1891 at Savona, British Columbia.

McLean, Donald*, clerk at Fort Colvile (Flathead House 1839), sent to Kamloops when Samuel Black murdered there in February 1841; son of Alexander McLean, a Selkirk settler who came to Red River with Archibald McDonald in 1814 and was one of the twenty-two killed with Governor Robert Semple at Seven Oaks in 1816; frequent visitor at Tshimakain mission, where his daughter Elisa lived with the Walkers in 1841-42; killed in 1864 at Chilcotin.

McLeod, Alexander Roderick (NWC 1802, HBC 1821), chief trader in Athabasca; to Fort Vancouver 1825; Umpqua expeditions 1827-28; helped establish Fort Langley 1827; in June 1828 he led the controversial expedition to avenge the murder of the McKenzie party by the Clallam (twenty-two Natives were killed); explored the Sacramento and Buenoventura Valleys; chief factor 1836; to Athabasca 1837; died 1840.

McLeod, John* (HBC 1811), chief trader 1821; preceded McDonald at Thompson River; Norway House (1826-30); St Maurice 1833-49; died of cholera in 1849 at Hochelaga, Lower Canada.

McLoughlin, David, second son of John Sr., grew up at Fort Vancouver; educated in Paris; returned to the Columbia with his father when he returned from leave in 1839; clerk at Fort Vancouver; resigned from HBC in 1846 and assisted his father at Oregon City; died in Idaho 1903.

McLoughlin, Dr John* (NWC 1806, partner 1814), HBC chief factor in charge of the Columbia District at Fort George and Fort Vancouver 1824-46; prominent in the development of Oregon City; died 1857.

McLoughlin, Dr John Jr.*, elder son of Chief Factor John Sr., studied medicine in Paris 1829-34; to Columbia 1837; surgeon at Fort McLoughlin 1837-38; Fort Vancouver 1838-40; assistant to W.G. Rae at Stikine 1840; murdered at Stikine April 1842.

McMillan, James* (NWC 1804), HBC chief trader in the Columbia 1821; explored lower Fraser River 1824; chief factor 1827; established Fort Langley; to Fort Vancouver 1828; left Columbia 1829; in charge of experimental farm at Red River 1830-34; retired to Scotland 1839; died 1858.

McNeill, Captain W.H., sailed on Northwest Coast for many years for Sturgis and Company of Boston; Duncan Finlayson purchased the *Lama* from him in 1832 and hired him for the HBC; commanded the *Beaver* in 1837; died in Victoria 1875.

McPherson, John* (HBC 1832), clerk at Colvile from 1840, in charge Flathead House and Kootenais; retired 1845.

McTavish, Dugald (HBC 1832), brother-in-law of James Hargrave; accountant at Fort Vancouver 1839-47; chief trader 1846; to Sandwich Islands 1847-52; chief factor 1851; manager HBC Oregon Department 1853-58; Fort Victoria 1859-63; died in Montreal 1871.

Manson, Donald* (HBC 1817), clerk at Langley with James McMillan 1827-28; clerk Fort Vancouver 1829; Nass 1831-34; Fort McLoughlin (Milbanke Sound) 1834-39; chief trader 1837; Thompson River 1841-42; Stikine 1843; succeeded Peter S. Ogden in charge at New Caledonia 1844-47; retired 1858; died in Oregon 1880.

Martineau, Alexis, middleman, Fort Colvile from 1837; left with Louis Brown to join DeSmet mission in 1840.

Martineau, Pierre (HBC 1828), middleman, boute, miller, Fort Colvile 1835-42; son-in-law of Canote Umphreville; both drowned at the OK Dalles in 1842.

Maxwell, Henry (HBC 1835), to Columbia 1840; retired 1864.

Mengarini, Father Gregorio, came to Oregon from St Louis with Father DeSmet and four other Jesuits in 1841.

Miles, Robert (HBC 1818), to Hudson Bay with McDonald and the Ermatinger brothers in 1818; accountant at York Factory 1821-34; chief trader 1828; furlough in Europe 1834-35; Rupert's House 1835-43; chief factor 1844.

Moncravier, J.B., American free trader in Flathead region.

Monique, Joseph (HBC 1829), Iroquois bout and guide at Fort Vancouver; died at Fort Vancouver 1845.

Montignis (Montigny), Edward, Thompson River middleman, horse keeper, interpreter, 1836-48.

Montour, Nicholas (NWC 1804), HBC clerk 1821, son of NWC partner; Snake country trapper; Fort Colvile (Kootenais) 1830-33; became a free trader, employed from time to time by HBC.

Moreau, Joseph, joined fur trade 1817; voyageur at Fort George 1822; Thompson River boute 1828-30; drowned at the Cascades 1831.

Morwick, William (HBC 1833), postmaster, shot by Natives at Fort Babine January 1843.

Mouselle, Joseph, one of the party who captured Samuel Black's murderer.

Nicolas (Hwistesmetxequen), Upper Okanagan Chief at Kamloops.

Nicollet, Father J.N., Roman Catholic missionary.

Noah, Harry Bell (NWC 1814), Sandwich Islander, at Fort George 1822; on board the *William and Ann* in 1825.

Ogden, Peter Skene* (NWC 1811, partner 1820), clerk HBC 1822; to Columbia District 1823; chief trader 1824; conducted Snake River expeditions 1824-30; to north Pacific coast 1830; established Fort Simpson (Nass) in 1832; chief factor 1834; in charge New Caledonia 1835-44; with James Douglas and John Work on HBC Board of Management after John McLoughlin retired in 1846; died at Oregon City 1854.

Onahargon, Lasard, Fort George 1822; Thompson River 1827-31; to Montreal 1831.

Ossin, Louis (NWC 1819, HBC 1821), New Caledonia 1824; settled in Willamette Valley 1841; died 1856.

Ouvrie, Jean Baptiste (Pacific Fur Company 1810, NWC 1813, HBC 1821), Fort George overseer 1822; middleman, interpreter; 1829 Cowlitz region; Fort Nisqually 1836-42; died c. 1849.

Pambrun, Pierre (HBC 1815), witness at trials following the deaths of Governor Robert Semple and nineteen settlers at Seven Oaks, Red River Colony, in 1816; to New Caledonia (Babines) 1825; Fort Walla Walla (Nez Percés) 1831; chief trader 1839; died in May 1841 after fall from horse.

Payette, François* (NWC 1814, HBC 1821), interpreter at Spokane House; Snake Country expeditions with John Work 1830-31; Fort Colvile 1833-35, Flathead and Kootenay posts; at Fort Boise (Idaho) 1835-1844 when he retired to Canada.

Pelly, George, cousin of Sir John Pelly, sailed from London December 1834; HBC representative in Hawaii 1834-51; removed in 1851; died 1866.

Pelly, Sir John*, HBC London Committee 1806; deputy-governor 1812; governor 1822 until his death in 1852.

Pépin, Étienne (HBC 1827), Fort Vancouver; blacksmith, many years at Fort Langley; retired 1860.

Picard, André, Thompson River from 1826; Colvile 1839-41.

Pion, William (HBC 1828), mixed-blood middleman, at Fort Colvile 1840-42.

Plamondon (Plomondon), Simon (NWC 1820, HBC 1821), middleman and trapper; to New Caledonia 1823; to Fort Langley 1827; settled in Cowlitz Valley 1837; died c. 1900.

Plante, Antoine, middleman, on Snake expeditions with Peter S. Ogden; Fort Colvile 1832-46; remained in Colvile area after he retired; died in Montana 1890.

Plouffe, Antoine (HBC 1828), middleman, Fort Colvile 1828-36; drowned in the Flathead River 1836.

Point, Father Nicholas, Roman Catholic missionary; to Bitter Root Valley (Racine Amer) from St Louis with Father DeSmet and four other Jesuits August 1841; established Coeur d'Alènes mission in 1843; returned east in 1847.

Presse, François, to HBC late 1830s; one of those charged in connection with the murder of John McLoughlin Jr. at Stikine.

Preveau (Proveau), Louis (HBC 1828), middleman, boat builder at Fort Colvile for eighteen years; died there in 1846.

Pritchard, John, had charge of Buffalo Wool Company at Red River 1822; later ran a school there.

Rae, W.G. (HBC 1827), to the Columbia as clerk in 1834; served at Colvile 1835-36 and

Walla Walla; clerk at Fort Vancouver 1837-38; married John McLoughlin's daughter Elisa in 1838; in charge at Stikine 1840; chief trader 1841 when he took charge of HBC interests in San Francisco; committed suicide in 1845.

Rivet, François (NWC 1813 Astoria), came to Pacific coast with Lewis and Clark 1804; HBC Spokane 1822, interpreter; on Snake River expeditions; interpreter at Fort Colvile 1827-37; retired to Willamette Valley, where he died in 1852.

Robertson, Colin (NWC 1804-9, HBC 1814), re-established Red River settlement 1815-16 after attack by NWC; joined McDonald at Sault Ste Marie 1816; involved in conflict with NWC at Fort Wedderburn 1818 and at Grand Rapids in 1820; chief factor 1821, in charge at Norway House; served later in Saskatchewan District, Island Lake, Churchill, Swan River, and New Brunswick; retired 1840; died at Montreal in 1842.

Rogers, Cornelius, came to Oregon with the ABCFM missionaries.

Ross, Charles (HBC 1818), to Hudson Bay with McDonald and the Ermatinger brothers in 1818; clerk in Babine country 1824-27; New Caledonia until 1832; to Athabasca; Fort McLoughlin November 1838; to Vancouver Island 1843, in charge at Fort Victoria; died June 1844.

Ross, Donald* (HBC 1816), 1824-26 at York Factory on Hudson Bay; Governor Simpson's confidential secretary at Montreal 1826-27; chief trader 1829; in charge at Norway House 1830-51; chief factor 1839; died 1852 at Fort Garry.

Rowand, John* (NWC 1804 Fort des Prairies), built Fort Edmonton 1808 and remained there most of his life; HBC chief trader 1821; chief factor 1826.

Ryan, Captain William*, to Columbia in command of the *Isabella* 1829; vessel wrecked at mouth of the river May 1830; took *Ganymede* back to England and returned with it in May 1833; later master of the *Cadboro;* returned to England on the *Dryad* 1836 and retired.

Satakarass, Pierre (NWC 1814), Iroquois, Fort George 1822; Thompson River 1827-29; Fort Colvile 1835-44; died at Victoria 1852.

Satakarata, Louis (NWC 1814), Fort George 1822; Fort Langley 1827, 1836-45; died at Victoria 1852.

Simpson, Lieutenant Aemilius (HBC 1826), to Fort Vancouver November 1826; commander of the schooner *Vancouver* 1827-30; chief trader 1830; commander of the brig *Dryad* to Northwest Coast and Sandwich Islands 1831; to Nass, where he died suddenly shortly after his arrival 1831.

Simpson, Alexander (HBC 1827), brother of Thomas, half-brother of Lieutenant Aemilius Simpson; clerk at Lachine; to Fort Vancouver in 1839, intended for Hawaii office but position given to George T. Allan; returned to England on hearing of death of his brother Thomas.

Simpson, Governor George* (HBC 1820), appointed governor of the northern region at time of the merger of the HBC and NWC in 1821; soon after became governor-in-chief of Rupert's Land; visited the Columbia District in 1824-25, 1828-29 and again as part of his journey around the world in 1841; he was knighted by Queen Victoria in 1841; died 1860.

Simpson, Thomas (HBC 1828), confidential clerk to Governor George Simpson, his cousin by marriage; half-brother of Lieutenant Aemilius Simpson; HBC Northern Discovery Expedition under Peter Warren Dease 1836; died under mysterious circumstances near Turtle River, North Dakota 14 June 1840.

Sinclair, James*, led HBC settlers from Red River Colony to Cowlitz Valley in 1841;

visited Colvile en route back east; career divided between Red River and western regions until 1852 when he became an HBC clerk and returned to Oregon; brought his family and another group of settlers to Walla Walla in 1854; killed in a Native attack at the Cascades in 1856.

Sinclair, Captain Thomas (HBC 1824), sloopmaster at York Factory 1824-26; to Columbia with Aemilius Simpson; first mate, later master of *Cadboro* 1827, during establishment of Fort Langley; returned to England on the *Ganymede* 1834.

Smith, Donald, later Lord Strathcona (HBC 1838), nephew of long-time HBC secretary William Smith; served on Labrador coast 1838-68; took charge of HBC Montreal office 1869; became HBC governor in Canada; appointed by government of Canada special commissioner to inquire into the troubles connected with the Northwest Rebellion 1869-70; represented Winnipeg in Manitoba Legislative Assembly 1870-74 and Selkirk in the Canadian House of Commons 1870-80; active in railway development, a key figure in the group involved in building the CPR; appointed Canadian high commissioner to London 1896 until his death in 1914.

Smith, William*, HBC secretary in London 1818 until his death in January 1843.

Smith, William G.*, son of William Smith, became HBC secretary in London in 1855, succeeding Archibald Barclay.

Spalding, Reverend Henry Harmon, ABCFM missionary, Lapwai mission.

Spokane Garry, one of two Native boys sent by HBC to Anglican mission school at Red River 1825-29 and 1830-31; friend of the Tshimakain mission.

Steel, James, to Columbia in 1839; farmer at Nisqually; returned east 1842.

Swan, Captain John P., first mate on *William and Ann* 1824; captain of the *Cadboro* 1826; captain of the *William and Ann* when it went down with all hands in March 1829.

Taylor, Hugh*, Montreal, financial advisor to HBC officers.

Therrien, Pierre, in fur trade from 1818; to Columbia 1827; middleman, served at Fort Langley until 1830 when he was fatally injured by the wadding of the *Vancouver's* parting cannon salute.

Thew, William (HBC 1834), New Caledonia 1837-42; troublesome clerk at Colvile 1842; returned to England 1843.

Thomas, Governor Thomas (HBC 1789), surgeon at York Factory 1789; governor of the Northern Department 1814-15; settled at Red River; died 1828.

Tod, John* (HBC 1811), Severn District and Island Lake; to New Caledonia 1823-32; 1832 to Nelson River; chief trader 1834; to Fort Vancouver 1838; Nisqually 1839; New Caledonia 1840; Thompson River District 1841-49; retired to Oak Bay, Victoria; member of the Provisional Council of Vancouver Island 1851; died 1882.

Tolmie, Dr W. Fraser* (HBC 1831), botanist; travelled overland from Fort Vancouver to Nisqually with McDonald in 1833; in charge at Nisqually and later Fort McLoughlin; to Victoria 1859 where he was a prominent citizen and member of the legislature; died in 1886.

Towai (NWC 1817), Sandwich Islander, middleman and labourer at Fort George and later Fort Vancouver; Umpqua expedition; retired near Fort Vancouver 1845.

Tranquille, Shuswap chief near Kamloops; his death in 1840 was ascribed to some 'spell' cast by Chief Factor Samuel Black and was avenged by his nephew, who murdered Black at the fort in February 1841. The murderer was tracked down by HBC men with help from other neighbouring Natives and summarily killed.

Umphreville, Canote, served more than thirty years in the Columbia; Fort Colvile 1826-42; long-time guide and trusted aide to McDonald; drowned at the OK Dalles 1842.

Umphreville, Pierre, 'Wacon,' son of Canote, Fort Colvile 1836-42.

Vital, Fabien, drowned at the Dalles des Morts October 1838.

Walker, Reverend Elkanah*, with Reverend Cushing Eells and their wives, under the auspices of the American Board of Commissioners for Foreign Missions (ABCFM), established the Tshimakain mission sixty miles south of Fort Colvile in 1838-39.

Wallace, Robert, travelling botanist, drowned at Dalles des Morts in October 1838.

White, Reverend Elijah, former member of the Oregon Methodist Mission brought settlers to Oregon in 1842.

Whitman, Marcus and wife Narcissa, ABCFM missionaries at Waiilatpu near Walla Walla 1836; both were murdered by Cayouse in 1847.

Wilkes, Captain Charles, leader of 1841 US Exploring Expedition.

Work, John (HBC 1814), to the Columbia District with Peter S. Ogden 1823; Spokane House 1823-24; Flathead House 1825-26; Fort Colvile 1826-29; Snake country expedition 1830; Sacramento Valley December 1834; manager of coasting trade at Fort Simpson 1834-40; chief factor 1846; 1853 appointed to HBC Board of Management for the Columbia District; retired to Victoria; died there 1861.

Yale, James Murray* (HBC 1815), involved in conflict with NWC at Fort Chipewyan 1817; New Caledonia 1821-26; Fort Vancouver 1827-28; 1828 clerk at Fort Langley with McDonald, in charge 1833-59; chief trader 1844; retired to Vancouver Island; died 1871.

The editor would like to thank Bruce M. Watson for his assistance in compiling the biographical information in this section.

Bibliography

Brown, Burt Barker, ed. *Letters of John McLoughlin, 1829-1832*. Portland: Oregon Historical Society, 1948.

Barman, Jean. *The West Beyond the West: A History of British Columbia*. Toronto: University of Toronto Press, 1991.

Brown, Jennifer. *Strangers in Blood: Fur Trade Company Families in Indian Country*. Vancouver: UBC Press, 1980.

Carstens, Peter. *The Queen's People: A Study of Hegemony, Coercion and Accomodation among the Okanagan of Canada*. Toronto: University of Toronto Press, 1991.

Cole, Jean Murray. 'Exile in the Wilderness, Archibald McDonald's Ten Years at Fort Colvile,' *The Beaver* (Summer 1972): 7-14.

–. *Exile in the Wilderness*. Toronto/Seattle: Burns and MacEachern/University of Washington Press, 1979.

–. 'Literary Leanings in the Fur Trade,' *Journal of Canadian Studies* (Summer 1981): 87-93.

–. 'Success or Survival? The Progress and Problems of the Tshimakain Mission,' *Idaho Yesterdays* (Spring/Summer 1987): 86-94.

–. 'Archibald McDonald's Fort Langley Letters,' *British Columbia Historical News* (Fall 1999): 31-36.

Chance, David H. *People of the Falls*. Colvile, WA: Kettle Falls Historical Centre, 1986.

Cullen, Mary. *History of Fort Langley, 1827-96*. Ottawa: National Historic Sites and Parks, 1979.

Dobbs, Arthur. *An Account of the Countries Adjoining to Hudson Bay*. London: J. Robinson, 1744.

Douglas, David. "Journals and Letters of David Douglas," *Oregon Historical Quarterly*, vols. 5 (1904) and 6 (1905).

Drury, C.M., ed. *First White Women over the Rockies*. Vols. 1 and 2. Glendale, CA: Clark, 1963.

–. *Nine Years with Spokane Indians: The Diary, 1838-1848, of Elkanah Walker*. Glendale, CA: Clark, 1976.

Fleming, R. Harvey, ed. *Minutes of Council, Northern Department of Rupert's Land, 1821-1831*. Toronto: Champlain Society, 1940.

Gibson, James R. *The Lifeline of the Oregon Country: The Fraser-Columbia Brigade System, 1811-47.* Vancouver: UBC Press, 1997.

Glazebrook, G.P. de T., ed. *The Hargrave Correspondence, 1821-1843.* Toronto: Champlain Society, 1938.

Halpenny, Francess G., and Jean Hamelin, eds., *Dictionary of Canadian Biography.* Vols. 7 and 8. Toronto: University of Toronto Press, 1988 and 1985.

Harris, R. Cole. *The Resettlement of British Columbia: Essays on Colonialism and Geographic Change.* Vancouver: UBC Press, 1997.

Harvey, A.G. *Douglas of the Fir.* Cambridge, MA: Harvard University Press, 1947.

Hayman, John, ed. *Robert Brown and the Vancouver Island Exploring Expedition.* Vancouver: UBC Press, 1989.

Judd, Carol M., and Arthur Ray, eds. *Old Trails and New Directions: Papers of the Third North American Fur Trade Conference.* Toronto: University of Toronto Press, 1980.

Klippenstein, Frieda. *The Role of the Carrier in the Fur Trade: A Report from Historical and Anthropological Sources.* Canadian Parks Service, March 1992.

Lent, D. Geneva. *West of the Mountains.* Seattle: University of Washington Press, 1963.

Lewis, W.S., and Naojiro Murakami, eds. *Ranald MacDonald: The Narrative of His Early Life.* Spokane, WA: Eastern Washington State Historical Society, 1923. Reprint Portland, OR: Oregon Historical Society, 1990.

McDonald, Lois Halliday. *Fur Trade Letters of Francis Ermatinger, 1818-1853.* Glendale, CA: Clark, 1980.

MacKay, Douglas. *The Honourable Company.* Toronto: Musson, 1938.

Mackie, Richard. *Trading Beyond the Mountains: The British Fur Trade in the Pacific, 1793-1843.* Vancouver: UBC Press, 1997.

Maclachlan, Morag, ed. *The Fort Langley Journals, 1827-30.* Vancouver: UBC Press, 1998.

McLeod, Malcolm. ed. *Peace River: A Canoe Voyage from Hudson's Bay to the Pacific ... in 1828. Journal of the late Chief Factor Archibald McDonald ...* Ottawa: J. Durie and Son, 1872. Reprint Toronto: Coles Canadian Collection, 1970; Edmonton: Hurtig, 1971.

Maude, Mary McD., ed., *Dictionary of Canadian Biography.* Vol. 9. Toronto: University of Toronto Press, 1976.

Merk, Frederick, ed. *Fur Trade and Empire: George Simpson's Journal, 1824-1825.* Rev. ed. 1968. Cambridge: Harvard University Press, 1931.

Morwood, William. *Traveler in a Vanished Landscape.* New York: Potter, 1973.

Rich, E.E., ed. *McLoughlin's Fort Vancouver Letters.* Vol. 1, *First Series, 1825-1838;* Vol. 2 *Second Series, 1839-1844;* Vol. 3, *Third Series, 1844-46.* Toronto: Champlain Society, 1941, 1943, and 1944.

–. ed. *Simpson's 1828 Journey to the Columbia: Part of a Dispatch from George Simpson ESQr Governor of Rupert's Land to the Governor & Committee of the Hudson's Bay company London.* Toronto/London: Champlain Society/Hudson's Bay Record Society, 1947.

–. *The Fur Trade and the Northwest to 1857.* Toronto: McClelland and Stewart, 1967.

Roe, Jo Ann. *Ranald MacDonald: Pacific Rim Adventurer.* Pullman, WA: Washington State University Press, 1997.

Ruggles, Richard I. *A Country So Interesting: The Hudson's Bay Company and Two Centuries of Mapping, 1670-1870.* Montreal and Kingston: McGill-Queen's University Press, 1991.

Simpson, George. *Narrative of a Journey Round the World during the Years 1841 and 1842.* London: Henry Colburn, 1847.

Tolmie, William Fraser. *Physician and Fur Trader: The Journals of William Fraser Tolmie.*
    Vancouver: Mitchell, 1963.
Van Kirk, Sylvia. *Many Tender Ties: Women in Fur-Trade Society in Western Canada, 1670–
    1870.* Winnipeg: Watson and Dwyer, 1980.
Vibert, Elizabeth. *Trader's Tales: Narrative of Cultural Encounters in the Columbia Plateau,
    1807-1846.* Norman and London: University of Oklahoma Press, 1997.

Unpublished Sources

Archibald McDonald Papers, Fort Colvile Journal and Letter Book, AB20 C72M BCA.
Directors' Correspondence, vol. 66, docs. 99, 100; vol. 63, docs. 313, 314, 316, Royal Botanic
    Gardens Archives, Kew, Richmond, Surrey, England.
Edmonton Correspondence Inward 1841, B.60/c/1 HBCA.
Ermatinger Papers. Archibald McDonald Letters, AB40 M142, BCA.
Farley, A.L. *Historical Cartography of British Columbia*, unpublished monograph, BCA.
Fort Langley Journal and Letter Book 1829-33, B.113/a/3, B.113/b/1, HBCA.
John McLeod Journals and Correspondence 1812-44, Archibald MacDonald Letters,
    AB40 M142A, BCA.
Kamloops Correspondence 1826-7, B.97/a/2 HBCA.
London Correspondence Inward, A.1/117 HBCA.
Walker-Whitman Papers, Coe Collection, Beinecke Rare Book and Manuscript Library,
    Yale University Library, New Haven, CT.

Index

Set in Stone by Brenda and Neil West, BN Typographics West

Printed and bound in Canada by Friesens

Copy editor: Joanne Richardson

Proofreader: Darcy Cullen

THE PIONEERS OF BRITISH COLUMBIA

❧

Visit the UBC Press web site at www.ubcpress.ca for information and
detailed descriptions of other UBC Press books

Ask for UBC Press books in your bookstore or contact us at info@ubcpress.ca

You can order UBC Press books directly from Raincoast,
TELEPHONE: 1-800-663-5714, FAX: 1-800-565-3770